Labor Law
Selected Statutes, Forms, and Agreements

EDITORIAL ADVISORY BOARD

Richard A. Epstein
James Parker Hall Distinguished Service Professor of Law
University of Chicago

E. Allan Farnsworth
Alfred McCormack Professor of Law
Columbia University

Ronald J. Gilson
Charles J. Meyers Professor of Law and Business
Stanford University
Marc and Eva Stern Professor of Law and Business
Columbia University

Geoffrey C. Hazard, Jr.
Trustee Professor of Law
University of Pennsylvania

James E. Krier
Earl Warren DeLano Professor of Law
University of Michigan

Elizabeth Warren
Leo Gottlieb Professor of Law
Harvard University

Bernard Wolfman
Fessenden Professor of Law
Harvard University

Labor Law

Selected Statutes, Forms, and Agreements

Michael C. Harper
Professor of Law
Boston University School of Law

Samuel Estreicher
Professor of Law
New York University School of Law

ASPEN LAW & BUSINESS
Aspen Publishers, Inc.

Copyright © 1996 by Michael C. Harper and
Samuel Estreicher

All rights reserved. No part of this book may be reproduced
in any form or by any electronic or mechanical means
including information storage and retrieval systems without
permission in writing from the publisher, except by a
reviewer who may quote brief passages in a review.

Library of Congress Catalog Card No. 96-76722

ISBN 0-316-32510-4

Second Printing

MV-NY

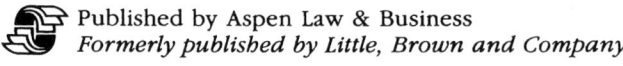
Published by Aspen Law & Business
Formerly published by Little, Brown and Company

Printed in the United States of America

Contents

SELECTED STATUTES	**1**
Sherman Act	1
Clayton Act	5
Norris-LaGuardia Act of 1933	7
Federal Arbitration Act	14
Railway Labor Act of 1926	20
National Labor Relations Act of 1935	51
Labor Management Relations Act of 1947	74
Labor-Management Reporting and Disclosure Act of 1959	92
Labor-Management Cooperation Act of 1978	122
Proposed Labor Reform Act of 1977	128
Postal Reorganization Act—Selected Provisions	138
Worker Adjustment and Retraining Notification Act of 1988	144
United States Bankruptcy Code—Selected Provisions	150
Montana Wrongful Discharge from Employment Act of 1987	156
Labour Relations Act of Ontario—Selected Provisions	159
SELECTED REGULATIONS AND FORMS	**213**
Regulations of the National Mediation Board—Selected Provisions	213
Forms of the National Mediation Board	239
Regulations of the National Labor Relations Board— Selected Provisions	242
Forms of the National Labor Relations Board	298

SELECTED AGREEMENTS **303**

1994-1997 Collective Bargaining Agreement Between General Electric Company and the International Union of Electronic, Electrical, Salaried, Machine and Furniture Workers (AFL-CIO)   303

1994 Memorandum of Agreement Between Saturn Corporation and the International Union, United Automobile, Aerospace and Agricultural Implement Workers of America (AFL-CIO)   364

Labor Law
Selected Statutes, Forms, and Agreements

Selected Statutes*

Sherman Act
26 Stat. 209 (1890), as amended, 15 U.S.C. §§1 et seq.

§1. (§1) Trusts, etc., in restraint of trade illegal; penalty

Every contract, combination in the form of trust or otherwise, or conspiracy, in restraint of trade or commerce among the several States, or with foreign nations, is declared to be illegal. Every person who shall make any contract or engage in any combination or conspiracy hereby declared to be illegal shall be deemed guilty of a felony, and, on conviction thereof, shall be punished by fine not exceeding $10,000,000 if a corporation, or, if any other person, $350,000, or by imprisonment not exceeding three years, or by both said punishments, in the discretion of the court.

(July 2, 1890, c.647, §1, 26 Stat. 209; Aug. 17, 1937, c.690, Title VIII, 50 Stat. 693; July 7, 1955, c.281, 69 Stat. 282; Dec. 21, 1974, Pub. L. 93-528, §3, 88 Stat. 1708; Dec. 12, 1975, Pub. L. 94-145, §2, 89 Stat. 801; Nov. 16, 1990, Pub. L. 101-588, §4(a), 104 Stat. 2880.)

§2. (§2) Monopolizing trade a felony; penalty

Every person who shall monopolize, or attempt to monopolize, or combine or conspire with any other person or persons, to monopolize

---

*The section numbers of the statute involved, as originally enacted, are followed (in parentheses) by the corresponding section numbers in the United States Code where appropriate. Unless otherwise indicated, the text of any federal statute is taken from the United States Code (1994 ed.). Captions indicated by italic run-in headings have been added in the interest of readability. —Eds.

any part of the trade or commerce among the several States, or with foreign nations, shall be deemed guilty of a felony, and, on conviction thereof, shall be punished by fine not exceeding $10,000,000 if a corporation, or, if any other person, $350,000, or by imprisonment not exceeding three years, or by both said punishments, in the discretion of the court.

(July 2, 1890, c.647, §2, 26 Stat. 209; July 7, 1955, c.281, 69 Stat. 282; Dec. 21, 1974, Pub. L. 93-528, §3, 88 Stat. 1708; Nov. 16, 1990, Pub. L. 101-588, §4(b), 104 Stat. 2880.)

§3. (§3) Trusts in Territories or District of Columbia illegal; combination a felony

Every contract, combination in form of trust or otherwise, or conspiracy, in restraint of trade or commerce in any Territory of the United States or of the District of Columbia, or in restraint of trade or commerce between any such Territory and another, or between any such Territory or Territories and any State or States or the District of Columbia, or with foreign nations, or between the District of Columbia and any State or States or foreign nations, is declared illegal. Every person who shall make any such contract or engage in any such combination or conspiracy, shall be deemed guilty of a felony, and, on conviction thereof, shall be punished by fine not exceeding $10,000,000 if a corporation, or, if any other person, $350,000, or by imprisonment not exceeding three years, or by both said punishments, in the discretion of the court.

(July 2, 1890, c.647, §3, 26 Stat. 209; July 7, 1955, c.281, 69 Stat. 282; Dec. 21, 1974, Pub. L. 93-528, §3, 88 Stat. 1708; Nov. 16, 1990, Pub. L. 101-588, §4(c), 104 Stat. 2880.)

§4. (§4) Jurisdiction of courts; duty of United States attorneys; procedure

The several district courts of the United States are invested with jurisdiction to prevent and restrain violations of sections 1 to 7 of this title; and it shall be the duty of the several United States attorneys, in their respective districts, under the direction of the Attorney General, to institute proceedings in equity to prevent and restrain such violations. Such proceedings may be by way of petition setting forth the case and praying that such violation shall be enjoined or otherwise prohibited. When the parties complained of shall have been duly notified of such petition the court shall proceed, as soon as may be, to the hearing and determination of the case; and pending such petition and before final decree, the court may at any time make such temporary restraining order or prohibition as shall be deemed just in the premises.

(July 2, 1890, c.647, §4, 26 Stat. 209; Mar. 3, 1911, c.231, §291, 36 Stat. 1167; June 25, 1948, c.646, §1, 62 Stat. 909.)

§5. (§5) Bringing in additional parties

Whenever it shall appear to the court before which any proceeding under section 4 of this title may be pending, that the ends of justice require that other parties should be brought before the court, the court may cause them to be summoned, whether they reside in the district in which the court is held or not; and subpoenas to that end may be served in any district by the marshal thereof.

(July 2, 1890, c.647, §5, 26 Stat. 210.)

§6. (§6) Forfeiture of property in transit

Any property owned under any contract or by any combination, or pursuant to any conspiracy (and being the subject thereof) mentioned in section 1 of this title, and being in the course of transportation from one State to another, or to a foreign country, shall be forfeited to the United States, and may be seized and condemned by like proceedings as those provided by law for the forfeiture, seizure, and condemnation of property imported into the United States contrary to law.

(July 2, 1890, c.647, §6, 26 Stat. 210.)

§7. (§6a) Conduct involving trade or commerce with foreign nations*

Sections 1 to 7 of this title shall not apply to conduct involving trade or commerce (other than import trade or import commerce) with foreign nations unless—

 (1) such conduct has a direct, substantial, and reasonably foreseeable effect—

  (A) on trade or commerce which is not trade or commerce with foreign nations, or on import trade or import commerce with foreign nations; or

---

*A prior §7 of Act of July 2, 1890, c.647, 26 Stat. 210, formerly appeared as 15 U.S.C. §15 and was repealed by Act of July 5, 1955, c.283, §3, 69 Stat. 283. The civil suit provisions are now codified at 15 U.S.C. §15, and set forth below as part of the Clayton Act.—EDS.

(B) on export trade or export commerce with foreign nations, of a person engaged in such trade or commerce in the United States; and
   (2) such effect gives rise to a claim under the provisions of sections 1 to 7 of this title, other than this section.

If sections 1 to 7 of this title apply to such conduct only because of the operation of paragraph (1) (B), then sections 1 to 7 of this title shall apply to such conduct only for injury to export business in the United States.

(July 2, 1890, c.647, §7, 26 Stat. 210, as added Oct. 8, 1982, Pub. L. 97-290, Title IV, §402, 96 Stat. 1246.)

§8. (§7) "Person" defined

The word "person", or "persons", wherever used in sections 1 to 7 of this title shall be deemed to include corporations and associations existing under or authorized by the laws of either the United States, the laws of any of the Territories, the laws of any State, or the laws of any foreign country.

(July 2, 1890, c.647, §8, 26 Stat. 210.)

(§8) Trusts in restraint of import trade illegal; penalty*

Every combination, conspiracy, trust, agreement, or contract is declared to be contrary to public policy, illegal, and void when the same is made by or between two or more persons or corporations, either of whom, as agent or principal, is engaged in importing any article from any foreign country into the United States, and when such combination, conspiracy, trust, agreement, or contract is intended to operate in restraint of lawful trade, or free competition in lawful trade or commerce, or to increase the market price in any part of the United States of any article or articles imported or intended to be imported into the United States, or of any manufacture into which such imported article enters or is intended to enter. Every person who shall be engaged in the importation of goods or any commodity from any foreign country in violation of this section, or who shall combine or conspire with another to violate the same, is guilty of a misdemeanor, and on conviction thereof in any court of the United States such person shall be fined in a sum not less than $100 and not exceeding $5,000,

---

*This and succeeding sections were enacted as part of the Act of Aug. 27, 1894, c.349, 28 Stat. 570, and not as part of the Sherman Act of 1890. —Eds.

and shall be further punished by imprisonment, in the discretion of the court, for a term not less than three months nor exceeding twelve months.

(Aug. 27, 1894, c.349, §73, 28 Stat. 570; Feb. 12, 1913, c.40, 37 Stat. 667.)

(§9) Jurisdiction of courts; duty of United States attorneys; procedure

The several district courts of the United States are invested with jurisdiction to prevent and restrain violations of section seventy-three of this Act; and it shall be the duty of the several United States attorneys, in their respective districts, under the direction of the Attorney General, to institute proceedings in equity to prevent and restrain such violations. Such proceedings may be by way of petitions setting forth the case and praying that such violations shall be enjoined or otherwise prohibited. When the parties complained of shall have been duly notified of such petition the court shall proceed, as soon as may be, to the hearing and determination of the case; and pending such petition and before final decree, the court may at any time make such temporary restraining order or prohibition as shall be deemed just in the premises.

(Aug. 27, 1894, c.349, §74, 28 Stat. 570; Mar. 3, 1911, c.231, §291, 36 Stat. 1167; June 25, 1948, c.646, §1, 62 Stat. 909.)

(§10) Bringing in additional parties

Whenever it shall appear to the court before which any proceeding under section 9 of this title may be pending, that the ends of justice require that other parties should be brought before the court, the court may cause them to be summoned, whether they reside in the district in which the court is held or not; and subpoenas to that end may be served in any district by the marshal thereof.

(Aug. 27, 1894, c.349, §75, 28 Stat. 570.)

Clayton Act
38 Stat. 730 (1914), as amended,
15 U.S.C. §§12 et seq.

Be it enacted by the Senate and House of Representatives of the United States of America in Congress assembled, That "anti-trust laws" as used herein, includes the Act entitled "An Act to protect trade and commerce against unlawful restraints and monopolies", approved July second, eighteen hundred and ninety [Sherman Act, supra]. . . .

§4. (§15) Suits by persons injured

[A]ny person who shall be injured in his business or property by reason of anything forbidden in the antitrust laws may sue therefor in any district court of the United States in the district in which the defendant resides or is found or has an agent, without regard to the amount in controversy, and shall recover threefold the damages by him sustained, and the cost of the suit, including a reasonable attorney's fee. . . .

(Oct. 15, 1914, c.323, §4, 38 Stat. 731; Sept. 12, 1980, Pub. L. 96-349, §4(a)(1), 94 Stat. 1156; Dec. 29, 1982, Pub. L. 97-393, §1, 96 Stat. 1964.)

§6. (§17) Antitrust laws not applicable to labor organizations

The labor of a human being is not a commodity or article of commerce. Nothing contained in the antitrust laws shall be construed to forbid the existence and operation of labor, agricultural, or horticultural organizations, instituted for the purposes of mutual help, and not having capital stock or conducted for profit, or to forbid or restrain individual members of such organizations from lawfully carrying out the legitimate objects thereof; nor shall such organizations, or the members thereof, be held or construed to be illegal combinations or conspiracies in restraint of trade, under the antitrust laws.

(Oct. 15, 1914, c.323, §6, 38 Stat. 731.)

§16. (§26) Injunctive relief for private parties; exception; costs

Any person, firm, corporation, or association shall be entitled to sue for and have injunctive relief, in any court of the United States having jurisdiction over the parties, against threatened loss or damage by a violation of the antitrust laws, including sections 13, 14, 18, and 19 of this title, when and under the same conditions and principles as injunctive relief against threatened conduct that will cause loss or damage is granted by courts of equity, under the rules governing such proceedings, and upon the execution of proper bond against damages for an injunction improvidently granted and a showing that the danger of irreparable loss or damage is immediate, a preliminary injunction may issue: *Provided*, That nothing herein contained shall be construed to entitle any person, firm, corporation, or association, except the United States, to bring suit for injunctive relief against any common carrier subject to the jurisdiction of the Surface Transportation Board under subtitle IV of Title 49. In any action under this section in which the plaintiff substantially prevails, the court shall award the cost of suit, including a reasonable attorney's fee, to such plaintiff.

(Oct. 15, 1914, c.323, §16, 38 Stat. 737; Sept. 30, 1976, Pub. L. 94-435, Title III, §302(3), 90 Stat. 1396; as amended, Dec. 29, 1995, Pub. L. 104-88, Title III, §318(3), 109 Stat. 949.)

§20. (§52) Statutory restriction of injunctive relief

No restraining order or injunction shall be granted by any court of the United States, or a judge or the judges thereof, in any case between an employer and employees, or between employers and employees, or between employees, or between persons employed and persons seeking employment, involving, or growing out of, a dispute concerning terms or conditions of employment, unless necessary to prevent irreparable injury to property, or to a property right, of the party making the application, for which injury there is no adequate remedy at law, and such property or property right must be described with particularity in the application, which must be in writing and sworn to by the applicant or by his agent or attorney.

And no such restraining order or injunction shall prohibit any person or persons, whether singly or in concert, from terminating any relation of employment, or from ceasing to perform any work or labor, or from recommending, advising, or persuading others by peaceful means so to do; or from attending at any place where any such person or persons may lawfully be, for the purpose of peacefully obtaining or communicating information, or from peacefully persuading any person to work or to abstain from working; or from ceasing to patronize or to employ any party to such dispute, or from recommending, advising, or persuading others by peaceful and lawful means so to do; or from paying or giving to, or withholding from, any person engaged in such dispute, any strike benefits or other moneys or things of value; or from peaceably assembling in a lawful manner, and for lawful purposes; or from doing any act or thing which might lawfully be done in the absence of such dispute by any party thereto; nor shall any of the acts specified in this paragraph be considered or held to be violations of any law of the United States.

(Oct. 15, 1914, c.323, §20, 38 Stat. 738.)

Norris-LaGuardia Act of 1933
47 Stat. 70 (1932), as amended, 29 U.S.C. §§101-115

§1. (§101) Issuance of restraining orders and injunctions; limitation; public policy

No court of the United States, as defined in this chapter, shall have jurisdiction to issue any restraining order or temporary or permanent injunction in a case involving or growing out of a labor dispute, except in a strict conformity with the provisions of this chapter; nor shall any such restraining order or temporary or permanent injunction be issued contrary to the public policy declared in this chapter.

(Mar. 23, 1932, c.90, §1, 47 Stat. 70.)

§2. (§102) Public policy in labor matters declared

In the interpretation of this chapter and in determining the jurisdiction and authority of the courts of the United States, as such jurisdiction and authority are defined and limited in this chapter, the public policy of the United States is declared as follows:

Whereas under prevailing economic conditions, developed with the aid of governmental authority for owners of property to organize in the corporate and other forms of ownership association, the individual unorganized worker is commonly helpless to exercise actual liberty of contract and to protect his freedom of labor, and thereby to obtain acceptable terms and conditions of employment, wherefore, though he should be free to decline to associate with his fellows, it is necessary that he have full freedom of association, self-organization, and designation of representatives of his own choosing, to negotiate the terms and conditions of his employment, and that he shall be free from the interference, restraint, or coercion of employers of labor, or their agents, in the designation of such representatives or in self-organization or in other concerted activities for the purpose of collective bargaining or other mutual aid or protection; therefore, the following definitions of and limitations upon the jurisdiction and authority of the courts of the United States are enacted.

(Mar. 23, 1932, c.90, §2, 47 Stat. 70.)

§3. (§103) Nonenforceability of undertakings in conflict with public policy; "yellow dog" contracts

Any undertaking or promise, such as is described in this section, or any other undertaking or promise in conflict with the public policy declared in section 102 of this title, is declared to be contrary to the public policy of the United States, shall not be enforceable in any court of the United States and shall not afford any basis for the granting of legal or equitable relief by any such court, including specifically the following:

Every undertaking or promise hereafter made, whether written or oral, express or implied, constituting or contained in any contract or agreement of hiring or employment between any individual, firm, company, association, or corporation, and any employee or prospective employee of the same, whereby

(a) Either party to such contract or agreement undertakes or promises not to join, become, or remain a member of any labor organization or of any employer organization; or

(b) Either party to such contract or agreement undertakes or promises that he will withdraw from an employment relation in the event that he joins, becomes, or remains a member of any labor organization or of any employer organization.

(Mar. 23, 1932, c.90, §3, 47 Stat. 70.)

§4. (§104) Enumeration of specific acts not subject to restraining orders or injunctions

No court of the United States shall have jurisdiction to issue any restraining order or temporary or permanent injunction in any case involving or growing out of any labor dispute to prohibit any person or persons participating or interested in such dispute (as these terms are herein defined) from doing, whether singly or in concert, any of the following acts:

(a) Ceasing or refusing to perform any work or to remain in any relation of employment;

(b) Becoming or remaining a member of any labor organization or of any employer organization, regardless of any such undertaking or promise as is described in section 103 of this title;

(c) Paying or giving to, or withholding from, any person participating or interested in such labor dispute, any strike or unemployment benefits or insurance, or other moneys or things of value;

(d) By all lawful means aiding any person participating or interested in any labor dispute who is being proceeded against in, or is prosecuting, any action or suit in any court of the United States or of any State;

(e) Giving publicity to the existence of, or the facts involved in, any labor dispute, whether by advertising, speaking, patrolling, or by any other method not involving fraud or violence;

(f) Assembling peaceably to act or to organize to act in promotion of their interests in a labor dispute;

(g) Advising or notifying any person of an intention to do any of the acts heretofore specified;

(h) Agreeing with other persons to do or not to do any of the acts heretofore specified; and

(i) Advising, urging, or otherwise causing or inducing without fraud or violence the acts heretofore specified, regardless of any such undertaking or promise as is described in section 103 of this title.

(Mar. 23, 1932, c.90, §4, 47 Stat. 70.)

§5. (§105) Doing in concert of certain acts as constituting unlawful combination or conspiracy subjecting person to injunctive remedies

No court of the United States shall have jurisdiction to issue a restraining order or temporary or permanent injunction upon the ground that any of the persons participating or interested in a labor dispute constitute or are engaged in an unlawful combination or conspiracy because of the doing in concert of the acts enumerated in section 104 of this title.

(Mar. 23, 1932, c.90, §5, 47 Stat. 71.)

§6. (§106) Responsibility of officers and members of associations or their organizations for unlawful acts of individual officers, members, and agents

No officer or member of any association or organization, and no association or organization participating or interested in a labor dispute, shall be held responsible or liable in any court of the United States for the unlawful acts of individual officers, members, or agents, except upon clear proof of actual participation in, or actual authorization of, such acts, or of ratification of such acts after actual knowledge thereof.

(Mar. 23, 1932, c.90, §6, 47 Stat. 71.)

§7. (§107) Issuance of injunctions in labor disputes; hearing; findings of court; notice to affected persons; temporary restraining order; undertakings

No court of the United States shall have jurisdiction to issue a temporary or permanent injunction in any case involving or growing out of a labor dispute, as defined in this chapter, except after hearing the testimony of witnesses in open court (with opportunity for cross-examination) in support of the allegations of a complaint made under oath, and testimony in opposition thereto, if offered, and except after findings of fact by the court, to the effect—

(a) That unlawful acts have been threatened and will be committed unless restrained or have been committed and will be continued unless restrained, but no injunction or temporary restraining order shall be issued on account of any threat or unlawful act excepting against the person or persons, association, or organization making the threat or committing the unlawful act or actually authorizing or ratifying the same after actual knowledge thereof;

(b) That substantial and irreparable injury to complainant's property will follow;

(c) That as to each item of relief granted greater injury will be inflicted upon complainant by the denial of relief than will be inflicted upon defendants by the granting of relief;

(d) That complainant has no adequate remedy at law; and

(e) That the public officers charged with the duty to protect complainant's property are unable or unwilling to furnish adequate protection.

Such hearing shall be held after due and personal notice thereof has been given, in such manner as the court shall direct, to all known persons against whom relief is sought, and also to the chief of those public officials of the county and city within which the unlawful acts have been threatened or committed charged with the duty to protect complainant's property: *Provided, however,* That if a complainant shall also allege that, unless a temporary restraining order shall be issued without notice, a substantial and irreparable injury to complainant's property will be unavoidable, such a temporary restraining order may be issued upon testimony under oath, sufficient, if sustained, to justify the court in issuing a temporary injunction upon a hearing after notice. Such a temporary restraining order shall be effective for no longer than five days and shall become void at the expiration of said five days. No temporary restraining order or temporary injunction shall be issued except on condition that complainant shall first file an undertaking with adequate security in an amount to be fixed by the court sufficient to recompense those enjoined for any loss, expense, or damage caused by the improvident or erroneous issuance of such order or injunction, including all reasonable costs (together with a reasonable attorney's fee) and expense of defense against the order or against the granting of any injunctive relief sought in the same proceeding and subsequently denied by the court.

The undertaking mentioned in this section shall be understood to signify an agreement entered into by the complainant and the surety upon which a decree may be rendered in the same suit or proceeding against said complainant and surety, upon a hearing to assess damages of which hearing complainant and surety shall have reasonable notice, the said complainant and surety submitting themselves to the jurisdiction of the court for that purpose. But nothing in this section contained shall deprive any party having a claim or cause of action under or upon such undertaking from electing to pursue his ordinary remedy by suit at law or in equity.

(Mar. 23, 1932, c.90, §7, 47 Stat. 71.)

§8. (§108) Noncompliance with obligations involved in labor disputes or failure to settle by negotiation or arbitration as preventing injunctive relief

No restraining order or injunctive relief shall be granted to any complainant who has failed to comply with any obligation imposed by law which is involved in the labor dispute in question, or who has failed to make every reasonable effort to settle such dispute either by negotiation or with the aid of any available governmental machinery of mediation or voluntary arbitration.

(Mar. 23, 1932, c.90, §8, 47 Stat. 72.)

§9. (§109) Granting of restraining order or injunction as dependent on previous findings of fact; limitation on prohibitions included in restraining orders and injunctions

No restraining order or temporary or permanent injunction shall be granted in a case involving or growing out of a labor dispute, except on the basis of findings of fact made and filed by the court in the record of the case prior to the issuance of such restraining order or injunction; and every restraining order or injunction granted in a case involving or growing out of a labor dispute shall include only a prohibition of such specific act or acts as may be expressly complained of in the bill of complaint or petition filed in such case and as shall be expressly included in said findings of fact made and filed by the court as provided in this chapter.

(Mar. 23, 1932, c.90, §9, 47 Stat. 72.)

§10. (§110) Review by Court of Appeals of issuance or denial of temporary injunctions; record

Whenever any court of the United States shall issue or deny any temporary injunction in a case involving or growing out of a labor dispute, the court shall, upon the request of any party to the proceedings and on his filing the usual bond for costs, forthwith certify as in ordinary cases the record of the case to the court of appeals for its review. Upon the filing of such record in the court of appeals, the appeal shall be heard and the temporary injunctive order affirmed, modified, or set aside expeditiously.

(Mar. 23, 1932, c.90, §10, 47 Stat. 72; June 25, 1948, c.646, §32(a), 62 Stat. 991; May 24, 1949, c.139, §127, 63 Stat. 107; Nov. 8, 1984, Pub. L. 98-620, Title IV, §402(30), 98 Stat. 3359.)

§§11, 12. (§§111, 112) [Repealed. June 25, 1948, c.645, §21, 62 Stat. 862, eff. Sept. 1, 1948.]*

§13. (§113) Definitions of terms and words used in chapter

When used in this chapter, and for the purposes of this chapter—

(a) A case shall be held to involve or to grow out of a labor dispute when the case involves persons who are engaged in the same industry, trade, craft, or occupation; or have direct or indirect interests therein; or who are employees of the same employer; or who are members of the same or an affiliated organization of employers or employees; whether such dispute is (1) between one or more employers or associations of employers and one or more employees or associations of employees; (2) between one or more employers or associations of employers and one or more employers or associations of employers; or (3) between one or more employees or associations of employees and one or more employees or associations of employees; or when the case involves any conflicting or competing interests in a "labor dispute" (as defined in this section) of "persons participating or interested" therein (as defined in this section).

(b) A person or association shall be held to be a person participating or interested in a labor dispute if relief is sought against him or it, and if he or it is engaged in the same industry, trade, craft, or occupation in which such dispute occurs, or has a direct or indirect interest therein, or is a member, officer, or agent of any association composed in whole or in part of employers or employees engaged in such industry, trade, craft, or occupation.

(c) The term "labor dispute" includes any controversy concerning terms or conditions of employment, or concerning the association or representation of persons in negotiating, fixing, maintaining, changing, or seeking to arrange terms or conditions of employment, regardless of whether or not the disputants stand in the proximate relation of employer and employee.

(d) The term "court of the United States" means any court of the United States whose jurisdiction has been or may be conferred or defined or limited by Act of Congress, including the courts of the District of Columbia.

(Mar. 23, 1932, c.90, §13, 47 Stat. 73.)

---

*The text of §11, dealing with the right of persons charged with contempt to "a speedy and public trial by an impartial jury of the state and district wherein the contempt shall have been committed," is now in 18 U.S.C. §3692. The subject of §12, dealing with recusal, is treated in Rule 42 of the Federal Rules of Criminal Procedure.—Eds.

§14. (§114) Separability of provisions

If any provision of this chapter or the application thereof to any person or circumstance is held unconstitutional or otherwise invalid, the remaining provisions of this chapter and the application of such provisions to other persons or circumstances shall not be affected thereby.

(Mar. 23, 1932, c.90, §14, 47 Stat. 73.)

§15. (§115) Repeal of conflicting acts

All acts and parts of acts in conflict with the provisions of this chapter are repealed.

(Mar. 23, 1932, c.90, §15, 47 Stat. 73.)

Federal Arbitration Act
61 Stat. 669 (1947), as amended, 9 U.S.C. §§1 et seq.*

§1. "Maritime transactions" and "commerce" defined; exceptions to operation of title

"Maritime transactions", as herein defined, means charter parties, bills of lading of water carriers, agreements relating to wharfage, supplies furnished vessels or repairs to vessels, collisions, or any other matters in foreign commerce which, if the subject of controversy, would be embraced within admiralty jurisdiction; "commerce", as herein defined, means commerce among the several States or with foreign nations, or in any Territory of the United States or in the District of Columbia, or between any such Territory and another, or between any such Territory and any State or foreign nation, or between the District of Columbia and any State or Territory or foreign nation, but nothing herein contained shall apply to contracts of employment of seamen, railroad employees, or any other class of workers engaged in foreign or interstate commerce.

(July 30, 1947, c.392, 61 Stat. 670.)

§2. Validity, irrevocability, and enforcement of agreements to arbitrate

A written provision in any maritime transaction or a contract evidencing a transaction involving commerce to settle by arbitration a controversy thereafter arising out of such contract or transaction, or the refusal to perform the whole or any part thereof, or an agreement in writ-

---

*This law is derived from Act of Feb. 12, 1925, c.213, 43 Stat. 883. —Eds.

Federal Arbitration Act

ing to submit to arbitration an existing controversy arising out of such a contract, transaction, or refusal, shall be valid, irrevocable, and enforceable, save upon such grounds as exist at law or in equity for the revocation of any contract.

(July 30, 1947, c.392, 61 Stat. 670.)

§3. Stay of proceedings where issue therein referable to arbitration

If any suit or proceeding be brought in any of the courts of the United States upon any issue referable to arbitration under an agreement in writing for such arbitration, the court in which such suit is pending, upon being satisfied that the issue involved in such suit or proceeding is referable to arbitration under such an agreement, shall on application of one of the parties stay the trial of the action until such arbitration has been had in accordance with the terms of the agreement, providing the applicant for the stay is not in default in proceeding with such arbitration.

(July 30, 1947, c.392, 61 Stat. 670.)

§4. Failure to arbitrate under agreement; petition to United States court having jurisdiction for order to compel arbitration; notice and service thereof; hearing and determination

A party aggrieved by the alleged failure, neglect, or refusal of another to arbitrate under a written agreement for arbitration may petition any United States district court which, save for such agreement, would have jurisdiction under Title 28, in a civil action or in admiralty of the subject matter of a suit arising out of the controversy between the parties, for an order directing that such arbitration proceed in the manner provided for in such agreement. Five days' notice in writing of such application shall be served upon the party in default. Service thereof shall be made in the manner provided by the Federal Rules of Civil Procedure. The court shall hear the parties, and upon being satisfied that the making of the agreement for arbitration or the failure to comply therewith is not in issue, the court shall make an order directing the parties to proceed to arbitration in accordance with the terms of the agreement. The hearing and proceedings, under such agreement, shall be within the district in which the petition for an order directing such arbitration is filed. If the making of the arbitration agreement or the failure, neglect, or refusal to perform the same be in issue, the court shall proceed summarily to the trial thereof. If no jury trial be demanded by the party alleged to be in default, or if the matter in dispute is within admiralty jurisdiction, the court shall hear and determine such issue. Where such an issue is raised, the party alleged to be in default may, except in cases of admiralty, on or before the return day of the notice of application, demand a jury trial of such issue, and upon such demand the court shall make an order referring the issue or issues to a jury in the manner provided by the Federal Rules of Civil Procedure, or may specially call a jury for that purpose. If the jury find that no agreement in writing for arbitration was made or that there is no default in proceeding thereunder, the proceeding shall be dismissed. If the jury find that an agreement for arbitration was made in writing and that there is a default in proceeding thereunder, the court shall make an order summarily directing the parties to proceed with the arbitration in accordance with the terms thereof.

(July 30, 1947, c.392, 61 Stat. 671; Sept. 3, 1954, c.1263, §19, 68 Stat. 1233.)

§5. Appointment of arbitrators or umpire

If in the agreement provision be made for a method of naming or appointing an arbitrator or arbitrators or an umpire, such method shall be followed; but if no method be provided therein, or if a method be provided and any party thereto shall fail to avail himself of such method, or if for any other reason there shall be a lapse in the naming of an arbitrator or arbitrators or umpire, or in filling a vacancy, then upon the application of either party to the controversy the court shall designate and appoint an arbitrator or arbitrators or umpire, as the case may require, who shall act under the said agreement with the same force and effect as if he or they had been specifically named therein; and unless otherwise provided in the agreement the arbitration shall be by a single arbitrator.

(July 30, 1947, c.392, 61 Stat. 671.)

§6. Application heard as motion

Any application to the court hereunder shall be made and heard in the manner provided by law for the making and hearing of motions, except as otherwise herein expressly provided.

(July 30, 1947, c.392, 61 Stat. 671.)

§7. Witnesses before arbitrators; fees; compelling attendance

The arbitrators selected either as prescribed in this title or otherwise, or a majority of them, may summon in writing any person to attend before them or any of them as a witness and in a proper case to bring with him or them any book, record, document, or paper which may be deemed material as evidence in the case. The fees for such attendance shall be the same as the fees of witnesses before masters of the United States courts. Said summons shall issue in the name of the arbitrator or arbitrators, or a majority of them, and shall be signed by the arbitrators, or a majority of them, and shall be directed to the said person and shall be served in the same manner as subpoenas to appear and testify before the court; if any person or persons so summoned to testify shall refuse or neglect to obey said summons, upon petition the United States district court for the district in which such arbitrators, or a majority of them, are sitting may compel the attendance of such person or persons before said arbitrator or arbitrators, or punish said person or persons for contempt in the same manner provided by law for securing the attendance of witnesses or their punishment for neglect or refusal to attend in the courts of the United States.

(July 30, 1947, c.392, 61 Stat. 672; Oct. 31, 1951, c.655, §14, 65 Stat. 715.)

§8. Proceedings begun by libel in admiralty and seizure of vessel or property

If the basis of jurisdiction be a cause of action otherwise justiciable in admiralty, then, notwithstanding anything herein to the contrary, the party claiming to be aggrieved may begin his proceeding hereunder by libel and seizure of the vessel or other property of the other party according to the usual course of admiralty proceedings, and the court shall then have jurisdiction to direct the parties to proceed with the arbitration and shall retain jurisdiction to enter its decree upon the award.

(July 30, 1947, c.392, 61 Stat. 672.)

§9. Award of arbitrators; confirmation; jurisdiction; procedure

If the parties in their agreement have agreed that a judgment of the court shall be entered upon the award made pursuant to the arbitration, and shall specify the court, then at any time within one year after the award is made any party to the arbitration may apply to the court so specified for an order confirming the award, and thereupon the court must grant such an order unless the award is vacated, modified, or corrected as prescribed in sections 10 and 11 of this title. If no court is specified in the agreement of the parties, then such application may be made to the United States court in and for the district within which such award was made. Notice of the application shall be served upon the adverse party, and thereupon the court shall have jurisdiction of such party as though he had appeared generally in the proceeding. If the adverse party is a resident of the district within which the award was made, such service shall be made upon the adverse party or his attorney as prescribed by law for service of notice of motion in an action in the same court. If the adverse party shall be a nonresident, then the notice of the application shall be served by the marshal of any district within which the adverse party may be found in like manner as other process of the court.

(July 30, 1947, c.392, 61 Stat. 672.)

§10. Same; vacation; grounds; rehearing

(a) In any of the following cases the United States court in and for the district wherein the award was made may make an order vacating the award upon the application of any party to the arbitration—

(1) Where the award was procured by corruption, fraud, or undue means.

(2) Where there was evident partiality or corruption in the arbitrators, or either of them.

(3) Where the arbitrators were guilty of misconduct in refusing to postpone the hearing, upon sufficient cause shown, or in refusing to hear evidence pertinent and material to the controversy; or of any other misbehavior by which the rights of any party have been prejudiced.

(4) Where the arbitrators exceeded their powers, or so imperfectly executed them that a mutual, final, and definite award upon the subject matter submitted was not made.

(5) Where an award is vacated and the time within which the agreement required the award to be made has not expired the court may, in its discretion, direct a rehearing by the arbitrators.

(b) The United States district court for the district wherein an award was made that was issued pursuant to section 580 of title 5 may make an order vacating the award upon the application of a person, other than a party to the arbitration, who is adversely affected or aggrieved by the award, if the use of arbitration or the award is clearly inconsistent with the factors set forth in section 572 of title 5.

(July 30, 1947, c.392, 61 Stat. 672; Nov. 15, 1990, Pub. L. 101-552, §5, 104 Stat. 2745; Aug. 26, 1992, Pub. L. 102-354, §5(b)(4), 106 Stat. 946.)

§11. Same; modification or correction; grounds; order

In either of the following cases the United States court in and for the district wherein the award was made may make an order modifying or correcting the award upon the application of any party to the arbitration—

(a) Where there was an evident material miscalculation of figures or an evident material mistake in the description of any person, thing, or property referred to in the award.

(b) Where the arbitrators have awarded upon a matter not submitted to them, unless it is a matter not affecting the merits of the decision upon the matter submitted.

(c) Where the award is imperfect in matter of form not affecting the merits of the controversy.

The order may modify and correct the award, so as to effect the intent thereof and promote justice between the parties.

(July 30, 1947, c.392, 61 Stat. 673.)

§12. Notice of motions to vacate or modify; service; stay of proceedings

Notice of a motion to vacate, modify, or correct an award must be served upon the adverse party or his attorney within three months after the award is filed or delivered. If the adverse party is a resident of the district within which the award was made, such service shall be made upon the adverse party or his attorney as prescribed by law for service of notice of motion in an action in the same court. If the adverse party shall be a non-resident then the notice of the application shall be served by the marshal of any district within which the adverse party may be found in like manner as other process of the court. For the purposes of the motion any judge who might make an order to stay the proceedings in an action brought in the same court may make an order, to be served with the notice of motion, staying the proceedings of the adverse party to enforce the award.

(July 30, 1947, c.392, 61 Stat. 673.)

§13. Papers filed with order on motions; judgment; docketing; force and effect; enforcement

The party moving for an order confirming, modifying, or correcting an award shall, at the time such order is filed with the clerk for the entry of judgment thereon, also file the following papers with the clerk:

(a) The agreement; the selection or appointment, if any, of an additional arbitrator or umpire; and each written extension of the time, if any, within which to make the award.

(b) The award.

(c) Each notice, affidavit, or other paper used upon an application to confirm, modify, or correct the award, and a copy of each order of the court upon such an application.

The judgment shall be docketed as if it was rendered in an action.

The judgment so entered shall have the some force and effect, in all respects, as, and be subject to all the provisions of law relating to, a judgment in an action; and it may be enforced as if it had been rendered in an action in the court in which it is entered.

(July 30, 1947, c.392, 61 Stat. 673.)

§14. **Contracts not affected**

This title shall not apply to contracts made prior to January 1, 1926.

(July 30, 1947, c.392, 61 Stat. 673.)

Railway Labor Act of 1926
44 Stat. 577 (1926), as amended, 45 U.S.C. §§151-188

SUBCHAPTER I.   GENERAL PROVISIONS

§1. (§151) **Definitions; short title**

When used in this chapter and for the purposes of this chapter—

First. The term "carrier" includes any express company, sleeping-car company, carrier by railroad, subject to subtitle IV of Title 49, and any company which is directly or indirectly owned or controlled by or under common control with any carrier by railroad and which operates any equipment or facilities or performs any service (other than trucking service) in connection with the transportation, receipt, delivery, elevation, transfer in transit, refrigeration or icing, storage, and handling of property transported by railroad, and any receiver, trustee, or other individual or body, judicial or otherwise, when in the possession of the business of any such "carrier": *Provided, however,* That the term "carrier" shall not include any street, interurban, or suburban electric railway, unless such railway is operating as a part of a general steam-railroad system of transportation, but shall not exclude any part of the general steam-railroad system of transportation now or hereafter operated by any other motive power. The Interstate Commerce Commission is authorized and directed upon request of the Mediation Board or upon complaint of any party interested to determine after hearing whether any line operated by electric power falls within the terms of this proviso. The term "carrier" shall not include any company by reason of its being engaged in the mining of coal, the supplying of coal to a carrier where delivery is not beyond the mine tipple, and the operation of equipment or facilities therefor, or in any of such activities.

Second. The term "Adjustment Board" means the National Railroad Adjustment Board created by this chapter.

Third. The term "Mediation Board" means the National Mediation Board created by this chapter.

Fourth. The term "commerce" means commerce among the several States or between any State, Territory, or the District of Columbia and any foreign nation, or between any Territory or the District of Columbia and any State, or between any Territory and any other Territory, or between any Territory and the District of Columbia, or within any Territory or the District of Columbia, or between points in the same State but through any other State or any Territory or the District of Columbia or any foreign nation.

Fifth. The term "employee" as used herein includes every person in the service of a carrier (subject to its continuing authority to supervise and direct the manner of rendition of his service) who performs any work defined as that of an employee or subordinate official in the orders of the Interstate Commerce Commission now in effect, and as the same may be amended or interpreted by orders hereafter entered by the Commission pursuant to the authority which is conferred upon it to enter orders amending or interpreting such existing orders: *Provided, however,* That no occupational classification made by order of the Interstate Commerce Commission shall be construed to define the crafts according to which railway employees may be organized by their voluntary action, nor shall the jurisdiction or powers of such employee organizations be regarded as in any way limited or defined by the provisions of this chapter or by the orders of the Commission.

The term "employee" shall not include any individual while such individual is engaged in the physical operations consisting of the mining of coal, the preparation of coal, the handling (other than movement by rail with standard railroad locomotives) of coal not beyond the mine tipple, or the loading of coal at the tipple.

Sixth. The term "representative" means any person or persons, labor union, organization, or corporation designated either by a carrier or group of carriers or by its or their employees, to act for it or them.

Seventh. The term "district court" includes the United States District Court for the District of Columbia; and the term "court of appeals" includes the United States Court of Appeals for the District of Columbia.

This chapter may be cited as the "Railway Labor Act."

(May 20, 1926, c.347, §1, 44 Stat. 577; June 7, 1934, c.426, 48 Stat. 926; June 21, 1934, c.691, §1, 48 Stat. 1185; June 25, 1936, c.804, 49 Stat. 1921; Aug. 13, 1940, c.664, §§2, 3, 54 Stat. 785, 786; June 25, 1948, c.646, §32(a), (b), 62 Stat. 991; May 24, 1949, c.139, §127, 63 Stat. 107.)

§2. (§151a) General purposes

The purposes of the chapter are: (1) To avoid any interruption to commerce or to the operation of any carrier engaged therein; (2) to forbid any limitation upon freedom of association among employees or any denial, as a condition of employment or otherwise, of the right of employees to join a labor organization; (3) to provide for the complete independence of carriers and of employees in the matter of self-organization to carry out the purposes of this chapter; (4) to provide for the prompt and orderly settlement of all disputes concerning rates of pay, rules, or working conditions; (5) to provide for the prompt and orderly settlement of all disputes growing out of grievances or out of the interpretation or application of agreements covering rates of pay, rules, or working conditions.

(May 20, 1926, c.347, §2, 44 Stat. 577; June 21, 1934, c.691, §2, 48 Stat. 1186.)

§2. (§152) General duties

First. Duty of carriers and employees to settle disputes

It shall be the duty of all carriers, their officers, agents, and employees to exert every reasonable effort to make and maintain agreements concerning rates of pay, rules, and working conditions, and to settle all disputes, whether arising out of the application of such agreements or otherwise, in order to avoid any interruption to commerce or to the operation of any carrier growing out of any dispute between the carrier and the employees thereof.

Second. Consideration of disputes by representatives

All disputes between a carrier or carriers and its or their employees shall be considered, and, if possible, decided, with all expedition, in conference between representatives designated and authorized so to confer, respectively, by the carrier or carriers and by the employees thereof interested in the dispute.

Third. Designation of representatives

Representatives, for the purposes of this chapter, shall be designated by the respective parties without interference, influence, or coercion by either party over the designation of representatives by the other; and neither party shall in any way interfere with, influence, or coerce the other in its choice of representatives. Representatives of employees for the purposes of this chapter need not be persons in the employ of the carrier, and no carrier shall, by interference, influence, or coercion seek in any manner to prevent the designation by its employees as their representatives of those who or which are not employees of the carrier.

Fourth. Organization and collective bargaining; freedom from interference by carrier; assistance in organizing or maintaining organization by carrier forbidden; deduction of dues from wages forbidden

Employees shall have the right to organize and bargain collectively through representatives of their own choosing. The majority of any craft or class of employees shall have the right to determine who shall be the representative of the craft or class for the purposes of this chapter. No carrier, its officers, or agents shall deny or in any way question the right of its employees to join, organize, or assist in organizing the labor organization of their choice, and it shall be unlawful for any carrier to interfere in any way with the organization of its employees, or to use the funds of the carrier in maintaining or assisting or contributing to any labor organization, labor representative, or other agency of collective bargaining, or in performing any work therefor, or to influence or coerce employees in an effort to induce them to join or remain or not to join or remain members of any labor organization, or to deduct from the wages of employees any dues, fees, assessments, or other contributions payable to labor organizations, or to collect or to assist in the collection of any such dues, fees, assessments, or other contributions: *Provided*, That nothing in this chapter shall be construed to prohibit a carrier from permitting an employee, individually, or local representatives of employees from conferring with management during working hours without loss of time, or to prohibit a carrier from furnishing free transportation to its employees while engaged in the business of a labor organization.

Fifth. Agreements to join or not to join labor organizations forbidden

No carrier, its officers, or agents shall require any person seeking employment to sign any contract or agreement promising to join or not to join a labor organization; and if any such contract has been enforced prior to the effective date of this chapter, then such carrier shall notify the employees by an appropriate order that such contract has been discarded and is no longer binding on them in any way.

Sixth. Conference of representatives; time; place; private agreements

In case of a dispute between a carrier or carriers and its or their employees, arising out of grievances or out of the interpretation or application of agreements concerning rates of pay, rules, or working conditions, it shall be the duty of the designated representative or representatives of such carrier or carriers and of such employees, within ten days after the receipt of notice of a desire on the part of either party to confer in respect to such dispute, to specify a time and place at which such conference shall be held: *Provided,* (1) That the place so specified shall be situated upon the line of the carrier involved or as otherwise mutually agreed upon; and (2) that the time so specified shall allow the designated conferees reasonable opportunity to reach such place of conference, but shall not exceed twenty days from the receipt of such notice: *And provided further*, That nothing in this chapter shall be construed to supersede the provisions of any agreement (as to conferences) then in effect between the parties.

Seventh. Change in pay, rules, or working conditions contrary to agreement or to section 156 forbidden

No carrier, its officers, or agents shall change the rates of pay, rules, or working conditions of its employees, as a class, as embodied in agreements except in the manner prescribed in such agreements or in section 156 of this title.

Eighth. Notices of manner of settlement of disputes; posting

Every carrier shall notify its employees by printed notices in such form and posted at such times and places as shall be specified by the Mediation Board that all disputes between the carrier and its employees will be handled in accordance with the requirements of this chapter, and in such notices there shall be printed verbatim, in large type, the third, fourth, and fifth paragraphs of this section. The provisions of said paragraphs are made a part of the contract of employment between the carrier and each employee, and shall be held binding upon the parties, regardless of any other express or implied agreements between them.

Ninth. Disputes as to identity of representatives; designation by Mediation Board; secret elections

If any dispute shall arise among a carrier's employees as to who are the representatives of such employees designated and authorized in accordance with the requirements of this chapter, it shall be the duty of the Mediation Board, upon request of either party to the dispute, to investigate such dispute and to certify to both parties, in writing, within thirty days after the receipt of the invocation of its services, the name or names of the individuals or organizations that have been designated and authorized to represent the employees involved in the dispute, and certify the same to the carrier. Upon receipt of such certification the carrier shall treat with the representative so certified as the representative of the craft or class for the purposes of this chapter. In such an investigation, the Mediation Board shall be authorized to take a secret ballot of the employees involved, or to utilize any other appropriate method of ascertaining the names of their duly designated and authorized representatives in such manner as shall insure the choice of representatives by the employees without interference, influence, or coercion exercised by the carrier. In the conduct of any election for the purposes herein indicated the Board shall designate who may participate in the election and establish the rules to govern the election, or may appoint a committee of three neutral persons who after hearing shall within ten days designate the employees who may participate in the election. The Board shall have access to and have power to make copies of the books and records of the carriers to obtain and utilize such information as may be deemed necessary by it to carry out the purposes and provisions of this paragraph.

Tenth. Violations; prosecution and penalties

The willful failure or refusal of any carrier, its officers or agents, to comply with the terms of the third, fourth, fifth, seventh, or eighth paragraph of this section shall be a misdemeanor, and upon conviction thereof the carrier, officer, or agent offending shall be subject to a fine of not less than $1,000, nor more than $20,000, or imprisonment for not more than six months, or both fine and imprisonment, for each offense, and each day during which such carrier, officer, or agent shall willfully fail or refuse to comply with the terms of the said paragraphs of this section shall constitute a separate offense. It shall be the duty of any United States attorney to whom any duly designated representative of a carrier's employees may apply to institute in the proper court and to prosecute under the direction of the Attorney General of the United States, all necessary proceedings for the enforcement of the provisions of this section, and for the punishment of all violations thereof and the costs and expenses of such prosecution shall be paid out of the appropriation for the expenses of the courts of the United States: *Provided*, That nothing in this chapter shall be construed to require an individual employee to render labor or service without his consent, nor shall anything in this chapter be construed to make the quitting of his labor by an individual employee an illegal act; nor shall any court issue any process to compel the performance by an individual employee of such labor or service, without his consent.

Eleventh. Union security agreements; check-off

Notwithstanding any other provisions of this chapter, or of any other statute or law of the United States, or Territory thereof, or of any State, any carrier or carriers as defined in this chapter and a labor organization or labor organizations duly designated and authorized to represent employees in accordance with the requirements of this chapter shall be permitted—

(a) to make agreements, requiring, as a condition of continued employment, that within sixty days following the beginning of such employment, or the effective date of such agreements, whichever is the later, all employees shall become members of the labor organization representing their craft or class: *Provided*, That no such agreement shall require such condition of employment with respect to employees to whom membership is not available upon the same terms and conditions as are generally applicable to any other member or with respect to employees to whom membership was denied or terminated for any reason other than the failure of the employee to tender the periodic dues, initiation fees, and assessments (not including fines and penalties) uniformly required as a condition of acquiring or retaining membership.

(b) to make agreements providing for the deduction by such carrier or carriers from the wages of its or their employees in a craft or class and payment to the labor organization representing the craft or class of such employees, of any periodic dues, initiation fees, and assessments (not including fines and penalties) uniformly required as a condition of acquiring or retaining membership: *Provided*, That no such agreement shall be effective with respect to any individual employee until he shall have furnished the employer with a written assignment to the labor organization of such membership dues, initiation fees, and assessments, which shall be revocable in writing after the expiration of one year or upon the termination date of the applicable collective agreement, whichever occurs sooner.

(c) The requirement of membership in a labor organization in an agreement made pursuant to subparagraph (a) of this paragraph shall be satisfied, as to both a present or future employee in engine, train, yard, or hostling service, that is, an employee engaged in any of the services or capacities covered in the First division of paragraph (h) of section 153 of this title defining the jurisdictional scope of the First Division of the National Railroad Adjustment Board, if said employee shall hold or acquire membership in any one of the labor organizations, national in scope, organized in accordance with this chapter and admitting to membership employees of a craft or class in any of said services; and no agreement made pursuant to subparagraph (b) of this paragraph shall provide for deductions from his wages for periodic dues, initiation fees, or assessments payable to any labor organization other than that in which he holds membership: *Provided, however*, That as to an employee in any of said services on a particular carrier at the effective date of any such agreement on a carrier, who is not a member of any one of the labor organizations, national in scope, organized in accordance with this chapter and admitting to membership employees of a craft or class in any of said services, such employee, as a condition of continuing his employment, may be required to become a member of the organization representing the craft in which he is employed on the effective date of the first agreement applicable to him: *Provided, further*, That nothing herein or in any such agreement or agreements shall prevent an employee from changing membership from one organization to another organization admitting to membership employees of a craft or class in any of said services.

(d) Any provisions in paragraphs Fourth and Fifth of this section in conflict herewith are to the extent of such conflict amended.

(May 20, 1926, c.347, §2, 44 Stat. 577; June 21, 1934, c.691, §2, 48 Stat. 1186; June 25, 1948, c.646, §1, 62 Stat. 909; Jan. 10, 1951, c.1220, 64 Stat. 1238.)

§3. (§153) National Railroad Adjustment Board

First. Establishment; composition; powers and duties; divisions; hearings and awards; judicial review

There is established a Board, to be known as the "National Railroad Adjustment Board", the members of which shall be selected within thirty days after June 21, 1934, and it is provided—

(a) That the said Adjustment Board shall consist of thirty-four members, seventeen of whom shall be selected by the carriers and seventeen by such labor organizations of the employees, national in scope, as have been or may be organized in accordance with the provisions of sections 151a and 152 of this title.

(b) The carriers, acting each through its board of directors or its receiver or receivers, trustee or trustees, or through an officer or officers designated for that purpose by such board, trustee or trustees, or receiver or receivers, shall prescribe the rules under which its representatives shall be selected and shall select the representatives of the carriers on the Adjustment Board and designate the division on which each such representative shall serve, but no carrier or system of carriers shall have more than one voting representative on any division of the Board.

(c) Except as provided in the second paragraph of subsection (h) of this section, the national labor organizations, as defined in paragraph (a) of this section, acting each through the chief executive or other medium designated by the organization or association thereof, shall prescribe the rules under which the labor members of the Adjustment Board shall be selected and shall select such members and designate the division on which each member shall serve; but no labor organization shall have more than one voting representative on any division of the Board.

(d) In case of a permanent or temporary vacancy on the Adjustment Board, the vacancy shall be filled by selection in the same manner as in the original selection.

(e) If either the carriers or the labor organizations of the employees fail to select and designate representatives to the Adjustment Board, as provided in paragraphs (b) and (c) of this section, respectively, within sixty days after June 21, 1934, in case of any original appointment to office of a member of the Adjustment Board, or in case of a vacancy in any such office within thirty days after such vacancy occurs, the Mediation Board shall thereupon directly make the appointment and shall select an individual associated in interest with the carriers or the group of labor organizations of employees, whichever he is to represent.

(f) In the event a dispute arises as to the right of any national labor organization to participate as per paragraph (c) of this section in the selection and designation of the labor members of the Adjustment Board, the

Secretary of Labor shall investigate the claim of such labor organization to participate, and if such claim in the judgment of the Secretary of Labor has merit, the Secretary shall notify the Mediation Board accordingly, and within ten days after receipt of such advice the Mediation Board shall request those national labor organizations duly qualified as per paragraph (c) of this section to participate in the selection and designation of the labor members of the Adjustment Board to select a representative. Such representative, together with a representative likewise designated by the claimant, and a third or neutral party designated by the Mediation Board, constituting a board of three, shall within thirty days after the appointment of the neutral member, investigate the claims of the labor organization desiring participation and decide whether or not it was organized in accordance with sections 151a and 152 of this title and is otherwise properly qualified to participate in the selection of the labor members of the Adjustment Board, and the findings of such boards of three shall be final and binding.

(g) Each member of the Adjustment Board shall be compensated by the party or parties he is to represent. Each third or neutral party selected under the provisions of paragraph (f) of this section shall receive from the Mediation Board such compensation as the Mediation Board may fix, together with his necessary traveling expenses and expenses actually incurred for subsistence, or per diem allowance in lieu thereof, subject to the provisions of law applicable thereto, while serving as such third or neutral party.

(h) The said Adjustment Board shall be composed of four divisions, whose proceedings shall be independent of one another, and the said divisions as well as the number of their members shall be as follows:

First division: To have jurisdiction over disputes involving train- and yard-service employees of carriers; that is, engineers, firemen, hostlers, and outside hostler helpers, conductors, trainmen, and yard-service employees. This division shall consist of eight members, four of whom shall be selected and designated by the carriers and four of whom shall be selected and designated by the labor organizations, national in scope and organized in accordance with sections 151a and 152 of this title and which represent employees in engine, train, yard, or hostling service: *Provided, however,* That each labor organization shall select and designate two members on the First Division and that no labor organization shall have more than one vote in any proceedings of the First Division or in the adoption of any award with respect to any dispute submitted to the First Division: *Provided further, however,* That the carrier members of the First Division shall cast no more than two votes in any proceedings of the division or in the adoption of any award with respect to any dispute submitted to the First Division.

Second division: To have jurisdiction over disputes involving machinists, boilermakers, blacksmiths, sheet-metal workers, electrical workers, carmen, the helpers and apprentices of all the foregoing, coach cleaners, power-house employees, and railroad-shop laborers. This division shall consist of ten members, five of whom shall be selected by the carriers and five by the national labor organizations of the employees.

Third division: To have jurisdiction over disputes involving station, tower, and telegraph employees, train dispatchers, maintenance-of-way men, clerical employees, freight handlers, express, station, and store employees, signal men, sleeping-car conductors, sleeping-car porters, and maids and dining-car employees. This division shall consist of ten members, five of whom shall be selected by the carriers and five by the national labor organizations of employees.

Fourth division: To have jurisdiction over disputes involving employees of carriers directly or indirectly engaged in transportation of passengers or property by water, and all other employees of carriers over which jurisdiction is not given to the first, second, and third divisions. This division shall consist of six members, three of whom shall be selected by the carriers and three by the national labor organizations of the employees.

(i) The disputes between an employee or group of employees and a carrier or carriers growing out of grievances or out of the interpretation or application of agreements concerning rates of pay, rules, or working conditions, including cases pending and unadjusted on June 21, 1934, shall be handled in the usual manner up to and including the chief operating officer of the carrier designated to handle such disputes; but, failing to reach an adjustment in this manner, the disputes may be referred by petition of the parties or by either party to the appropriate division of the Adjustment Board with a full statement of the facts and all supporting data bearing upon the disputes.

(j) Parties may be heard either in person, by counsel, or by other representatives, as they may respectively elect, and the several divisions of the Adjustment Board shall give due notice of all hearings to the employee or employees and the carrier or carriers involved in any disputes submitted to them.

(k) Any division of the Adjustment Board shall have authority to empower two or more of its members to conduct hearings and make findings upon disputes, when properly submitted, at any place designated by the division: *Provided, however,* That except as provided in paragraph (h) of this section, final awards as to any such dispute must be made by the entire division as hereinafter provided.

(*l*) Upon failure of any division to agree upon an award because of a deadlock or inability to secure a majority vote of the division members, as provided in paragraph (n) of this section, then such division shall forthwith agree upon and select a neutral person, to be known as "referee", to sit with the division as a member thereof, and make an award. Should the division fail to agree upon and select a referee within ten days of the date of the deadlock or inability to secure a majority vote, then the division, or any member thereof, or the parties or either party to the dispute may certify that fact to the Mediation Board, which Board shall, within ten days from the date of receiving such certificate, select and name the referee to sit with the division as a member thereof and make an award. The Mediation Board shall be bound by the same provisions in the appointment of these neutral referees as are provided elsewhere in this chapter for the appointment of arbitrators and shall fix and pay the compensation of such referees.

(m) The awards of the several divisions of the Adjustment Board shall be stated in writing. A copy of the awards shall be furnished to the respective parties to the controversy, and the awards shall be final and binding upon both parties to the dispute. In case a dispute arises involving an interpretation of the award, the division of the Board upon request of either party shall interpret the award in the light of the dispute.

(n) A majority vote of all members of the division of the Adjustment Board eligible to vote shall be competent to make an award with respect to any dispute submitted to it.

(*o*) In case of an award by any division of the Adjustment Board in favor of petitioner, the division of the Board shall make an order, directed to the carrier, to make the award effective and, if the award includes a requirement for the payment of money, to pay to the employee the sum to which he is entitled under the award on or before a day named. In the event any division determines that an award favorable to the petitioner should not be made in any dispute referred to it, the division shall make an order to the petitioner stating such determination.

(p) If a carrier does not comply with an order of a division of the Adjustment Board within the time limit in such order, the petitioner, or any person for whose benefit such order was made, may file in the District Court of the United States for the district in which he resides or in which is located the principal operating office of the carrier, or through which the carrier operates, a petition setting forth briefly the causes for which he claims relief, and the order of the division of the Adjustment Board in the premises. Such suit in the District Court of the United States shall proceed in all respects as other civil suits, except that on the trial of such suit the findings and order of the division of the Adjustment Board shall be conclusive on the parties, and except that the petitioner shall not be liable for costs in the district court nor for costs at any subsequent stage of the proceedings, unless they accrue upon his appeal, and such costs shall be paid out of the appropriation for the expenses of the courts of the United States. If the petitioner shall finally prevail he shall be allowed a reasonable attorney's fee, to be taxed and collected as a part of the costs of the suit. The district courts are empowered, under the rules of the court governing actions at law, to make such order and enter such judgment, by writ of mandamus or otherwise, as may be appropriate to enforce or set aside the order of the division of the Adjustment Board: *Provided, however,* That such order may not be set aside except for failure of the division to comply with the requirements of this chapter, for failure of the order to conform, or confine itself, to matters within the scope of the division's jurisdiction, or for fraud or corruption by a member of the division making the order.

(q) If any employee or group of employees, or any carrier, is aggrieved by the failure of any division of the Adjustment Board to make an award in a dispute referred to it, or is aggrieved by any of the terms of an award or by the failure of the division to include certain terms in such award, then such employee or group of employees or carrier may file in any United States district court in which a petition under paragraph (p) could be filed, a petition for review of the division's order. A copy of the petition shall be forthwith transmitted by the clerk of the court to the Adjustment Board. The Adjustment Board shall file in the court the record of the proceedings on which it based its action. The court shall have jurisdiction to affirm the order of the division or to set it aside, in whole or in part, or it may remand the proceeding to the division for such further action as it may direct. On such review, the findings and order of the division shall be conclusive on the parties, except that the order of the division may be set aside, in whole or in part, or remanded to the division, for failure of the division to comply with the requirements of this chapter, for failure of the order to conform, or confine itself, to matters within the scope of the division's jurisdiction, or for fraud or corruption by a member of the division making the order. The judgment of the court shall be subject to review as provided in sections 1291 and 1254 of Title 28.

(r) All actions at law based upon the provisions of this section shall be begun within two years from the time the cause of action accrues under the award of the division of the Adjustment Board, and not after.

(s) The several divisions of the Adjustment Board shall maintain headquarters in Chicago, Illinois, meet regularly, and continue in session so long as there is pending before the division any matter within its jurisdiction which has been submitted for its consideration and which has not been disposed of.

(t) Whenever practicable, the several divisions or subdivisions of the Adjustment Board shall be supplied with suitable quarters in any Federal building located at its place of meeting.

(u) The Adjustment Board may, subject to the approval of the Mediation Board, employ and fix the compensations of such assistants as it deems necessary in carrying on its proceedings. The compensation of such employees shall be paid by the Mediation Board.

(v) The Adjustment Board shall meet within forty days after June 21, 1934, and adopt such rules as it deems necessary to control proceedings before the respective divisions and not in conflict with the provisions of this section. Immediately following the meeting of the entire Board and the adoption of such rules, the respective divisions shall meet and organize by the selection of a chairman, a vice chairman, and a secretary. Thereafter each division shall annually designate one of its members to act as chairman and one of its members to act as vice chairman: *Provided, however,* That the chairmanship and vice-chairmanship of any division shall alternate as between the groups, so that both the chairmanship and vice-chairmanship shall be held alternately by a representative of the carriers and a representative of the employees. In case of a vacancy, such vacancy shall be filled for the unexpired term by the selection of a successor from the same group.

(w) Each division of the Adjustment Board shall annually prepare and submit a report of its activities to the Mediation Board, and the substance of such report shall be included in the annual report of the Mediation Board to the Congress of the United States. The reports of each division of the Adjustment Board and the annual report of the Mediation Board shall state in detail all cases heard, all actions taken, the names, salaries, and duties of all agencies, employees, and officers receiving compensation from the United States under the authority of this chapter, and an account of all moneys appropriated by Congress pursuant to the authority conferred by this chapter and disbursed by such agencies, employees, and officers.

(x) Any division of the Adjustment Board shall have authority, in its discretion, to establish regional adjustment boards to act in its place and stead for such limited period as such division may determine to be necessary. Carrier members of such regional boards shall be designated in keeping with rules devised for this purpose by the carrier members of the Adjustment Board and the labor members shall be designated in keeping with rules devised for this purpose by the labor members of the Adjustment Board. Any such regional board shall, during the time for which it is appointed, have the same authority to conduct hearings, make findings upon disputes and adopt the same procedure as the division of the Adjustment Board appointing it, and its decisions shall be enforceable to the same extent and under the same processes. A neutral person, as referee, shall be appointed for service in connection with any such regional adjustment board in the same circumstances and manner as provided in paragraph (*l*) of this section, with respect to a division of the Adjustment Board.

Second. System, group, or regional boards: establishment by voluntary agreement; special adjustment boards: establishment, composition, designation of representatives by Mediation Board, neutral member, compensation, quorum, finality and enforcement of awards

Nothing in this section shall be construed to prevent any individual carrier, system, or group of carriers and any class or classes of its or their employees, all acting through their representatives, selected in accordance with the provisions of this chapter, from mutually agreeing to the establishment of system, group, or regional boards of adjustment for the purpose of adjusting and deciding disputes of the character specified in this section. In the event that either party to such a system, group, or regional board of adjustment is dissatisfied with such arrangement, it may upon ninety days' notice to the other party elect to come under the jurisdiction of the Adjustment Board.

If written request is made upon any individual carrier by the representative of any craft or class of employees of such carrier for the establishment of a special board of adjustment to resolve disputes otherwise referable to the Adjustment Board, or any dispute which has been pending before the Adjustment Board for twelve months from the date the dispute (claim) is received by the Board, or if any carrier makes such a request upon any such representative, the carrier or the representative upon whom such request is made shall join in an agreement establishing such a board within thirty days from the date such request is made. The cases which may be considered by such board shall be defined in the agreement establishing it. Such board shall consist of one person designated by the carrier and one person designated by the representative of the employees. If such carrier or such representative fails to agree upon the establishment of such a board as provided herein, or to exercise its rights to designate a member of the board, the carrier or representative making the request for the establishment of the special board may request the Mediation Board to designate a member of the special board on behalf of the carrier or representative upon whom such request was made. Upon receipt of a request for such designation the Mediation Board shall promptly make such designation and shall select an individual associated in interest with the carrier or representative he is to represent, who, with the member appointed by the carrier or representative requesting the establishment of the special board, shall constitute the board. Each member of the board shall be compensated by the party he is to represent. The members of the board so designated shall determine all matters not previously agreed upon by the carrier and the representative of the employees with respect to the establishment and jurisdiction of the board. If they are unable to agree such matters shall be determined by a neutral member of the board selected or appointed and compensated in the same manner as is hereinafter provided with respect to situations where the members of the board are unable to agree upon an award. Such neutral member shall cease to be a member of the board when he has determined such matters. If with respect to any dispute or group of disputes the members of the board designated by the carrier and the representative are unable to agree upon an award disposing of the dispute or group of disputes they shall by mutual agreement select a neutral person to be a member of the board for the consideration and disposition of such dispute or group of disputes. In the event the members of the board designated by the parties are unable, within ten days after their failure to agree upon an award, to agree upon the selection of such neutral person, either member of the board may request the Mediation Board to appoint such neutral person and upon receipt of such request the Mediation Board shall promptly make such appointment. The neutral person so selected or appointed shall be compensated and reimbursed for expenses by the Mediation Board. Any two members of the board shall be competent to render an award. Such awards shall be final and binding upon both parties to the dispute and if in favor of the petitioner, shall direct the other party to comply therewith on or before the day named. Compliance with such awards shall be enforcible by proceedings in the United States district courts in the same manner and subject to the same provisions that apply to proceedings for enforcement of compliance with awards of the Adjustment Board.

(May 20, 1926, c.347, §3, 44 Stat. 578; June 21, 1934, c.691, §3, 48 Stat. 1189; June 20, 1966, Pub. L. 89-456, §§1, 2, 80 Stat. 208, 209; Apr. 23, 1970, Pub. L. 91-234, §§1-6, 84 Stat. 199, 200.)

§4. (§154) National Mediation Board

First. Board of Mediation abolished; National Mediation Board established; composition; term of office; qualifications; salaries; removal

The Board of Mediation is abolished, effective thirty days from June 21, 1934, and the members, secretary, officers, assistants, employees, and agents thereof, in office upon June 21, 1934, shall continue to function and receive their salaries for a period of thirty days from such date in the same manner as though this chapter had not been passed. There is established, as an independent agency in the executive branch of the Government, a board to be known as the "National Mediation Board", to be composed of three members appointed by the President, by and with the advice and consent of the Senate, not more than two of whom shall be of the same political party. Each member of the Mediation Board in office on January 1, 1965, shall be deemed to have been appointed for a term of office which shall expire on July 1 of the year his term would have otherwise expired. The terms of office of all successors shall expire three years after the expiration of the terms for which their predecessors were appointed; but any member appointed to fill a vacancy occurring prior to the expiration of the term for which his predecessor was appointed shall be appointed only for the unexpired term of his predecessor. Vacancies in the Board shall not impair the powers nor affect the duties of the Board nor of the remaining members of the Board. Two of the members in office shall constitute a quorum for the transaction of the business of the Board. Each member of the Board shall receive necessary traveling and subsistence expenses, or per diem allowance in lieu thereof, subject to the provisions of law applicable thereto, while away from the principal office of the Board on business required by this chapter. No person in the employment of or who is pecuniarily or otherwise interested in any organization of employees or any carrier shall enter upon the duties of or continue to be a member of the Board. Upon the expiration of his term of office a member shall continue to serve until his successor is appointed and shall have qualified.

All cases referred to the Board of Mediation and unsettled on June 21, 1934, shall be handled to conclusion by the Mediation Board.

A member of the Board may be removed by the President for inefficiency, neglect of duty, malfeasance in office, or ineligibility, but for no other cause.

Second. Chairman; principal office; delegation of powers; oaths; seal; report

The Mediation Board shall annually designate a member to act as chairman. The Board shall maintain its principal office in the District of Columbia, but it may meet at any other place whenever it deems it necessary so to do. The Board may designate one or more of its members to exercise the functions of the Board in mediation proceedings. Each member of the Board shall have power to administer oaths and affirmations. The Board shall have a seal which shall be judicially noticed. The Board shall make an annual report to Congress.

Third. Appointment of experts and other employees; salaries of employees; expenditures

The Mediation Board may (1) subject to the provisions of the civil service laws, appoint such experts and assistants to act in a confidential capacity and such other officers and employees as are essential to the effective transaction of the work of the Board; (2) in accordance with chapter 51 and subchapter III of chapter 53 of Title 5, fix the salaries of such experts, assistants, officers, and employees; and (3) make such expenditures (including expenditures for rent and personal services at the seat of government and elsewhere, for law books, periodicals, and books of reference, and for printing and binding, and including expenditures for salaries and compensation, necessary traveling expenses and expenses actually incurred for subsistence, and other necessary expenses of the Mediation Board, Adjustment Board, Regional Adjustment Boards established under paragraph (w) of section 153 of this title, and boards of arbitration, in accordance with the provisions of this section and sections 153 and 157 of this title, respectively), as may be necessary for the execution of the functions vested in the Board, in the Adjustment Board and in the boards of arbitration, and as may be provided for by the Congress from time to time. All expenditures of the Board shall be allowed and paid on the presentation of itemized vouchers therefor approved by the chairman.

Fourth. Delegation of powers and duties

The Mediation Board is authorized by its order to assign, or refer, any portion of its work, business, or functions arising under this chapter or any other Act of Congress, or referred to it by Congress or either branch thereof, to an individual member of the Board or to an employee or employees of the Board to be designated by such order for action thereon, and by its order at any time to amend, modify, supplement, or rescind any such assignment or reference. All such orders shall take effect forthwith and remain in effect until otherwise ordered by the Board. In conformity with and subject to the order or orders of the Mediation Board in the premises, [and] such individual member of the Board or employee designated shall have power and authority to act as to any of said work, business, or functions so assigned or referred to him for action by the Board.

Fifth. Transfer of officers and employees of Board of Mediation; transfer of appropriation

All officers and employees of the Board of Mediation (except the members thereof, whose offices are abolished) whose services in the judgment of the Mediation Board are necessary to the efficient operation of the Board are transferred to the Board, without change in classification or compensation; except that the Board may provide for the adjustment of such classification or compensation to conform to the duties to which such officers and employees may be assigned.

All unexpended appropriations for the operation of the Board of Mediation that are available at the time of the abolition of the Board of Mediation shall be transferred to the Mediation Board and shall be available for its use for salaries and other authorized expenditures.

(May 20, 1926, c.347, §4, 44 Stat. 579; June 21, 1934, c.691, §4, 48 Stat. 1193; Oct. 28, 1949, c.782, Title XI, §1106(a), 63 Stat. 972; Aug. 31, 1964, Pub. L. 88-542, 78 Stat. 748.)

§5. (§155) Functions of Mediation Board

First. Disputes within jurisdiction of Mediation Board

The parties, or either party, to a dispute between an employee or group of employees and a carrier may invoke the services of the Mediation Board in any of the following cases:

(a) A dispute concerning changes in rates of pay, rules, or working conditions not adjusted by the parties in conference.

(b) Any other dispute not referable to the National Railroad Adjustment Board and not adjusted in conference between the parties or where conferences are refused.

The Mediation Board may proffer its services in case any labor emergency is found by it to exist at any time.

In either event the said Board shall promptly put itself in communica-

Railway Labor Act of 1926

tion with the parties to such controversy, and shall use its best efforts, by mediation, to bring them to agreement. If such efforts to bring about an amicable settlement through mediation shall be unsuccessful, the said Board shall at once endeavor as its final required action (except as provided in paragraph third of this section and in section 160 of this title) to induce the parties to submit their controversy to arbitration, in accordance with the provisions of this chapter.

If arbitration at the request of the Board shall be refused by one or both parties, the Board shall at once notify both parties in writing that its mediatory efforts have failed and for thirty days thereafter, unless in the intervening period the parties agree to arbitration, or an emergency board shall be created under section 160 of this title, no change shall be made in the rates of pay, rules, or working conditions or established practices in effect prior to the time the dispute arose.

Second. Interpretation of agreement

In any case in which a controversy arises over the meaning or the application of any agreement reached through mediation under the provisions of this chapter, either party to the said agreement, or both, may apply to the Mediation Board for an interpretation of the meaning or application of such agreement. The said Board shall upon receipt of such request notify the parties to the controversy, and after a hearing of both sides give its interpretation within thirty days.

Third. Duties of Board with respect to arbitration of disputes; arbitrators; acknowledgment of agreement; notice to arbitrators; reconvening of arbitrators; filing contracts with Board; custody of records and documents

The Mediation Board shall have the following duties with respect to the arbitration of disputes under section 157 of this title:

(a) On failure of the arbitrators named by the parties to agree on the remaining arbitrator or arbitrators within the time set by section 157 of this title, it shall be the duty of the Mediation Board to name such remaining arbitrator or arbitrators. It shall be the duty of the Board in naming such arbitrator or arbitrators to appoint only those whom the Board shall deem wholly disinterested in the controversy to be arbitrated and impartial and without bias as between the parties to such arbitration. Should, however, the Board name an arbitrator or arbitrators not so disinterested and impartial, then, upon proper investigation and presentation of the facts, the Board shall promptly remove such arbitrator.

If an arbitrator named by the Mediation Board, in accordance with the provisions of this chapter, shall be removed by such Board as provided by this chapter, or if such an arbitrator refuses or is unable to serve, it shall be the duty of the Mediation Board, promptly, to select another arbitrator, in the same manner as provided in this chapter for an original appointment by the Mediation Board.

(b) Any member of the Mediation Board is authorized to take the acknowledgment of an agreement to arbitrate under this chapter. When so acknowledged, or when acknowledged by the parties before a notary public or the clerk of a district court or a court of appeals of the United States, such agreement to arbitrate shall be delivered to a member of said Board or transmitted to said Board, to be filed in its office.

(c) When an agreement to arbitrate has been filed with the Mediation Board, or with one of its members, as provided by this section, and when the said Board has been furnished the names of the arbitrators chosen by the parties to the controversy it shall be the duty of the Board to cause a notice in writing to be served upon said arbitrators, notifying them of their appointment, requesting them to meet promptly to name the remaining arbitrator or arbitrators necessary to complete the Board of Arbitration, and advising them of the period within which, as provided by the agreement to arbitrate, they are empowered to name such arbitrator or arbitrators.

(d) Either party to an arbitration desiring the reconvening of a board of arbitration to pass upon any controversy arising over the meaning or application of an award may so notify the Mediation Board in writing, stating in such notice the question or questions to be submitted to such reconvened Board. The Mediation Board shall thereupon promptly communicate with the members of the Board of Arbitration, or a subcommittee of such Board appointed for such purpose pursuant to a provision in the agreement to arbitrate, and arrange for the reconvening of said Board of Arbitration or subcommittee, and shall notify the respective parties to the controversy of the time and place at which the Board, or the subcommittee, will meet for hearings upon the matters in controversy to be submitted to it. No evidence other than that contained in the record filed with the original award shall be received or considered by such reconvened Board or subcommittee, except such evidence as may be necessary to illustrate the interpretations suggested by the parties. If any member of the original Board is unable or unwilling to serve on such reconvened Board or subcommittee thereof, another arbitrator shall be named in the same manner and with the same powers and duties as such original arbitrator.

(e) Within sixty days after June 21, 1934, every carrier shall file with the Mediation Board a copy of each contract with its employees in effect on the 1st day of April 1934, covering rates of pay, rules, and working conditions. If no contract with any craft or class of its employees has been entered into, the carrier shall file with the Mediation Board a statement of that fact, including also a statement of the rates of pay, rules, and working conditions applicable in dealing with such craft or class. When any new contract is executed or change is made in an existing contract with any class or craft of its employees covering rates of pay, rules, or working conditions, or in those rates of pay, rules, and working conditions of employees not covered by contract, the carrier shall file the same with the Mediation Board within thirty days after such new contract or change in existing contract has been executed or rates of pay, rules, and working conditions have been made effective.

(f) The Mediation Board shall be the custodian of all papers and documents heretofore filed with or transferred to the Board of Mediation bearing upon the settlement, adjustment, or determination of disputes between carriers and their employees or upon mediation or arbitration proceedings held under or pursuant to the provisions of any Act of Congress in respect thereto; and the President is authorized to designate a custodian of the records and property of the Board of Mediation until the transfer and delivery of such records to the Mediation Board and to require the transfer and delivery to the Mediation Board of any and all such papers and documents filed with it or in its possession.

(May 20, 1926, c.347, §5, 44 Stat. 580; June 21, 1934, c.691, §5, 48 Stat. 1195; June 25, 1948, c.646, §32(a), 62 Stat. 991; May 24, 1949, c.139, §127, 63 Stat. 107.)

§6. (§156) Procedure in changing rates of pay, rules, and working conditions

Carriers and representatives of the employees shall give at least thirty days' written notice of an intended change in agreements affecting rates of pay, rules, or working conditions, and the time and place for the beginning of conference between the representatives of the parties interested in such intended changes shall be agreed upon within ten days after the receipt of said notice, and said time shall be within the thirty days provided in the notice. In every case where such notice of intended change has been given, or conferences are being held with reference thereto, or the services of the Mediation Board have been requested by either party, or said Board has proffered its services, rates of pay, rules, or working conditions shall not be altered by the carrier until the controversy has been finally acted upon, as required by section 155 of this title, by the Mediation Board, unless a period of ten days has elapsed after termination of conferences without request for or proffer of the services of the Mediation Board.

(May 20, 1926, c.347, §6, 44 Stat. 582; June 21, 1934, c.691, §6, 48 Stat. 1197.)

§7. (§157) Arbitration

First. Submission of controversy to arbitration

Whenever a controversy shall arise between a carrier or carriers and its or their employees which is not settled either in conference between representatives of the parties or by the appropriate adjustment board or through mediation, in the manner provided in sections 151 to 156 of this title, such controversy may, by agreement of the parties to such controversy, be submitted to the arbitration of a board of three (or, if the parties to the controversy so stipulate, of six) persons: *Provided, however,* That the failure or refusal of either party to submit a controversy to arbitration shall not be construed as a violation of any legal obligation imposed upon such party by the terms of this chapter or otherwise.

Second. Manner of selecting board of arbitration

Such board of arbitration shall be chosen in the following manner:

(a) In the case of a board of three the carrier or carriers and the representatives of the employees, parties respectively to the agreement to arbitrate, shall each name one arbitrator; the two arbitrators thus chosen shall select a third arbitrator. If the arbitrators chosen by the parties shall fail to name the third arbitrator within five days after their first meeting, such third arbitrator shall be named by the Mediation Board.

(b) In the case of a board of six the carrier or carriers and the representatives of the employees, parties respectively to the agreement to arbitrate, shall each name two arbitrators; the four arbitrators thus chosen shall, by a majority vote, select the remaining two arbitrators. If the arbitrators chosen by the parties shall fail to name the two arbitrators within fifteen days after their first meeting, the said two arbitrators, or as many of them as have not been named, shall be named by the Mediation Board.

Third. Board of arbitration; organization; compensation; procedure

(a) Notice of selection or failure to select arbitrators. When the arbitrators selected by the respective parties have agreed upon the remaining arbitrator or arbitrators, they shall notify the Mediation Board; and, in the event of their failure to agree upon any or upon all of the necessary arbitrators within the period fixed by this chapter, they shall, at the expiration of such period, notify the Mediation Board of the arbitrators selected, if any, or of their failure to make or to complete such selection.

(b) Organization of board; procedure. The board of arbitration shall organize and select its own chairman and make all necessary rules for conducting its hearings: *Provided, however,* That the board of arbitration shall be bound to give the parties to the controversy a full and fair hearing, which shall include an opportunity to present evidence in support of their claims, and an opportunity to present their case in person, by counsel, or by other representative as they may respectively elect.

(c) Duty to reconvene; questions considered. Upon notice from the Mediation Board that the parties, or either party, to an arbitration desire the reconvening of the board of arbitration (or a subcommittee of such board of arbitration appointed for such purpose pursuant to the agreement to arbi-

trate) to pass upon any controversy over the meaning or application of their award, the board, or its subcommittee, shall at once reconvene. No question other than, or in addition to, the questions relating to the meaning or application of the award, submitted by the party or parties in writing, shall be considered by the reconvened board of arbitration or its subcommittee.

Such rulings shall be acknowledged by such board or subcommittee thereof in the same manner, and filed in the same district court clerk's office, as the original award and become a part thereof.

(d) *Competency of arbitrators.* No arbitrator, except those chosen by the Mediation Board, shall be incompetent to act as an arbitrator because of his interest in the controversy to be arbitrated, or because of his connection with or partiality to either of the parties to the arbitration.

(e) *Compensation and expenses.* Each member of any board of arbitration created under the provisions of this chapter named by either party to the arbitration shall be compensated by the party naming him. Each arbitrator selected by the arbitrators or named by the Mediation Board shall receive from the Mediation Board such compensation as the Mediation Board may fix, together with his necessary traveling expenses and expenses actually incurred for subsistence, while serving as an arbitrator.

(f) *Award; disposition of original and copies.* The board of arbitration shall furnish a certified copy of its award to the respective parties to the controversy, and shall transmit the original, together with the papers and proceedings and a transcript of the evidence taken at the hearings, certified under the hands of at least a majority of the arbitrators, to the clerk of the district court of the United States for the district wherein the controversy arose or the arbitration is entered into, to be filed in said clerk's office as hereinafter provided. The said board shall also furnish a certified copy of its award, and the papers and proceedings, including testimony relating thereto, to the Mediation Board to be filed in its office; and in addition a certified copy of its award shall be filed in the office of the Interstate Commerce Commission: *Provided, however,* That such award shall not be construed to diminish or extinguish any of the powers or duties of the Interstate Commerce Commission, under subtitle IV of Title 49.

(g) *Compensation of assistants to board of arbitration; expenses; quarters.* A board of arbitration may, subject to the approval of the Mediation Board, employ and fix the compensation of such assistants as it deems necessary in carrying on the arbitration proceedings. The compensation of such employees, together with their necessary traveling expenses and expenses actually incurred for subsistence, while so employed, and the necessary expenses of boards of arbitration, shall be paid by the Mediation Board.

Whenever practicable, the board shall be supplied with suitable quarters in any Federal building located at its place of meeting or at any place where the board may conduct its proceedings or deliberations.

(h) *Testimony before a board; oaths; attendance of witnesses; production of documents; subpoenas; fees.* All testimony before said board shall be given under oath or affirmation, and any member of the board shall have the power to administer oaths or affirmations. The board of arbitration, or any member thereof, shall have the power to require the attendance of witnesses and the production of such books, papers, contracts, agreements, and documents as may be deemed by the board of arbitration material to a just determination of the matters submitted to its arbitration, and may for that purpose request the clerk of the district court of the United States for the district wherein said arbitration is being conducted to issue the necessary subpoenas, and upon such request the said clerk or his duly authorized deputy shall be, and he is, authorized, and it shall be his duty, to issue such subpoenas.

Any witness appearing before a board of arbitration shall receive the same fees and mileage as witnesses in courts of the United States, to be paid by the party securing the subpoena.

(May 20, 1926, c.347, §7, 44 Stat. 582; June 21, 1934, c.691, §7, 48 Stat. 1197; Oct. 15, 1970, Pub. L. 91-452, Title II, §238, 84 Stat. 930.)

§8. (§158) Agreement to arbitrate; form and contents; signatures and acknowledgment; revocation

The agreement to arbitrate—

(a) Shall be in writing;

(b) Shall stipulate that the arbitration is had under the provisions of this chapter;

(c) Shall state whether the board of arbitration is to consist of three or of six members;

(d) Shall be signed by the duly accredited representatives of the carrier or carriers and the employees, parties respectively to the agreement to arbitrate, and shall be acknowledged by said parties before a notary public, the clerk of a district court or court of appeals of the United States, or before a member of the Mediation Board, and, when so acknowledged, shall be filed in the office of the Mediation Board;

(e) Shall state specifically the questions to be submitted to the said board for decision; and that, in its award or awards, the said board shall confine itself strictly to decisions as to the questions so specifically submitted to it;

(f) Shall provide that the questions, or any one or more of them, submitted by the parties to the board of arbitration may be withdrawn from arbitration on notice to that effect signed by the duly accredited representatives of all the parties and served on the board of arbitration;

(g) Shall stipulate that the signatures of a majority of said board of arbitration affixed to their award shall be competent to constitute a valid and binding award;

(h) Shall fix a period from the date of the appointment of the arbitrator or arbitrators necessary to complete the board (as provided for in the agreement) within which the said board shall commence its hearings;

(i) Shall fix a period from the beginning of the hearings within which the said board shall make and file its award: *Provided*, That the parties may agree at any time upon an extension of this period;

(j) Shall provide for the date from which the award shall become effective and shall fix the period during which the award shall continue in force;

(k) Shall provide that the award of the board of arbitration and the evidence of the proceedings before the board relating thereto, when certified under the hands of at least a majority of the arbitrators, shall be filed in the clerk's office of the district court of the United States for the district wherein the controversy arose or the arbitration was entered into, which district shall be designated in the agreement; and, when so filed, such award and proceedings shall constitute the full and complete record of the arbitration;

(*l*) Shall provide that the award, when so filed, shall be final and conclusive upon the parties as to the facts determined by said award and as to the merits of the controversy decided;

(m) Shall provide that any difference arising as to the meaning, or the application of the provisions, of an award made by a board of arbitration shall be referred back for a ruling to the same board, or, by agreement, to a subcommittee of such board; and that such ruling, when acknowledged in the same manner, and filed in the same district court clerk's office, as the original award, shall be a part of and shall have the same force and effect as such original award; and

(n) Shall provide that the respective parties to the award will each faithfully execute the same.

The said agreement to arbitrate, when properly signed and acknowledged as herein provided, shall not be revoked by a party to such agreement: *Provided, however*, That such agreement to arbitrate may at any time be revoked and canceled by the written agreement of both parties, signed by their duly accredited representatives, and (if no board of arbitration has yet been constituted under the agreement) delivered to the Mediation Board or any member thereof; or, if the board of arbitration has been constituted as provided by this chapter, delivered to such board of arbitration.

(May 20, 1926, c.347, §8, 44 Stat. 584; June 21, 1934, c.691, §7, 48 Stat. 1197; June 25, 1948, c.646, §32(a), 62 Stat. 991; May 24, 1949, c.139, §127, 63 Stat. 107.)

§9. (§159) Award and judgment thereon; effect of chapter on individual employee

First. Filing of award

The award of a board of arbitration, having been acknowledged as herein provided, shall be filed in the clerk's office of the district court designated in the agreement to arbitrate.

Second. Conclusiveness of award; judgment

An award acknowledged and filed as herein provided shall be conclusive on the parties as to the merits and facts of the controversy submitted to arbitration, and unless, within ten days after the filing of the award, a petition to impeach the award, on the grounds hereinafter set forth, shall be filed in the clerk's office of the court in which the award has been filed, the court shall enter judgment on the award, which judgment shall be final and conclusive on the parties.

Third. Impeachment of awards; grounds

Such petition for the impeachment or contesting of any award so filed shall be entertained by the court only on one or more of the following grounds:

(a) That the award plainly does not conform to the substantive requirements laid down by this chapter for such awards, or that the proceedings were not substantially in conformity with this chapter;

(b) That the award does not conform, nor confine itself, to the stipulations of the agreement to arbitrate; or

(c) That a member of the board of arbitration rendering the award was guilty of fraud or corruption; or that a party to the arbitration practiced fraud or corruption which fraud or corruption affected the result of the arbitration: *Provided, however,* That no court shall entertain any such petition on the ground that an award is invalid for uncertainty; in such case the proper remedy shall be a submission of such award to a reconvened board, or subcommittee thereof, for interpretation, as provided by this chapter: *Provided further,* That an award contested as herein provided shall be construed liberally by the court, with a view to favoring its validity, and that no award shall be set aside for trivial irregularity or clerical error, going only to form and not to substance.

Fourth. Effect of partial invalidity of award

If the court shall determine that a part of the award is invalid on some ground or grounds designated in this section as a ground of invalidity, but shall determine that a part of the award is valid, the court shall set aside the entire award: *Provided, however,* That, if the parties shall agree thereto, and if such valid and invalid parts are separable, the court shall set aside the invalid part, and order judgment to stand as to the valid part.

Fifth. Appeal; record

At the expiration of 10 days from the decision of the district court upon the petition filed as aforesaid, final judgment shall be entered in accordance with said decision, unless during said 10 days either party shall appeal therefrom to the court of appeals. In such case only such portion of the record shall be transmitted to the appellate court as is necessary to the proper understanding and consideration of the questions of law presented by said petition and to be decided.

Sixth. Finality of decision of court of appeals

The determination of said court of appeals upon said questions shall be final, and, being certified by the clerk thereof to said district court, judgment pursuant thereto shall thereupon be entered by said district court.

Seventh. Judgment where petitioner's contentions are sustained

If the petitioner's contentions are finally sustained, judgment shall be entered setting aside the award in whole or, if the parties so agree, in part; but in such case the parties may agree upon a judgment to be entered disposing of the subject matter of the controversy, which judgment when entered shall have the same force and effect as judgment entered upon an award.

Eighth. Duty of employee to render service without consent; right to quit

Nothing in this chapter shall be construed to require an individual employee to render labor or service without his consent, nor shall anything in this chapter be construed to make the quitting of his labor or service by an individual employee an illegal act; nor shall any court issue any process to compel the performance by an individual employee of such labor or service, without his consent.

(May 20, 1926, c.347, §9, 44 Stat. 585; June 25, 1948, c.646, §32(a), 62 Stat. 991; May 24, 1949, c.139, §127, 63 Stat. 107.)

§9A. (§159a) Special procedure for commuter service

(a) Applicability of provisions. Except as provided in section 590(h) of this title, the provisions of this section shall apply to any dispute subject to this chapter between a publicly funded and publicly operated carrier providing rail commuter service (including the Amtrak Commuter Services Corporation) and its employees.

(b) Request for establishment of emergency board. If a dispute between the parties described in subsection (a) of this section is not adjusted under the foregoing provisions of this chapter and the President does not, under section 160 of this title, create an emergency board to investigate and report on such dispute, then any party to the dispute or the Governor of any State through which the service that is the subject of the dispute is operated may request the President to establish such an emergency board.

(c) Establishment of emergency board. (1) Upon the request of a party or a Governor under subsection (b) of this section, the President shall create an emergency board to investigate and report on the dispute in accordance with section 160 of this title. For purposes of this subsection, the period during which no change, except by agreement, shall be made by the parties in the conditions out of which the dispute arose shall be 120 days from the day of the creation of such emergency board.

(2) If the President, in his discretion, creates a board to investigate and report on a dispute between the parties described in subsection (a) of this section, the provisions of this section shall apply to the same extent as if such board had been created pursuant to paragraph (1) of this subsection.

(d) Public hearing by National Mediation Board upon failure of emergency board to effectuate settlement of dispute. Within 60 days after the creation of an emergency board under this section, if there has been no settlement between the parties, the National Mediation Board shall conduct a public hearing on the dispute at which each party shall appear and provide testimony setting forth the reasons it has not accepted the recommendations of the emergency board for settlement of the dispute.

(e) Establishment of second emergency board. If no settlement in the dispute is reached at the end of the 120-day period beginning on the date of the creation of the emergency board, any party to the dispute or the Governor of any State through which the service that is the subject of the dispute is operated may request the President to establish another emergency board, in which case the President shall establish such emergency board.

(f) Submission of final offers to second emergency board by parties. Within 30 days after creation of a board under subsection (e) of this section, the parties to the dispute shall submit to the board final offers for settlement of the dispute.

(g) Report of second emergency board. Within 30 days after the submission of final offers under subsection (f) of this section, the emergency board shall submit a report to the President setting forth its selection of the most reasonable offer.

(h) Maintenance of status quo during dispute period. From the time a request to establish a board is made under subsection (e) of this section until 60 days after such board makes its report under subsection (g) of this section, no change, except by agreement, shall be made by the parties in the conditions out of which the dispute arose.

(i) Work stoppages by employees subsequent to carrier offer selected; eligibility of employees for benefits. If the emergency board selects the final offer submitted by the carrier and, after the expiration of the 60-day period described in subsection (h) of this section, the employees of such carrier engage in any work stoppage arising out of the dispute, such employees shall not be eligible during the period of such work stoppage for benefits under the Railroad Unemployment Insurance Act [45 U.S.C. §351 et seq.].

Railway Labor Act of 1926

(j) Work stoppages by employees subsequent to employees offer selected; eligibility of employer for benefits. If the emergency board selects the final offer submitted by the employees and, after the expiration of the 60-day period described in subsection (h) of this section, the carrier refuses to accept the final offer submitted by the employees and the employees of such carrier engage in any work stoppage arising out of the dispute, the carrier shall not participate in any benefits of any agreement between carriers which is designed to provide benefits to such carriers during a work stoppage.

(May 20, 1926, c.347, §9A, as added Aug. 13, 1981, Pub. L. 97-35, Title XI, §1157, 95 Stat. 681.)

§10. (§160) Emergency Board

If a dispute between a carrier and its employees be not adjusted under the foregoing provisions of this chapter and should, in the judgment of the Mediation Board, threaten substantially to interrupt interstate commerce to a degree such as to deprive any section of the country of essential transportation service, the Mediation Board shall notify the President, who may thereupon, in his discretion, create a board to investigate and report respecting such dispute. Such board shall be composed of such number of persons as to the President may seem desirable: *Provided, however,* That no member appointed shall be pecuniarily or otherwise interested in any organization of employees or any carrier. The compensation of the members of any such board shall be fixed by the President. Such board shall be created separately in each instance and it shall investigate promptly the facts as to the dispute and make a report thereon to the President within thirty days from the date of its creation.

There is authorized to be appropriated such sums as may be necessary for the expenses of such board, including the compensation and the necessary traveling expenses and expenses actually incurred for subsistence, of the members of the board. All expenditures of the board shall be allowed and paid on the presentation of itemized vouchers therefor approved by the chairman.

After the creation of such board and for thirty days after such board has made its report to the President, no change, except by agreement, shall be made by the parties to the controversy in the conditions out of which the dispute arose.

(May 20, 1926, c.347, §10, 44 Stat. 586; June 21, 1934, c.691, §7, 48 Stat. 1197.)

§11. (§161) Effect of partial invalidity of chapter

If any section, subsection, sentence, clause, or phrase of this chapter is for any reason held to be unconstitutional, such decision shall not affect the validity of the remaining portions of this chapter. All Acts or parts of Acts inconsistent with the provisions of this chapter are repealed.

(May 20, 1926, c.347, §11, 44, Stat. 587; June 21, 1934, c.691, §8, 48 Stat. 1197.)

§12. (§162) Authorization of appropriations

There is authorized to be appropriated such sums as may be necessary for expenditure by the Mediation Board in carrying out the provisions of this chapter.

(May 20, 1926, c.347, §12, 44 Stat. 587; June 21, 1934, c.691, §7, Stat. 1197.)

§14. (§163) Repeal of prior legislation; exception

Chapters 6 and 7 of this title, providing for mediation, conciliation, and arbitration, and all Acts and parts of Acts in conflict with the provisions of this chapter are repealed, except that the members, secretary, officers, employees, and agents of the Railroad Labor Board, in office on May 20, 1926, shall receive their salaries for a period of 30 days from such date, in the same manner as though this chapter had not been passed.

(May 20, 1926, c.347, §14, 44 Stat. 587.)

Subchapter II. Carriers by Air

§201. (§181) Application of subchapter I to carriers by air

All of the provisions of subchapter I of this chapter except section 153 of this title are extended to and shall cover every common carrier by air engaged in interstate or foreign commerce, and every carrier by air transporting mail for or under contract with the United States Government, and every air pilot or other person who performs any work as an employee or subordinate official of such carrier or carriers, subject to its or their continuing authority to supervise and direct the manner of rendition of his service.

(May 20, 1926, c.347, §201, as added Apr. 10, 1936, c.166, 49 Stat. 1189.)

§202. (§182) Duties, penalties, benefits, and privileges of subchapter I applicable

The duties, requirements, penalties, benefits, and privileges prescribed and established by the provisions of subchapter I of this chapter except section 153 of this title shall apply to said carriers by air and their employees in the same manner and to the same extent as though such carriers and their employees were specifically included within the definition of "carrier" and "employee", respectively, in section 151 of this title.

(May 20, 1926, c.347, §202, as added Apr. 10, 1936, c.166, 49 Stat. 1189.)

§203. (§183) Disputes within jurisdiction of Mediation Board

The parties or either party to a dispute between an employee or a group of employees and a carrier or carriers by air may invoke the services of the National Mediation Board and the jurisdiction of said Mediation Board is extended to any of the following cases:

(a) A dispute concerning changes in rates of pay, rules, or working conditions not adjusted by the parties in conference.

(b) Any other dispute not referable to an adjustment board, as hereinafter provided, and not adjusted in conference between the parties, or where conferences are refused.

The National Mediation Board may proffer its services in case any labor emergency is found by it to exist at any time.

The services of the Mediation Board may be invoked in a case under this subchapter in the same manner and to the same extent as are the disputes covered by section 155 of this title.

(May 20, 1926, c.347, §203, as added Apr. 10, 1936, c.166, 49 Stat. 1189.)

§204. (§184) System, group, or regional boards of adjustment

The disputes between an employee or group of employees and a carrier or carriers by air growing out of grievances, or out of the interpretation or application of agreements concerning rates of pay, rules, or working conditions, including cases pending and unadjusted on April 10, 1936 before the National Labor Relations Board, shall be handled in the usual manner up to and including the chief operating officer of the carrier designated to handle such disputes; but, failing to reach an adjustment in this manner, the disputes may be referred by petition of the parties or by either party to an appropriate adjustment board, as hereinafter provided, with a full statement of the facts and supporting data bearing upon the disputes.

It shall be the duty of every carrier and of its employees, acting through their representatives, selected in accordance with the provisions of this subchapter, to establish a board of adjustment of jurisdiction not exceeding the jurisdiction which may be lawfully exercised by system, group, or regional boards of adjustment, under the authority of section 153 of this title.

Such boards of adjustment may be established by agreement between employees and carriers either on any individual carrier, or system, or group of carriers by air and any class or classes of its or their employees; or pending the establishment of a permanent National Board of Adjustment as hereinafter provided. Nothing in this chapter shall prevent said carriers by air, or any class or classes of their employees, both acting through their representatives selected in accordance with provisions of this subchapter, from mutually agreeing to the establishment of a National Board of Adjustment of temporary duration and of similarly limited jurisdiction.

(May 20, 1926, c.347, §204, as added Apr. 10, 1936, c.166, 49 Stat. 1189.)

§205. (§185) National Air Transport Adjustment Board

When, in the judgment of the National Mediation Board, it shall be necessary to have a permanent national board of adjustment in order to provide for the prompt and orderly settlement of disputes between said carriers by air, or any of them, and its or their employees, growing out of grievances or out of the interpretation or application of agreements between said carriers by air or any of them, and any class or classes of its or their employees, covering rates of pay, rules, or working conditions, the National Mediation Board is empowered and directed, by its order duly made, published, and served, to direct the said carriers by air and such labor organizations of their employees, national in scope, as have been or may be recognized in accordance with the provisions of this chapter, to select and designate four representatives who shall constitute a board which shall be known as the "National Air Transport Adjustment Board." Two members of said National Air Transport Adjustment Board shall be selected by said carriers by air and two members by the said labor organizations of the employees, within thirty days after the date of the order of the National Mediation Board, in the manner and by the procedure prescribed by section 153 of this title for the selection and designation of members of the National Railroad Adjustment Board. The National Air Transport Adjustment Board shall meet within forty days after the date of the order of the National Mediation Board directing the selection and designation of its members and shall organize and adopt rules for conducting its proceedings, in the manner prescribed in section 153 of this title. Vacancies in membership or office shall be filled, members shall be appointed in case of failure of the carriers or of labor organizations of the employees to select and designate representatives, members of the National Air Transport Adjustment Board shall be compensated, hearings shall be held, findings and awards made, stated, served, and enforced, and the number and compensation of any necessary assistants shall be determined and the compensation of such employees shall be paid, all in the same manner and to the same extent as provided with reference to the National Railroad Adjustment Board by section 153 of this title. The powers and duties prescribed and established by the provisions of section 153 of this title with reference to the National Railroad Adjustment Board and the several divisions thereof are conferred upon and shall be exercised and performed in like manner and to the same extent by the said National Air Transport Adjustment Board, not exceeding, however, the jurisdiction conferred upon said National Air Transport Adjustment Board by the provisions of this subchapter. From and after the organization of the National Air Transport Adjustment Board, if any system, group, or regional board of adjustment established by any carrier or carriers by air and any class or classes of its or their employees is not satisfactory to either party thereto, the said party, upon ninety days' notice to the other party, may elect to come under the jurisdiction of the National Air Transport Adjustment Board.

(May 20, 1926, c.347, §205, as added Apr. 10, 1936, c.166, 49 Stat. 1190.)

§207. (§187) Separability of provisions

If any provision of this subchapter or application thereof to any person or circumstance is held invalid, the remainder of such sections and the application of such provision to other persons or circumstances shall not be affected thereby.

(May 20, 1926, c.347, §207, as added Apr. 10, 1936, c.166, 49 Stat. 1191.)

§208. (§188) Authorization of appropriations

There is authorized to be appropriated such sums as may be necessary for expenditure by the Mediation Board in carrying out the provisions of this chapter.

(May 20, 1926, c.347, §208, as added Apr. 10, 1936, c.166, 49 Stat. 1191.)

National Labor Relations Act of 1935[*]
49 Stat. 449 (1935), as amended, 29 U.S.C. §§151-169

FINDINGS AND POLICIES

§1. (§151) The denial by employers of the right of employees to organize and the refusal by employers to accept the procedure of collective bargaining

---

[*]Internal section references are to the NLRA of 1935 (Wagner Act), as amended, and not to the United States Code. The text of the original Wagner Act is printed in regular roman type; the Taft-Hartley amendments of 1947 are in boldface type; the Landrum-Griffin amendments of 1959 are in italics; the 1974 amendments are underscored. Deleted matter is in brackets; bracketed matter in regular roman type was deleted in 1947, and bracketed matter in boldface type was deleted in 1959. Other amendments and deletions are specifically noted. In view of the information provided, legislative histories will not be appended at the end of each section. Also, to minimize confusion, section numbers for the NLRA will be set out in roman type.—EDS.

lead to strikes and other forms of industrial strife or unrest, which have the intent or the necessary effect of burdening or obstructing commerce by (a) impairing the efficiency, safety, or operation of the instrumentalities of commerce; (b) occurring in the current of commerce; (c) materially affecting, restraining, or controlling the flow of raw materials or manufactured or processed goods from or into the channels of commerce, or the prices of such materials or goods in commerce; or (d) causing diminution of employment and wages in such volume as substantially to impair or disrupt the market for goods flowing from or into the channels of commerce.

The inequality of bargaining power between employees who do not possess full freedom of association or actual liberty of contract, and employers who are organized in the corporate or other forms of ownership association substantially burdens and affects the flow of commerce, and tends to aggravate recurrent business depressions, by depressing wage rates and the purchasing power of wage earners in industry and by preventing the stabilization of competitive wage rates and working conditions within and between industries.

Experience has proved that protection by law of the right of employees to organize and bargain collectively safeguards commerce from injury, impairment, or interruption, and promotes the flow of commerce by removing certain recognized sources of industrial strife and unrest, by encouraging practices fundamental to the friendly adjustment of industrial disputes arising out of differences as to wages, hours, or other working conditions, and by restoring equality of bargaining power between employers and employees.

Experience has further demonstrated that certain practices by some labor organizations, their officers, and members have the intent or the necessary effect of burdening or obstructing commerce by preventing the free flow of goods in such commerce through strikes and other forms of industrial unrest or through concerted activities which impair the interest of the public in the free flow of such commerce. The elimination of such practices is a necessary condition to the assurance of the rights herein guaranteed.

It is hereby declared to be the policy of the United States to eliminate the causes of certain substantial obstructions to the free flow of commerce and to mitigate and eliminate these obstructions when they have occurred by encouraging the practice and procedure of collective bargaining and by protecting the exercise by workers of full freedom of association, self-organization, and designation of representatives of their own choosing, for the purpose of negotiating the terms and conditions of their employment or other mutual aid or protection.

Definitions

§2. (§152) When used in this Act—

(1) The term "person" includes one or more individuals, partnerships, associations, corporations, legal representatives, trustees, trustees in bankruptcy, or receivers.

National Labor Relations Act of 1935

(2) The term "employer" includes any person acting [in the interest of*] **as an agent** of an employer, directly or indirectly, but shall not include the United States **or any wholly owned Government corporation, or any Federal Reserve Bank**, or any State or political subdivision thereof, [**or any corporation or association operating a hospital, if no part of the net earnings inures to the benefit of any private shareholder or individual,***] or any person subject to the Railway Labor Act, as amended from time to time, or any labor organization (other than when acting as an employer), or anyone acting in the capacity of officer or agent of such labor organization.

(3) The term "employee" shall include any employee, and shall not be limited to the employees of a particular employer, unless the Act explicitly states otherwise, and shall include any individual whose work has ceased as a consequence of, or in connection with, any current labor dispute or because of any unfair labor practice, and who has not obtained any other regular and substantially equivalent employment, but shall not include any individual employed as an agricultural laborer, or in the domestic service of any family or person at his home, or any individual employed by his parent or spouse, **or any individual having the status of an independent contractor, or any individual employed as a supervisor, or any individual employed by an employer subject to the Railway Labor Act, as amended from time to time, or by any other person who is not an employer as herein defined.**

(4) The term "representatives" includes any individual or labor organization.

(5) The term "labor organization" means any organization of any kind, or any agency or employee representation committee or plan, in which employees participate and which exists for the purpose, in whole or in part, of dealing with employers concerning grievances, labor disputes, wages, rates of pay, hours of employment, or conditions of work.

(6) The term "commerce" means trade, traffic, commerce, transportation, or communication among the several States, or between the District of Columbia or any Territory of the United States and any State or other Territory, or between any foreign country and any State, Territory, or the District of Columbia, or within the District of Columbia or any Territory, or between points in the same State but through any other State or any Territory or the District of Columbia or any foreign country.

(7) The term "affecting commerce" means in commerce, or burdening or obstructing commerce or the free flow of commerce, or having led or tending to lead to a labor dispute burdening or obstructing commerce or the free flow of commerce.

(8) The term "unfair labor practice" means any unfair labor practice listed in section 8.

(9) The term "labor dispute" includes any controversy concerning terms, tenure or conditions of employment, or concerning the association

---

*The bracketed matter was deleted in 1974 by 88 Stat. 395.—EDS.

or representation of persons in negotiating, fixing, maintaining, changing, or seeking to arrange terms or conditions of employment, regardless of whether the disputants stand in the proximate relation of employer and employee.

(10) The term "National Labor Relations Board" means the National Labor Relations Board provided for in section 3 of this Act.

(11) The term "supervisor" means any individual having authority, in the interest of the employer, to hire, transfer, suspend, lay off, recall, promote, discharge, assign, reward, or discipline other employees, or responsibly to direct them, or to adjust their grievances, or effectively to recommend such action, if in connection with the foregoing the exercise of such authority is not of a merely routine or clerical nature, but requires the use of independent judgment.

(12) The term "professional employee" means—

(a) any employee engaged in work (i) predominantly intellectual and varied in character as opposed to routine mental, manual, mechanical, or physical work; (ii) involving the consistent exercise of discretion and judgment in its performance; (iii) of such a character that the output produced or the result accomplished cannot be standardized in relation to a given period of time; (iv) requiring knowledge of an advanced type in a field of science or learning customarily acquired by a prolonged course of specialized intellectual instruction and study in an institution of higher learning or a hospital, as distinguished from a general academic education or from an apprenticeship or from training in the performance of routine mental, manual, or physical processes; or

(b) any employee, who (i) has completed the courses of specialized intellectual instruction and study described in clause (iv) of paragraph (a), and (ii) is performing related work under the supervision of a professional person to qualify himself to become a professional employee as defined in paragraph (a).

(13) In determining whether any person is acting as an "agent" of another person so as to make such other person responsible for his acts, the question of whether the specific acts performed were actually authorized or subsequently ratified shall not be controlling.

(14) <u>The term "health care institution" shall include any hospital, convalescent hospital, health maintenance organization, health clinic, nursing home, extended care facility, or other institution devoted to the care of sick, infirm, or aged person.</u>

NATIONAL LABOR RELATIONS BOARD

§3. (§153) **(a) The National Labor Relations Board (hereinafter called the "Board") created by this Act prior to its amendment by the Labor Management Relations Act, 1947, is hereby continued as an agency of the**

United States, except that the Board shall consist of five instead of three members, appointed by the President by and with the advice and consent of the Senate. Of the two additional members so provided for, one shall be appointed for a term of five years and the other for a term of two years. Their successors, and the successors of the other members, shall be appointed for terms of five years each, excepting that any individual chosen to fill a vacancy shall be appointed only for the unexpired term of the member whom he shall succeed. The President shall designate one member to serve as Chairman of the Board. Any member of the Board may be removed by the President, upon notice and hearing, for neglect of duty or malfeasance in office, but for no other cause.

(b) The Board is authorized to delegate to any group of three or more members any or all of the powers which it may itself exercise. *The Board is also authorized to delegate to its regional directors its powers under section 9 to determine the unit appropriate for the purpose of collective bargaining, to investigate and provide for hearings, and determine whether a question of representation exists, and to direct an election or take a secret ballot under subsection (c) or (e) of section 9 and certify the results thereof, except that upon the filing of a request therefor with the Board by any interested person, the Board may review any action of a regional director delegated to him under this paragraph, but such a review shall not, unless specifically ordered by the Board, operate as a stay of any action taken by the regional director.* A vacancy in the Board shall not impair the right of the remaining members to exercise all of the powers of the Board, and three members of the Board shall, at all times, constitute a quorum of the Board, except that two members shall constitute a quorum of any group designated pursuant to the first sentence hereof. The Board shall have an official seal which shall be judicially noticed.

(c) The Board shall at the close of each fiscal year make a report in writing to Congress and to the President stating in detail the cases it has heard, the decisions it has rendered, the names, salaries, and duties of all employees and officers in the employ or under the supervision of the Board, and an account of all moneys it has disbursed.

(d) There shall be a General Counsel of the Board who shall be appointed by the President, by and with the advice and consent of the Senate, for a term of four years. The General Counsel of the Board shall exercise general supervision over all attorneys employed by the Board (other than trial examiners and legal assistants to Board members) and over the officers and employees in the regional offices. He shall have final authority, on behalf of the Board, in respect of the investigation of charges and issuance of complaints under section 10, and in respect of the prosecution of such complaints before the Board, and shall have such other duties as the Board may prescribe or as may be provided by law. *In case of a vacancy in the office of the General Counsel the President is authorized to designate the officer or employee who shall act as General Counsel during such vacancy, but no person or persons so designated shall so act (1) for more than forty days when the Congress is in session unless a nomination to fill such vacancy shall have been submitted to the Senate, or (2) after the adjournment sine die of the session of the Senate in which such nomination was submitted.*

§4. (§154) **(a) Each member of the Board and the General Counsel of the Board [shall receive a salary of $12,000 a year,] shall be eligible for reappointment, and shall not engage in any other business, vocation, or employment. The Board shall appoint an executive secretary, and such attorneys, examiners, and regional directors, and such other employees as it may from time to time find necessary for the proper performance of its duties. The Board may not employ any attorneys for the purpose of reviewing transcripts of hearings or preparing drafts of opinions except that any attorney employed for assignment as a legal assistant to any Board member may for such Board member review such transcripts and prepare such drafts. No trial examiner's report shall be reviewed, either before or after its publication, by any person other than a member of the Board or his legal assistant, and no trial examiner shall advise or consult with the Board with respect to exceptions taken to his findings, rulings, or recommendations. The Board may establish or utilize such regional, local, or other agencies, and utilize such voluntary and uncompensated services, as may from time to time be needed. Attorneys appointed under this section may, at the direction of the Board, appear for and represent the Board in any case in court. Nothing in this Act shall be construed to authorize the Board to appoint individuals for the purpose of conciliation or mediation, or for economic analysis.**

(b) All of the expenses of the Board, including all necessary traveling and subsistence expenses outside the District of Columbia incurred by the members or employees of the Board under its orders, shall be allowed and paid on the presentation of itemized vouchers therefor approved by the Board or by any individual it designates for that purpose.

§5. (§155) The principal office of the Board shall be in the District of Columbia, but it may meet and exercise any or all of its powers at any other place. The Board may, by one or more of its members or by such agents or agencies as it may designate, prosecute any inquiry necessary to its functions in any part of the United States. A member who participates in such an inquiry shall not be disqualified from subsequently participating in a decision of the Board in the same case.

§6. (§156) The Board shall have authority from time to time to make, amend, and rescind, **in the manner prescribed by the Administrative Procedure Act,*** such rules and regulations as may be necessary to carry out the provisions of this Act. [Such rules and regulations shall be effective upon publication in the manner which the Board shall prescribe.]

---

*5 U.S.C. §§551 et seq.—Eds.

Rights of Employees

§7. (§157) Employees shall have the right to self-organization, to form, join, or assist labor organizations, to bargain collectively through representatives of their own choosing, and to engage in other concerted activities for the purpose of collective bargaining or other mutual aid or protection, **and shall also have the right to refrain from any or all of such activities except to the extent that such right may be affected by an agreement requiring membership in labor organization as a condition of employment as authorized in section 8(a)(3).**

Unfair Labor Practices

§8. (§158) (a) It shall be an unfair labor practice for an employer—
 (1) to interfere with, restrain, or coerce employees in the exercise of the rights guaranteed in section 7;
 (2) to dominate or interfere with the formation or administration of any labor organization or contribute financial or other support to it: *Provided*, That subject to rules and regulations made and published by the Board pursuant to section 6, an employer shall not be prohibited from permitting employees to confer with him during working hours without loss of time or pay;
 (3) by discrimination in regard to hire or tenure of employment or any term or condition of employment to encourage or discourage membership in any labor organization: *Provided*, That nothing in this Act, or in any other statute of the United States, shall preclude an employer from making an agreement with a labor organization (not established, maintained, or assisted by any action defined in **section 8(a)** of this Act as an unfair labor practice) to require as a condition of employment membership therein **on or after the thirtieth day following the beginning of such employment or the effective date of such agreement, whichever is the later, (i)** if such labor organization is the representative of the employees as provided in section 9(a), in the appropriate collective-bargaining unit covered by such agreement when made, [**and has at the time the agreement was made or within the preceding twelve months received from the Board a notice of compliance with section 9(f), (g), (h)**], **and (ii) unless following an election as in section 9(e) within one year preceding the effective date of such agreement, the Board shall have certified that at least a majority of the employees eligible to vote in such election have voted to rescind the authority of such labor organization to make such an agreement:*** *Provided further*, That no employer shall justify any discrimi-

---

*Clause (ii) was added in 1951 by 65 Stat. 601.

nation against an employee for nonmembership in a labor organization (A) if he has reasonable grounds for believing that such membership was not available to the employee on the same terms and conditions generally applicable to other members, or (B) if he has reasonable grounds for believing that membership was denied or terminated for reasons other than the failure of the employee to tender the periodic dues and the initiation fees uniformly required as a condition of acquiring or retaining membership;

(4) to discharge or otherwise discriminate against an employee because he has filed charges or given testimony under this Act;

(5) to refuse to bargain collectively with the representatives of his employees, subject to the provisions of section 9(a).

(b) It shall be an unfair labor practice for a labor organization or its agents—

(1) to restrain or coerce (A) employees in the exercise of the rights guaranteed in section 7: *Provided*, That this paragraph shall not impair the right of a labor organization to prescribe its own rules with respect to the acquisition or retention of membership therein; or (B) an employer in the selection of his representatives for the purposes of collective bargaining or the adjustment of grievances;

(2) to cause or attempt to cause an employer to discriminate against an employee in violation of subsection (a)(3) or to discriminate against an employee with respect to whom membership in such organization has been denied or terminated on some ground other than his failure to tender the periodic dues and the initiation fees uniformly required as a condition of acquiring or retaining membership;

(3) to refuse to bargain collectively with an employer, provided it is the representative of his employees subject to the provisions of section 9(a);

(4)(i) to engage in, or to induce or encourage [the employees of any employer] *any individual employed by any person engaged in commerce or in an industry affecting commerce* to engage in, a strike or a [concerted] refusal in the course of [their] *his* employment to use, manufacture, process, transport, or otherwise handle or work on any goods, articles, materials, or commodities or to perform any services[,]; *or (ii) to threaten, coerce, or restrain any person engaged in commerce or in an industry affecting commerce, where in either case* an object thereof is—

(A) forcing or requiring any employer or self-employed person to join any labor or employer organization [or any employer or other person to cease using, selling, handling, transporting, or otherwise dealing in the products of any other producer, processor, or manufacturer, or to cease doing business with any other person;] *or to enter into any agreement which is prohibited by subsection (e) of this section;*

(B) forcing or requiring any person to cease using, selling, handling, transporting, or otherwise dealing in the products of any other producer, proces-

sor, or manufacturer, or to cease doing business with any other person, **or forcing or requiring any other employer to recognize or bargain with a labor organization as the representative of his employees unless such labor organization has been certified as the representative of such employees under the provisions of section 9[;]:** *Provided, That nothing contained in this clause (B) shall be construed to make unlawful, where not otherwise unlawful, any primary strike or primary picketing;*

(C) forcing or requiring any employer to recognize or bargain with a particular labor organization as the representative of his employees if another labor organization has been certified as the representative of such employees under the provisions of section 9;

(D) forcing or requiring any employer to assign particular work to employees in a particular labor organization or in a particular trade, craft, or class rather than to employees in another labor organization or in another trade, craft, or class, unless such employer is failing to conform to an order or certification of the Board determining the bargaining representative for employees performing such work:
Provided, **That nothing contained in subsection (b) shall be construed to make unlawful a refusal by any person to enter upon the premises of any employer (other than his own employer), if the employees of such employer are engaged in a strike ratified or approved by a representative of such employees whom such employer is required to recognize under this Act:** *Provided further, That for the purposes of this paragraph (4) only, nothing contained in such paragraph shall be construed to prohibit publicity, other than picketing, for the purpose of truthfully advising the public, including consumers and members of a labor organization, that a product or products are produced by an employer with whom the labor organization has a primary dispute and are distributed by another employer, as long as such publicity does not have an effect of inducing any individual employed by any person other than the primary employer in the course of his employment to refuse to pick up, deliver, or transport any goods, or not to perform any services, at the establishment of the employer engaged in such distribution;*

(5) to require of employees covered by an agreement authorized under subsection (a)(3) of this section the payment, as a condition precedent to becoming a member of such organization, of a fee in an amount which the Board finds excessive or discriminatory under all the circumstances. In making such a finding, the Board shall consider, among other relevant factors, the practices and customs of labor organizations in the particular industry, and the wages currently paid to the employees affected; [and]

(6) to cause or attempt to cause an employer to pay or deliver or agree to pay or deliver any money or other thing of value, in the nature of an exaction, for services which are not performed or not to be performed[.]; *and*

(7) to picket or cause to be picketed, or threaten to picket or cause to be picketed, any employer where an object thereof is forcing or requiring an employer to rec-

ognize or bargain with a labor organization as the representative of his employees, or forcing or requiring the employees of an employer to accept or select such labor organization as their collective bargaining representative, unless such labor organization is currently certified as the representative of such employees:

(A) where the employer has lawfully recognized in accordance with this Act any other labor organization and a question concerning representation may not appropriately be raised under section 9(c) of this Act,

(B) where within the preceding twelve months a valid election under section 9(c) of this Act has been conducted, or

(C) where such picketing has been conducted without a petition under section 9(c) of this Act being filed within a reasonable period of time not to exceed thirty days from the commencement of such picketing: Provided, That when such a petition has been filed the Board shall forthwith, without regard to the provisions of section 9(c) of this Act or the absence of a showing of a substantial interest on the part of the labor organization, direct an election in such unit as the Board finds to be appropriate and shall certify the results thereof: Provided further, That nothing in this subparagraph (C) shall be construed to prohibit any picketing or other publicity for the purpose of truthfully advising the public (including consumers) that an employer does not employ members of, or have a contract with, a labor organization, unless an effect of such picketing is to induce any individual employed by any other person in the course of his employment, not to pick up, deliver or transport any goods or not to perform any services.

Nothing in this paragraph (7) shall be construed to permit any act which would otherwise be an unfair labor practice under this section 8(b).

(c) The expressing of any views, argument, or opinion, or the dissemination thereof, whether in written, printed, graphic, or visual form, shall not constitute or be evidence of an unfair labor practice under any of the provisions of this Act, if such expression contains no threat of reprisal or force or promise of benefit.

(d) For the purposes of this section, to bargain collectively is the performance of the mutual obligation of the employer and the representative of the employees to meet at reasonable times and confer in good faith with respect to wages, hours, and other terms and conditions of employment, or the negotiation of an agreement, or any question arising thereunder, and the execution of a written contract incorporating any agreement reached if requested by either party, but such obligation does not compel either party to agree to a proposal or require the making of a concession: *Provided,* **That where there is in effect a collective-bargaining contract covering employees in an industry affecting commerce, the duty to bargain collectively shall also mean that no party to such contract shall terminate or modify such contract, unless the party desiring such termination or modification—**

(1) serves a written notice upon the other party to the contract of the proposed termination or modification sixty days prior to the expiration date thereof, or in the event such contract contains no expiration date,

sixty days prior to the time it is proposed to make such termination or modification;

(2) offers to meet and confer with the other party for the purpose of negotiating a new contract or a contract containing the proposed modifications;

(3) notifies the Federal Mediation and Conciliation Service within thirty days after such notice of the existence of a dispute, and simultaneously therewith notifies any State or Territorial agency established to mediate and conciliate disputes within the State or Territory where the dispute occurred, provided no agreement has been reached by that time; and

(4) continues in full force and effect, without resorting to strike or lock-out, all the terms and conditions of the existing contract for a period of six days after such notice is given or until the expiration date of such contract, whichever occurs later:

The duties imposed upon employers, employees, and labor organizations by paragraphs (2), (3), and (4) shall become inapplicable upon an intervening certification of the Board, under which the labor organization or individual, which is a party to the contract, has been superseded as or ceased to be the representative of the employees subject to the provisions of section 9(a), and the duties so imposed shall not be construed as requiring either party to discuss or agree to any modification of the terms and conditions contained in a contract for a fixed period, if such modification is to become effective before such terms and conditions can be reopened under the provisions of the contract. Any employee who engages in a strike within the [sixty-day] any notice period specified in this subsection, or who engages in any strike within the appropriate period specified in subsection (g) of this section, shall lose his status as an employee of the employer engaged in the particular labor dispute, for the purposes of sections 8, 9, and 10 of this Act, but such loss of status for such employee shall terminate if and when he is reemployed by such employer. Whenever the collective bargaining involves employees of a health care institution, the provisions of this subsection shall be modified as follows:

(A) The notice of paragraph (1) of this subsection shall be ninety days; the notice of paragraph (3) of this subsection shall be sixty days; and the contract period of paragraph (4) of this subsection shall be ninety days.

(B) Where the bargaining is for an initial agreement following certification or recognition, at least thirty days' notice of the existence of a dispute shall be given by the labor organization to the agencies set forth in paragraph (3) of this subsection.

(C) After notice is given to the Federal Mediation and Conciliation Service under either clause (A) or (B) of this sentence, the Service shall promptly communicate with the parties and use its best efforts, by mediation and conciliation, to bring them to agreement. The parties shall participate fully and promptly in such meetings as may be undertaken by the Service for the purpose of aiding in a settlement of the dispute.

(e) It shall be an unfair labor practice for any labor organization and any employer to enter into any contract or agreement, express or implied, whereby such employer ceases or refrains or agrees to cease or refrain from handling, using, selling, transporting or otherwise dealing in any of the products of any other employer, or to cease doing business with any other person, and any contract or agreement entered into heretofore or hereafter containing such an agreement shall be to such extent unenforcible and void: Provided, That nothing in this subsection (e) shall apply to an agreement between a labor organization and an employer in the construction industry relating to the contracting or subcontracting of work to be done at the site of the construction, alteration, painting, or repair of a building, structure, or other work: Provided further, That for the purposes of this subsection (e) and subsection (b)(4)(B) of this section the terms "any employer", "any person engaged in commerce or an industry affecting commerce", and "any person" when used in relation to the terms "any other producer, processor, or manufacturer", "any other employer", or "any other person" shall not include persons in the relation of a jobber, manufacturer, contractor, or subcontractor working on the goods or premises of the jobber or manufacturer or performing parts of an integrated process of production in the apparel and clothing industry: Provided further, That nothing in this Act shall prohibit the enforcement of any agreement which is within the foregoing exception.

(f) *It shall not be an unfair labor practice under subsections (a) and (b) of this section for an employer engaged primarily in the building and construction industry to make an agreement covering employees engaged (or who, upon their employment, will be engaged) in the building and construction industry with a labor organization of which building and construction employees are members (not established, maintained, or assisted by any action defined in subsection (a) of this section as an unfair labor practice) because (1) the majority status of such labor organization has not been established under the provisions of section 9 of this Act prior to the making of such agreement, or (2) such agreement requires as a condition of employment, membership in such labor organization after the seventh day following the beginning of such employment or the effective date of the agreement, whichever is later, or (3) such agreement requires the employer to notify such labor organization of opportunities for employment with such employer, or gives such labor organization an opportunity to refer qualified applicants for such employment, or (4) such agreement specifies minimum training or experience qualifications for employment or provides for priority in opportunities for employment based upon length of service with such employer, in the industry or in the particular geographical area: Provided, That nothing in this sub-

---

*Sec. 8(f) was inserted in the Act by Sec. 705(a) of Public Law 86-257. Sec. 705(b) provides:

> Nothing contained in the amendment made by subsection (a) shall be construed as authorizing the execution or application of agreements requiring membership in a labor organization as a condition of employment in any State or Territory in which such execution or application is prohibited by State or Territorial Law.

section shall set aside the final proviso to section 8(a)(3) of this Act: Provided further, That any agreement which would be invalid, but for clause (1) of this subsection, shall not be a bar to a petition filed pursuant to section 9(c) or 9(e).

(g) A labor organization before engaging in any strike, picketing, or other concerted refusal to work at any health care institution shall, not less than ten days prior to such action, notify the institution in writing and the Federal Mediation and Conciliation Service of that intention, except that in the case of bargaining for an initial agreement following certification or recognition the notice required by this subsection shall not be given until the expiration of the period specified in clause (B) of the last sentence of section (8)(d) of this Act. The notice shall state the date and time that such action will commence. The notice, once given, may be extended by the written agreement of both parties.

REPRESENTATIVES AND ELECTIONS

§9. (§159) (a) Representatives designated or selected for the purposes of collective bargaining by the majority of the employees in a unit appropriate for such purposes, shall be the exclusive representatives of all the employees in such unit for the purposes of collective bargaining in respect to rates of pay, wages, hours of employment, or other conditions of employment: *Provided,* That any individual employee or a group of employees shall have the right at any time to present grievances to their employer **and to have such grievances adjusted, without the intervention of the bargaining representative, as long as the adjustment is not inconsistent with the terms of a collective-bargaining contract or agreement then in effect:** *Provided further,* **That the bargaining representative has been given opportunity to be present at such adjustment.**

(b) The Board shall decide in each case whether, in order to assure to employees the fullest freedom in exercising the rights guaranteed by this Act, the unit appropriate for the purposes of collective bargaining shall be the employer unit, craft unit, plant unit, or subdivision thereof: **Provided, That the Board shall not (1) decide that any unit is appropriate for such purposes if such unit includes both professional employees and employees who are not professional employees unless a majority of such professional employees vote for inclusion in such unit; or (2) decide that any craft unit is inappropriate for such purposes on the ground that a different unit has been established by a prior Board determination, unless a majority of the employees in the proposed craft unit vote against separate representation or (3) decide that any unit is appropriate for such purposes if it includes, together with other employees, any individual employed as a guard to enforce against employees and other persons rules to protect property of the employer or to protect the safety of persons on the employer's premises; but no labor organization shall be certified as the representative** of employees in a bargaining unit of guards if such organization admits to membership, or is affiliated directly or indirectly with an organization which admits to membership, employees other than guards.

[(c) Whenever a question affecting commerce arises concerning the representation of employees, the Board may investigate such controversy and certify to the parties, in writing, the name or names of the representatives that have been designated or selected. In any such investigation, the Board shall provide for an appropriate hearing upon due notice, either in conjunction with a proceeding under section 10 or otherwise, and may take a secret ballot of employees, or utilize any other suitable method to ascertain such representatives.]

(c)(1) Whenever a petition shall have been filed, in accordance with such regulations as may be prescribed by the Board—

(A) by an employee or group of employees or any individual or labor organization acting in their behalf alleging that a substantial number of employees (i) wish to be represented for collective bargaining and that their employer declines to recognize their representative as the representative defined in section 9(a), or (ii) assert that the individual or labor organization, which has been certified or is being currently recognized by their employer as the bargaining representative, is no longer a representative as defined in section 9(a); or

(B) by an employer, alleging that one or more individuals or labor organizations have presented to him a claim to be recognized as the representative defined in section 9(a);

the Board shall investigate such petition and if it has reasonable cause to believe that a question of representation affecting commerce exists shall provide for an appropriate hearing upon due notice. Such hearing may be conducted by an officer or employee of the regional office, who shall not make any recommendations with respect thereto. If the Board finds upon the record of such hearing that such a question of representation exists, it shall direct an election by secret ballot and shall certify the results thereof.

(2) In determining whether or not a question of representation affecting commerce exists, the same regulations and rules of decision shall apply irrespective of the identity of the persons filing the petition or the kind of relief sought and in no case shall the Board deny a labor organization a place on the ballot by reason of an order with respect to such labor organization or its predecessor not issued in conformity with section 10(c).

(3) No election shall be directed in any bargaining unit or any subdivision within which, in the preceding twelve-month period, a valid election shall have been held. Employees [on strike] *engaged in an economic strike* who are not entitled to reinstatement shall [not] be eligible to vote *under such regulations as the Board shall find are consistent with the purposes and provisions of this Act in any election conducted within twelve months after the commencement of the strike.* In any election where none of the choices

on the ballot receives a majority, a run-off shall be conducted, the ballot providing for a selection between the two choices receiving the largest and second largest number of valid votes cast in the election.

(4) Nothing in this section shall be construed to prohibit the waiving of hearings by stipulation for the purpose of a consent election in conformity with regulations and rules of decision of the Board.

(5) In determining whether a unit is appropriate for the purposes specified in subsection (b) the extent to which the employees have organized shall not be controlling.

(d) Whenever an order of the Board made pursuant to section 10(c) is based in whole or in part upon facts certified following an investigation pursuant to subsection (c) of this section and there is a petition for the enforcement or review of such order, such certification and the record of such investigation shall be included in the transcript of the entire record required to be filed under section 10(e) or 10(f), and thereupon the decree of the court enforcing, modifying, or setting aside in whole or in part the order of the Board shall be made and entered upon the pleadings, testimony, and proceedings set forth in such transcript.

(e)(1) *Upon the filing with the Board, by 30 per centum or more of the employees in a bargaining unit covered by an agreement between their employer and a labor organization made pursuant to section 8(a)(3), of a petition alleging they desire that such authority be rescinded, the Board shall take a secret ballot of the employees in such unit, and shall certify the results thereof to such labor organization and to the employer.

(2) No election shall be conducted pursuant to this subsection in any bargaining unit or any subdivision within which, in the preceding twelve-month period, a valid election shall have been held.

[Subsections (f), (g), and (h) were deleted by the Labor-Management Reporting and Disclosure Act.—EDS.]

PREVENTION OF UNFAIR LABOR PRACTICES

§10. (§160) (a) The Board is empowered, as hereinafter provided, to prevent any person from engaging in any unfair labor practice (listed in section 8) affecting commerce. This power shall not be affected by any other means of adjustment or prevention that has been or may be established by agreement, law, or otherwise: *Provided*, **That the Board is empowered by agreement with any agency of any State or Territory to cede to such agency**

---

*As enacted in 1947, Section 9(e) had three subsections. In 1951, the first subsection was deleted and the two remaining subsections were renumbered (1) and (2). 65 Stat. 601. The deleted subsection required, as a condition to the inclusion of a union-shop clause in a labor agreement, that a majority of employees authorize such a clause in a Board-conducted election.—EDS.

jurisdiction over any cases in any industry (other than mining, manufacturing, communications, and transportation except where predominantly local in character) even though such cases may involve labor disputes affecting commerce, unless the provision of the State or Territorial statute applicable to the determination of such cases by such agency is inconsistent with the corresponding provision of this Act or has received a construction inconsistent therewith.

(b) Whenever it is charged that any person has engaged in or is engaging in any such unfair labor practice, the Board, or any agent or agency designated by the Board for such purposes, shall have power to issue and cause to be served upon such person a complaint stating the charges in that respect, and containing a notice of hearing before the Board or a member thereof, or before a designated agent or agency, at a place therein fixed, not less than five days after the serving of said complaint: *Provided,* **That no complaint shall issue based upon any unfair labor practice occurring more than six months prior to the filing of the charge with the Board and the service of a copy thereof upon the person against whom such charge is made, unless the person aggrieved thereby was prevented from filing such charge by reason of service in the armed forces, in which event the six-month period shall be computed from the day of his discharge.** Any such complaint may be amended by the member, agent, or agency conducting the hearing or the Board in its discretion at any time prior to the issuance of an order based thereon. The person so complained of shall have the right to file an answer to the original or amended complaint and to appear in person or otherwise and give testimony at the place and time fixed in the complaint. In the discretion of the member, agent, or agency conducting the hearing or the Board, any other person may be allowed to intervene in the said proceeding and to present testimony. [In any such proceeding the rules of evidence prevailing in courts of law or equity shall not be controlling.] **Any such proceeding shall, so far as practicable, be conducted in accordance with the rules of evidence applicable in the district courts of the United States under the rules of civil procedure for the district courts of the United States, adopted by the Supreme Court of the United States pursuant to section 2072 of Title 28.**

(c) The testimony taken by such member, agent, or agency or the Board shall be reduced to writing and filed with the Board. Thereafter, in its discretion, the Board upon notice may take further testimony or hear argument. If upon [all] **the preponderance of** the testimony taken the Board shall be of the opinion that any person named in the complaint has engaged in or is engaging in any such unfair labor practice, then the Board shall state its findings of fact and shall issue and cause to be served on such person an order requiring such person to cease and desist from such unfair labor practice, and to take such affirmative action including reinstatement of employees with or without back pay, as will effectuate the policies of this

Act: *Provided,* That where an order directs reinstatement of an employee, back pay may be required of the employer or labor organization, as the case may be, responsible for the discrimination suffered by him: *And provided further,* That in determining whether a complaint shall issue alleging a violation of section 8(a)(1) or section 8(a)(2), and in deciding such cases, the same regulations and rules of decision shall apply irrespective of whether or not the labor organization affected is affiliated with a labor organization national or international in scope. Such order may further require such person to make reports from time to time showing the extent to which it has complied with the order. If upon [all] **the preponderance of** the testimony taken the Board shall not be of the opinion that the person named in the complaint has engaged in or is engaging in any such unfair labor practice, then the Board shall state its findings of fact and shall issue an order dismissing the said complaint. **No order of the Board shall require the reinstatement of any individual as an employee who has been suspended or discharged, or the payment to him of any back pay, if such individual was suspended or discharged for cause. In case the evidence is presented before a member of the Board, or before an administrative law judge or judges thereof, such member, or such judge or judges as the case may be, shall issue and cause to be served on the parties to the proceeding a proposed report, together with a recommended order, which shall be filed with the Board, and if no exceptions are filed within twenty days after service thereof upon such parties, or within such further period as the Board may authorize, such recommended order shall become the order of the Board and become effective as therein prescribed.**

(d) Until **[a transcript of]** the record in a case shall have been filed in a court, as hereinafter provided, the Board may at any time upon reasonable notice and in such manner as it shall deem proper, modify or set aside, in whole or in part, any finding or order made or issued by it.

(e) The Board shall have power to petition any [United States] court of appeals of the United States [(including the United States court of appeals for the District of Columbia)], or if all the courts of appeals to which application may be made are in vacation, any [United States] district court *of the United States,* within any circuit or district, respectively, wherein the unfair labor practice in question occurred or wherein such person resides or transacts business, for the enforcement of such order and for appropriate temporary relief or restraining order, and shall file in the court the record in the proceedings, *as provided in section 2112 of Title 28.* Upon [such filing] *the filing of such petition,* the court shall cause notice thereof to be served upon such person, and thereupon shall have jurisdiction of the proceeding and of the question determined therein, and shall have power to grant such temporary relief or restraining order as it deems just and proper, and to make and enter [upon the pleadings, testimony, and proceedings set forth in such transcript] a decree enforcing, modifying and enforcing as so modified, or setting aside in whole or in part the order of the Board. No objection that has not been urged before the Board, its member, agent, or agency, shall be considered by the court, unless the failure or neglect to urge such objection shall be excused because of extraordinary circumstances. The findings of the Board with respect to questions of fact if supported by **substantial** evidence **on the record considered as a whole** shall be conclusive. If either party shall apply to the court for leave to adduce additional evidence and shall show to the satisfaction of the court that such additional evidence is material and that there were reasonable grounds for the failure to adduce such evidence in the hearing before the Board, its member, agent, or agency, the court may order such additional evidence to be taken before the Board, its member, agent, or agency, and to be made a part of the [transcript] *record*. The Board may modify its findings as to the facts, or make new findings by reason of additional evidence so taken and filed, and it shall file such modified or new findings, which findings with respect to questions of fact if supported by **substantial** evidence **on the record considered as a whole** shall be conclusive, and shall file its recommendations, if any, for the modification or setting aside of its original order. *Upon the filing of the record with it* the jurisdiction of the court shall be exclusive and its judgment and decree shall be final, except that the same shall be subject to review by the appropriate United States court of appeals if application was made to the district court as hereinabove provided, and by the Supreme Court of the United States upon writ of certiorari or certification as provided in section 1254 of Title 28.

(f) Any person aggrieved by a final order of the Board granting or denying in whole or in part the relief sought may obtain a review of such order in any United States court of appeals in the circuit wherein the unfair labor practice in question was alleged to have been engaged in or wherein such person resides or transacts business, or in the United States Court of Appeals for the District of Columbia, by filing in such a court a written petition praying that the order of the Board be modified or set aside. A copy of such petition shall be forthwith [served upon the Board] *transmitted by the clerk of the court to the Board*, and thereupon the aggrieved party shall file in the court [a transcript of] the [entire] record in the proceeding, certified by the Board [including the pleading and testimony upon which the order complained of was entered and the findings and order of the Board] *as provided in section 2112 of Title 28*. Upon [such filing] *the filing of such petition*, the court shall proceed in the same manner as in the case of an application by the Board under subsection (e) of this section, and shall have the same jurisdiction to grant to the Board such temporary relief or restraining order as it deems just and proper, and in like manner to make and enter a decree enforcing, modifying, and enforcing as so modified, or setting aside in whole or in part the order of the Board; the findings of the Board with respect to questions of fact if supported by **substantial** evidence **on the record considered as a whole** shall in like manner be conclusive.

(g) The commencement of proceedings under subsection (e) or (f) of this section shall not, unless specifically ordered by the court, operate as a stay of the Board's order.

(h) When granting appropriate temporary relief or a restraining order, or making and entering a decree enforcing, modifying, and enforcing as so modified or setting aside in whole or in part an order of the Board, as provided in this section, the jurisdiction of courts sitting in equity shall not be limited by the Act entitled "An Act to amend the Judicial Code and to define and limit the jurisdiction of courts sitting in equity, and for other purposes", approved March 23, 1932 (U.S.C., Supp. VII, title 29, secs. 101-115).*

(i) Repealed.

(j) **The Board shall have power, upon issuance of a complaint as provided in subsection (b) charging that any person has engaged in or is engaging in an unfair labor practice, to petition any district court of the United States (including the District Court of the United States for the District of Columbia), within any district wherein the unfair labor practice in question is alleged to have occurred or wherein such person resides or transacts business, for appropriate temporary relief or restraining order. Upon the filing of any such petition the court shall cause notice thereof to be served upon such person, and thereupon shall have jurisdiction to grant to the Board such temporary relief or restraining order as it deems just and proper.**

(k) Whenever it is charged that any person has engaged in an unfair labor practice within the meaning of paragraph (4)(D) of section 8(b), the Board is empowered and directed to hear and determine the dispute out of which such unfair labor practice shall have arisen, unless, within ten days after notice that such charge has been filed, the parties to such dispute submit to the Board satisfactory evidence that they have adjusted, or agreed upon methods for the voluntary adjustment of, the dispute. Upon compliance by the parties to the dispute with the decision of the Board or upon such voluntary adjustment of the dispute, such charge shall be dismissed.

(l) Whenever it is charged that any person has engaged in an unfair labor practice within the meaning of paragraph (4)(A), (B), or (C) of section 8(b), the preliminary investigation of such charge shall be made forthwith and given priority over all other cases except cases of like character in the office where it is filed or to which it is referred. If, after such investigation, the officer or regional attorney to whom the matter may be referred has reasonable cause to believe such charge is true and that a complaint should issue, he shall, on behalf of the Board, petition any district court of the United States (including the District Court of the United States for the District of Columbia) within any district where the unfair labor practice in question has occurred, is alleged to have occurred, or wherein such person resides or transacts business, for appropriate injunctive relief pending the

---

*The Norris-LaGuardia Act of 1932.—EDS.

final adjudication of the Board with respect to such matter. Upon the filing of any such petition the district court shall have jurisdiction to grant such injunctive relief or temporary restraining order as it deems just and proper, notwithstanding any other provision of law: *Provided further*, That no temporary restraining order shall be issued without notice unless a petition alleges that substantial and irreparable injury to the charging party will be unavoidable and such temporary restraining order shall be effective for no longer than five days and will become void at the expiration of such period[.]: *Provided further, That such officer or regional attorney shall not apply for any restraining order under section 8(b)(7) if a charge against the employer under section 8(a)(2) has been filed and after the preliminary investigation, he has reasonable cause to believe that such charge is true and that a complaint should issue.* Upon filing of any such petition the courts shall cause notice thereof to be served upon any person involved in the charge and such person, including the charging party, shall be given an opportunity to appear by counsel and present any relevant testimony: *Provided further*, That for the purposes of this subsection district courts shall be deemed to have jurisdiction of a labor organization (1) in the district in which such organization maintains its principal office, or (2) in any district in which its duly authorized officers or agents are engaged in promoting or protecting the interests of employee members. The service of legal process upon such officer or agent shall constitute service upon the labor organization and make such organization a party to the suit. In situations where such relief is appropriate the procedure specified herein shall apply to charges with respect to section 8(b)(4)(D).

(m) *Whenever it is charged that any person has engaged in an unfair labor practice within the meaning of subsection (a)(3) or (b)(2) of section 8, such charge shall be given priority over all other cases except cases of like character in the office where it is filed or to which it is referred and cases given priority under subsection (l) of this section.*

INVESTIGATORY POWERS

§11. (§161) For the purpose of all hearings and investigations, which, in the opinion of the Board, are necessary and proper for the exercise of the powers vested in it by section 9 and section 10—

(1) The Board, or its duly authorized agents or agencies, shall at all reasonable times have access to, for the purpose of examination, and the right to copy any evidence of any person being investigated or proceeded against that relates to any matter under investigation or in question. The Board, or any member thereof, shall upon application of any party to such proceedings, forthwith issue to such party subpenas requiring the attendance and testimony of witnesses or the production of any evidence in such

proceeding or investigation requested in such application. **Within five days after the service of a subpena on any person requiring the production of any evidence in his possession or under this control, such person may petition the Board to revoke, and the Board shall revoke, such subpena if in its opinion the evidence whose production is required does not relate to any matter under investigation, or any matter in question in such proceedings, or if in its opinion such subpena does not describe with sufficient particularity the evidence whose production is required.** Any member of the Board, or any agent or agency designated by the Board for such purposes, may administer oaths and affirmations, examine witnesses, and receive evidence. Such attendance of witnesses and the production of such evidence may be required from any place in the United States or any Territory or possession thereof, at any designated place of hearing.

(2) In case of contumacy or refusal to obey a subpena issued to any person, any district court of the United States or the United States courts of any Territory or possession, or the District Court of the United States for the District of Columbia, within the jurisdiction of which the inquiry is carried on or within the jurisdiction of which said person guilty of contumacy or refusal to obey is found or resides or transacts business, upon application by the Board shall have jurisdiction to issue to such person an order requiring such person to appear before the Board, its member, agent, or agency, there to produce evidence if so ordered, or there to give testimony touching the matter under investigation or in question; and any failure to obey such order of the court may be punished by said court as a contempt thereof.

[(3) No person shall be excused from attending and testifying or from producing books, records, correspondence, documents, or other evidence in obedience to the subpena of the Board, on the ground that the testimony or evidence required of him may tend to incriminate him or subject him to a penalty or forfeiture; but no individual shall be prosecuted or subjected to any penalty or forfeiture for or on account of any transaction, matter, or thing concerning which he is compelled, after having claimed his privilege against self-incrimination, to testify or produce evidence, except that such individual so testifying shall not be exempt from prosecution and punishment for perjury committed in so testifying.*]

(4) Complaints, orders, and other process and papers of the Board, its member, agent, or agency, may be served either personally or by registered mail or by telegraph or by leaving a copy thereof at the principal office or place of business of the person required to be served. The verified return by the individual so serving the same setting forth the manner of such service shall be proof of the same, and the return post office receipt or telegraph

---

*Section 11(3) was repealed in 1970, by 84 Stat. 930. Similar provisions were substituted; see 18 U.S.C. §§6001, 6002, 6004 (1970).

receipt therefor when registered and mailed or telegraphed as aforesaid shall be proof of service of the same. Witnesses summoned before the Board, its member, agent, or agency, shall be paid the same fees and mileage that are paid witnesses in the courts of the United States, and witnesses whose depositions are taken and the persons taking the same shall severally be entitled to the same fees as are paid for like services in the courts of the United States.

(5) All process of any court to which application may be made under this Act may be served in the judicial district wherein the defendant or other person required to be served resides or may be found.

(6) The several departments and agencies of the Government, when directed by the President, shall furnish the Board, upon its request, all records, papers, and information in their possession relating to any matter before the Board.

§12. (§162) Any person who shall willfully resist, prevent, impede, or interfere with any member of the Board or any of its agents or agencies in the performance of duties pursuant to this Act shall be punished by a fine of not more than $5,000 or by imprisonment for not more than one year, or both.

Limitations

§13. (§163) Nothing in this Act, **except as specifically provided for herein,** shall be construed so as either to interfere with or impede or diminish in any way the right to strike, **or affect the limitations or qualifications on that right.**

§14. (§164) **(a) Nothing herein shall prohibit any individual employed as a supervisor from becoming or remaining a member of a labor organization, but no employer subject to this Act shall be compelled to deem individuals defined herein as supervisors as employees for the purpose of any law, either national or local, relating to collective bargaining.**

(b) Nothing in this Act shall be construed as authorizing the execution or application of agreements requiring membership in a labor organization as a condition of employment in any State or Territory in which such execution or application is prohibited by State or Territorial Law.

(c) (1) The Board, in its discretion, may, by rule of decision or by published rules adopted pursuant to the Administrative Procedure Act, decline to assert jurisdiction over any labor dispute involving any class or category of employers, where, in the opinion of the Board, the effect of such labor dispute on commerce is not sufficiently substantial to warrant the exercise of its jurisdiction: Provided, That the Board shall

not decline to assert jurisdiction over any labor dispute over which it would assert jurisdiction under the standards prevailing upon August 1, 1959.

(2) Nothing in this subchapter shall be deemed to prevent or bar any agency or the courts of any State or Territory (including the Commonwealth of Puerto Rico, Guam, and the Virgin Islands), from assuming and asserting jurisdiction over labor disputes over which the Board declines, pursuant to paragraph (1) of this subsection, to assert jurisdiction.

§15. (§165) [Reference to repealed provisions of Bankruptcy Act of 1898.—EDS.]

§16. (§166) If any provision of this Act, or the application of such provision to any person or circumstances, shall be held invalid, the remainder of this Act, or the application of such provision to persons or circumstances other than those as to which it is held invalid, shall not be affected thereby.

§17. (§167) This Act may be cited as the "National Labor Relations Act."

§18. (§168) [Reference to repealed sections 9(f), (g), and (h).—EDS.]

§19. (§169) Any employee who is a member of and adheres to established and traditional tenets or teachings of a bona fide religion, body, or sect which has historically held conscientious objections to joining or financially supporting labor organizations shall not be required to join or financially support any labor organization as a condition of employment; except that such employee may be required in a contract between such employees' employer and a labor organization in lieu of periodic dues and initiation fees, to pay sums equal to such dues and initiation fees to a nonreligious, nonlabor organization charitable fund exempt from taxation under section 501(c)(3) of the Internal Revenue Service, chosen by such employee from a list of at least three such funds, designated in such contract or if the contract fails to designate such funds, then to any such fund chosen by the employee. If such employee who holds conscientious objections pursuant to this section requests the labor organization to use the grievance-arbitration procedure on the employee's behalf, the labor organization is authorized to charge the employee for the reasonable cost of using such procedure.*

---

*This section was added by Pub. L. 93-360, July 26, 1974, 88 Stat. 397, and amended, Pub. L. 96-593, Dec. 24, 1980, 94 Stat. 3452.—EDS.

Labor Management Relations Act of 1947[*]
61 Stat. 136 (1947), as amended, 29 U.S.C. §§141-197

Short Title and Declaration of Policy

§1. (§141) (a) This Act may be cited as the "Labor Management Relations Act, 1947."

(b) Industrial strife which interferes with the normal flow of commerce and with the full production of articles and commodities for commerce, can be avoided or substantially minimized if employers, employees, and labor organizations each recognize under law one another's legitimate rights in their relations with each other, and above all recognize under law that neither party has any right in its relations with any other to engage in acts or practices which jeopardize the public health, safety, or interest.

It is the purpose and policy of this Act, in order to promote the full flow of commerce, to prescribe the legitimate rights of both employees and employers in their relations affecting commerce, to provide orderly and peaceful procedures for preventing the interference by either with the legitimate rights of the other, to protect the rights of individual employees in their relations with labor organizations whose activities affect commerce, to define and proscribe practices on the part of labor and management which affect commerce and are inimical to the general welfare, and to protect the rights of the public in connection with labor disputes affecting commerce.

TITLE I. AMENDMENT OF NATIONAL LABOR RELATIONS ACT

§101. [The text of the National Labor Relations Act as amended is set forth supra.]

TITLE II. CONCILIATION OF LABOR DISPUTES; NATIONAL EMERGENCIES

§201. (§171) It is the policy of the United States that—

(a) sound and stable industrial peace and the advancement of the general welfare, health, and safety of the Nation and of the best interests of employers and employees can most satisfactorily be secured by the settlement of issues between employers and employees through the processes of

---

[*]Unless otherwise indicated, internal section references are to the NLRA or LMRA, and not to the United States Code. Provisions added by the LMRDA (1959) are in italics; provisions added by the Health Care Institutions Act (1974) are capitalized. Material deleted by the amendments is enclosed in brackets. Other amendments and deletions are specifically noted. In view of the information provided, legislative histories will not be appended at the end of each section.—EDS.

conference and collective bargaining between employers and the representatives of their employees;

(b) the settlement of issues between employers and employees through collective bargaining may be advanced by making available full and adequate government facilities for conciliation, mediation, and voluntary arbitration to aid and encourage employers and the representatives of their employees to reach and maintain agreements concerning rates of pay, hours, and working conditions, and to make all reasonable efforts to settle their differences by mutual agreement reached through conferences and collective bargaining or by such methods as may be provided for in any applicable agreement for the settlement of disputes; and

(c) certain controversies which arise between parties to collective-bargaining agreements may be avoided or minimized by making available full and adequate governmental facilities for furnishing assistance to employers and the representatives of their employees in formulating for inclusion within such agreements provision for adequate notice of any proposed changes in the terms of such agreements, for the final adjustment of grievances or questions regarding the application or interpretation of such agreements, and other provisions designed to prevent the subsequent arising of such controversies.

§202. (§172) (a) There is hereby created an independent agency to be known as the Federal Mediation and Conciliation Service (herein referred to as the "Service", except that for sixty days after June 23, 1947, such term shall refer to the Conciliation Service of the Department of Labor). The Service shall be under the direction of a Federal Mediation and Conciliation Director (hereinafter referred to as the "Director"), who shall be appointed by the President by and with the advice and consent of the Senate. The Director shall not engage in any other business, vocation or employment.

(b) The Director is authorized, subject to the civil service laws, to appoint such clerical and other personnel as may be necessary for the execution of the functions of the Service, and shall fix their compensation in accordance with the Classification Act of 1949, and may, without regard to the provisions of the civil service laws, appoint such conciliators and mediators as may be necessary to carry out the functions of the Service. The Director is authorized to make such expenditures for supplies, facilities, and services as he deems necessary. Such expenditures shall be allowed and paid upon presentation of itemized vouchers therefor approved by the Director or by any employee designated by him for that purpose.

(c) The principal office of the Service shall be in the District of Columbia, but the Director may establish regional offices convenient to localities in which labor controversies are likely to arise. The Director may by order, subject to revocation at any time, delegate any authority and discretion conferred upon him by this Act to any regional director, or other officer or employee of the Service. The Director may establish suitable procedures for cooperation with State and local mediation agencies. The Director shall make an annual report in writing to Congress at the end of the fiscal year.

(d) All mediation and conciliation functions of the Secretary of Labor or the United States Conciliation Service under section 8 of the Act entitled "An Act to Create a Department of Labor", approved March 4, 1913 (U.S.C., title 29, sec. 51), and all functions of the United States Conciliation Service under any other law are transferred to the Federal Mediation and Conciliation Service, together with the personnel and records of the United States Conciliation Service. Such transfer shall take effect upon the sixtieth day after June 23, 1947. Such transfer shall not affect any proceedings pending before the United States Conciliation Service or any certification, order, rule, or regulation theretofore made by it or by the Secretary of Labor. The Director and the Service shall not be subject in any way to the jurisdiction or authority of the Secretary of Labor or any official or division of the Department of Labor.

Functions of the Service

§203. (§173) (a) It shall be the duty of the Service, in order to prevent or minimize interruptions of the free flow of commerce growing out of labor disputes, to assist parties to labor disputes in industries affecting commerce to settle such disputes through conciliation and mediation.

(b) The Service may proffer its services in any labor dispute in any industry affecting commerce, either upon its own motion or upon the request of one or more of the parties to the dispute, whenever in its judgment such dispute threatens to cause a substantial interruption of commerce. The Director and the Service are directed to avoid attempting to mediate disputes which would have only a minor effect on interstate commerce if State or other conciliation services are available to the parties. Whenever the Service does proffer its services in any dispute, it shall be the duty of the Service promptly to put itself in communication with the parties and to use its best efforts, by mediation and conciliation, to bring them to agreement.

(c) If the Director is not able to bring the parties to agreement by conciliation within a reasonable time, he shall seek to induce the parties voluntarily to seek other means of settling the dispute without resort to strike, lock-out, or other coercion, including submission to the employees in the bargaining unit of the employer's last offer of settlement for approval or rejection in a secret ballot. The failure or refusal of either party to agree to any procedure suggested by the Director shall not be deemed a violation of any duty or obligation imposed by this Act.

Labor Management Relations Act of 1947 77

(d) Final adjustment by a method agreed upon by the parties is declared to be the desirable method for settlement of grievance disputes arising over the application or interpretation of an existing collective-bargaining agreement. The Service is directed to make its conciliation and mediation services available in the settlement of such grievance disputes only as a last resort and in exceptional cases.

(e)* The Service is authorized and directed to encourage and support the establishment and operation of joint labor management activities conducted by plant, area, and industrywide committees designed to improve labor management relationships, job security and organizational effectiveness, in accordance with the provisions of section 205A.

§204. (§174) (a) In order to prevent or minimize interruptions of the free flow of commerce growing out of labor disputes, employers and employees and their representatives, in any industry affecting commerce, shall—

(1) exert every reasonable effort to make and maintain agreements concerning rates of pay, hours, and working conditions, including provision for adequate notice of any proposed change in the terms of such agreements;

(2) whenever a dispute arises over the terms or application of a collective-bargaining agreement and a conference is requested by a party or prospective party thereto, arrange promptly for such a conference to be held and endeavor in such conference to settle such dispute expeditiously; and

(3) in case such dispute is not settled by conference, participate fully and promptly in such meetings as may be undertaken by the Service under this Act for the purpose of aiding in a settlement of the dispute.

§205. (§175) (a) There is created a National Labor-Management Panel which shall be composed of twelve members appointed by the President, six of whom shall be selected from among persons outstanding in the field of management and six of whom shall be selected from among persons outstanding in the field of labor. Each member shall hold office for a term of three years, except that any member appointed to fill a vacancy occurring prior to the expiration of the term for which his predecessor was appointed shall be appointed for the remainder of such term, and the terms of office of the members first taking office shall expire, as designated by the President at the time of appointment, four at the end of the first year, four at the end of the second year, and four at the end of the third year after the date of appointment. Members of the panel, when serving on business of the panel, shall be paid compensation at the rate of $25 per day, and shall also

---

*Subsection (e) was added in 1978, by Pub. L. 95-524, §6(c)(1), 92 Stat. 2020.

be entitled to receive an allowance for actual and necessary travel and subsistence expenses while so serving away from their places of residence.

(b) It shall be the duty of the panel, at the request of the Director, to advise in the avoidance of industrial controversies and the manner in which mediation and voluntary adjustment shall be administered, particularly with reference to controversies affecting the general welfare of the country.

§205A. (§175a)* (a)(1) The Service is authorized and directed to provide assistance in the establishment and operation of plant, area and industrywide labor management committees which—

(A) have been organized jointly by employers and labor organizations representing employees in that plant, area, or industry; and

(B) are established for the purpose of improving labor management relationships, job security, organizational effectiveness, enhancing economic development or involving workers in decisions affecting their jobs including improving communication with respect to subjects of mutual interest and concern.

(2) The Service is authorized and directed to enter into contracts and to make grants, where necessary or appropriate, to fulfill its responsibilities under this section.

(b)(1) No grant may be made, no contract may be entered into and no other assistance may be provided under the provisions of this section to a plant labor management committee unless the employees in that plant are represented by a labor organization and there is in effect at that plant a collective bargaining agreement.

(2) No grant may be made, no contract may be entered into and no other assistance may be provided under the provisions of this section to an area or industrywide labor management committee unless its participants include any labor organizations certified or recognized as the representative of the employees of an employer participating in such committee. Nothing in this clause shall prohibit participation in an area or industrywide committee by an employer whose employees are not represented by a labor organization.

(3) No grant may be made under the provisions of this section to any labor management committee which the Service finds to have as one of its purposes the discouragement of the exercise of rights contained in section 7 of the National Labor Relations Act (29 U.S.C. §157) [section 157 of this title], or the interference with collective bargaining in any plant, or industry.

(c) The Service shall carry out the provisions of this section through an office established for that purpose.

(d) There are authorized to be appropriated to carry out the provisions of this section $10,000,000 for the fiscal year 1979, and such sums as may be necessary thereafter.

---

*This section was added in 1978, by Pub. L. 95-524, §6(c)(2), 92 Stat. 2020.

Labor Management Relations Act of 1947

National Emergencies

§206. (§176) Whenever in the opinion of the President of the United States, a threatened or actual strike or lock-out affecting an entire industry or a substantial part thereof engaged in trade, commerce, transportation, transmission, or communication among the several States or with foreign nations, or engaged in the production of goods for commerce, will, if permitted to occur or to continue, imperil the national health or safety, he may appoint a board of inquiry to inquire into the issues involved in the dispute and to make a written report to him within such time as he shall prescribe. Such report shall include a statement of the facts with respect to the dispute, including each party's statement of its position but shall not contain any recommendations. The President shall file a copy of such report with the Service and shall make its contents available to the public.

§207. (§177) (a) A board of inquiry shall be composed of a chairman and such other members as the President shall determine, and shall have power to sit and act in any place within the United States and to conduct such hearings either in public or in private, as it may deem necessary or proper, to ascertain the facts with respect to the causes and circumstances of the dispute.

(b) Members of a board of inquiry shall receive compensation at the rate of $50 for each day actually spent by them in the work of the board, together with necessary travel and subsistence expenses.

(c) For the purpose of any hearing or inquiry conducted by any board appointed under this title, the provisions of sections 49 and 50 of title 18 (relating to the attendance of witnesses and the production of books, papers, and documents) are made applicable to the powers and duties of such board.

§208. (§178) (a) Upon receiving a report from a board of inquiry the President may direct the Attorney General to petition any district court of the United States having jurisdiction of the parties to enjoin such strike or lock-out or the continuing thereof, and if the court finds that such threatened or actual strike or lock-out—

(i) affects an entire industry or a substantial part thereof engaged in trade, commerce, transportation, transmission, or communication among the several States or with foreign nations, or engaged in the production of goods for commerce; and

(ii) if permitted to occur or to continue, will imperil the national health or safety, it shall have jurisdiction to enjoin any such strike or lock-out, or the continuing thereof, and to make such other orders as may be appropriate.

(b) In any case, the provisions of the Act of March 23, 1932, entitled "An Act to amend the Judicial Code and to define and limit the jurisdiction of courts sitting in equity, and for other purposes", shall not be applicable.

(c) The order or orders of the court shall be subject to review by the appropriate United States court of appeals and by the Supreme Court upon writ of certiorari or certification as provided in section 1254 of title 28.

§209. (§179) (a) Whenever a district court has issued an order under section 208 enjoining acts or practices which imperil or threaten to imperil the national health or safety, it shall be the duty of the parties to the labor dispute giving rise to such order to make every effort to adjust and settle their differences, with the assistance of the Service created by this Act. Neither party shall be under any duty to accept, in whole or in part, any proposal of settlement made by the Service.

(b) Upon the issuance of such order, the President shall reconvene the board of inquiry which has previously reported with respect to the dispute. At the end of a sixty-day period (unless the dispute has been settled by that time), the board of inquiry shall report to the President the current position of the parties and the efforts which have been made for settlement, and shall include a statement by each party of its position and a statement of the employer's last offer of settlement. The President shall make such report available to the public. The National Labor Relations Board, within the succeeding fifteen days, shall take a secret ballot of the employees of each employer involved in the dispute on the question of whether they wish to accept the final offer of settlement made by their employer as stated by him and shall certify the results thereof to the Attorney General within five days thereafter.

§210. (§180) Upon the certification of the results of such ballot or upon a settlement being reached, whichever happens sooner, the Attorney General shall move the court to discharge the injunction, which motion shall then be granted and the injunction discharged. When such motion is granted, the President shall submit to the Congress a full and comprehensive report of the proceedings, including the findings of the board of inquiry and the ballot taken by the National Labor Relations Board, together with such recommendations as he may see fit to make for consideration and appropriate action.

Compilation of Collective Bargaining Agreements, etc.

§211. (§181) (a) For the guidance and information of interested representatives of employers, employees, and the general public, the Bureau of Labor Statistics of the Department of Labor shall maintain a file of copies of all available collective bargaining agreements and other available agreements and actions thereunder settling or adjusting labor disputes. Such file shall be open to inspection under appropriate conditions prescribed by the

Labor Management Relations Act of 1947

Secretary of Labor, except that no specific information submitted in confidence shall be disclosed.

(b) The Bureau of Labor Statistics in the Department of Labor is authorized to furnish upon request of the Service, or employers, employees, or their representatives, all available data and factual information which may aid in the settlement of any labor dispute, except that no specific information submitted in confidence shall be disclosed.

Exemption of Railway Labor Act

§212. (§182) The provisions of this title shall not be applicable with respect to any matter which is subject to the provisions of the Railway Labor Act, as amended from time to time.

Conciliation of Labor Disputes in the Health Care Industry*

§213. (§183) (a) IF, IN THE OPINION OF THE DIRECTOR OF THE FEDERAL MEDIATION AND CONCILIATION SERVICE A THREATENED OR ACTUAL STRIKE OR LOCKOUT AFFECTING A HEALTH CARE INSTITUTION WILL, IF PERMITTED TO OCCUR OR TO CONTINUE, SUBSTANTIALLY INTERRUPT THE DELIVERY OF HEALTH CARE IN THE LOCALITY CONCERNED, THE DIRECTOR MAY FURTHER ASSIST IN THE RESOLUTION OF THE IMPASSE BY ESTABLISHING WITHIN 30 DAYS AFTER THE NOTICE TO THE FEDERAL MEDIATION AND CONCILIATION SERVICE UNDER CLAUSE (A) OF THE LAST SENTENCE OF SECTION 8(d) (WHICH IS REQUIRED BY CLAUSE (3) OF SUCH SECTION 8(d)), OR WITHIN 10 DAYS AFTER THE NOTICE UNDER CLAUSE (B), AN IMPARTIAL BOARD OF INQUIRY TO INVESTIGATE THE ISSUES INVOLVED IN THE DISPUTE AND TO MAKE A WRITTEN REPORT THEREON TO THE PARTIES WITHIN FIFTEEN (15) DAYS AFTER THE ESTABLISHMENT OF SUCH A BOARD. THE WRITTEN REPORT SHALL CONTAIN THE FINDINGS OF FACT TOGETHER WITH THE BOARD'S RECOMMENDATIONS FOR SETTLING THE DISPUTE, WITH THE OBJECTIVE OF ACHIEVING A PROMPT, PEACEFUL AND JUST SETTLEMENT OF THE DISPUTE. EACH SUCH BOARD SHALL BE COMPOSED OF SUCH NUMBER OF INDIVIDUALS AS THE DIRECTOR MAY DEEM DESIRABLE. NO MEMBER APPOINTED UNDER THIS SECTION SHALL HAVE ANY INTEREST OR INVOLVEMENT IN THE HEALTH CARE INSTITUTIONS OR THE EMPLOYEE ORGANIZATIONS INVOLVED IN THE DISPUTE.

---

*Added by Act of July 26, 1974, Pub. L. 93-360, §2, 88 Stat. 396.—EDS.

(b)(1) MEMBERS OF ANY BOARD ESTABLISHED UNDER THIS SECTION WHO ARE OTHERWISE EMPLOYED BY THE FEDERAL GOVERNMENT SHALL SERVE WITHOUT COMPENSATION BUT SHALL BE REIMBURSED FOR TRAVEL, SUBSISTENCE, AND OTHER NECESSARY EXPENSES INCURRED BY THEM IN CARRYING OUT ITS DUTIES UNDER THIS SECTION.

(2) MEMBERS OF ANY BOARD ESTABLISHED UNDER THIS SECTION WHO ARE NOT SUBJECT TO PARAGRAPH (1) SHALL RECEIVE COMPENSATION AT A RATE PRESCRIBED BY THE DIRECTOR BUT NOT TO EXCEED THE DAILY RATE PRESCRIBED FOR GS-18 OF THE GENERAL SCHEDULE UNDER SECTION 5332 OF TITLE 5, INCLUDING TRAVEL FOR EACH DAY THEY ARE ENGAGED IN THE PERFORMANCE OF THEIR DUTIES UNDER THIS SECTION AND SHALL BE ENTITLED TO REIMBURSEMENT FOR TRAVEL, SUBSISTENCE, AND OTHER NECESSARY EXPENSES INCURRED BY THEM IN CARRYING OUT THEIR DUTIES UNDER THIS SECTION.

(c) AFTER THE ESTABLISHMENT OF A BOARD UNDER SUBSECTION (a) OF THIS SECTION AND FOR 15 DAYS AFTER ANY SUCH BOARD HAS ISSUED ITS REPORT, NO CHANGE IN THE STATUS QUO IN EFFECT PRIOR TO THE EXPIRATION OF THE CONTRACT IN THE CASE OF NEGOTIATIONS FOR A CONTRACT RENEWAL, OR IN EFFECT PRIOR TO THE TIME OF THE IMPASSE IN THE CASE OF AN INITIAL BARGAINING NEGOTIATION, EXCEPT BY AGREEMENT, SHALL BE MADE BY THE PARTIES TO THE CONTROVERSY.

(d) THERE ARE AUTHORIZED TO BE APPROPRIATED SUCH SUMS AS MAY BE NECESSARY TO CARRY OUT THE PROVISIONS OF THIS SECTION.

TITLE III. SUITS BY AND AGAINST LABOR ORGANIZATIONS

§301. (§185) (a) Suits for violation of contracts between an employer and a labor organization representing employees in an industry affecting commerce as defined in this Act, or between any such labor organizations, may be brought in any district court of the United States having jurisdiction of the parties, without respect to the amount in controversy or without regard to the citizenship of the parties.

(b) Any labor organization which represents employees in an industry affecting commerce as defined in this Act and any employer whose activities affect commerce as defined in this Act shall be bound by the acts of its agents. Any such labor organization may sue or be sued as an entity and in behalf of the employees whom it represents in the courts of the United States. Any money judgment against a labor organization in a district court of the United States shall be enforceable only against the organization as an

Labor Management Relations Act of 1947

entity and against its assets, and shall not be enforceable against any individual member or his assets.

(c) For the purposes of actions and proceedings by or against labor organizations in the district courts of the United States, district courts shall be deemed to have jurisdiction of a labor organization (1) in the district in which such organization maintains its principal office, or (2) in any district in which its duly authorized officers or agents are engaged in representing or acting for employee members.

(d) The service of summons, subpena, or other legal process of any court of the United States upon an officer or agent of a labor organization, in his capacity as such, shall constitute service upon the labor organization.

(e) For the purposes of this section, in determining whether any person is acting as an "agent" of another person so as to make such other person responsible for his acts, the question of whether the specific acts performed were actually authorized or subsequently ratified shall not be controlling.

Restrictions on Payments to Employee Representatives

§302. (§186) (a) It shall be unlawful for any employer or *association of employers or any person who acts as a labor relations expert, adviser, or consultant to an employer or who acts in the interest of an employer* to pay, *lend*, or deliver, or [to] agree to pay, *lend*, or deliver, any money or other thing of value—

(1) to any representative of any of his employees who are employed in an industry affecting commerce[.]; or

(2) *to any labor organization, or any officer or employee thereof, which represents, seeks to represent, or would admit to membership, any of the employees of such employer who are employed in an industry affecting commerce; or*

(3) *to any employee or group or committee of employees of such employer employed in an industry affecting commerce in excess of their normal compensation for the purpose of causing such employee or group or committee directly or indirectly to influence any other employees in the exercise of the right to organize and bargain collectively through representatives of their own choosing; or*

(4) *to any officer or employee of a labor organization engaged in an industry affecting commerce with intent to influence him in respect to any of his actions, decisions, or duties as a representative of employees or as such officer or employee of such labor organization,*

(b) (1) It shall be unlawful for any [representative of any employees who are employed in an industry affecting commerce] *person to request, demand,* [to] receive or accept, or [to] agree to *receive or accept* [from the employer of such employees] *any payment, loan, or delivery of any money or other thing of value* [.] *prohibited by subsection (a) of this section.*

(2) *It shall be unlawful for any labor organization, or for any person acting as an officer, agent, representative, or employee of such labor organization, to*

demand or accept from the operator of any motor vehicle (as defined in section 10102 of title 49) employed in the transportation of property in commerce, or the employer of any such operator, any money or other thing of value payable to such organization or to an officer, agent, representative or employee thereof as a fee or charge for the unloading, or in connection with the unloading, of the cargo of such vehicle: Provided, That nothing in this paragraph shall be construed to make unlawful any payment by an employer to any of his employees as compensation for their services as employees.

(c) The provisions of this section shall not be applicable (1) [with] *in* respect to any money or other thing of value payable by an employer *to* any *of his employees whose established duties include acting openly for such employer in matters of labor relations or personnel administration or to any representative of his employees, or to any officer or employee or a labor organization,* who is *also* an employee or former employee of such employer, as compensation for, or by reason of, his service[s] as an employee of such employer; (2) with respect to the payment or delivery of any money or other thing of value in satisfaction of a judgment of any court or a decision or award of an arbitrator or impartial chairman or in compromise, adjustment, settlement, or release of any claim, complaint, grievance, or dispute in the absence of fraud or duress; (3) with respect to the sale or purchase of an article or commodity at the prevailing market price in the regular course of business; (4) with respect to money deducted from the wages of employees in payment of membership dues in a labor organization: *Provided,* That the employer has received from each employee, on whose account such deductions are made, a written assignment which shall not be irrevocable for a period of more than one year, or beyond the termination date of the applicable collective agreement, whichever occurs sooner; [or] (5) with respect to money or other thing of value paid to a trust fund established by such representative, for the sole and exclusive benefit of the employees of such employer, and their families and dependents (or of such employees, families, and dependents jointly with the employees of other employers making similar payments, and their families and dependents): *Provided,* That (A) such payments are held in trust for the purpose of paying, either from principal or income or both, for the benefit of employees, their families and dependents, for medical or hospital care, pensions on retirement or death of employees, compensation for injuries or illness resulting from occupational activity or insurance to provide any of the foregoing, or unemployment benefits or life insurance, disability and sickness insurance, or accident insurance; (B) the detailed basis on which such payments are to be made is specified in a written agreement with the employer, and employees and employers are equally represented in the administration of such fund, together with such neutral persons as the representatives of the employers and the representatives of [the] employees may agree upon and in the event the employer and employee groups deadlock on the administration of such fund and there are no neutral persons empowered to break such deadlock, such agreement provides that the two groups shall agree on an impartial umpire to decide such dispute, or in event of their failure to agree within a reasonable length of time, an impartial umpire to decide such dispute shall, on petition of either group, be appointed by the district court of the United States for the district where the trust fund has its principal office, and shall also contain provisions for an annual audit of the trust fund, a statement of the results of which shall be available for inspection by interested persons at the principal office of the trust fund and at such other places as may be designated in such written agreement; and (C) such payments as are intended to be used for the purpose of providing pensions or annuities for employees are made to a separate trust which provides that the funds held therein cannot be used for any purpose other than paying such pensions or annuities[.]; *(6) with respect to money or other thing of value paid by any employer to a trust fund established by such representative for the purpose of pooled vacation, holiday, severance or similar benefits, or defraying costs of apprenticeship or other training programs: Provided, That the requirements of clause (B) of the proviso to clause (5) of this subsection shall apply to such trust funds;* (7) with respect to money or other thing of value paid by any employer to a pooled or individual trust fund established by such representative for the purpose of (A) scholarships for the benefit of employees, their families, and dependents for study at educational institutions, or (B) child care centers for preschool and school age dependents of employees: *Provided,* That no labor organization or employer shall be required to bargain on the establishment of any such trust fund, and refusal to do so shall not constitute an unfair labor practice: *Provided further,* That the requirements of clause (B) of the proviso to clause (5) of this subsection shall apply to such trust funds;* (8) with respect to money or any other thing of value paid by any employer to a trust fund established by such representative for the purpose of defraying the costs of legal services for employees, their families, and dependents for counsel or plan of their choice: *Provided,* That the requirements of clause (B) of the proviso to clause (5) of this subsection shall apply to such trust funds: *Provided further,* That no such legal services shall be furnished: (A) to initiate any proceeding directed (i) against any such employer or its officers or agents except in workman's compensation cases, or (ii) against such labor organization, or its parent or subordinate bodies, or their officers or agents, or (iii) against any other employer or labor organization, or their officers or agents, in any matter arising under the National Labor Relations Act, as amended, or this Act; and (B) in any proceeding where a labor organization would be prohibited from defraying the costs of legal services by the provisions of the Labor-Management Reporting and Disclosure Act of

---

*Clause (7) of §302(c) was added by Pub. L. 91-96, Oct. 14, 1969, 83 Stat. 133.—Eds.

1959; or (9) with respect to money or other things of value paid by an employer to a plant, area or industrywide labor management committee established for one or more of the purposes set forth in section 5(b) of the Labor Management Cooperation Act of 1978.*

(d)(1) Any person who participates in a transaction involving a payment, loan, or delivery of money or other thing of value to a labor organization in payment of membership dues or to a joint labor-management trust fund as defined by clause (B) of the proviso to clause (5) of subsection (c) of this section or to a plant, area, or industry-wide labor-management committee that is received and used by such labor organization, trust fund, or committee, which transaction does not satisfy all the applicable requirements of subsections (c)(4) through (c)(9) of this section, and willfully and with intent to benefit himself or to benefit other persons he knows are not permitted to receive a payment, loan, money, or other thing of value under subsections (c)(4) through (c)(9) violates this subsection, shall, upon conviction thereof, be guilty of a felony and be subject to a fine of not more than $15,000, or imprisoned for not more than five years, or both; but if the value of the amount of money or thing of value involved in any violation of the provisions of this section does not exceed $1,000, such person shall be guilty of a misdemeanor and be subject to a fine of not more than $10,000, or imprisoned for not more than one year, or both.

(2) Except for violations involving transactions covered by subsection (d)(1) of this section, any person who willfully violates this section shall, upon conviction thereof, be guilty of a felony and be subject to a fine of not more than $15,000 or imprisoned for not more than five years, or both; but if the value of the amount of money or thing of value involved in any violation of the provisions of this section does not exceed $1,000, such person shall be guilty of a misdemeanor and be subject to a fine of not more than $10,000, or imprisoned for not more than one year, or both.**

(e) The district courts of the United States and the United States courts of the Territories and possessions shall have jurisdiction, for cause shown, and subject to the provisions of section 381 of title 28 (relating to notice to opposite party) to restrain violations of this section, without regard to the provisions of section 17 of title 15 and section 52 of title 29, and the provisions of the Act entitled "An Act to amend the Judicial Code and to define and limit the jurisdiction of courts sitting in equity, and for other purposes", approved March 23, 1932 (U.S.C., title 29, secs. 101-115).

---

*Clause (8) of §302(c) was added by Pub. L. 93-95, Aug. 15, 1973, 87 Stat. 314. Clause (9) was added by Pub. L. 95-524, Oct. 27, 1978, 92 Stat. 2021.—Eds.

**Section 302(d) was amended by Pub. L. 98-473, Oct. 12, 1984, 98 Stat. 2131.—Eds.

(f) This section shall not apply to any contract in force on June 23, 1947, until the expiration of such contract, or until July 1, 1948, whichever first occurs.

(g) Compliance with the restrictions contained in subsection (c)(5)(B) of this section upon contributions to trust funds, otherwise lawful, shall not be applicable to contributions to such trust funds established by collective agreement prior to January 1, 1946, nor shall subsection (c)(5)(A) of this section be construed as prohibiting contributions to such trust funds if prior to January 1, 1947, such funds contained provisions for pooled vacation benefits.

Boycotts and Other Unlawful Combinations

§303. (§187) (a) It shall be unlawful, for the purpose[s] of this section only, in an industry or activity affecting commerce, for any labor organization to engage in *any activity or conduct defined as an unfair labor practice in section 8(b)(4) of the National Labor Relations Act, as amended.* [or to induce or encourage the employees of any employer to engage in, a strike or a concerted refusal in the course of their employment to use, manufacture, process, transport, or otherwise handle or work on any goods, articles, materials, or commodities or to perform any services, where an object thereof is—

(1) forcing or requiring any employer or self-employed person to join any labor or employer organization or any employer or other person to cease using, selling, handling, transporting, or otherwise dealing in the products of any other producer, processor, or manufacturer, or to cease doing business with any other person;

(2) forcing or requiring any other employer to recognize or bargain with a labor organization as the representative of his employees unless such labor organization has been certified as the representative of such employees under the provisions of section 9 of the National Labor Relations Act;

(3) forcing or requiring any employer to recognize or bargain with a particular labor organization as the representative of his employees if another labor organization has been certified as the representative of such employees under the provisions of section 9 of the National Labor Relations Act;

(4) forcing or requiring any employer to assign particular work to employees in a particular labor organization or in a particular trade, craft, or class rather than to employees in another labor organization or in another trade, craft, or class unless such employer is failing to conform to an order or certification of the National Labor Relations Board determining the bargaining representative for employees performing such

work. Nothing contained in this subsection shall be construed to make unlawful a refusal by any person to enter upon the premises of any employer (other than his own employer), if the employees of such employer are engaged in a strike ratified or approved by a representative of such employees whom such employer is required to recognize under the National Labor Relations Act.]

(b) Whoever shall be injured in his business or property by reason of any violation of subsection (a) may sue therefor in any district court of the United States subject to the limitations and provisions of section 301 hereof without respect to the amount in controversy, or in any other court having jurisdiction of the parties, and shall recover the damages by him sustained and the cost of the suit.

Restriction on Political Contributions

[Section 304 of the LMRA (c.120, 61 Stat. 159 (1947)) amended §313 of the Federal Corrupt Practices Act (chs. 368, 369, 43 Stat. 1074 (1925)). Section 304 was repealed by c.645, 62 Stat. 868 (1948). The same chapter that repealed §304 enacted 18 U.S.C. §610 (1970) in c.645, 62 Stat. 723 (1948), which was repealed by Pub. L. 94-283, Title II, §201(a), May 11, 1976, 90 Stat. 496. Section 321 was enacted by the Federal Election Campaign Act, Pub. L. 94-283, Title I, §112(a), May 11, 1976, 90 Stat. 490, and was renumbered (to §316) and amended, Pub. L. 96-187, Title I, §§105(5), 112(d), Jan. 8, 1980, 93 Stat. 1354, 1366. Relevant parts of that Act are reprinted below.—EDS.]

Contributions or Expenditures by National Banks, Corporations, or Labor Organizations

§316. (2 U.S.C. §441b) (a) It is unlawful for any national bank, or any corporation organized by authority of any law of Congress, to make a contribution or expenditure in connection with any election to any political office, or in connection with any primary election or political convention or caucus held to select candidates for any political office, or for any corporation whatever, or any labor organization, to make a contribution or expenditure in connection with any election at which presidential and vice presidential electors or a Senator or Representative in, or a Delegate or Resident Commissioner to, Congress are to be voted for, or in connection with any primary election or political convention or caucus held to select candidates for any of the foregoing offices, or for any candidate, political committee, or other person knowingly to accept or receive any contribution prohibited by this section, or any officer or any director of any corporation or any national bank or any officer of any labor organization to consent to any contribution or expenditure by the corporation, national bank, or labor

Labor Management Relations Act of 1947

organization, as the case may be, prohibited by this section.

(b)(1) For the purposes of this section the term "labor organization" means any organization of any kind, or any agency or employee representation committee or plan, in which employees participate and which exists for the purpose, in whole or in part, of dealing with employers concerning grievances, labor disputes, wages, rates of pay, hours of employment, or conditions of work.

(2) For purposes of this section and section 12(h) of the Public Utility Holding Company Act (15 U.S.C. 791(h)), the term "contribution or expenditure" shall include any direct or indirect payment, distribution, loan, advance, deposit, or gift of money, or any services, or anything of value (except a loan of money by a national or State bank made in accordance with the applicable banking laws and regulations and in the ordinary course of business) to any candidate, campaign committee, or political party or organization, in connection with any election to any of the offices referred to in this section, but shall not include (A) communications by a corporation to its stockholders and executive or administrative personnel and their families or by a labor organization to its members and their families on any subject; (B) nonpartisan registration and get-out-the-vote campaigns by a corporation aimed at its stockholders and executive or administrative personnel and their families, or by a labor organization aimed at its members and their families; and (C) the establishment, administration, and solicitation of contributions to a separate segregated fund to be utilized for political purposes by a corporation, labor organization, membership organization, cooperative, or corporation without capital stock.

(3) It shall be unlawful—

(A) For such a fund to make a contribution or expenditure by utilizing money on anything of value secured by physical force, job discrimination, financial reprisals, or the threat of force, job discrimination, or financial reprisal; or by dues, fees, or other moneys required as a condition of membership in a labor organization or as a condition of employment, or by moneys obtained in any commercial transaction;

(B) for any person soliciting an employee for a contribution to such a fund to fail to inform such employee of the political purposes of such fund at the time of such solicitation; and

(C) for any person soliciting an employee for a contribution to such a fund to fail to inform such employee, at the time of such solicitation, of his right to refuse to so contribute without any reprisal.

(4)(A) Except as provided in subparagraphs (B), (C), and (D), it shall be unlawful—

(i) for a corporation, or a separate segregated fund established by a corporation, to solicit contributions to such a fund from any person other than its stockholders and their families and its executive or administrative personnel and their families, and

(ii) for a labor organization, or a separate segregated fund established by a labor organization, to solicit contributions to such a fund from any person other than its members and their families.

(B) It shall not be unlawful under this section for a corporation, a labor organization, or a separate segregated fund established by such corporation or such labor organization, to make 2 written solicitations for contributions during the calendar year from any stockholder, executive or administrative personnel, or employee of a corporation or the families of such persons. A solicitation under this subparagraph may be made only by mail addressed to stockholders, executive or administrative personnel, or employees at their residence and shall be so designed that the corporation, labor organization, or separate segregated fund conducting such solicitation cannot determine who makes a contribution of $50 or less as a result of such solicitation and who does not make such a contribution.

(C) This paragraph shall not prevent a membership organization, cooperative, or corporation without capital stock, or a separate segregated fund established by a membership organization, cooperative, or corporation without capital stock, from soliciting contributions to such a fund from members of such organization, cooperative, or corporation without capital stock.

(D) This paragraph shall not prevent a trade association or a separate segregated fund established by a trade association from soliciting contributions from the stockholders and executive or administrative personnel of the member corporations of such trade association and the families of such stockholders or personnel to the extent that such solicitation of such stockholders and personnel, and their families, has been separately and specifically approved by the member corporation involved, and such member corporation does not approve any such solicitation by more than one such trade association in any calendar year.

(5) Notwithstanding any other law, any method of soliciting voluntary contributions or of facilitating the making of voluntary contributions to a separate segregated fund established by a corporation, permitted by law to corporations with regard to stockholders and executive or administrative personnel, shall also be permitted to labor organizations with regard to their members.

6) Any corporation, including its subsidiaries, branches, divisions, and affiliates, that utilizes a method of soliciting voluntary contributions or facilitating the making of voluntary contributions, shall make available such method, on written request and at a cost sufficient only to reimburse the corporation for the expenses incurred thereby, to a labor organization representing any members working for such corporation, its subsidiaries, branches, divisions, and affiliates.

(7) For purposes of this section, the term "executive or administrative personnel" means individuals employed by a corporation who are paid on a salary, rather than hourly, basis and who have policymaking, managerial, professional, or supervisory responsibilities.

Strikes by Government Employees [Repealed]*

§305. (§188) It shall be unlawful for any individual employed by the United States or any agency thereof including wholly owned Government corporations to participate in any strike. Any individual employed by the United States or by any such agency who strikes shall be discharged immediately from his employment, and shall forfeit his civil-service status, if any, and shall not be eligible for reemployment for three years by the United States or any such agency.

TITLE IV. CREATION OF JOINT COMMITTEE TO STUDY AND REPORT ON BASIC PROBLEMS AFFECTING FRIENDLY LABOR RELATIONS AND PRODUCTIVITY

[Text omitted.]

TITLE V. DEFINITIONS

§501. (§142) When used in this Act—
(1) The term "industry affecting commerce" means any industry or activity in commerce or in which a labor dispute would burden or obstruct commerce or tend to burden or obstruct commerce or the free flow of commerce.
(2) The term "strike" includes any strike or other concerted stoppage of work by employees (including a stoppage by reason of the expiration of a collective-bargaining agreement) and any concerted slow-down or other concerted interruption of operations by employees.

---

*Section 305 was repealed by Act of Aug. 9, 1955, c.690, §4(3), 69 Stat. 625. Congress instead enacted 5 U.S.C. §§118p-118r (now 5 U.S.C. §§3333, 7311; 18 U.S.C. §1918). Those provisions make strikes by federal employees a felony, and the Civil Service Reform Act of 1978 also makes strikes and other stoppages unfair labor practices (5 U.S.C. §§7116(b)(7)(A) and (B)) and provides for decertification of a union that strikes (5 U.S.C. §7120(f)).—EDS.

(3) The terms "commerce," "labor disputes," "employer," "employee," "labor organization," "representative," "person," and "supervisor" shall have the same meaning as when used in the National Labor Relations Act as amended by this Act.

Saving Provision

§502. (§143) Nothing in this Act shall be construed to require an individual employee to render labor or service without his consent, nor shall anything in this Act be construed to make the quitting of his labor by an individual employee an illegal act; nor shall any court issue any process to compel the performance by an individual employee of such labor or service, without his consent; nor shall the quitting of labor by an employee or employees in good faith because of abnormally dangerous conditions for work at the place of employment of such employee or employees be deemed a strike under this Act.

Separability

§503. (§144) If any provision of this Act, or the application of such provision to any person or circumstance, shall be held invalid, the remainder of this Act, or the application of such provision to persons or circumstances other than those as to which it is held invalid, shall not be affected thereby.

Labor-Management Reporting and Disclosure Act of 1959
73 Stat. 519 (1959), as amended, 29 U.S.C. §§401-531

§2. (§401) Congressional declaration of findings, purposes, and policy

(a) *Standards for labor-management relations.* The Congress finds that, in the public interest, it continues to be the responsibility of the Federal Government to protect employees' rights to organize, choose their own representatives, bargain collectively, and otherwise engage in concerted activities for their mutual aid or protection; that the relations between employers and labor organizations and the millions of workers they represent have a substantial impact on the commerce of the Nation; and that in order to accomplish the objective of a free flow of commerce it is essential that labor organizations, employers, and their officials adhere to the highest standards of responsibility and ethical conduct in administering the affairs of their organizations, particularly as they affect labor-management relations.

(b) *Protection of rights of employees and the public.* The Congress further finds, from recent investigations in the labor and management fields, that there have been a number of instances of breach of trust, corruption, disregard of the rights of individual employees, and other failures to observe high standards of responsibility and ethical conduct which require further and supplementary legislation that will afford necessary protection of the rights and interests of employees and the public generally as they relate to the activities of labor organizations, employers, labor relations consultants, and their officers and representatives.

(c) *Necessity to eliminate or prevent improper practices.* The Congress, therefore, further finds and declares that the enactment of this chapter is necessary to eliminate or prevent improper practices on the part of labor organizations, employers, labor relations consultants, and their officers and representatives which distort and defeat the policies of the Labor Management Relations Act, 1947, as amended [29 U.S.C. §141 et seq.], and the Railway Labor Act, as amended [45 U.S.C. §151 et seq.], and have the tendency or necessary effect of burdening or obstructing commerce by (1) impairing the efficiency, safety, or operation of the instrumentalities of commerce; (2) occurring in the current of commerce; (3) materially affecting, restraining, or controlling the flow of raw materials or manufactured or processed goods into or from the channels of commerce, or the prices of such materials or goods in commerce; or (4) causing diminution of employment and wages in such volume as substantially to impair or disrupt the market for goods flowing into or from the channels of commerce.

(Pub. L. 86-257, §2, Sept. 14, 1959, 73 Stat. 519.)

§3. (§402) Definitions

For the purposes of this chapter—

(a) "Commerce" means trade, traffic, commerce, transportation, transmission, or communication among the several States or between any State and any place outside thereof.

(b) "State" includes any State of the United States, the District of Columbia, Puerto Rico, the Virgin Islands, American Samoa, Guam, Wake Island, the Canal Zone, and Outer Continental Shelf lands defined in the Outer Continental Shelf Lands Act [43 U.S.C. §1331 et seq.].

(c) "Industry affecting commerce" means any activity, business, or industry in commerce or in which a labor dispute would hinder or obstruct commerce or the free flow of commerce and includes any activity or industry "affecting commerce" within the meaning of the Labor Management Relations Act, 1947, as amended [29 U.S.C. §141 et seq.], or the Railway Labor Act, as amended [45 U.S.C. §151 et seq.].

(d) "Person" includes one or more individuals, labor organizations, partnerships, associations, corporations, legal representatives, mutual companies, joint-stock companies, trusts, unincorporated organizations, trustees, trustees in cases under title 11, or receivers.

(e) "Employer" means any employer or any group or association of employers engaged in an industry affecting commerce (1) which is, with respect to employees engaged in an industry affecting commerce, an employer within the meaning of any law of the United States relating to the employment of any employees or (2) which may deal with any labor organization concerning grievances, labor disputes, wages, rates of pay, hours of employment, or conditions of work, and includes any person acting directly or indirectly as an employer or as an agent of an employer in relation to an employee but does not include the United States or any corporation wholly owned by the Government of the United States or any State or political subdivision thereof.

(f) "Employee" means any individual employed by an employer, and includes any individual whose work has ceased as a consequence of, or in connection with, any current labor dispute or because of any unfair labor practice or because of exclusion or expulsion from a labor organization in any manner or for any reason inconsistent with the requirements of this chapter.

(g) "Labor dispute" includes any controversy concerning terms, tenure, or conditions of employment, or concerning the association or representation of persons in negotiating, fixing, maintaining, changing, or seeking to arrange terms or conditions of employment, regardless of whether the disputants stand in the proximate relation of employer and employee.

(h) "Trusteeship" means any receivership, trusteeship, or other method of supervision or control whereby a labor organization suspends the autonomy otherwise available to a subordinate body under its constitution or bylaws.

(i) "Labor organization" means a labor organization engaged in an industry affecting commerce and includes any organization of any kind, any agency, or employee representation committee, group, association, or plan so engaged in which employees participate and which exists for the purpose, in whole or in part, of dealing with employers concerning grievances, labor disputes, wages, rates of pay, hours, or other terms or conditions of employment, and any conference, general committee, joint or system board, or joint council so engaged which is subordinate to a national or international labor organization, other than a State or local central body.

(j) A labor organization shall be deemed to be engaged in an industry affecting commerce if it—

(1) is the certified representative of employees under the provisions of the National Labor Relations Act, as amended [29 U.S.C. §151 et seq.], or the Railway Labor Act, as amended [45 U.S.C. §151 et seq.]; or

(2) although not certified, is a national or international labor organization or a local labor organization recognized or acting as the representative of employees of an employer or employers engaged in an industry affecting commerce; or

(3) has chartered a local labor organization or subsidiary body which is representing or actively seeking to represent employees of employers within the meaning of paragraph (1) or (2); or

(4) has been chartered by a labor organization representing or actively seeking to represent employees within the meaning of paragraph (1) or (2) as the local or subordinate body through which such employees may enjoy membership or become affiliated with such labor organization; or

(5) is a conference, general committee, joint or system board, or joint council, subordinate to a national or international labor organization, which includes a labor organization engaged in an industry affecting commerce within the meaning of any of the preceding paragraphs of this subsection, other than a State or local central body.

(k) "Secret ballot" means the expression by ballot, voting machine, or otherwise, but in no event by proxy, of a choice with respect to any election or vote taken upon any matter, which is cast in such a manner that the person expressing such choice cannot be identified with the choice expressed.

(*l*) "Trust in which a labor organization is interested" means a trust or other fund or organization (1) which was created or established by a labor organization, or one or more of the trustees or one or more members of the governing body of which is selected or appointed by a labor organization, and (2) a primary purpose of which is to provide benefits for the members of such labor organization or their beneficiaries.

(m) "Labor relations consultant" means any person who, for compensation, advises or represents an employer, employer organization, or labor organization concerning employee organizing, concerted activities, or collective bargaining activities.

(n) "Officer" means any constitutional officer, any person authorized to perform the functions of president, vice president, secretary, treasurer, or other executive functions of a labor organization, and any member of its executive board or similar governing body.

(o) "Member" or "member in good standing", when used in reference to a labor organization, includes any person who has fulfilled the requirements for membership in such organization, and who neither has voluntarily withdrawn from membership nor has been expelled or suspended from membership after appropriate proceedings consistent with lawful provisions of the constitution and bylaws of such organization.

(p) "Secretary" means the Secretary of Labor.

(q) "Officer, agent, shop steward, or other representative," when used with respect to a labor organization, includes elected officials and key administrative personnel, whether elected or appointed (such as business agents, heads of departments or major units, and organizers who exercise substantial independent authority), but does not include salaried non-supervisory professional staff, stenographic, and service personnel.

(r) "District court of the United States" means a United States district court and a United States court of any place subject to the jurisdiction of the United States.

(Pub. L. 86-257, §3, Sept. 14, 1959, 73 Stat. 520; Pub. L. 96-598, Title III, §320, Nov. 6, 1978, 92 Stat. 2678.)

TITLE I. BILL OF RIGHTS OF MEMBERS OF LABOR ORGANIZATION

§101. (§411) Bill of rights; constitution and bylaws of labor organizations

(a)(1) *Equal rights.* Every member of a labor organization shall have equal rights and privileges within such organization to nominate candidates, to vote in elections or referendums of the labor organization, to attend membership meetings, and to participate in the deliberations and voting upon the business of such meetings, subject to reasonable rules and regulations in such organization's constitution and bylaws.

(2) *Freedom of speech and assembly.* Every member of any labor organization shall have the right to meet and assemble freely with other members; and to express any views, arguments, or opinions; and to express at meetings of the labor organization his views, upon candidates in an election of the labor organization or upon any business properly before the meeting, subject to the organization's established and reasonable rules pertaining to the conduct of meetings: *Provided,* That nothing herein shall be construed to impair the right of a labor organization to adopt and enforce reasonable rules as to the responsibility of every member toward the organization as an institution and to his refraining from conduct that would interfere with its performance of its legal or contractual obligations.

(3) *Dues, initiation fees, and assessments.* Except in the case of a federation of national or international labor organizations, the rates of dues and initiation fees payable by members of any labor organization in effect on September 14, 1959 shall not be increased, and no general or special assessment shall be levied upon such members, except—

(A) in the case of a local labor organization, (i) by majority vote by secret ballot of the members in good standing voting at a general or

Labor-Management Reporting and Disclosure Act of 1959

special membership meeting, after reasonable notice of the intention to vote upon such question, or (ii) by majority vote of the members in good standing voting in a membership referendum conducted by secret ballot; or

(B) in the case of a labor organization, other than a local labor organization or a federation of national or international labor organizations, (i) by majority vote of the delegates voting at a regular convention, or at a special convention of such labor organization held upon not less than thirty days' written notice to the principal office of each local or constituent labor organization entitled to such notice, or (ii) by majority vote of the members in good standing of such labor organization voting in a membership referendum conducted by secret ballot, or (iii) by majority vote of the members of the executive board or similar governing body of such labor organization, pursuant to express authority contained in the constitution and bylaws of such labor organization: *Provided*, That any such action on the part of the executive board or similar governing body shall be effective only until the next regular convention of such labor organization.

(4) *Protection of the right to sue.* No labor organization shall limit the right of any member thereof to institute an action in any court, or in a proceeding before any administrative agency, irrespective of whether or not the labor organization or its officers are named as defendants or respondents in such action or proceeding, or the right of any member of a labor organization to appear as a witness in any judicial, administrative, or legislative proceeding, or to petition any legislature or to communicate with any legislator: *Provided*, That such member may be required to exhaust reasonable hearing procedures (but not to exceed a four-month lapse of time) within such organization, before instituting legal or administrative proceedings against such organizations or any officer thereof: *And provided further*, That no interested employer or employer association shall directly or indirectly finance, encourage, or participate in, except as a party, any such action, proceeding, appearance, or petition.

(5) *Safeguards against improper disciplinary action.* No member of any labor organization may be fined, suspended, expelled, or otherwise disciplined except for nonpayment of dues by such organization or by any officer thereof unless such organization or by any officer thereof unless such member has been (A) served with written specific charges; (B) given a reasonable time to prepare his defense; (C) afforded a full and fair hearing.

(b) *Invalidity of constitution and bylaws.* Any provision of the constitution and bylaws of any labor organization which is inconsistent with the provisions of this section shall be of no force or effect.

(Pub. L. 86-257, Title I, §101, Sept. 14, 1959, 73 Stat. 522.)

§102. (§412) Civil action for infringement of rights; jurisdiction

Any person whose rights secured by the provisions of this subchapter have been infringed by any violation of this subchapter may bring a civil action in a district court of the United States for such relief (including injunctions) as may be appropriate. Any such action against a labor organization shall be brought in the district court of the United States for the district where the alleged violation occurred, or where the principal office of such labor organization is located.

(Pub. L. 86-257, Title I, §102, Sept. 14, 1959, 73 Stat. 523.)

§103. (§413) Retention of existing rights of members

Nothing contained in this subchapter shall limit the rights and remedies of any member of a labor organization under any State or Federal law or before any court or other tribunal, or under the constitution and bylaws of any labor organization.

(Pub. L. 86-257, Title I, §103, Sept. 14, 1959, 73 Stat. 523.)

§104. (§414) Right to copies of collective bargaining agreements

It shall be the duty of the secretary or corresponding principal officer of each labor organization, in the case of a local labor organization, to forward a copy of each collective bargaining agreement made by such labor organization with any employer to any employee who requests such a copy and whose rights as such employee are directly affected by such agreement, and in the case of a labor organization other than a local labor organization, to forward a copy of any such agreement to each constituent unit which has members directly affected by such agreement; and such officer shall maintain at the principal office of the labor organization of which he is an officer copies of any such agreement made or received by such labor organization, which copies shall be available for inspection by any member or by any employee whose rights are affected by such agreement. The provisions of section 440 of this title shall be applicable in the enforcement of this section.

(Pub. L. 86-257, Title I, §104, Sept. 14, 1959, 73 Stat. 523.)

§105. (§415) Information to members of provisions of chapter

Every labor organization shall inform its members concerning the provisions of this chapter.

(Pub. L. 86-257, Title I, §105, Sept. 14, 1959, 73 Stat. 523.)

Labor-Management Reporting and Disclosure Act of 1959

TITLE II. REPORTING BY LABOR ORGANIZATIONS, OFFICERS AND EMPLOYEES OF LABOR ORGANIZATIONS, AND EMPLOYERS

§201. (§431) Report of labor organizations

(a) *Adoption and filing of constitution and bylaws; contents of report.* Every labor organization shall adopt a constitution and bylaws and shall file a copy thereof with the Secretary, together with a report, signed by its president and secretary or corresponding principal officers, containing the following information—

(1) the name of the labor organization, its mailing address, and any other address at which it maintains its principal office or at which it keeps the records referred to in this subchapter;

(2) the name and title of each of its officers;

(3) the initiation fee or fees required from a new or transferred member and fees for work permits required by the reporting labor organization;

(4) the regular dues or fees or other periodic payments required to remain a member of the reporting labor organization; and

(5) detailed statements, or references to specific provisions of documents filed under this subsection which contain such statements, showing the provision made and procedures followed with respect to each of the following: (A) qualifications for or restrictions on membership, (B) levying of assessments, (C) participation in insurance or other benefit plans, (D) authorization for disbursement of funds of the labor organization, (E) audit of financial transactions of the labor organization, (F) the calling of regular and special meetings, (G) the selection of officers and stewards and of any representatives to other bodies composed of labor organizations' representatives, with a specific statement of the manner in which each officer was elected, appointed, or otherwise selected, (H) discipline or removal of officers or agents for breaches of their trust, (I) imposition of fines, suspensions, and expulsions of members, including the grounds for such action and any provision made for notice, hearing, judgment on the evidence, and appeal procedures, (J) authorization for bargaining demands, (K) ratification of contract terms, (L) authorization for strikes, and (M) issuance of work permits. Any change in the information required by this subsection shall be reported to the Secretary at the time the reporting labor organization files with the Secretary the annual financial report required by subsection (b) of this section.

(b) *Annual financial report; filing; contents.* Every labor organization shall file annually with the Secretary a financial report signed by its president and treasurer or corresponding principal officers containing the following information in such detail as may be necessary accurately to disclose its financial condition and operations for its preceding fiscal year—

(1) assets and liabilities at the beginning and end of the fiscal year;

(2) receipts of any kind and the sources thereof;

(3) salary, allowances, and other direct or indirect disbursements (including reimbursed expenses) to each officer and also to each employee who, during such fiscal year, received more than $10,000 in the aggregate from such labor organization and any other labor organization affiliated with it or with which it is affiliated, or which is affiliated with the same national or international labor organization;

(4) direct and indirect loans made to any officer, employee, or member, which aggregated more than $250 during the fiscal year, together with a statement of the purpose, security, if any, and arrangements for repayment;

(5) direct and indirect loans to any business enterprise, together with a statement of the purpose, security, if any, and arrangements for repayment; and

(6) other disbursements made by it including the purposes thereof; all in such categories as the Secretary may prescribe.

(c) *Availability of information to members; examination of books, records, and accounts.* Every labor organization required to submit a report under this subchapter shall make available the information required to be contained in such report to all of its members, and every such labor organization and its officers shall be under a duty enforceable at the suit of any member of such organization in any State court of competent jurisdiction or in the district court of the United States for the district in which such labor organization maintains its principal office, to permit such member for just cause to examine any books, records, and accounts necessary to verify such report. The court in such action may, in its discretion, in addition to any judgment awarded to the plaintiff or plaintiffs, allow a reasonable attorney's fee to be paid by the defendant, and costs of the action.

(Pub. L. 86-257, Title II, §201(a)-(c), Sept. 14, 1959, 73 Stat. 524.)

§202 (§432) Report of officers and employees of labor organizations

(a) *Filing; contents of report.* Every officer of a labor organization and every employee of a labor organization (other than an employee performing exclusively clerical or custodial services) shall file with the Secretary a signed report listing and describing for his preceding fiscal year—

(1) any stock, bond, security, or other interest, legal or equitable, which he or his spouse or minor child directly or indirectly held in, and any income or any other benefit with monetary value (including reimbursed expenses) which he or his spouse or minor child derived directly or indirectly from, an employer whose employees such labor organization represents or is actively seeking to represent, except payments and other benefits received as a bona fide employee of such employer;

(2) any transaction in which he or his spouse or minor child engaged, directly or indirectly, involving any stock, bond, security, or loan to or from, or other legal or equitable interest in the business of an

employer whose employees such labor organization represents or is actively seeking to represent;

(3) any stock, bond, security, or other interest, legal or equitable, which he or his spouse or minor child directly or indirectly held in, and any income or any other benefit with monetary value (including reimbursed expenses) which he or his spouse or minor child directly or indirectly derived from, any business a substantial part of which consists of buying from, selling or leasing to, or otherwise dealing with, the business of an employer whose employees such labor organization represents or is actively seeking to represent;

(4) any stock, bond, security, or other interest, legal or equitable, which he or his spouse or minor child directly or indirectly held in, and any income or any other benefit with monetary value (including reimbursed expenses) which he or his spouse or minor child directly or indirectly derived from, a business any part of which consists of buying from, or selling or leasing directly or indirectly to, or otherwise dealing with such labor organization;

(5) any direct or indirect business transaction or arrangement between him or his spouse or minor child and any employer whose employees his organization represents or is actively seeking to represent, except work performed and payments and benefits received as a bona fide employee of such employer and except purchases and sales of goods or services in the regular course of business at prices generally available to any employee of such employer; and

(6) any payment of money or other thing of value (including reimbursed expenses) which he or his spouse or minor child received directly or indirectly from any employer or any person who acts as a labor relations consultant to an employer, except payments of the kinds referred to in section 186(c) of this title.

(b) *Report of certain bona fide investments.* The provisions of paragraphs (1), (2), (3), (4), and (5) of subsection (a) of this section shall not be construed to require any such officer or employee to report his bona fide investments in securities traded on a securities exchange registered as a national securities exchange under the Securities Exchange Act of 1934 [15 U.S.C. §78a et seq.], in shares in an investment company registered under the Investment Company Act of 1940 [15 U.S.C. §80a-1 et seq.], or in securities of a public utility holding company registered under the Public Utility Holding Company Act of 1935 [15 U.S.C. §79 et seq.], or to report any income derived therefrom.

(c) *Exemption from filing requirement.* Nothing contained in this section shall be construed to require any officer or employee of a labor organization to file a report under subsection (a) of this section unless he or his spouse or minor child holds or has held an interest, has received income or any other benefit with monetary value or a loan, or has engaged in a transaction described therein.

(Pub. L. 86-257, Title II, §202, Sept. 14, 1959, 73 Stat. 525.)

§203. (§433) Report of employers

(a) *Filing and contents of report of payments, loans, promises, agreements, or arrangements.* Every employer who in any fiscal year made—

(1) any payment or loan, direct or indirect, of money or other thing of value (including reimbursed expenses), or any promise or agreement therefor, to any labor organization or officer, agent, shop steward, or other representative of a labor organization, or employee of any labor organization, except (A) payments or loans made by any national or State bank, credit union, insurance company, savings and loan association or other credit institution and (B) payments of the kind referred to in section 186(c) of this title;

(2) any payment (including reimbursed expenses) to any of his employees, or any group or committee of such employees, for the purpose of causing such employee or group or committee of employees to persuade other employees to exercise or not to exercise, or as the manner of exercising, the right to organize and bargain collectively through representatives of their own choosing unless such payments were contemporaneously or previously disclosed to such other employees;

(3) any expenditure, during the fiscal year, where an object thereof, directly or indirectly, is to interfere with, restrain, or coerce employees in the exercise of the right to organize and bargain collectively through representatives of their own choosing, or is to obtain information concerning the activities of employees or a labor organization in connection with a labor dispute involving such employer, except for use solely in conjunction with an administrative or arbitral proceeding or a criminal or civil judicial proceeding;

(4) any agreement or arrangement with a labor relations consultant or other independent contractor or organization pursuant to which such person undertakes activities where an object thereof, directly or indirectly, is to persuade employees to exercise or not to exercise, or persuade employees as to the manner of exercising, the right to organize and bargain collectively through representatives of their own choosing, or undertakes to supply such employer with information concerning the activities of employees or a labor organization in connection with a labor dispute involving such employer, except information for use solely in conjunction with an administrative or arbitral proceeding or a criminal or civil judicial proceeding; or

(5) any payment (including reimbursed expenses) pursuant to an agreement or arrangement described in subdivision (4);

shall file with the Secretary a report, in a form prescribed by him, signed by its president and treasurer or corresponding principal officers showing in detail the date and amount of each such payment, loan, promise, agreement, or arrangement and the name, address, and position, if any, in any

Labor-Management Reporting and Disclosure Act of 1959

firm or labor organization of the person to whom it was made and a full explanation of the circumstances of all such payments, including the terms of any agreement or understanding pursuant to which they were made.

(b) *Persuasive activities relating to the right to organize and bargain collectively; supplying information of activities in connection with labor disputes; filing and contents of report of agreement or arrangement.* Every person who pursuant to any agreement or arrangement with an employer undertakes activities where an object thereof is, directly or indirectly—

(1) to persuade employees to exercise or not to exercise, or persuade employees as to the manner of exercising, the right to organize and bargain collectively through representatives of their own choosing; or

(2) to supply an employer with information concerning the activities of employees or a labor organization in connection with a labor dispute involving such employer, except information for use solely in conjunction with an administrative or arbitral proceeding or a criminal or civil judicial proceeding;

shall file within thirty days after entering into such agreement or arrangement a report with the Secretary, signed by its president and treasurer or corresponding principal officers, containing the name under which such person is engaged in doing business and the address of its principal office, and a detailed statement of the terms and conditions of such agreement or arrangement. Every such person shall file annually, with respect to each fiscal year during which payments were made as a result of such an agreement or arrangement, a report with the Secretary, signed by its president and treasurer or corresponding principal officers, containing a statement (A) of its receipts of any kind from employers on account of labor relations advice or services, designating the sources thereof, and (B) of its disbursements of any kind, in connection with such services and the purposes thereof. In each such case such information shall be set forth in such categories as the Secretary may prescribe.

(c) *Advisory or representative services exempt from filing requirements.* Nothing in this section shall be construed to require any employer or other person to file a report covering the services of such person by reason of his giving or agreeing to give advice to such employer or representing or agreeing to represent such employer before any court, administrative agency, or tribunal of arbitration or engaging or agreeing to engage in collective bargaining on behalf of such employer with respect to wages, hours, or other terms or conditions of employment or the negotiation of an agreement or any question arising thereunder.

(d) *Exemption from filing requirements generally.* Nothing contained in this section shall be construed to require an employer to file a report under subsection (a) of this section unless he has made an expenditure, payment, loan, agreement, or arrangement of the kind described therein. Nothing contained in this section shall be construed to require any other person to file a report under subsection (b) of this section unless he was a party to an agreement or arrangement of the kind described therein.

(e) *Services by and payments to regular officers, supervisors, and employees of employer.* Nothing contained in this section shall be construed to require any regular officer, supervisor, or employee of an employer to file a report in connection with services rendered to such employer nor shall any employer be required to file a report covering expenditures made to any regular officer, supervisor, or employee of an employer as compensation for service as a regular officer, supervisor, or employee of such employer.

(f) *Rights protected by section 158(c) of this title.* Nothing contained in this section shall be construed as an amendment to, or modification of the rights protected by, section 158(c) of this title.

(g) *Definition.* The term "interfere with, restrain, or coerce" as used in this section means interference, restraint, and coercion which, if done with respect to the exercise of rights guaranteed in section 157 of this title, would, under section 158(a) of this title, constitute an unfair labor practice.

(Pub. L. 86-257, Title II, §203, Sept. 14, 1959, 73 Stat. 526.)

§204. (§434) Exemption of attorney-client communications

Nothing contained in this chapter shall be construed to require an attorney who is a member in good standing of the bar of any State, to include in any report required to be filed pursuant to the provisions of this chapter any information which was lawfully communicated to such attorney by any of his clients in the course of a legitimate attorney-client relationship.

(Pub. L. 86-257, Title II, §204, Sept. 14, 1959, 73 Stat. 528.)

§205. (§435) Reports and documents as public information

(a) *Publication; statistical and research purposes.* The contents of the reports and documents filed with the Secretary pursuant to sections 431, 432, 433, and 441 of this title shall be public information, and the Secretary may publish any information and data which he obtains pursuant to the provisions of this subchapter. The Secretary may use the information and data for statistical and research purposes, and compile and publish such studies, analyses, reports, and surveys based thereon as he may deem appropriate.

(b) *Inspection and examination of information and data.* The Secretary shall by regulation make reasonable provision for the inspection and examination, on the request of any person, of the information and data contained

Labor-Management Reporting and Disclosure Act of 1959

in any report or other document filed with him pursuant to section 431, 432, 433, or 441, of this title.

(c) *Copies of reports or documents; availability to State agencies.* The Secretary shall by regulation provide for the furnishing by the Department of Labor of copies of reports or other documents filed with the Secretary pursuant to this subchapter, upon payment of a charge based upon the cost of the service. The Secretary shall make available without payment of a charge, or require any person to furnish, to such State agency as is designated by law or by the Governor of the State in which such person has his principal place of business or headquarters, upon request of the Governor of such State, copies of any reports and documents filed by such person with the Secretary pursuant to section 431, 432, 433, or 441 of this title, or of information and data contained therein. No person shall be required by reason of any law of any State to furnish to any officer or agency of such State any information included in a report filed by such person with the Secretary pursuant to the provisions of this subchapter, if a copy of such report, or of the portion thereof containing such information, is furnished to such officer or agency. All moneys received in payment of such charges fixed by the Secretary pursuant to this subsection shall be deposited in the general fund of the Treasury.

(Pub. L. 86-257, Title II, §205, Sept. 14, 1959, 73 Stat. 528; Pub. L. 89-216, §2(a)-(c), Sept. 29, 1965, 79 Stat. 888.)

§206. (§436) Retention of records

Every person required to file any report under this subchapter shall maintain records of the matters required to be reported which will provide in sufficient detail the necessary basic information and data from which the documents filed with the Secretary may be verified, explained, or clarified, and checked for accuracy and completeness, and shall include vouchers, worksheets, receipts, and applicable resolutions, and shall keep such records available for examination for a period of not less than five years after the filing of the documents based on the information which they contain.

(Pub. L. 86-257, Title II, §206, Sept. 14, 1959, 73 Stat. 529.)

§207. (§437) Time for making reports

(a) Each labor organization shall file the initial report required under section 431(a) of this title within ninety days after the date on which it first becomes subject to this chapter.

(b) Each person required to file a report under section 431(b), 432, 433(a), the second sentence of 433(b), or section 441 of this title shall file such report within ninety days after the end of each of its fiscal years; except that where such person is subject to section 431(b), 432, 433(a), the second sentence of 433(b), or section 441 of this title, as the case may be, for only a portion of such a fiscal year (because September 14, 1959, occurs during such person's fiscal year or such person becomes subject to this chapter during its fiscal year) such person may consider that portion as the entire fiscal year in making such report.

(Pub. L. 86-257, Title II, §207, Sept. 14, 1959, 73 Stat. 529; Pub. L. 89-216, §2(d), Sept. 29, 1965, 79 Stat. 888.)

§208. (§438) Rules and regulations; simplified reports

The Secretary shall have authority to issue, amend, and rescind rules and regulations prescribing the form and publication of reports required to be filed under this subchapter and such other reasonable rules and regulations (including rules prescribing reports concerning trusts in which a labor organization is interested) as he may find necessary to prevent the circumvention or evasion of such reporting requirements. In exercising his power under this section the Secretary shall prescribe by general rule simplified reports for labor organizations or employers for whom he finds that by virtue of their size a detailed report would be unduly burdensome, but the Secretary may revoke such provision for simplified forms of any labor organization or employer if he determines, after such investigation as he deems proper and due notice and opportunity for a hearing, that the purposes of this section would be served thereby.

(Pub. L. 86-257, Title II, §208, Sept. 14, 1959, 73 Stat. 529.)

§209. (§439) Violations and penalties

(a) *Willful violations of provisions of subchapter.* Any person who willfully violates this subchapter shall be fined not more than $10,000 or imprisoned for not more than one year, or both.

(b) *False statements or representation of fact with knowledge of falsehood.* Any person who makes a false statement or representation of a material fact, knowing it to be false, or who knowingly fails to disclose a material fact, in any document, report, or other information required under the provisions of this subchapter shall be fined not more than $10,000 or imprisoned for not more than one year, or both.

(c) *False entry in or willful concealment, etc., of books and records.* Any person who willfully makes a false entry in or willfully conceals, withholds, or

Labor-Management Reporting and Disclosure Act of 1959   107

destroys any books, records, reports, or statements required to be kept by any provision of this subchapter shall be fined not more than $10,000 or imprisoned for not more than one year, or both.

(d) *Personal responsibility of individuals required to sign reports.* Each individual required to sign reports under sections 431 and 433 of this title shall be personally responsible for the filing of such reports and for any statement contained therein which he knows to be false.

(Pub. L. 86-257, Title II, §209, Sept. 14, 1959, 73 Stat. 529.)

§210. (§440) Civil action for enforcement by Secretary; jurisdiction

Whenever it shall appear that any person has violated or is about to violate any of the provisions of this subchapter, the Secretary may bring a civil action for such relief (including injunctions) as may be appropriate. Any such action may be brought in the district court of the United States where the violation occurred or, at the option of the parties, in the United States District Court for the District of Columbia.

(Pub. L. 86-257, Title II, §210, Sept. 14, 1959, 73 Stat. 530.)

§211. (§441) Surety company reports; contents; waiver or modification of requirements respecting contents of reports

Each surety company which issues any bond required by this chapter or the Employee Retirement Income Security Act of 1974 [29 U.S.C. §1001 et seq.] shall file annually with the Secretary, with respect to each fiscal year during which any such bond was in force, a report, in such form and detail as he may prescribe by regulation, filed by the president and treasurer or corresponding principal officers of the surety company, describing its bond experience under each such chapter or Act, including information as to the premiums received, total claims paid, amounts recovered by way of subrogation, administrative and legal expenses and such related data and information as the Secretary shall determine to be necessary in the public interest and to carry out the policy of the chapter. Notwithstanding the foregoing, if the Secretary finds that any such specific information cannot be practicably ascertained or would be uninformative, the Secretary may modify or waive the requirement for such information.

(Pub. L. 86-257, Title II, §211, as added Pub. L. 89-216, §3, Sept. 29, 1965, 79 Stat. 888, and amended Pub. L. 93-406, Title I, §111(a)(2)(D), Sept. 2, 1974, 88 Stat. 852.)

Title III. Trusteeships

§301. (§461) Reports

(a) *Filing and contents; annual financial report.* Every labor organization which has or assumes trusteeship over any subordinate labor organization shall file with the Secretary within thirty days after September 14, 1959 or the imposition of any such trusteeship, and semiannually thereafter, a report, signed by its president and treasurer or corresponding principal officers, as well as by the trustees of such subordinate labor organization, containing the following information: (1) the name and address of the subordinate organization; (2) the date of establishing the trusteeship; (3) a detailed statement of the reason or reasons for establishing or continuing the trusteeship; and (4) the nature and extent of participation by the membership of the subordinate organization in the selection of delegates to represent such organization in regular or special conventions or other policy-determining bodies and in the election of officers of the labor organization which has assumed trusteeship over such subordinate organization. The initial report shall also include a full and complete account of the financial condition of such subordinate organization as of the time trusteeship was assumed over it. During the continuance of a trusteeship the labor organization which has assumed trusteeship over a subordinate labor organization shall file on behalf of the subordinate labor organization the annual financial report required by section 431(b) of this title signed by the president and treasurer or corresponding principal officers of the labor organization which has assumed such trusteeship and the trustees of the subordinate labor organization.

(b) *Applicability of other laws.* The provisions of sections 431(c), 435, 436, 438, and 440 of this title shall be applicable to reports filed under this subchapter.

(c) *Penalty for violations.* Any person who willfully violates this section shall be fined not more than $10,000 or imprisoned for not more than one year, or both.

(d) *False statements and entries; failure to disclose material facts; withholding, concealing or destroying documents, books, records, reports, or statements; penalty.* Any person who makes a false statement or representation of a material fact, knowing it to be false, or who knowingly fails to disclose a material fact, in any report required under the provisions of this section or willfully makes any false entry in or willfully withholds, conceals, or destroys any documents, books, records, reports, or statements upon which such report is based, shall be fined not more than $10,000 or imprisoned for not more than one year, or both.

(e) *Personal liability.* Each individual required to sign a report under this section shall be personally responsible for the filing of such report and for any statement contained therein which he knows to be false.

(Pub. L. 86-257, Title III, §301, Sept. 14, 1959, 73 Stat. 530.)

§302. (§462) Purposes for establishment of trusteeship

Trusteeships shall be established and administered by a labor organization over a subordinate body only in accordance with the constitution and bylaws of the organization which has assumed trusteeship over the subordinate body and for the purpose of correcting corruption or financial malpractice, assuring the performance of collective bargaining agreements or other duties of a bargaining representative, restoring democratic procedures, or otherwise carrying out the legitimate objects of such labor organization.

(Pub. L. 86-257, Title III, §302, Sept. 14, 1959, 73 Stat. 531.)

§303. (§463) Unlawful acts relating to labor organization under trusteeship

(a) During any period when a subordinate body of a labor organization is in trusteeship, it shall be unlawful (1) to count the vote of delegates from such body in any convention or election of officers of the labor organization unless the delegates have been chosen by secret ballot in an election in which all the members in good standing of such subordinate body were eligible to participate, or (2) to transfer to such organization any current receipts or other funds of the subordinate body except the normal per capita tax and assessments payable by subordinate bodies not in trusteeship: *Provided,* That nothing herein contained shall prevent the distribution of the assets of a labor organization in accordance with its constitution and bylaws upon the bona fide dissolution thereof.

(b) Any person who willfully violates this section shall be fined not more than $10,000 or imprisoned for not more than one year, or both.

(Pub. L. 86-257, Title III, §303, Sept. 14, 1959, 73 Stat. 531.)

§304. (§464) Civil action for enforcement

(a) *Complaint; investigation; commencement of action by Secretary, member or subordinate body of labor organization; jurisdiction.* Upon the written complaint of any member or subordinate body of a labor organization alleging that such organization has violated the provisions of this subchapter (except section 461 of this title) the Secretary shall investigate the complaint and if the Secretary finds probable cause to believe that such violation has occurred and has not been remedied he shall, without disclosing the identity of the complainant, bring a civil action in any district court of the United States having jurisdiction of the labor organization for such relief (including injunctions) as may be appropriate. Any member of subordinate body of a labor organization affected by any violation of this subchapter (except section 461 of this title) may bring a civil action in any district court of the United States having jurisdiction of the labor organization for such relief (including injunctions) as may be appropriate.

(b) *Venue.* For the purpose of actions under this section, district courts of the United States shall be deemed to have jurisdiction of a labor organization (1) in the district in which the principal office of such labor organization is located, or (2) in any district in which its duly authorized officers or agents are engaged in conducting the affairs of the trusteeship.

(c) *Presumptions of validity or invalidity of trusteeship.* In any proceeding pursuant to this section a trusteeship established by a labor organization in conformity with the procedural requirements of its constitution and bylaws and authorized or ratified after a fair hearing either before the executive board or before such other body as may be provided in accordance with its constitution or bylaws shall be presumed valid for a period of eighteen months from the date of its establishment and shall not be subject to attack during such period except upon clear and convincing proof that the trusteeship was not established or maintained in good faith for a purpose allowable under section 462 of this title. After the expiration of eighteen months the trusteeship shall be presumed invalid in any such proceeding and its discontinuance shall be decreed unless the labor organization shall show by clear and convincing proof that the continuation of the trusteeship is necessary for a purpose allowable under section 462 of this title. In the latter event the court may dismiss the complaint or retain jurisdiction of the cause on such conditions and for such period as it deems appropriate.

(Pub. L. 86-257, Title III, §304, Sept. 14, 1959, 73 Stat. 531.)

§305. (§465) Report to Congress

The Secretary shall submit to the Congress at the expiration of three years from September 14, 1959, a report upon the operation of this subchapter.

(Pub. L. 86-257, Title III, §305, Sept. 14, 1959, 73 Stat. 532.)

§306. (§466) Additional rights and remedies; exclusive jurisdiction of district court; res judicata

The rights and remedies provided by this subchapter shall be in addition to any and all other rights and remedies at law or in equity: *Provided,* That upon the filing of a complaint by the Secretary the jurisdiction of the district court over such trusteeship shall be exclusive and the final judgment shall be res judicata.

(Pub. L. 86-257, Title III, §306, Sept. 14, 1959, 73 Stat. 532.)

Labor-Management Reporting and Disclosure Act of 1959

TITLE IV. ELECTIONS

§401. (§481) Terms of office and election procedures

(a) *Officers of national or international labor organizations; manner of election.* Every national or international labor organization, except a federation of national or international labor organization, shall elect its officers not less often than once every five years either by secret ballot among the members in good standing or at a convention of delegates chosen by secret ballot.

(b) *Officers of local labor organizations; manner of election.* Every local labor organization shall elect its officers not less often than once every three years by secret ballot among the members in good standing.

(c) *Requests for distribution of campaign literature; civil action for enforcement; jurisdiction; inspection of membership lists; adequate safeguards to insure fair election.* Every national or international labor organization, except a federation of national or international labor organizations, and every local labor organization, and its officers, shall be under a duty, enforceable at the suit of any bona fide candidate for office in such labor organization in the district court of the United States in which such labor organization maintains its principal office, to comply with all reasonable requests of any candidate to distribute by mail or otherwise at the candidate's expense campaign literature in aid of such person's candidacy to all members in good standing of such labor organization and to refrain from discrimination in favor of or against any candidate with respect to the use of lists of members, and whenever such labor organizations or its officers authorize the distribution by mail or otherwise to members of campaign literature on behalf of any candidate or of the labor organization itself with reference to such election, similar distribution at the request of any other bona fide candidate shall be made by such labor organization and its officers, with equal treatment as to the expense of such distribution. Every bona fide candidate shall have the right, once within 30 days prior to an election of a labor organization in which he is a candidate, to inspect a list containing the names and last known addresses of all members of the labor organization who are subject to a collective bargaining agreement requiring membership therein as a condition of employment, which list shall be maintained and kept at the principal office of such labor organization by a designated official thereof. Adequate safeguards to insure a fair election shall be provided, including the right of any candidate to have an observer at the polls and at the counting of the ballots.

(d) *Officers of intermediate bodies; manner of election.* Officers of intermediate bodies, such as general committees, system boards, joint boards, or joint councils, shall be elected not less often than once every four years by secret ballot among the members in good standing or by labor organization officers representative of such members who have been elected by secret ballot.

(e) *Nomination of candidates; eligibility; notice of election; voting rights; counting and publication of results; preservation of ballots and records.* In any election required by this section which is to be held by secret ballot a reasonable opportunity shall be given for the nomination of candidates and every member in good standing shall be eligible to be a candidate and to hold office (subject to section 504 of this title and to reasonable qualifications uniformly imposed) and shall have the right to vote for or otherwise support the candidate or candidates of his choice, without being subject to penalty, discipline, or improper interference or reprisal of any kind by such organization or any member thereof. Not less than fifteen days prior to the election notice thereof shall be mailed to each member at his last known home address. Each member in good standing shall be entitled to one vote. No member whose dues have been withheld by his employer for payment to such organization pursuant to his voluntary authorization provided for in a collective bargaining agreement shall be declared ineligible to vote or be a candidate for office in such organization by reason of alleged delay or default in the payment of dues. The votes cast by members of each local labor organization shall be counted, and the results published, separately. The election officials designated in the constitution and bylaws or the secretary, if no other official is designated, shall preserve for one year the ballots and other records pertaining to the election. The election shall be conducted in accordance with the constitution and bylaws of such organization insofar as they are not inconsistent with the provisions of this subchapter.

(f) *Election of officers by convention of delegates; manner of conducting convention; preservation of records.* When officers are chosen by a convention of delegates elected by secret ballot, the convention shall be conducted in accordance with the constitution and bylaws of the labor organization insofar as they are not inconsistent with the provisions of this subchapter. The officials designated in the constitution and bylaws or the secretary, if no other is designated, shall preserve for one year the credentials of the delegates and all minutes and other records of the convention pertaining to the election of officers.

(g) *Use of dues, assessments or similar levies, and funds of employer for promotion of candidacy of person.* No moneys received by any labor organization by way of dues, assessment, or similar levy, and no moneys of an employer shall be contributed or applied to promote the candidacy of any person in any election subject to the provisions of this subchapter. Such moneys of a labor organization may be utilized for notices, factual statements of issues not involving candidates, and other expenses necessary for the holding of an election.

(h) *Removal of officers guilty of serious misconduct.* If the Secretary, upon application of any member of a local labor organization, finds after hearing

Labor-Management Reporting and Disclosure Act of 1959 113

in accordance with subchapter II of chapter 5 of Title 5 that the constitution and bylaws of such labor organization do not provide an adequate procedure for the removal of an elected officer guilty of serious misconduct, such officer may be removed, for cause shown and after notice and hearing, by the members in good standing voting in a secret ballot, conducted by the officers of such labor organization in accordance with its constitution and bylaws insofar as they are not inconsistent with the provisions of this subchapter.

(i) *Rules and regulations for determining adequacy of removal procedures.* The Secretary shall promulgate rules and regulations prescribing minimum standards and procedures for determining the adequacy of the removal procedures to which reference is made in subsection (h) of this section.

(Pub. L. 86-257, Title IV, §401, Sept. 14, 1959, 73 Stat. 532.)

§402. (§482) Enforcement

(a) *Filing of complaint; presumption of validity of challenged election.* A member of a labor organization—

(1) who has exhausted the remedies available under the constitution and bylaws of such organization and of any parent body, or

(2) who has invoked such available remedies without obtaining a final decision within three calendar months after their invocation,

may file a complaint with the Secretary within one calendar month thereafter alleging the violation of any provision of section 481 of this title (including violation of the constitution and bylaws of the labor organization pertaining to the election and removal of officers). The challenged election shall be presumed valid pending a final decision thereon (as hereinafter provided) and in the interim the affairs of the organization shall be conducted by the officers elected or in such other manner as its constitution and bylaws may provide.

(b) *Investigation of complaint; commencement of civil action by Secretary; jurisdiction; preservation of assets.* The Secretary shall investigate such complaint and, if he finds probable cause to believe that a violation of this subchapter has occurred and has not been remedied, he shall, within sixty days after the filing of such complaint, bring a civil action against the labor organization as an entity in the district court of the United States in which such labor organization maintains its principal office to set aside the invalid election, if any, and to direct the conduct of an election or hearing and vote upon the removal of officers under the supervision of the Secretary and in accordance with the provisions of this subchapter and such rules and regulations as the Secretary may prescribe. The court shall have power to take such action as it deems proper to preserve the assets of the labor organization.

(c) *Declaration of void election; order for new election; certification of election to court; decree; certification of result of vote for removal of officers.* If, upon a preponderance of the evidence after a trial upon the merits, the court finds—

>(1) that an election has not been held within the time prescribed by section 481 of this title, or

>(2) that the violation of section 481 of this title may have affected the outcome of an election,

the court shall declare the election, if any, to be void and direct the conduct of a new election under supervision of the Secretary and, so far as lawful and practicable, in conformity with the constitution and bylaws of the labor organization. The Secretary shall promptly certify to the court the names of the persons elected, and the court shall thereupon enter a decree declaring such persons to be the officers of the labor organization. If the proceeding is for the removal of officers pursuant to subsection (h) of section 481 of this title, the Secretary shall certify the results of the vote and the court shall enter a decree declaring whether such persons have been removed as officers of the labor organization.

(d) *Review of orders; stay of order directing election.* An order directing an election, dismissing a complaint, or designating elected officers of a labor organization shall be appealable in the same manner as the final judgment in a civil action, but an order directing an election shall not be stayed pending appeal.

(Pub. L. 86-257, Title IV, §402, Sept. 14, 1959, 73 Stat. 534.)

§403. (§483) Application of other laws; existing rights and remedies; exclusiveness of remedy for challenging election

No labor organization shall be required by law to conduct elections of officers with greater frequency or in a different form or manner than is required by its own constitution or bylaws, except as otherwise provided by this subchapter. Existing rights and remedies to enforce the constitution and bylaws of a labor organization with respect to elections prior to the conduct thereof shall not be affected by the provisions of this subchapter. The remedy provided by this subchapter for challenging an election already conducted shall be exclusive.

(Pub. L. 86-257, Title IV, §403, Sept. 14, 1959, 73 Stat. 534.)

Labor-Management Reporting and Disclosure Act of 1959

TITLE V. SAFEGUARDS FOR LABOR ORGANIZATIONS

§501. (§501) Fiduciary responsibility of officers of labor organizations

(a) *Duties of officers; exculpatory provisions and resolutions void.* The officers, agents, shop stewards, and other representatives of a labor organization occupy positions of trust in relation to such organization and its members as a group. It is, therefore, the duty of each such person, taking into account the special problems and functions of a labor organization, to hold its money and property solely for the benefit of the organization and its members and to manage, invest, and expend the same in accordance with its constitution and bylaws and any resolutions of the governing bodies adopted thereunder, to refrain from dealing with such organization as an adverse party or in behalf of an adverse party in any matter connected with his duties and from holding or acquiring any pecuniary or personal interest which conflicts with the interests of such organization, and to account to the organization for any profit received by him in whatever capacity in connection with transactions conducted by him or under his direction on behalf of the organization. A general exculpatory provision in the constitution and bylaws of such a labor organization or a general exculpatory resolution of a governing body purporting to relieve any such person of liability for breach of the duties declared by this section shall be void as against public policy.

(b) *Violation of duties; action by member after refusal or failure by labor organization to commence proceedings; jurisdiction; leave of court; counsel fees and expenses.* When any officer, agent, shop steward, or representative of any labor organization is alleged to have violated the duties declared in subsection (a) of this section and the labor organization or its governing board or officers refuse or fail to sue or recover damages or secure an accounting or other appropriate relief within a reasonable time after being requested to do so by any member of the labor organization, such member may sue such officer, agent, shop steward, or representative in any district court of the United States or in any State court of competent jurisdiction to recover damages or secure an accounting or other appropriate relief for the benefit of the labor organization. No such proceeding shall be brought except upon leave of the court obtained upon verified application and for good cause shown, which application may be made ex parte. The trial judge may allot a reasonable part of the recovery in any action under this subsection to pay the fees of counsel prosecuting the suit at the instance of the member of the labor organization and to compensate such member for any expenses necessarily paid or incurred by him in connection with the litigation.

(c) *Embezzlement of assets; penalty.* Any person who embezzles, steals, or unlawfully and willfully abstracts or converts to his own use, or the use of another, any of the moneys, funds, securities, property, or other assets of a labor organization of which he is an officer, or by which he is employed, directly or indirectly, shall be fined not more than $10,000 or imprisoned for not more than five years, or both.

(Pub. L. 86-257, Title V, §501, Sept. 14, 1959, 73 Stat. 535.)

§502. (§502) Bonding of officers and employees of labor organizations; amount, form, and placement of bonds; penalty for violation

(a) Every officer, agent, shop steward, or other representative or employee of any labor organization (other than a labor organization whose property and annual financial receipts do not exceed $5,000 in value), or of a trust in which a labor organization is interested, who handles funds or other property thereof shall be bonded to provide protection against loss by reason of acts of fraud or dishonesty on his part directly or through connivance with others. The bond of each such person shall be fixed at the beginning of the organization's fiscal year and shall be in an amount not less than 10 per centum of the funds handled by him and his predecessor or predecessors, if any, during the preceding fiscal year, but in no case more than $500,000. If the labor organization or the trust in which a labor organization is interested does not have a preceding fiscal year, the amount of the bond shall be, in the case of a local labor organization, not less than $1,000, and in the case of any other labor organization or of a trust in which a labor organization is interested, not less than $10,000. Such bonds shall be individual or schedule in form, and shall have a corporate surety company as surety thereon. Any person who is not covered by such bonds shall not be permitted to receive, handle, disburse, or otherwise exercise custody or control of the funds or other property of a labor organization or of a trust in which a labor organization is interested. No such bond shall be placed through an agent or broker or with a surety company in which any labor organization or any officer, agent, shop steward, or other representative of a labor organization has any direct or indirect interest. Such surety company shall be a corporate surety which holds a grant of authority from the Secretary of the Treasury under sections 9304-9308 of Title 31, as an acceptable surety on Federal bonds: *Provided*, That when in the opinion of the Secretary a labor organization has made other bonding arrangements which would provide the protection required by this section at comparable cost or less, he may exempt such labor organization from placing a bond through a surety company holding such grant of authority.

(b) Any person who willfully violates this section shall be fined not more than $10,000 or imprisoned for not more than one year, or both.

(Pub. L. 86-257, Title V, §502, Sept. 14, 1959, 73 Stat. 536; Pub. L. 89-216, §1, Sept. 29, 1965, 79 Stat. 888.)

§504. (§504) Prohibition against certain persons holding office

(a) *Membership in Communist Party; persons convicted of robbery, bribery, etc.* No person who is or has been a member of the Communist Party or who has been convicted of, or served any part of a prison term resulting from his conviction of, robbery, bribery, extortion, embezzlement, grand larceny, burglary, arson, violation of narcotics laws, murder, rape, assault with intent to kill, assault which inflicts grievous bodily injury, or a violation of subchapter III or IV of this chapter, any felony involving abuse or misuse of such person's position or employment in a labor organization or employee benefit plan to seek or obtain an illegal gain at the expense of the members of the labor organization or the beneficiaries of the employee benefit plan, or conspiracy to commit any such crimes or attempt to commit any such crimes, or a crime in which any of the foregoing crimes is an element, shall serve or be permitted to serve—

(1) as a consultant or adviser to any labor organization,

(2) as an officer, director, trustee, member of any executive board or similar governing body, business agent, manager, organizer, employee, or representative in any capacity of any labor organization,

(3) as a labor relations consultant or adviser to a person engaged in an industry or activity affecting commerce, or as an officer, director, agent, or employee of any group or association of employers dealing with any labor organization, or in a position having specific collective bargaining authority or direct responsibility in the area of labor-management relations in any corporation or association engaged in an industry or activity affecting commerce, or

(4) in a position which entitles its occupant to a share of the proceeds of, or as an officer or executive or administrative employee of, any entity whose activities are in whole or substantial part devoted to providing goods or services to any labor organization, or

(5) in any capacity, other than in his capacity as a member of such labor organization, that involves decisionmaking authority concerning, or decisionmaking authority over, or custody of, or control of the moneys, funds, assets, or property of any labor organization,

during or for the period of thirteen years after such conviction or after the end of such imprisonment, whichever is later, unless the sentencing court on the motion of the person convicted sets a lesser period of at least three years after such conviction or after the end of such imprisonment, whichever is later, or unless prior to the end of such period, in the case of a person so convicted or imprisoned, (A) his citizenship rights, having been revoked as a result of such conviction, have been fully restored, or (B) if the offense is a Federal offense, the sentencing judge or, if the offense is a State or local offense, the United States district court for the district in which the offense was committed, pursuant to sentencing guidelines and policy statements under section 994(a) of Title 28, determines that such person's service in any capacity referred to in clauses (1) through (5) would not be contrary to the purposes of this chapter. Prior to making any such determination the court shall hold a hearing and shall give notice of such proceeding by certified mail to the Secretary of Labor and to State, county, and Federal prosecuting officials in the jurisdiction or jurisdictions in which such person was convicted. The court's determination in any such proceeding shall be final. No person shall knowingly hire, retain, employ, or otherwise place any other person to serve in any capacity in violation of this subsection.

(b) *Penalty for violations.* Any person who willfully violates this section shall be fined not more than $10,000 or imprisoned for not more than five years, or both.

(c) *Definitions.* For the purpose of this section —

(1) A person shall be deemed to have been "convicted" and under the disability of "conviction" from the date of the judgment of the trial court, regardless of whether that judgment remains under appeal.

(2) A period of parole shall not be considered as part of a period of imprisonment.

(d) *Salary of persons barred from labor organization office during appeal of conviction.* Whenever any person —

(1) by operation of this section, has been barred from office or other position in a labor organization as a result of a conviction, and

(2) has filed an appeal of that conviction,

any salary which would be otherwise due such person by virtue of such office or position, shall be placed in escrow by the individual employer or organization responsible for payment of such salary. Payment of such salary into escrow shall continue for the duration of the appeal or for the period of time during which such salary would be otherwise due, whichever period is shorter. Upon the final reversal of such person's conviction on appeal, the amounts in escrow shall be paid to such person. Upon the final sustaining of such person's conviction on appeal, the amounts in escrow shall be returned to the individual employer or organization responsible for payment of those amounts. Upon final reversal of such person's conviction, such person shall no longer be barred by this statute from assuming any position from which such person was previously barred.

(Pub. L. 86-257, Title V, §504, Sept. 14, 1959, 73 Stat. 536; Pub. L. 98-473, Title II, §803, Oct. 12, 1984, 98 Stat. 2133; Pub. L. 100-182, §15(a), Dec. 7, 1987, 101 Stat. 1269.)

Title VI. Miscellaneous Provisions

§601. (§521) Investigations by Secretary; applicability of other laws

(a) The Secretary shall have power when he believes it necessary in order to determine whether any person has violated or is about to violate any provision of this chapter (except subchapter II of this chapter) to make an investigation and in connection therewith he may enter such places and inspect such records and accounts and question such persons as he may deem necessary to enable him to determine the facts relative thereto. The Secretary may report to interested persons or officials concerning the facts required to be shown in any report required by this chapter and concerning the reasons for failure or refusal to file such a report or any other matter which he deems to be appropriate as a result of such an investigation.

(b) For the purpose of any investigation provided for in this chapter, the provisions of sections 49 and 50 of title 15 (relating to the attendance of witnesses and the production of books, papers, and documents), are made applicable to the jurisdiction, powers, and duties of the Secretary or any officers designated by him.

(Pub. L. 86-257, Title VI, §601, Sept. 14, 1959, 73 Stat. 539.)

§602. (§522) Extortionate picketing; penalty for violation

(a) It shall be unlawful to carry on picketing on or about the premises of any employer for the purpose of, or as part of any conspiracy or in furtherance of any plan or purpose for, the personal profit or enrichment of any individual (except a bona fide increase in wages or other employee benefits) by taking or obtaining any money or other thing of value from such employer against his will or with his consent.

(b) Any person who willfully violates this section shall be fined not more than $10,000 or imprisoned not more than twenty years, or both.

(Pub. L. 86-257, Title VI, §602, Sept. 14, 1959, 73 Stat. 539.)

§603. (§523) Retention of rights under other Federal and State laws

(a) Except as explicitly provided to the contrary, nothing in this chapter shall reduce or limit the responsibilities of any labor organization or any officer, agent, shop steward, or other representative of a labor organization, or of any trust in which a labor organization is interested, under any other Federal law or under the laws of any State, and, except as explicitly provided to the contrary, nothing in this chapter shall take away any right or bar any remedy to which members of a labor organization are entitled under such other Federal law or law of any State.

(b) Nothing contained in this chapter and section 186(a)–(c) of this title shall be construed to supersede or impair or otherwise affect the provisions of the Railway Labor Act, as amended [45 U.S.C. §151 et seq.], or any of the obligations, rights, benefits, privileges, or immunities of any carrier, employee, organization, representative, or person subject thereto; nor shall anything contained in this chapter be construed to confer any rights, privileges, immunities, or defenses upon employers, or to impair or otherwise affect the rights of any person under the National Labor Relations Act, as amended [29 U.S.C. §151 et seq.].

(Pub. L. 86-257, Title VI, §603, Sept. 14, 1959, 73 Stat. 540.)

§604. (§524) Effect on State laws

Nothing in this chapter shall be construed to impair or diminish the authority of any State to enact and enforce general criminal laws with respect to robbery, bribery, extortion, embezzlement, grand larceny, burglary, arson, violation of narcotics laws, murder, rape, assault with intent to kill, or assault which inflicts grievous bodily injury, or conspiracy to commit any of such crimes.

(Pub. L. 86-257, Title VI, §604, Sept. 14, 1959, 73 Stat. 540.)

§2201. (§524a) Elimination of racketeering activities threat; State legislation governing collective bargaining representative

Notwithstanding this or any other Act regulating labor-management relations, each State shall have the authority to enact and enforce, as part of a comprehensive statutory system to eliminate the threat of pervasive racketeering activity in an industry that is, or over time has been, affected by such activity, a provision of law that applies equally to employers, employees, and collective bargaining representatives, which provision of law governs service in any position in a local labor organization which acts or seeks to act in that State as a collective bargaining representative pursuant to the National Labor Relations Act [29 U.S.C. §151 et seq.], in the industry that is subject to that program.

(Pub. L. 98-473, Title II, §2201, Oct. 12, 1984, 98 Stat. 2192.)

§605. (§525) Service of process

For the purposes of this chapter, service of summons, subpena, or other legal process of a court of the United States upon an officer or agent of a labor organization in his capacity as such shall constitute service upon the labor organization.

(Pub. L. 86-257, Title VI, §605, Sept. 14, 1959, 73 Stat. 540.)

§606. (§526) Applicability of administrative procedure provisions

The provisions of subchapter II of chapter 5, and chapter 7, of title 5 shall be applicable to the issuance, amendment, or rescission of any rules or regulations, or any adjudication authorized or required pursuant to the provisions of this chapter.

(Pub. L. 86-257, Title VI, §606, Sept. 14, 1959, 73 Stat. 540.)

Labor-Management Reporting and Disclosure Act of 1959

§607. (§527) Cooperation with other agencies and departments

In order to avoid unnecessary expense and duplication of functions among Government agencies, the Secretary may make such arrangements or agreements for cooperation or mutual assistance in the performance of his functions under this chapter and the functions of any such agency as he may find to be practicable and consistent with law. The Secretary may utilize the facilities or services of any department, agency, or establishment of the United States or of any State or political subdivision of a State, including the services of any of its employees, with the lawful consent of such department, agency, or establishment; and each department, agency, or establishment of the United States is authorized and directed to cooperate with the Secretary and, to the extent permitted by law, to provide such information and facilities as he may request for his assistance in the performance of his functions under this chapter. The Attorney General or his representative shall receive from the Secretary for appropriate action such evidence developed in the performance of his functions under this chapter as may be found to warrant consideration for criminal prosecution under the provisions of this chapter or other Federal law.

[Pub. L. 86-257, Title VI, §607, Sept. 14, 1959, 73 Stat. 540.)

§608. (§528) Criminal contempt

No person shall be punished for any criminal contempt allegedly committed outside the immediate presence of the court in connection with any civil action prosecuted by the Secretary or any other person in any court of the United States under the provisions of this chapter unless the facts constituting such criminal contempt are established by the verdict of the jury in a proceeding in the district court of the United States, which jury shall be chosen and empaneled in the manner prescribed by the law governing trial juries in criminal prosecutions in the district courts of the United States.

(Pub. L. 86-257, Title VI, §608, Sept. 14, 1959, 73 Stat. 541.)

§609. (§529) Prohibition on certain discipline by labor organization

It shall be unlawful for any labor organization, or any officer, agent, shop steward, or other representative of a labor organization, or any employee thereof to fine, suspend, expel, or otherwise discipline any of its members for exercising any right to which he is entitled under the provisions of this chapter. The provisions of section 412 of this title shall be applicable in the enforcement of this section.

(Pub. L. 86-257, Title VI, §609, Sept. 14, 1959, 73 Stat. 541.)

§610. (§530) Deprivation of rights by violence; penalty

It shall be unlawful for any person through the use of force or violence, or threat of the use of force or violence, to restrain, coerce, or intimidate, or attempt to restrain, coerce, or intimidate any member of a labor organization for the purpose of interfering with or preventing the exercise of any right to which he is entitled under the provisions of this chapter. Any person who willfully violates this section shall be fined not more than $1,000 or imprisoned for not more than one year, or both.

(Pub. L. 86-257, Title VI, §610, Sept. 14, 1959, 73 Stat. 541.)

§611. (§531) Separability of provisions

If any provision of this chapter, or the application of such provision to any person or circumstances, shall be held invalid, the remainder of this chapter or the application of such provision to persons or circumstances other than those as to which it is held invalid, shall not be affected thereby.

(Pub. L. 86-257, Title VI, §611, Sept. 14, 1959, 73 Stat. 541.)

Labor-Management Cooperation Act of 1978
61 Stat. 153, as amended, 29 U.S.C. §§173, 175(a), 186*

§203. (§173) Functions of [the Federal Mediation Conciliation] Service

(a) *Settlement of disputes through conciliation and mediation.* It shall be the duty of the Service, in order to prevent or minimize interruptions of the free flow of commerce growing out of labor disputes, to assist parties to labor disputes in industries affecting commerce to settle such disputes through conciliation and mediation.

(b) *Intervention on motion of Service or request of parties; avoidance of mediation of minor disputes.* The Service may proffer its services in any labor dispute in any industry affecting commerce, either upon its own motion or upon the request of one or more of the parties to the dispute, whenever in its judgment such dispute threatens to cause a substantial interruption of commerce. The Director and the Service are directed to avoid attempting to mediate disputes which would have only a minor effect on interstate commerce if State or other conciliation services are available to the parties. Whenever the Service does proffer its services in any dispute, it shall be the duty of the Service promptly to put itself in communication with the parties and to use its best efforts, by mediation and conciliation, to bring them to agreement.

---

*Provisions relating to the establishment of plant, area, and industrywide labor-management committees have been grouped together for the reader's convenience.—EDS.

(c) *Settlement of dispute by other means upon failure of conciliation.* If the Director is not able to bring the parties to agreement by conciliation within a reasonable time, he shall seek to induce the parties voluntarily to seek other means of settling the dispute without resort to strike, lock-out, or other coercion, including submission to the employees in the bargaining unit of the employer's last offer of settlement for approval or rejection in a secret ballot. The failure or refusal of either party to agree to any procedure suggested by the Director shall not be deemed a violation of any duty or obligation imposed by this chapter.

(d) *Use of conciliation and mediation services as last resort.* Final adjustment by a method agreed upon by the parties is declared to be the desirable method for settlement of grievance disputes arising over the application or interpretation of an existing collective-bargaining agreement. The Service is directed to make its conciliation and mediation services available in the settlement of such grievance disputes only as a last resort and in exceptional cases.

(e) *Encouragement and support of establishment and operation of joint labor management activities conducted by committees.* The Service is authorized and directed to encourage and support the establishment and operation of joint labor management activities conducted by plant, area, and industrywide committees designed to improve labor management relationships, job security and organizational effectiveness, in accordance with the provisions of section 175a of this title.

(f) *Alternative means of dispute resolution.* The Service may make its services available to Federal agencies to aid in the resolution of disputes under the provisions of subchapter IV of chapter 5 of Title 5. Functions performed by the Service may include assisting parties to disputes related to administrative programs, training persons in skills and procedures employed in alternative means of dispute resolution, and furnishing officers and employees of the Service to act as neutrals. Only officers and employees who are qualified in accordance with section 573 of Title 5, may be assigned to act as neutrals. The Service shall consult with the Administrative Conference of the United States and other agencies in maintaining rosters of neutrals and arbitrators, and to adopt such procedures and rules as are necessary to carry out the services authorized in this subsection.

(June 23, 1947, c.120, Title II, §203, 61 Stat. 153; Oct. 27, 1978, Pub. L. 95-524, §6(c)(1), 92 Stat. 2020, Nov. 15, 1990, Pub. L. 101-552, §7, 104 Stat. 2746; Aug. 26, 1992, Pub. L. 102-354, §5(b)(5), 106 Stat. 946.)

§205(A). (§175a) Assistance to plant, area, and industrywide labor management committees

(a) *Establishment and operation of plant, area, and industrywide committees.*
(1) The Service is authorized and directed to provide assistance in the establishment and operation of plant, area and industrywide labor management committees which—

(A) have been organized jointly by employers and labor organizations representing employees in that plant, area, or industry; and

(B) are established for the purpose of improving labor management relationships, job security, organizational effectiveness, enhancing economic development or involving workers in decisions affecting their jobs including improving communication with respect to subjects of mutual interest and concern.

(2) The Service is authorized and directed to enter into contracts and to make grants, where necessary or appropriate, to fulfill its responsibilities under this section.

(b) *Restriction on grants, contracts, or other assistance.*

(1) No grant may be made, no contract may be entered into and no other assistance may be provided under the provisions of this section to a plant labor management committee unless the employees in that plant are represented by a labor organization and there is in effect at that plant a collective bargaining agreement.

(2) No grant may be made, no contract may be entered into and no other assistance may be provided under the provisions of this section to an area or industrywise labor management committee unless its participants include any labor organizations certified or recognized as the representative of the employees of an employer participating in such committee. Nothing in this clause shall prohibit participation in an area or industrywide committee by an employer whose employees are not represented by a labor organization.

(3) No grant may be made under the provisions of this section to any labor management committee which the Service finds to have as one of its purposes the discouragement of the exercise of rights contained in section 157 of this title, or the interference with collective bargaining in any plant, or industry.

(c) *Establishment of office.* The Service shall carry out the provisions of this section through an office established for that purpose.

(d) *Authorization of appropriation.* There are authorized to be appropriated to carry out the provisions of this section $10,000,000 for the fiscal year 1979, and such sums as may be necessary thereafter.

(June 23, 1947, c.120, Title II, §205A, as added Oct. 27, 1978, Pub. L. 95-524, §6(c)(2), 92 Stat. 2020.)

§302. (§186) Restrictions on financial transactions

(a) *Payment or lending, etc., of money by employer or agent to employees, representatives, or labor organizations.* It shall be unlawful for any employer or association of employers or any person who acts as a labor relations expert, adviser, or consultant to an employer or who acts in the interest of an employer to pay, lend, or deliver, or agree to pay, lend, or deliver, any money or other thing of value—

(1) to any representative of any of his employees who are employed in an industry affecting commerce; or

(2) to any labor organization, or any officer or employee thereof, which represents, seeks to represent, or would admit to membership, any of the employees of such employer who are employed in an industry affecting commerce; or

(3) to any employee or group or committee of employees of such employer employed in an industry affecting commerce in excess of their normal compensation for the purpose of causing such employee or group or committee directly or indirectly to influence any other employees in the exercise of the right to organize and bargain collectively through representatives of their own choosing; or

(4) to any officer or employee of a labor organization engaged in an industry affecting commerce with intent to influence him in respect to any of his actions, decisions, or duties as a representative of employees or as such officer or employee of such labor organization.

(b) *Request, demand, etc., for money or other thing of value.*

(1) It shall be unlawful for any person to request, demand, receive, or accept, or agree to receive or accept, any payment, loan, or delivery of any money or other thing of value prohibited by subsection (a) of this section.

(2) It shall be unlawful for any labor organization, or for any person acting as an officer, agent, representative, or employee of such labor organization, to demand or accept from the operator of any motor vehicle (as defined in section 10102 of Title 49) employed in the transportation of property in commerce, or the employer of any such operator, any money or other thing of value payable to such organization or to an officer, agent, representative or employee thereof as a fee or charge for the unloading, or in connection with the unloading, of the cargo of such vehicle: *Provided*, That nothing in this paragraph shall be construed to make unlawful any payment by an employer to any of his employees as compensation for their services as employees.

(c) *Exceptions.* The provisions of this section shall not be applicable (1) in respect to any money or other thing of value payable by an employer to any of his employees whose established duties include acting openly for such employer in matters of labor relations or personnel administration or to any representative of his employees, or to any officer or employee of a labor organization, who is also an employee or former employee of such employer, as compensation for, or by reason of, his service as an employee of such employer; (2) with respect to the payment or delivery of any money or other thing of value in satisfaction of a judgment of any court or a decision or award of an arbitrator or impartial chairman or in compromise, adjustment, settlement, or release of any claim, complaint, grievance, or dispute in the absence of fraud or duress; (3) with respect to the sale or purchase of an article or commodity at the prevailing market price in the regular course of business; (4) with respect to money deducted from the wages of employees in payment of membership dues in a labor organization: *Provided*, That the employer has received from each employee, on whose account such deductions are made, a written assignment which shall not be irrevocable for a period of more than one year, or beyond the termination date of the applicable collective agreement, whichever occurs sooner; (5) with respect to money or other thing of value paid to a trust fund established by such representative, for the sole and exclusive benefit of the employees of such employer, and their families and dependents (or of such employees, families, and dependents jointly with the employees of other employers making similar payments, and their families and dependents): *Provided*, That (A) such payments are held in trust for the purpose of paying, either from principal or income or both, for the benefit of employees, their families and dependents, for medical or hospital care, pensions on retirement or death of employees, compensation for injuries or illness resulting from occupational activity or insurance to provide any of the foregoing, or unemployment benefits or life insurance, disability and sickness insurance, or accident insurance; (B) the detailed basis on which such payments are to be made is specified in a written agreement with the employer, and employees and employers are equally represented in the administration of such fund, together with such neutral persons as the representatives of the employers and the representatives of employees may agree upon and in the event the employer and employee groups deadlock on the administration of such fund and there are no neutral persons empowered to break such deadlock, such agreement provides that the two groups shall agree on an impartial umpire to decide such dispute, or in event of their failure to agree within a reasonable length of time, an impartial umpire to decide such dispute shall, on petition of either group, be appointed by the district court of the United States for the district where the trust fund has its principal office, and shall also contain provisions for an annual audit of the trust fund, a statement of the results of which shall be available for inspection by interested persons at the principal office of the trust fund and at such other places as may be designated in such written agreement; and (C) such payments as are intended to be used for the purpose of providing pensions or annuities for employees are made to a separate trust which provides the funds held therein cannot be used for any purpose other than paying such pensions or annuities; (6) with respect to money or other thing of value paid by any employer to a trust fund established by such representative for the purpose of pooled vacation, holiday, severance or similar benefits, or defraying costs of apprenticeship or other training programs: *Provided*, That the requirements of clause (B) of the proviso to clause (5) of this subsection shall apply to such trust funds: (7) with respect to money or other thing of value paid by any employer to a pooled or individual trust fund established

Labor-Management Cooperation Act of 1978

by such representative for the purpose of (A) scholarships for the benefit of employees, their families, and dependents for study at educational institutions, (B) child care centers for preschool and school age dependents of employees, or (C) financial assistance for employee housing: *Provided*, That no labor organization or employer shall be required to bargain on the establishment of any such trust fund, and refusal to do so shall not constitute an unfair labor practice: *Provided further*, That the requirements of clause (B) of the proviso to clause (5) of this subsection shall apply to such trust funds; (8) with respect to money or any other thing of value paid by any employer to a trust fund established by such representative for the purpose of defraying the costs of legal services for employees, their families, and dependents for counsel or plan of their choice: *Provided*, That the requirements of clause (B) of the proviso to clause (5) of this subsection shall apply to such trust funds: *Provided further*, That no such legal services shall be furnished: (A) to initiate any proceeding directed (i) against any such employer or its officers or agents except in workman's compensation cases, or (ii) against such labor organization, or its parent or subordinate bodies, or their officers or agents, or (iii) against any other employer or labor organization, or their officers or agents, in any matter arising under subchapter II of this chapter or this chapter; and (B) in any proceeding where a labor organization would be prohibited from defraying the costs of legal services by the provisions of the Labor-Management Reporting and Disclosure Act of 1959 [29 U.S.C. §401 et seq.]; or (9) with respect to money or other things of value paid by an employer to a plant, area or industrywide labor management committee established for one or more of the purposes set forth in section 5(b) of the Labor Management Cooperation Act of 1978.*

(d) *Penalty for violations*.

(1) Any person who participates in a transaction involving a payment, loan, or delivery of money or other thing of value to a labor organization in payment of membership dues or to a joint labor-management trust fund as defined by clause (B) of the proviso to clause (5) of subsection (c) of this section or to a plant, area, or industrywide labor-management committee that is received and used by such labor organization, trust fund, or committee, which transaction does not satisfy all the applicable requirements of subsections (c)(4) through (c)(9) of this section, and willfully and with intent to benefit himself or to benefit other persons he knows are not permitted to receive a payment, loan, money, or other thing of value under subsections (c)(4) through (c)(9) violates this subsection, [and] shall, upon conviction thereof, be guilty of a felony and be subject to a fine of not more than $15,000, or imprisoned for not more than five years, or both; but if the value of the amount of money or thing of value involved in any violation of the provisions of this section does not

---

*This probably refers to §6(b) of Pub. L. 95-424, which is set out as a note under 29 U.S.C. §175a.—EDS.

exceed $1,000, such person shall be guilty of a misdemeanor and be subject to a fine of not more than $10,000, or imprisoned for not more than one year, or both.

(2) Except for violations involving transactions covered by subsection (d)(1) of this section, any person who willfully violates this section shall upon conviction thereof, be guilty of a felony and be subject to a fine of not more than $15,000, or imprisoned for not more than five years, or both; but if the value of the amount of money or thing of value involved in any violation of the provisions of this section does not exceed $1,000, such person shall be guilty of a misdemeanor and be subject to a fine of not more than $10,000, or imprisoned for not more than one year, or both.

(e) *Jurisdiction of courts.* The district courts of the United States and the United States courts of the Territories and possessions shall have jurisdiction, for cause shown, and subject to the provisions of section 381 of Title 28 (relating to notice to opposite party) to restrain violations of this section, without regard to the provisions of section 17 of Title 15 and section 52 of this title, and the provisions of chapter 6 of this title.

(f) *Effective date of provisions.* This section shall not apply to any contract in force on June 23, 1947, until the expiration of such contract, or until July 1, 1948, whichever first occurs.

(g) *Contributions to trust funds.* Compliance with the restrictions contained in subsection (c)(5)(B) of this section upon contributions to trust funds, otherwise lawful, shall not be applicable to contributions to such trust funds established by collective agreement prior to January 1, 1946, nor shall subsection (c)(5)(A) of this section be construed as prohibiting contributions to such trust funds if prior to January 1, 1947, such funds contained provisions for pooled vacation benefits.

(June 23, 1947, c.120, Title III, §302, 61 Stat. 157; Sept. 14, 1959, Pub. L. 86-257, Title V, §505, 73 Stat. 537; Oct. 14, 1969, Pub. L. 91-86, 83 Stat. 133; Aug. 15, 1973, Pub. L. 93-95, 87 Stat. 314; Oct. 27, 1978, Pub. L. 95-524, §6(d), 92 Stat. 2021; Oct. 12, 1984, Pub. L. 98-473, Title II, §801, 98 Stat. 2131; Apr. 18, 1990, Pub. L. 101-273, §1, 104 Stat. 138.)

Proposed Labor Reform Act of 1977*
H.R. 8410, 95th Cong., 1st Sess. (1977)

To amend the National Labor Relations Act to strengthen the remedies and expedite the procedures under such Act.

Be it enacted by the Senate and House of Representatives of the United States of

---

*Text of bill that passed the U.S. House of Representatives on October 6, 1977. A similar bill, S. 1883, was considered in the Senate but did not emerge from the relevant committee.—EDS.

America in Congress assembled. That (a) this Act may be cited as the "Labor Reform Act of 1977".

(b) Except as otherwise specifically provided, whenever in this Act an amendment or repeal is expressed in terms of an amendment to, or repeal of, a section or other provision, the reference shall be considered to be made to a section or other provision of the National Labor Relations Act.

§2. (a) Section 3(a) of the National Labor Relations Act is amended to read as follows:

"Sec. 3. (a) The National Labor Relations Board (hereinafter called the 'Board') created by this Act prior to its amendment by the Labor-Management Relations Act, 1947, and by the Labor Reform Act of 1977, is hereby continued as an agency of the United States, except that the Board shall consist of seven instead of five members, appointed by the President by and with the advice and consent of the Senate. Of the two additional members so provided for, one shall be appointed for a term of five years and the other for a term of six years. Their successors, and the successors of the other members, shall be appointed for terms of seven years each, excepting that any individual chosen to fill a vacancy shall be appointed only for the unexpired term of the member whom that individual shall succeed. The President shall designate one member to serve as Chairman of the Board. No more than a simple majority of the members of the Board shall be members of the same political party. Any member of the Board may be removed by the President, upon notice and hearing, for neglect of duty or malfeasance in office, but for no other cause."

(b)(1) The third sentence of section 3(b) is amended by striking "three" and substituting "four".

(2) Section 3(b) is further amended by inserting after the third sentence the following new sentence: "The Board shall within ninety days after the date of enactment of the Labor Reform Act of 1977 establish a procedure, upon conditions stated in the rule, pursuant to which a group designated pursuant to the first sentence of this subsection may, in appropriate cases, upon motion of the prevailing party in a decision of an administrative law judge after a hearing under section 10(b), summarily affirm such decision. A motion for summary affirmance shall be filed within ten days after the decision of the administrative law judge, any response shall be filed within twenty days thereafter, and the motion and response shall then be presented for decision to a group designated pursuant to the first sentence of this subsection."

§3. Section 6 is amended to read as follows:

"Sec. 6. (a) The Board is authorized to make, amend, and rescind (in the manner prescribed by subchapter II of chapter 5 of title 5, United States Code) such rules and regulations as may be necessary to carry out the provisions of this Act.

"(b)(1) The Board shall within twelve months after the date of enactment of the Labor Reform Act of 1977 issue regulations to implement the provisions of section 9(c)(6)* including rules—

"(A) which shall, subject to reasonable conditions, including due regard for the needs of the employer to maintain the continuity of production, provide that if an employer or employer representative addresses the employees on its premises or during working time on issues relating to representation by a labor organization during a period of time that employees are seeking representation by a labor organization, the employees shall be assured an equal opportunity to obtain in an equivalent manner information concerning such issues from such labor organization, and, with due regard for the rights declared in section 7, the right of such labor organizations to conduct meetings without undue interference, and the right of the employees to the privacy of their homes, provide also that the employees are assured an equal opportunity overall to obtain such information from the employer and such labor organization: *Provided*, That the rule shall apply to elections conducted pursuant to sections 9(c)(1) and 9(e):

"(B) to facilitate agreements concerning the eligibility of voters; and

"(C) to govern the holding of elections in cases in which an appeal has not been decided prior to the date of the election.

"(2) The Board shall, to the fullest extent practicable, exercise its authority under subsection (a) of this section to promulgate rules declaring certain units to be appropriate for the purposes of collective bargaining.

"(3) A rule or regulation issued by the Board with respect to the subject matter set forth in paragraph (1) or (2) of this subsection shall be judicially reviewable only in a proceeding under section 10 of this Act and only on the grounds that the Board prejudicially violated the requirements of subchapter II of chapter 5 of title 5, United States Code, or that a rule or regulation of the Board is arbitrary or capricious, contrary to a specific prohibition of this Act, or of the Constitution. The failure of the Board to comply with the time requirements set forth in paragraph (1) of this subsection, or to institute a rulemaking proceeding with respect to the subject matter set forth in paragraph (2) of this subsection, within a reasonable period of time after a request for such a rulemaking procedure has been filed with the Board pursuant to section 553(e) of title 5, United States Code, [or] to complete such a procedure within a reasonable period after its institution, may be reviewed upon the petition of any aggrieved party in the court of appeals of the judicial circuit in which the petitioner resides or has its principal office, or in the United States Court of Appeals for the District of Columbia Circuit. The court of appeals shall have jurisdiction to grant appropriate relief.

---

*Text of proposed §9(c)(6) is provided below.—Eds.

"(4)(a) Notwithstanding any other provision of this Act, simultaneously with promulgation or repromulgation of any rule or regulation, the National Labor Relations Board promulgating or repromulgating the rule or regulation shall transmit a copy thereof to the Secretary of the Senate and the Clerk of the House of Representatives. Except as provided in paragraph (2), the rule or regulation shall not become effective, if—

"(1) within ninety calendar days of continuous session of Congress after the date of promulgation, both Houses of Congress adopt a concurrent resolution, the matter after the resolving clause of which is as follows: 'That Congress disapproves the rule or regulation promulgated by the National Labor Relations Board dealing with the matter of _____, which rule or regulation was transmitted to Congress on _____,' the blank spaces therein being appropriately filled; or

"(2) within sixty calendar days of continuous session of Congress after the date of promulgating, one House of Congress adopts such a concurrent resolution and transmits such resolution to the other House, and such resolution is not disapproved by such other House within thirty calendar days of continuous session of Congress after such transmittal.

"(b) If at the end of sixty calendar days of continuous session of Congress after the date of promulgation of a rule or regulation, no committee of either House of Congress has reported or been discharged from further consideration of a concurrent resolution disapproving the rule or regulation, and neither House has adopted such a resolution, the rule or regulation may go into effect immediately. If, within such sixty calendar days, such a committee has reported or been discharged from further consideration of such a resolution, or either House has adopted such a resolution, the rule or regulation may go into effect not sooner than ninety calendar days of continuous session of Congress after its promulgation unless disapproved as provided in paragraph (1)(A)[sic].

"(c) Congressional inaction on, or rejection of, a resolution of disapproval under this subsection shall not be deemed an expression of approval of the rule involved.

"(C) For the purposes of subparagraphs (A) and (B)[sic] of this paragraph—

"(i) continuity of session is broken only by an adjournment of Congress sine die; and

"(ii) the days on which either House is not in session because of an adjournment of more than three days to a day certain are excluded in the computation of thirty, sixty, and ninety calendar days of continuous session of Congress."

§4. Section 9(b)(3) is amended by striking, "or is affiliated directly or indirectly with an organization which admits to membership, employees other than guards." and substituting "nonguard employees of the same employer at the same location, or if such organization is directly affiliated with any national or international labor organization which represents nonguard employees of the same employer at the same location".

§5. Section 9(c) is amended by adding at the end thereof the following new paragraph:

"(6)(A) Notwithstanding any other provisions of section 9, whenever a petition shall have been filed and served on the employer, or a labor organization pursuant to subsection [(c)(1)(A)] or (e)(1) of this section 9, or the individual or the labor organization that is the representative defined in subsection (a) of this section, in accordance with such regulations as may be prescribed by the Board, by an employee or group of employees or any individual or labor organization acting in their behalf alleging that their employer declines to recognize their representative as the representative defined in subsection (a) in a unit appropriate for the purposes of collective bargaining under a rule established by the Board pursuant to section 6 or a decision in the applicable industry, that a majority of the employees in that unit have designated that individual or labor organization as their representative defined in subsection (a), and that no individual or labor organization is currently certified or recognized as the exclusive representative of any of the employees in the bargaining unit defined in the petition, or that a majority of employees in a unit currently certified or recognized designate that they no longer desire representation, or that a majority of the employees covered by an agreement made pursuant to section 8(a)(3) designate that such authority be rescinded, the Board shall investigate such petition. If the Board finds that the unit there specified is a unit covered by an agreement pursuant to section 8(a)(3), or is a unit where the certified or currently recognized representative is no longer desired, or is a unit appropriate for the purposes of collective bargaining under a rule established by the Board pursuant to section 6 or a decision in the applicable industry, and if the Board has reasonable cause to believe that a question of representation affecting commerce exists and that the other conditions specified in this subsection have been met, the Board shall within seventeen days after the filing and serving of the petition direct an election by secret ballot not more than twenty-five days after a petition is filed and served under this subparagraph and shall so notify the representative named in the petition and the employer. [If a petition is filed asserting] that a majority of the employees in a unit appropriate for the purposes of collective bargaining do not wish to be represented by the individual or labor organization which has been certified or is being currently recognized by their employer as the representative defined in subsection (a), or do not wish to be covered by an agreement between their employer and a labor organization made pursuant to subsection (a)(3) of section 8, the Board shall investigate such petition. If the Board has reasonable cause to believe that a question of representation affecting commerce, or a question covering an agreement made pursuant to subsection (a)(3) of section 8, exists and that the other conditions specified in this subsection have been met, the Board shall within seventeen days after the filing and serving of the petition direct an election by secret ballot which shall take place within eight days after such election is directed by the Board, and in no event more than twenty-five days after a petition is filed and served under this subparagraph, and the Board shall so notify the representative named in the petition and the employer.

"(B) In any proceeding under this subsection in which the Board directs an election by secret ballot, and which is not governed by subparagraph (A) of this paragraph, the Board shall direct the election on a date not more than fifty days after the filing and serving of the petition and shall inform the representative named in the petition, the employer, and all other interested parties of the election date not less than fifteen days prior to the election except that, where the Board determines that the proceeding presents issues of exceptional novelty or complexity, the Board may direct the election on a date not more than seventy-five days after the filing and serving of said petition. In computing the time limits stated in this paragraph the days of the week during which a majority of the employees involved in the election are on vacation shall not be included.

"(C) After an election conducted pursuant to subparagraph (A) or (B) of this paragraph is completed, the Board shall, unless under a rule adopted pursuant to subsection (b)(1)(D) [sic] of section 6, the ballots have been impounded, promptly serve the parties with a tally of the ballots.

"(D)(i) Any party to the election conducted pursuant to subparagraphs (A) and (B) of this paragraph may, within five days after such election, object to the election on the ground that conduct contrary to a rule relating to election[s] declared by the Board pursuant to its authority under section 6 or conduct contrary to a rule of decision declared by the Board in a proceeding under section 10 did affect the result of the election.

"(ii) With regard to challenged ballots, the Board shall, where such ballots are sufficient in number to affect the outcome of the election, investigate the challenges and serve a report upon the parties on challenges: *Provided*, That nothing contained herein shall preclude resolution of the eligibility questions raised by such challenges in a subsequent unit clarification proceeding.

"(iii) The Board shall move expeditiously to resolve any issues raised by the objections or regarding eligibility and to certify the results of the election: *Provided*, That an objection that an election was conducted under subparagraph (A) instead of subparagraph (B) shall not be a basis for setting the election aside.".

§6. Section 9(d) is amended by inserting immediately before the period at the end thereof a comma and the following: "except that no such certification shall be set aside unless the Board in issuing such certification prejudicially violated the procedural requirements of this Act or of subchapter II of chapter 5, United States Code, or acted arbitrarily or capriciously, or contrary to a specific prohibition of this Act or of the Constitution, or made findings with respect to questions of fact which are not supported by substantial evidence on the record considered as a whole.".

§7. The first sentence of subsection (10)(b) is amended to read as follows:

"(b) Whenever—

"(1) it is charged that any person has engaged in or is engaging in any such unfair labor practice, or

"(2) it is charged that any person has engaged in or is engaging in a willful violation of—

"(A) any final order of the Board entered pursuant to subsection (c) of this section and which is not and has not been the subject to a proceeding under subsection (c) or (f) of this section, or

"(B) any final order of a court of appeals of the United States entered in a proceeding under subsection (e) or (f) of this section, prohibiting interference with, restraint or coercion of employees in the exercise of the rights guaranteed in section 7 or discrimination against employees to encourage or discourage membership in a labor organization,

and that said violation occurred within three years of the entry of the order violated,

the Board, or any agent or agency designated by the Board for such purposes, is authorized to issue and cause to be served upon such person a complaint stating the charges. Such complaint shall contain a notice of hearing before the Board or member thereof, or before a designated agent or agency, at a place therein fixed, not less than five days after the serving of such complaint. No complaint shall be issued based upon any unfair labor practice or willful violation of a final order occurring more than six months prior to the filing of the charge with the Board and the service of a copy thereof upon the person against whom such charge is made, unless the person aggrieved thereby was prevented from filing such charge by reason of service in the Armed Forces, in which event the six-month period shall be computed from the day of his discharge.".

§8. Section 10(c) is amended by—

(1) inserting "(1)" after "(e)";

(2) striking out the fifth sentence of paragraph (1) (as redesignated by this section) and inserting in lieu thereof the following: "If upon the preponderance of the testimony taken the Board shall not be of the opinion that the person named in the complaint has engaged in or is engaging in any such unfair labor practice, or has willfully violated or is willfully

violating a final order as specified in subsection (b) of this section, then the Board shall state its findings of fact and shall issue an order dismissing the said complaint.";

(3) by adding at the end thereof the following new paragraphs:

"(2) If upon the preponderance of testimony taken the Board shall be of the opinion that the allegation in the complaint that a person has willfully violated or is willfully violating a final order as specified in subsection (b) of this section has been sustained, then the Board shall state its findings of fact and shall issue and cause to be served on such person an order certifying the identification of that person to the Secretary of Labor. Notwithstanding any other law, unless the Secretary of Labor determines that because of unusual circumstances the national interest requires otherwise, the Secretary shall certify the identity of such person to the Comptroller General. The Comptroller General shall distribute a list to all agencies of the United States containing the names of persons certified by the Secretary of Labor pursuant to this subsection. Unless the agency of the United States concerned, after notice and opportunity for hearing to all interested parties, certifies to the Secretary of Labor that there is no other source of material or services furnished by the person affected by the Board order, no contracts shall be awarded to such person for a reasonable, definitely stated period of time commensurate with the seriousness of the violation, as determined by the Secretary of Labor, but such period shall not exceed three years. A debarment may be removed or the period may be reduced by the Secretary of Labor upon the submission of an application, supported by documentary evidence, setting forth appropriate grounds for the granting of relief, including without limitation compliance with the final order found to have been willfully violated, bona fide change of ownership or management, a fraud or misrepresentation of the charging party: *Provided*, That this subparagraph shall restrict the award of contracts solely to the products or services performed at the particular facility or facilities where the willful violation occurs of the business entity legally responsible for the willful violation or to the local, intermediate, national or international labor organization legally responsible for the willful violation.

"(3) In a case in which the Board determines that any person has engaged in an unfair labor practice within the meaning of subsection (a)(1), (2)(3), (b)(1), or (b)(2) of section 8 which deprives an employee of employment while employees in a bargaining unit which includes that employee are seeking representation by a labor organization or during the period after a labor organization has first been recognized as a representative defined in subsection (a) of section 9 in such unit until the first collective-bargaining contract is entered into between the employer and the representative, the measure of backpay for the period until a valid offer of reinstatement is made shall be double the employee's wage rate at the time of the unfair labor practice less the wages the employee has earned during that period. In a case in which the Board determines that an unlawful refusal to bargain prior to the entry into the first collective-bargaining contract between the employer and the representative selected or designated by a majority of the employees in the bargaining unit has taken place, the Board may award to the employees in that unit compensation for the delay in bargaining caused by the unfair labor practice which shall be measured by the difference between (i) the wages and other benefits received by such employees during the period of delay, and (ii) the wages and fringe benefits such employees were receiving at the time of the unfair labor practice multiplied by the percentage change in wages and other benefits stated in the Bureau of Labor Statistics' average wage and benefit settlements, [sic] quarterly report of major collective-bargaining settlements, for the quarter in which the delay began. If the Secretary of Labor certifies to the Board that the Bureau has, subsequent to the effective date of the Labor Reform Act of 1977, instituted regular issuance of a statistical compilation of bargaining settlements which the Secretary determines would better effectuate the purposes of this subsection than the compilation specified herein, the Board shall, in administering this subsection, use the compilation certified by the Secretary.".

§9. (a) The third sentence of subsection 10(e) is amended by inserting immediately before the period at the end thereof a comma and the following: "nor shall any objection be considered by the court unless a petition for review pursuant to subsection (f) of this section has been timely filed by the party stating the objection".

(b) The fourth sentence of section 10(e) is amended to read as follows: "The findings of the Board with respect to questions of fact if supported by substantial evidence on the record considered as a whole shall be conclusive: *Provided*, That no finding of the Board that a representative is the exclusive representative of the employees in a unit for purposes of collective bargaining shall be accepted by the court unless such representative has been certified by the Board after a secret ballot election conducted in accordance with subsection (c) of section 9 or has been determined to be a representative defined in subsection (a) of section 9 by the Board in an order entered pursuant to subsection (c) of this section: *Provided further*, That no such order shall be entered where the employer has not engaged in conduct, unlawful under this Act, which undermines a free and fair election under subsection (c) of section 9: *Provided further*, That any representative designated or selected prior to the effective date of this Act shall remain such representative under this provision unless such designation or selection is withdrawn by the employees in the unit appropriate for the purposes of collective bargaining in an election under subsection (c) of section 9: *Provided further*, That where the employer agrees to recognize an individual or labor organization as a representative defined in subsection (a) of section 9 on the basis of proof of majority support other than a Board certification and such support is in fact demonstrated, the individual or labor organization so chosen shall be considered to be a representative for purposes of subsection (a) of section 9."

(c) The first sentence of subsection 10(f) is amended by—

(1) inserting "within thirty days" after "by filing", and

(2) inserting before the period at the end thereof the following: "except that, if a petition for review has been timely filed, any other party to that Board proceeding, aggrieved by the order, may, within fifteen days of service on it of said petition, file a further petition for review".

§10. The first sentence of section 10(l) is amended to read as follows:

"(l) Whenever it is charged that any person has engaged in an unfair labor practice within the meaning of—

"(1) subsection (a)(3) or (b)(2) of section 8 which deprives an employee of employment while employees in a bargaining unit which includes [sic] that employees are seeking representation by a labor organization or during the period after a labor organization has first been recognized as a representative defined in subsection (a) of section 9 in such unit until the first collective-bargaining contract is entered into between the employer and the representative, or

"(2) subsection 4(A), (B), or (C) of section 8(b) or section 8(e) or section 8(b)(7),

the preliminary investigation of such charge shall be made forthwith and given priority over all other cases except cases of like character in the office where it is filed or to which it is referred.".

§11. Section 10(m) is amended by inserting "under circumstances not subject to section 10(l)," after "section 8,".

§12. Section 10 of the National Labor Relations Act, as amended, is amended by adding at the end thereof the following new subsection:

"(n) Where there exists an agreement between an employer and a labor organization, whether express or implied, not to strike, picket or lockout, the Board, if it finds that the public interest would be served thereby, shall have the power to petition any district court of the United States (including the District Court of the United States for the District of Columbia) within any district where either or both of the parties reside or transact business, for such temporary injunctive relief or restraining order as is necessary to prevent any person not authorized by a representative of employees of the employer being struck or picketed within the meaning of subsection (a) of section 9 from engaging in, or inducing or encouraging any employee of the employer to engage in, conduct in breach of such agreement, irrespective of the nature of the dispute underlying such strike, picket or lockout, and such court shall have jurisdiction to grant to such party or the Board such temporary injunctive relief or restraining order as it deems just and proper.".

§13. Except as otherwise specifically provided in this Act, the amendments made by this Act shall take effect sixty days after the date of enactment of this Act.
Passed the House of Representatives October 6, 1977.

Postal Reorganization Act — Selected Provisions
84 Stat. 719, 39 U.S.C. §§101 et seq.

§1201. Definition

As used in this chapter, "guards" means —
(1) maintenance guards who, on the effective date of this chapter, are in key position KP-5 under the provisions of former section 3514 of title 39; and
(2) security guards, who may be employed in the Postal Service and whose primary duties shall include the exercise of authority to enforce rules to protect the safety of property, mail, or persons on the premises.

(Pub. L. 91-375, Aug. 12, 1970, 84 Stat. 733.)

§1202. Bargaining units

The National Labor Relations Board shall decide in each case the unit appropriate for collective bargaining in the Postal Service. The National Labor Relations Board shall not include in any bargaining unit —
(1) any management official or supervisor;
(2) any employee engaged in personnel work in other than a purely nonconfidential clerical capacity;
(3) both professional employees and employees who are not professional employees unless a majority of such professional employees vote for inclusion in such unit; or
(4) together with other employees, any individual employed as a security guard to enforce against employees and other persons, rules to protect property of the Postal Service or to protect the safety of property,

mail, or persons on the premises of the Postal Service; but no labor organization shall be certified as the representative of employees in a bargaining unit of security guards if such organization admits to membership, or is affiliated directly or indirectly with an organization which admits to membership, employees other than guards.

(Pub. L. 91-375, Aug. 12, 1970, 84 Stat. 733.)

§1203. Recognition of labor organizations

(a) The Postal Service shall accord exclusive recognition to a labor organization when the organization has been selected by a majority of the employees in an appropriate unit as their representative.

(b) Agreements and supplements in effect on the date of enactment of this section covering employees in the former Post Office Department shall continue to be recognized by the Postal Service until altered or amended pursuant to law.

(c) When a petition has been filed, in accordance with such regulations as may be prescribed by the National Labor Relations Board—

(1) by an employee, a group of employees, or any labor organization acting in their behalf, alleging that (A) a substantial number of employees wish to be represented for collective bargaining by a labor organization and that the Postal Service declines to recognize such labor organization as the representative; or (B) the labor organization which has been certified or is being currently recognized by the Postal Service as the bargaining representative is no longer a representative; or

(2) by the Postal Service, alleging that one or more labor organizations has presented to it a claim to be recognized as the representative;

the National Labor Relations Board shall investigate such petition and, if it has reasonable cause to believe that a question of representation exists, shall provide for an appropriate hearing upon due notice. Such hearing may be conducted by an officer or employee of the National Labor Relations Board, who shall not make any recommendations with respect thereto. If the National Labor Relations Board finds upon the record of such hearing that such a question of representation exists, it shall direct an election by secret ballot and shall certify the results thereof.

(d) A petition filed under subsection (c)(1) of this section shall be accompanied by a statement signed by at least 30 percent of the employees in the appropriate unit stating that they desire that an election be conducted for either of the purposes set forth in such subsection.

(e) Nothing in this section shall be construed to prohibit the waiving of hearings by stipulation for the purpose of a consent election in conformity with regulations and rules of decision of the National Labor Relations Board.

(Pub. L. 91-375, Aug. 12, 1970, 84 Stat. 734.)

§1204. Elections

(a) All elections authorized under this chapter shall be conducted under the supervision of the National Labor Relations Board, or persons designated by it, and shall be by secret ballot. Each employee eligible to vote shall be provided the opportunity to choose the labor organization he wishes to represent him, from among those on the ballot, or "no union".

(b) In any election where none of the choices on the ballot receives a majority, a runoff shall be conducted, the ballot providing for a selection between the 2 choices receiving the largest and second largest number of valid votes cast in the election. In the event of a tie vote, additional runoff elections shall be conducted until one of the choices has received a majority of the votes.

(c) No election shall be held in any bargaining unit within which, in the preceding 12-month period, a valid election has been held.

(Pub. L. 91-375, Aug. 12, 1970, 84 Stat. 735.)

§1205. Deductions of dues

(a) When a labor organization holds exclusive recognition, or when an organization of personnel not subject to collective-bargaining agreements has consultation rights under section 1004 of this title, the Postal Service shall deduct the regular and periodic dues of the organization from the pay of all members of the organization in the unit of recognition if the Post Office Department or the Postal Service has received from each employee, on whose account such deductions are made, a written assignment which shall be irrevocable for a period of not more than one year.

(b) Any agreement in effect immediately prior to the date of enactment of the Postal Reorganization Act between the Post Office Department and any organization of postal employees which provides for deduction by the Department of the regular and periodic dues of the organization from the pay of its members, shall continue in full force and effect and the obligation for such deductions shall be assumed by the Postal Service. No such deduction shall be made from the pay of any employee except on his written assignment, which shall be irrevocable for a period of not more than one year.

(Pub. L. 91-375, Aug. 12, 1970, 84 Stat. 735.)

§1206. Collective-bargaining agreements

(a) Collective-bargaining agreements between the Postal Service and bargaining representatives recognized under section 1203 of this title shall be effective for not less than 2 years.

(b) Collective-bargaining agreements between the Postal Service and bargaining representatives recognized under section 1203 may include any procedures for resolution by the parties of grievances and adverse actions arising under the agreement, including procedures culminating in binding third-party arbitration, or the parties may adopt any such procedures by mutual agreement in the event of a dispute.

(c) The Postal Service and bargaining representatives recognized under section 1203 may by mutual agreement adopt procedures for the resolution of disputes or impasses arising in the negotiation of a collective-bargaining agreement.

(Pub. L. 91-375, Aug. 12, 1970, 84 Stat. 735.)

§1207. Labor disputes

(a) If there is a collective-bargaining agreement in effect, no party to such agreement shall terminate or modify such agreement unless the party desiring such termination or modification serves written notice upon the other party to the agreement of the proposed termination or modification not less than 90 days prior to the expiration date thereof, or not less than 90 days prior to the time it is proposed to make such termination or modification. The party serving such notice shall notify the Federal Mediation and Conciliation Service of the existence of a dispute within 45 days of such notice, if no agreement has been reached by that time.

(b) If the parties fail to reach agreement or to adopt a procedure providing for a binding resolution of a dispute by the expiration date of the agreement in effect, or the date of the proposed termination or modification, the Director of the Federal Mediation and Conciliation Service shall direct the establishment of a factfinding panel consisting of 3 persons. For this purpose, he shall submit to the parties a list of not less than 15 names, from which list each party, within 10 days, shall select 1 person. The 2 so selected shall then choose from the list a third person who shall serve as chairman of the fact-finding panel. If either of the parties fails to select a person or if the 2 members are unable to agree on the third person within 3 days, the selection shall be made by the Director. The factfinding panel shall issue after due investigation a report of its findings, with or without recommendations, to the parties no later than 45 days from the date the list of names is submitted.

(c)(1) If no agreement is reached within 90 days after the expiration or termination of the agreement or the date on which the agreement became subject to modification under subsection (a) of this section, or if the parties decide upon arbitration but do not agree upon the procedures therefor, an arbitration board shall be established consisting of 3 members, not members of the factfinding panel, 1 of whom shall be selected by the Postal Service, 1 by the bargaining representative of the employees, and the third by the 2 thus selected. If either of the parties fails to select a member, or if the members chosen by the parties fail to agree on the third person within 5 days after their first meeting, the selection shall be made by the Director. If the parties do not agree on the framing of the issues to be submitted, the factfinding panel shall frame the issues and submit them to the arbitration board.

(2) The arbitration board shall give the parties a full and fair hearing, including an opportunity to present evidence in support of their claims, and an opportunity to present their case in person, by counsel or by other representative as they may elect. Decisions of the arbitration board shall be conclusive and binding upon the parties. The arbitration board shall render its decision within 45 days after its appointment.

(3) Costs of the arbitration board and factfinding panel shall be shared equally by the Postal Service and the bargaining representative.

(d) In the case of a bargaining unit whose recognized collective-bargaining representative does not have an agreement with the Postal Service, if the parties fail to reach agreement within 90 days of the commencement of collective bargaining, a factfinding panel will be established in accordance with the terms of subsection (b) of this section, unless the parties have previously agreed to another procedure for a binding resolution of their differences. If the parties fail to reach agreement within 180 days of the commencement of collective bargaining, and if they have not agreed to another procedure for binding resolution, an arbitration board shall be established to provide conclusive and binding arbitration in accordance with the terms of subsection (c) of this section.

(Pub. L. 91-375, Aug. 12, 1970, 84 Stat. 735.)

§1208. Suits

(a) The courts of the United States shall have jurisdiction with respect to actions brought by the National Labor Relations Board under this chapter to the same extent that they have jurisdiction with respect to actions under title 29.

(b) Suits for violation of contracts between the Postal Service and a labor organization representing Postal Service employees, or between any such labor organizations, may be brought in any district court of the United States having jurisdiction of the parties, without respect to the amount in controversy.

(c) A labor organization and the Postal Service shall be bound by the authorized acts of their agents. Any labor organization may sue or be sued as an entity and in behalf of the employees whom it represents in the courts of the United States. Any money judgment against a labor organization in a district court of the United States shall be enforcible only against the organization as an entity and against its assets, and shall not be enforcible against any individual member or his assets.

(d) For the purposes of actions and proceedings by or against labor organizations in the district courts of the United States, district courts shall be deemed to have jurisdiction of a labor organization (1) in the district in which such organization maintains its principal offices, or (2) in any district in which its duly authorized officers or agents are engaged in representing or acting for employee members.

(e) The service of summons, subpena, or other legal process of any court of the United States upon an officer or agent of a labor organization, in his capacity as such, shall constitute service upon the labor organization.

(Pub. L. 91-375, Aug. 12, 1970, 84 Stat. 736.)

§1209. Applicability of Federal labor laws

(a) Employee-management relations shall, to the extent not inconsistent with provisions of this title, be subject to the provisions of subchapter II of chapter 7 of title 29.

(b) The provisions of chapter 11 of title 29 shall be applicable to labor organizations that have or are seeking to attain recognition under section 1203 of this title, and to such organizations' officers, agents, shop stewards, other representatives, and members to the extent to which such provisions would be applicable if the Postal Service were an employer under section 402 of title 29. In addition to the authority conferred on him under section 438 of title 29, the Secretary of Labor shall have authority, by regulation issued with the written concurrence of the Postal Service, to prescribe simplified reports for any such labor organization. The Secretary of Labor may revoke such provision for simplified forms of any such labor organization if he determines, after such investigation as he deems proper and after due notice and opportunity for a hearing, that the purposes of this chapter and of chapter 11 of title 29 would be served thereby.

(c) Each employee of the Postal Service shall have the right, freely and without fear of penalty or reprisal, to form, join, and assist a labor organization or to refrain from any such activity, and each employee shall be protected in the exercise of this right.

(Pub. L. 91-375, Aug. 12, 1970, 84 Stat. 737.)

Worker Adjustment and Retraining Notification Act of 1988
102 Stat. 890 (1988), 29 U.S.C. §§2101-2109

§2. (§2101) Definitions; exclusions from definition of loss of employment

(a) *Definitions.*
As used in this chapter—

(1) the term "employer" means any business enterprise that employs—

(A) 100 or more employees, excluding part-time employees; or

(B) 100 or more employees who in the aggregate work at least 4,000 hours per week (exclusive of hours of overtime);

(2) the term "plant closing" means the permanent or temporary shutdown of a single site of employment, or one or more facilities or operating units within a single site of employment, if the shutdown results in an employment loss at the single site of employment during any 30-day period for 50 or more employees excluding any part-time employees;

(3) the term "mass layoff" means a reduction of force which—

(A) is not the result of a plant closing; and

(B) results in an employment loss at the single site of employment during any 30-day period for—

(i)(I) at least 33 percent of the employees (excluding any part-time employees); and

(II) at least 50 employees (excluding any part-time employee); or

(ii) at least 500 employees (excluding any part-time employees);

(4) the term "representative" means an exclusive representative of employees within the meaning of section 159(a) or 158(f) of this title or section 152 of Title 45;

(5) the term "affected employees" means employees who may reasonably be expected to experience an employment loss as a consequence of a proposed plant closing or mass layoff by their employer;

(6) subject to subsection (b) of this section, the term "employment loss" means (A) an employment termination, other than a discharge for cause, voluntary departure, or retirement, (B) a layoff exceeding 6 months, or (C) a reduction in hours of work of more than 50 percent during each month of any 6-month period;

(7) the term "unit of local government" means any general purpose political subdivision of a State which has the power to levy taxes and spend funds, as well as general corporate and police powers; and

Worker Adjustment and Retraining Notification Act of 1988

(8) the term "part-time employee" means an employee who is employed for an average of fewer than 20 hours per week or who has been employed for fewer than 6 of the 12 months preceding the date on which notice is required.

(b) *Exclusions from definition of employment loss.*

(1) In the case of a sale of part or all of an employer's business, the seller shall be responsible for providing notice for any plant closing or mass layoff in accordance with section 2102 of this title, up to and including the effective date of the sale. After the effective date of the sale of part or all of an employer's business, the purchaser shall be responsible for providing notice for any plant closing or mass layoff in accordance with section 2102 of this title. Notwithstanding any other provision of this chapter, any person who is an employee of the seller (other than a part-time employee) as of the effective date of the sale shall be considered an employee of the purchaser immediately after the effective date of the sale.

(2) Notwithstanding subsection (a)(6) of this section, an employee may not be considered to have experienced an employment loss if the closing or layoff is the result of the relocation or consolidation of part or all of the employer's business and, prior to the closing or layoff—

(A) the employer offers to transfer the employee to a different site of employment within a reasonable commuting distance with no more than a 6-month break in employment; or

(B) the employer offers to transfer the employee to any other site of employment regardless of distance with no more than a 6-month break in employment, and the employee accepts within 30 days of the offer or of the closing or layoff, whichever is later.

(Pub. L. 100-379, §2, Aug. 4, 1988, 102 Stat. 890.)

§3. (§2102) Notice required before plant closings and mass layoffs

(a) *Notice to employees, state dislocated worker units, and local governments.* An employer shall not order a plant closing or mass layoff until the end of a 60-day period after the employer serves written notice of such an order—

(1) to each representative of the affected employees as of the time of the notice or, if there is no such representative at that time, to each affected employee; and

(2) to the State dislocated worker unit (designated or created under title III of the Job Training Partnership Act [29 U.S.C. §1651 et seq.]) and the chief elected official of the unit of local government within which such closing or layoff is to occur.

If there is more than one such unit, the unit of local government which the employer shall notify is the unit of local government to which the employer pays the highest taxes for the year preceding the year for which the determination is made.

(b) *Reduction of notification period.*

(1) An employer may order the shutdown of a single site of employment before the conclusion of the 60-day period if as of the time that notice would have been required the employer was actively seeking capital or business which, if obtained, would have enabled the employer to avoid or postpone the shutdown and the employer reasonably and in good faith believed that giving the notice required would have precluded the employer from obtaining the needed capital or business.

(2)(A) An employer may order a plant closing or mass layoff before the conclusion of the 60-day period if the closing or mass layoff is caused by business circumstances that were not reasonably foreseeable as of the time that notice would have been required.

(B) No notice under this chapter shall be required if the plant closing or mass layoff is due to any form of natural disaster, such as a flood, earthquake, or the drought currently ravaging the farmlands of the United States.

(3) An employer relying on this subsection shall give as much notice as is practicable and at that time shall give a brief statement of the basis for reducing the notification period.

(c) *Extension of layoff period.* A layoff of more than 6 months which, at its outset, was announced to be a layoff of 6 months or less, shall be treated as an employment loss under this chapter unless—

(1) the extension beyond 6 months is caused by business circumstances (including unforeseeable changes in price or cost) not reasonably foreseeable at the time of the initial layoff; and

(2) notice is given at the time it becomes reasonably foreseeable that the extension beyond 6 months will be required.

(d) *Determination with respect to employment loss.* For purposes of this section, in determining whether a plant closing or mass layoff has occurred or will occur, employment losses for 2 or more groups at a single site of employment, each of which is less than the minimum number of employees specified in section 2101(a)(2) or (3) of this title but which in the aggregate exceed that minimum number, and which occur within any 90-day period shall be considered to be a plant closing or mass layoff unless the employer demonstrates that the employment losses are the result of separate and distinct actions and causes and are not an attempt by the employer to evade the requirements of this chapter.

(Pub. L. 100-379, §3, Aug. 4, 1988, 102 Stat. 891.)

Worker Adjustment and Retraining Notification Act of 1988

§4. (§2103) Exemptions

This chapter shall not apply to a plant closing or mass layoff if—

(1) the closing is of a temporary facility or the closing or layoff is the result of the completion of a particular project or undertaking, and the affected employees were hired with the understanding that their employment was limited to the duration of the facility or the project or undertaking; or

(2) the closing or layoff constitutes a strike or constitutes a lockout not intended to evade the requirements of this chapter. Nothing in this chapter shall require an employer to serve written notice pursuant to section 2102(a) of this title when permanently replacing a person who is deemed to be an economic striker under the National Labor Relations Act [29 U.S.C. §151 et seq.]: *Provided,* That nothing in this chapter shall be deemed to validate or invalidate any judicial or administrative ruling relating to the hiring of permanent replacements for economic strikers under the National Labor Relations Act.

(Pub. L. 100-379, §4, Aug. 4, 1988, 102 Stat. 892.)

§5. (§2104) Administration and enforcement of requirements

(a) *Civil actions against employers.*

(1) Any employer who orders a plant closing or mass layoff in violation of section 2102 of this title shall be liable to each aggrieved employee who suffers an employment loss as a result of such closing or layoff for—

(A) back pay for each day of violation at a rate of compensation not less than the higher of—

(i) the average regular rate received by such employee during the last 3 years of the employee's employment, or

(ii) the final regular rate received by such employee; and

(B) benefits under an employee benefit plan described in section 1002(3) of this title, including the cost of medical expenses incurred during the employment loss which would have been covered under an employee benefit plan if the employment loss had not occurred.

Such liability shall be calculated for the period of the violation, up to a maximum of 60 days, but in no event for more than one-half the number of days the employee was employed by the employer.

(2) The amount for which an employer is liable under paragraph (1) shall be reduced by—

(A) any wages paid by the employer to the employee for the period of the violation;

(B) any voluntary and unconditional payment by the employer to the employee that is not required by any legal obligation; and

(C) any payment by the employer to a third party or trustee (such as premiums for health benefits or payments to a defined contribution pension plan) on behalf of and attributable to the employee for the period of the violation.

In addition, any liability incurred under paragraph (1) with respect to a defined benefit pension plan may be reduced by crediting the employee with service for all purposes under such a plan for the period of the violation.

(3) Any employer who violates the provisions of section 2102 of this title with respect to a unit of local government shall be subject to a civil penalty of not more than $500 for each day of such violation, except that such penalty shall not apply if the employer pays to each aggrieved employee the amount for which the employer is liable to that employee within 3 weeks from the date the employer orders the shutdown or layoff.

(4) If an employer which has violated this chapter proves to the satisfaction of the court that the act or omission that violated this chapter was in good faith and that the employer had reasonable grounds for believing that the act or omission was not a violation of this chapter the court may, in its discretion, reduce the amount of the liability or penalty provided for in this section.

(5) A person seeking to enforce such liability, including a representative of employees or a unit of local government aggrieved under paragraph (1) or (3), may sue either for such person or for other persons similarly situated, or both, in any district court of the United States for any district in which the violation is alleged to have occurred, or in which the employer transacts business.

(6) In any such suit, the court, in its discretion, may allow the prevailing party a reasonable attorney's fee as part of the costs.

(7) For purposes of this subsection, the term, "aggrieved employee" means an employee who has worked for the employer ordering the plant closing or mass layoff and who, as a result of the failure by the employer to comply with section 2102 of this title did not receive timely notice either directly or through his or her representative as required by section 2102 of this title.

(b) *Exclusivity of remedies.* The remedies provided for in this section shall be the exclusive remedies for any violation of this chapter. Under this chapter, a Federal court shall not have authority to enjoin a plant closing or mass layoff.

(Pub. L. 100-379, §5, Aug. 4, 1988, 102 Stat. 893.)

Worker Adjustment and Retraining Notification Act of 1988

§6. (§2105) Procedure in addition to other rights of employees

The rights and remedies provided to employees by this chapter are in addition to, and not in lieu of, any other contractual or statutory rights and remedies of the employees, and are not intended to alter or affect such rights and remedies, except that the period of notification required by this chapter shall run concurrently with any period of notification required by contract or by any other statute.

(Pub. L. 100-379, §6, Aug. 4, 1988, 102 Stat. 894.)

§7. (§2106) Procedure encouraged where not required

It is the sense of Congress that an employer who is not required to comply with the notice requirements of section 2102 of this title should, to the extent possible, provide notice to its employees about a proposal to close a plant or permanently reduce its workforce.

(Pub. L. 100-379, §7, Aug. 4, 1988, 102 Stat. 894.)

§8. (§2107) Authority to prescribe regulations

(a) The Secretary of Labor shall prescribe such regulations as may be necessary to carry out this chapter. Such regulations shall, at a minimum, include interpretative regulations describing the methods by which employers may provide for appropriate service of notice as required by this chapter.

(b) The mailing of notice to an employee's last known address or inclusion of notice in the employee's paycheck will be considered acceptable methods for fulfillment of the employer's obligation to give notice to each affected employee under this chapter.

(Pub. L. 100-379, §8, Aug. 4, 1988, 102 Stat. 894.)

§9. (§2108) Effect on other laws

The giving of notice pursuant to this chapter, if done in good faith compliance with this chapter, shall not constitute a violation of the National Labor Relations Act [29 U.S.C. §151 et seq.] or the Railway Labor Act [45 U.S.C. §151 et seq.].

(Pub. L. 100-379, §9, Aug. 4, 1988, 102 Stat. 894.)

§10. (§2109) Report on employment and international competitiveness

Two years after Aug. 4, 1988, the Comptroller General shall submit to the Committee on Small Business of both the House and Senate, the Committee on Labor and Human Resources, and the Committee on Education and Labor a report containing a detailed and objective analysis of the effect of this chapter on employers (especially small- and medium-sized businesses), the economy (international competitiveness), and employees (in terms of levels and conditions of employment). The Comptroller General shall assess both costs and benefits, including the effect on productivity, competitiveness, unemployment rates and compensation, and worker retraining and readjustment.

(Pub. L. 100-379, §10, Aug. 4, 1988, 102 Stat. 894.)

United States Bankruptcy Code—Selected Provisions
92 Stat. 2549, as amended, 11 U.S.C. §§101 et seq.

§1113. Rejection of collective bargaining agreements*

(a) The debtor in possession, or the trustee if one has been appointed under the provisions of this chapter, other than a trustee in a case covered by subchapter IV of this chapter and by title I of the Railway Labor Act, may assume or reject a collective bargaining agreement only in accordance with the provisions of this section.

(b)(1) Subsequent to filing a petition and prior to filing an application seeking rejection of a collective bargaining agreement, the debtor in possession or trustee (hereinafter in this section, "trustee" shall include a debtor in possession), shall—

    (A) make a proposal to the authorized representative of the employees covered by such agreement, based on the most complete and reliable information available at the time of such proposal, which provides for those necessary modifications in the employees benefits and protections that are necessary to permit the reorganization of the debtor and assures that all creditors, the debtor and all of the affected parties are treated fairly and equitably; and

    (B) provide, subject to subsection (d)(3), the representative of the employees with such relevant information as is necessary to evaluate the proposal.

    (2) During the period beginning on the date of the making of a proposal provided for in paragraph (1) and ending on the date of the

---

*Section references are to the United States Code.—Eds.

hearing provided for in subsection (d)(1), the trustee shall meet, at reasonable times, with the authorized representative to confer in good faith in attempting to reach mutually satisfactory modifications of such agreement.

(c) The court shall approve an application for rejection of a collective bargaining agreement only if the court finds that—

(1) the trustee has, prior to the hearing, made a proposal that fulfills the requirements of subsection (b)(1);

(2) the authorized representative of the employees has refused to accept such proposal without good cause; and

(3) the balance of the equities clearly favors rejection of such agreement.

(d)(1) Upon the filing of an application for rejection the court shall schedule a hearing to be held not later than fourteen days after the date of the filing of such application. All interested parties may appear and be heard at such hearing. Adequate notice shall be provided to such parties at least ten days before the date of such hearing. The court may extend the time for the commencement of such hearing for a period not exceeding seven days where the circumstances of the case, and the interests of justice require such extension, or for additional periods of time to which the trustee and representative agree.

(2) The court shall rule on such application for rejection within thirty days after the date of the commencement of the hearing. In the interests of justice, the court may extend such time for ruling for such additional period as the trustee and the employees' representative may agree to. If the court does not rule on such application within thirty days after the date of the commencement of the hearing, or within such additional time as the trustee and the employees' representative may agree to, the trustee may terminate or alter any provisions of the collective bargaining agreement pending the ruling of the court on such application.

(3) The court may enter such protective orders, consistent with the need of the authorized representative of the employee to evaluate the trustee's proposal and the application for rejection, as may be necessary to prevent disclosure of information provided to such representative where such disclosure could compromise the position of the debtor with respect to its competitors in the industry in which it is engaged.

(e) If during a period when the collective bargaining agreement continues in effect, and if essential to the continuation of the debtor's business, or in order to avoid irreparable damage to the estate, the court, after notice and a hearing, may authorize the trustee to implement interim changes in the terms, conditions, wages, benefits, or work rules provided by a collective bargaining agreement. Any hearing under this paragraph shall be scheduled in accordance with the needs of the trustee. The implementation of such interim changes shall not render the application for rejection moot.

(f) No provision of this title shall be construed to permit a trustee to unilaterally terminate or alter any provisions of a collective bargaining agreement prior to compliance with the provisions of this section.

(Added Pub. L. 98-353, Title III, §541(a), July 10, 1984, 98 Stat. 390.)

§1114. Payment of insurance benefits to retired employees

(a) For purposes of this section, the term "retiree benefits" means payments to any entity or person for the purpose of providing or reimbursing payments for retired employees and their spouses and dependents, for medical, surgical, or hospital care benefits, or benefits in the event of sickness, accident, disability, or death under any plan, fund, or program (through the purchase of insurance or otherwise) maintained or established in whole or in part by the debtor prior to filing a petition commencing a case under this title.

(b)(1) For purposes of this section, the term "authorized representative" means the authorized representative designated pursuant to subsection (c) for persons receiving any retiree benefits covered by a collective bargaining agreement or subsection (d) in the case of persons receiving retiree benefits not covered by such an agreement.

(2) Committees of retired employees appointed by the court pursuant to this section shall have the same rights, powers, and duties as committees appointed under sections 1102 and 1103 of this title for the purpose of carrying out the purposes of sections 1114 and 1129(a)(13) and, as permitted by the court, shall have the power to enforce the rights of persons under this title as they relate to retiree benefits.

(c)(1) A labor organization shall be, for purposes of this section, the authorized representative of those persons receiving any retiree benefits covered by any collective bargaining agreement to which that labor organization is signatory, unless (A) such labor organization elects not to serve as the authorized representative of such persons, or (B) the court, upon a motion by any party in interest, after notice and hearing, determines that different representation of such persons is appropriate.

(2) In cases where the labor organization referred to in paragraph (1) elects not to serve as the authorized representative of those persons receiving any retiree benefits covered by any collective bargaining agreement to which that labor organization is signatory, or in cases where the court, pursuant to paragraph (1) finds different representation of such persons appropriate, the court, upon a motion by any party in interest, and after notice and a hearing, shall appoint a committee of retired employees if the debtor seeks to modify or not pay the retiree benefits or if the court otherwise determines that it is appropriate, from among such

persons, to serve as the authorized representative of such persons under this section.

(d) The court, upon a motion by any party in interest, and after notice and a hearing, shall appoint a committee of retired employees if the debtor seeks to modify or not pay the retiree benefits or if the court otherwise determines that it is appropriate, to serve as the authorized representative, under this section, of those persons receiving any retiree benefits not covered by a collective bargaining agreement.

(e)(1) Notwithstanding any other provision of this title, the debtor in possession, or the trustee if one has been appointed under the provisions of this chapter (hereinafter in this section "trustee" shall include a debtor in possession), shall timely pay and shall not modify any retiree benefits, except that—

> (A) the court, on motion of the trustee or authorized representative, and after notice and a hearing, may order modification of such payments, pursuant to the provisions of subsections (g) and (h) of this section, or
>
> (B) the trustee and the authorized representative of the recipients of those benefits may agree to modification of such payments,

after which such benefits as modified shall continue to be paid by the trustee.

> (2) Any payment for retiree benefits required to be made before a plan confirmed under section 1129 of this title is effective has the status of an allowed administrative expense as provided in section 503 of this title.

(f)(1) Subsequent to filing a petition and prior to filing an application seeking modification of the retiree benefits, the trustee shall—

> (A) make a proposal to the authorized representative of the retirees, based on the most complete and reliable information available at the time of such proposal, which provides for those necessary modifications in the retiree benefits that are necessary to permit the reorganization of the debtor and assures that all creditors, the debtor and all of the affected parties are treated fairly and equitably; and
>
> (B) provide, subject to subsection (k)(3), the representative of the retirees with such relevant information as is necessary to evaluate the proposal.
>
> (2) During the period beginning on the date of the making of a proposal provided for in paragraph (1), and ending on the date of the hearing provided for in subsection (k)(1), the trustee shall meet, at reasonable times, with the authorized representative to confer in good faith in attempting to reach mutually satisfactory modifications of such retiree benefits.

(g) The court shall enter an order providing for modification in the payment of retiree benefits if the court finds that—

(1) the trustee has, prior to the hearing, made a proposal that fulfills the requirements of subsection (f);

(2) the authorized representative of the retirees has refused to accept such proposal without good cause; and

(3) such modification is necessary to permit the reorganization of the debtor and assures that all creditors, the debtor, and all of the affected parties are treated fairly and equitably, and is clearly favored by the balance of the equities;

except that in no case shall the court enter an order providing for such modification which provides for a modification to a level lower than that proposed by the trustee in the proposal found by the court to have complied with the requirements of this subsection and subsection (f): *Provided, however,* That at any time after an order is entered providing for modification in the payment of retiree benefits, or at any time after an agreement modifying such benefits is made between the trustee and the authorized representative of the recipients of such benefits, the authorized representative may apply to the court for an order increasing those benefits which order shall be granted if the increase in retiree benefits sought is consistent with the standard set forth in paragraph (3): *Provided further,* That neither the trustee nor the authorized representative is precluded from making more than one motion for a modification order governed by this subsection.

(h)(1) Prior to a court issuing a final order under subsection (g) of this section, if essential to the continuation of the debtor's business, or in order to avoid irreparable damage to the estate, the court, after notice and a hearing, may authorize the trustee to implement interim modifications in retiree benefits.

(2) Any hearing under this subsection shall be scheduled in accordance with the needs of the trustee.

(3) The implementation of such interim changes does not render the motion for modification moot.

(i) No retiree benefits paid between the filing of the petition and the time a plan confirmed under section 1129 of this title becomes effective shall be deducted or offset from the amounts allowed as claims for any benefits which remain unpaid, or from the amounts to be paid under the plan with respect to such claims for unpaid benefits, whether such claims for unpaid benefits are based upon or arise from a right to future unpaid benefits or from any benefits not paid as a result of modifications allowed pursuant to this section.

(j) No claim for retiree benefits shall be limited by section 502(b)(7) of this title.

(k)(1) Upon the filing of an application for modifying retiree benefits, the court shall schedule a hearing to be held not later than fourteen days after the date of the filing of such application. All interested parties may appear and be heard at such hearing. Adequate notice shall be provided to such parties at least ten days before the date of such hearing. The court may extend the time for the commencement of such hearing for a period not exceeding seven days where the circumstances of the case, and the interests of justice require such extension, or for additional periods of time to which the trustee and the authorized representative agree.

(2) The court shall rule on such application for modification within ninety days after the date of the commencement of the hearing. In the interests of justice, the court may extend such time for ruling for such additional period as the trustee and the authorized representative may agree to. If the court does not rule on such application within ninety days after the date of the commencement of the hearing, or within such additional time as the trustee and the authorized representative may agree to, the trustee may implement the proposed modifications pending the ruling of the court on such application.

(3) The court may enter such protective orders, consistent with the need of the authorized representative of the retirees to evaluate the trustee's proposal and the application for modification, as may be necessary to prevent disclosure of information provided to such representative where such disclosure could compromise the position of the debtor with respect to its competitors in the industry in which it is engaged.

(*l*) This section shall not apply to any retiree, or the spouse or dependents of such retiree, if such retiree's gross income for the twelve months preceding the filing of the bankruptcy petition equals or exceeds $250,000, unless such retiree can demonstrate to the satisfaction of the court that he is unable to obtain health, medical, life, and disability coverage for himself, his spouse, and his dependents who would otherwise be covered by the employer's insurance plan, comparable to the coverage provided by the employer on the day before the filing of a petition under this title.

(Added Pub. L. 100-334, §2(a), June 16, 1988, 102 Stat. 610.)

§1167. Collective bargaining agreements

Notwithstanding section 365 of this title, neither the court nor the trustee may change the wages or working conditions of employees of the debtor established by a collective bargaining agreement that is subject to the Railway Labor Act except in accordance with section 6 of such Act.

(Pub. L. 95-598, Nov. 6, 1978, 92 Stat. 2642; Pub. L. 103-394, §501(d), October 22, 1994, 108 Stat. 4106.)

Montana Wrongful Discharge from Employment Act of 1987
Mont. Rev. Stat. §§39-2-901 to 39-2-915

§39-2-901. Short title

This part may be cited as the "Wrongful Discharge From Employment Act".

§39-2-902. Purpose

This part sets forth certain rights and remedies with respect to wrongful discharge. Except as limited in this part, employment having no specified term may be terminated at the will of either the employer or the employee on notice to the other for any reason considered sufficient by the terminating party. Except as provided in 39-2-912, this part provides the exclusive remedy for a wrongful discharge from employment.

§39-2-903. Definitions

In this part, the following definitions apply:

(1) "Constructive discharge" means the voluntary termination of employment by an employee because of a situation created by an act or omission of the employer which an objective, reasonable person would find so intolerable that voluntary termination is the only reasonable alternative. Constructive discharge does not mean voluntary termination because of an employer's refusal to promote the employee or improve wages, responsibilities, or other terms and conditions of employment.

(2) "Discharge" includes a constructive discharge as defined in subsection (1) and any other termination of employment, including resignation, elimination of the job, layoff for lack of work, failure to recall or rehire, and any other cutback in the number of employees for a legitimate business reason.

(3) "Employee" means a person who works for another for hire. The term does not include a person who is an independent contractor.

(4) "Fringe benefits" means the value of any employer-paid vacation leave, sick leave, medical insurance plan, disability insurance plan, life insurance plan, and pension benefit plan in force on the date of the termination.

(5) "Good cause" means reasonable job-related grounds for dismissal based on a failure to satisfactorily perform job duties, disruption of the

employer's operation, or other legitimate business reason. The legal use of a lawful product by an individual off the employer's premises during non-working hours is not a legitimate business reason, unless the employer acts within the provisions of 39-2-313 (3) or (4).

(6) "Lost wages" means the gross amount of wages that would have been reported to the internal revenue service [sic] as gross income on Form W-2 and includes additional compensation deferred at the option of the employee.

(7) "Public policy" means a policy in effect at the time of the discharge concerning the public health, safety, or welfare established by constitutional provision, statute, or administrative rule.

§39-2-904. Elements of wrongful discharge

A discharge is wrongful only if:

(1) it was in retaliation for the employee's refusal to violate public policy or for reporting a violation of public policy;

(2) the discharge was not for good cause and the employee had completed the employer's probationary period of employment; or

(3) the employer violated the express provisions of its own written personnel policy.

§39-2-905. Remedies

(1) If an employer has committed a wrongful discharge, the employee may be awarded lost wages and fringe benefits for a period not to exceed 4 years from the date of discharge, together with interest thereon. Interim earnings, including amounts the employee could have earned with reasonable diligence, must be deducted from the amount awarded for lost wages. Before interim earnings are deducted from lost wages, there must be deducted from the interim earnings any reasonable amounts expended by the employee in searching for, obtaining, or relocating to new employment.

(2) The employee may recover punitive damages otherwise allowed by law if it is established by clear and convincing evidence that the employer engaged in actual fraud or actual malice in the discharge of the employee in violation of 39-2-904(1).

(3) There is no right under any legal theory to damages for wrongful discharge under this part for pain and suffering, emotional distress, compensatory damages, punitive damages, or any other form of damages, except as provided for in subsections (1) and (2).

(§§39-2-906 through 39-2-910 reserved.)

§39-2-911. Limitation of actions

(1) An action under this part must be filed within 1 year after the date of discharge.

(2) If an employer maintains written internal procedures, other than those specified in 39-2-912, under which an employee may appeal a discharge within the organizational structure of the employer, the employee shall first exhaust those procedures prior to filing an action under this part. The employee's failure to initiate or exhaust available internal procedures is a defense to an action brought under this part. If the employer's internal procedures are not completed within 90 days from the date the employee initiates the internal procedures, the employee may file an action under this part and for purposes of this subsection the employer's internal procedures are considered exhausted. The limitation period in subsection (1) is tolled until the procedures are exhausted. In no case may the provisions of the employer's internal procedures extend the limitation period in subsection (1) more than 120 days.

(3) If the employer maintains written internal procedures under which an employee may appeal a discharge within the organizational structure of the employer, the employer shall within 7 days of the date of the discharge notify the discharged employee of the existence of such procedures and shall supply the discharged employee with a copy of them. If the employer fails to comply with this subsection, the discharged employee need not comply with subsection (2).

§39-2-912. Exemptions

This part does not apply to a discharge:

(1) that is subject to any other state or federal statute that provides a procedure or remedy for contesting the dispute. Such statutes include those that prohibit discharge for filing complaints, charges, or claims with administrative bodies or that prohibit unlawful discrimination based on race, national origin, sex, age, handicap, creed, religion, political belief, color, marital status, and other similar grounds.

(2) of an employee covered by a written collective bargaining agreement or a written contract of employment for a specific term.

§39-2-913. Preemption of common-law remedies

Except as provided in this part, no claim for discharge may arise from tort or express or implied contract.

Labour Relations Act of Ontario

§39-2-913. Arbitration

(1) A party may make a written offer to arbitrate a dispute that otherwise could be adjudicated under this part.

(2) An offer to arbitrate must be in writing and contain the following provisions:

    (a) A neutral arbitrator must be selected by mutual agreement or, in the absence of agreement, as provided in 27-5-211.

    (b) The arbitration must be governed by the Uniform Arbitration Act, Title 27, chapter 5. If there is a conflict between the Uniform Arbitration Act and this part, this part applies.

    (c) The arbitrator is bound by this part.

(3) If a complaint is filed under this part, the offer to arbitrate must be made within 60 days after service of the complaint and must be accepted in writing within 30 days after the date the offer is made.

(4) A discharged employee who makes a valid offer to arbitrate that is accepted by the employer and who prevails in such arbitration is entitled to have the arbitrator's fee and all costs of arbitration paid by the employer.

(5) If a valid offer to arbitrate is made and accepted, arbitration is the exclusive remedy for the wrongful discharge dispute and there is no right to bring or continue a lawsuit under this part. The arbitrator's award is final and binding, subject to review of the arbitrator's decision under the provisions of the Uniform Arbitration Act.

§39-2-915. Effect of rejection of offer to arbitrate

A party who makes a valid offer to arbitrate that is not accepted by the other party and who prevails in an action under this part is entitled as an element of costs to reasonable attorney fees incurred subsequent to the date of the offer.

Labour Relations Act of Ontario—Selected Provisions
Bill 7, ch. 1, R.S.O., 1st Sess., 36th Legislature, 44 Eliz. II, 1995

Schedule A

1. (1) In this Act,

"accredited employers' organization" means an organization of employers that is accredited under this Act as the bargaining agent for a unit of employers; ("association patronale accréditée") "agriculture" includes farming in all its branches, including dairying, beekeeping, aquaculture, the raising of livestock including non-traditional livestock, furbearing animals and poultry, the production, cultivation, growing and harvesting of agricultural commodities, including eggs, maple products, mushrooms and tobacco, and any practices performed as an integral part of an agricultural operation, but does not include anything that was not or would not have been determined to be agriculture under section 2 of the predecessor to this Act as it read on June 22, 1994; ("agriculture")

"bargaining unit" means a unit of employees appropriate for collective bargaining, whether it is an employer unit or a plant unit or a subdivision of either of them; ("unité de négociation")

"Board" means the Ontario Labour Relations Board; ("Commission")

"certified council of trade unions" means a council of trade unions that is certified under this Act as the bargaining agent for a bargaining unit of employees of an employer; ("conseil de syndicats accrédité")

"collective agreement" means an agreement in writing between an employer or an employers' organization, on the one hand, and a trade union that, or a council of trade unions that, represents employees of the employer or employees of members of the employers' organization, on the other hand, containing provisions respecting terms or conditions of employment or the rights, privileges or duties of the employer, the employers' organization, the trade union or the employees, and includes a provincial agreement; ("convention collective")

"construction industry" means the businesses that are engaged in constructing, altering, decorating, repairing or demolishing buildings, structures, roads, sewers, water or gas mains, pipe lines, tunnels, bridges, canals or other works at the site; ("industrie de la construction")

"council of trade unions" includes an allied council, a trades council, a joint board and any other association of trade unions; ("conseil de syndicats")

"dependent contractor" means a person, whether or not employed under a contract of employment, and whether or not furnishing tools, vehicles, equipment, machinery, material, or any other thing owned by the dependent contractor, who performs work or services for another person for compensation or reward on such terms and conditions that the dependent contractor is in a position of economic dependence upon, and under an obligation to perform duties for, that person more closely resembling the relationship of an employee than that of an independent contractor; ("entrepreneur dépendant")

"employee" includes a dependent contractor; ("employé")

"employers' organization" means an organization of employers formed for purposes that include the regulation of relations between employers and employees and includes an accredited employers' organization and a designated or accredited employer bargaining agency; ("association patronale")

"lock-out" includes the closing of a place of employment, a suspension of work or a refusal by an employer to continue to employ a number of employees, with a view to compel or induce the employees, or to aid another employer to compel or induce that employer's employees, to refrain from exercising any rights or privileges under this Act or to agree to provisions or changes in provisions respecting terms or conditions of employment or the rights, privileges or duties of the employer, an employers' organization, the trade union, or the employees; ("lock-out")

"member", when used with reference to a trade union, includes a person who has applied for membership in the trade union; ("membre")

"Minister" means the Minister of Labour; ("ministre")

"professional engineer" means an employee who is a member of the engineering profession entitled to practise in Ontario and employed in a professional capacity; ("ingénieur")

"strike" includes a cessation of work, a refusal to work or to continue to work by employees in combination or in concert or in accordance with a common understanding, or a slow-down or other concerted activity on the part of employees designed to restrict or limit output; ("grève")

"trade union" means an organization of employees formed for purposes that include the regulation of relations between employees and employers and includes a provincial, national, or international trade union, a certified council of trade unions and a designated or certified employee bargaining agency. ("syndicat") R.S.O. 1990, c. L.2, s. 1 (1); 1993, c. 27, Sched., *amended.*

(2) For the purposes of this Act, no person shall be deemed to have ceased to be an employee by reason only of the person's ceasing to work for the person's employer as the result of a lock-out or strike or by reason only of being dismissed by the person's employer contrary to this Act or to a collective agreement.

(3) Subject to section 97, for the purposes of this Act, no person shall be deemed to be an employee,

(a) who is a member of the architectural, dental, land surveying, legal or medical profession entitled to practise in Ontario and employed in a professional capacity; or

(b) who, in the opinion of the Board, exercises managerial functions or is employed in a confidential capacity in matters relating to labour relations.

(4) Where, in the opinion of the Board, associated or related activities or businesses are carried on, whether or not simultaneously, by or through more than one corporation, individual, firm, syndicate or association or any combination thereof, under common control or direction, the Board may, upon the application of any person, trade union or council of trade unions concerned, treat the corporations, individuals, firms, syndicates or associations or any combination thereof as constituting one employer for the purposes of this Act and grant such relief, by way of declaration or otherwise as it may deem appropriate.

(5) Where, in an application made pursuant to subsection (4), it is alleged that more than one corporation, individual, firm, syndicate or association or any combination thereof are or were under common control or direction, the respondents to the application shall adduce at the hearing all facts within their knowledge that are material to the allegation. R.S.O. 1990, c. L.2, s. 1(2-5).

Purposes and Application of Act

2. The following are the purposes of the Act:

1. To facilitate collective bargaining between employers and trade unions that are the freely-designated representatives of the employees.
2. To recognize the importance of workplace parties adapting to change.
3. To promote flexibility, productivity and employee involvement in the workplace.
4. To encourage communication between employers and employees in the workplace.
5. To recognize the importance of economic growth as the foundation for mutually beneficial relations amongst employers, employees and trade unions.
6. To encourage co-operative participation of employers and trade unions in resolving workplace issues.
7. To promote the expeditious resolution of workplace disputes. *New.*

3. This Act does not apply,
   (a) to a domestic employed in a private home;
   (b) to a person employed in agriculture, hunting or trapping;
   (c) to a person, other than an employee of a municipality or a person employed in silviculture, who is employed in horticulture by an employer whose primary business is agriculture or horticulture;
   (d) to a member of a police force within the meaning of the *Police Services Act;*
   (e) to a full-time firefighter within the meaning of the *Fire Departments Act;*

(f) to a teacher as defined in the *School Boards and Teachers Collective Negotiations Act*, expect as provided in that Act;

(g) to a member of the Ontario Provincial Police Force;

(h) to an employee within the meaning of the *Colleges Collective Bargaining Act*;

(i) to a provincial judge; or

(j) to a person employed as a labour mediator or labour conciliator. R.S.O. 1990, c. L.2, s. 2; 1993, c. 38, s. 67(1), *amended.*

4. (1) This Act binds agencies of the Crown other than,

(a) those that employ Crown employees as defined in the *Public Service Act*; and

(b) those that are designated under clause 29.1(1)(a) of the *Public Service Act.*

(2) Except as provided in subsection (1), this Act does not bind the Crown. *New.*

Freedoms

5. Every person is free to join a trade union of the person's own choice and to participate in its lawful activities. R.S.O. 1990, c. L.2, s. 3.

6. Every person is free to join an employers' organization of the person's own choice and to participate in its lawful activities. R.S.O. 1990, c. L.2, s. 4.

Establishment of Bargaining Rights by Certification

7. (1) Where no trade union has been certified as bargaining agent of the employees of an employer in a unit that a trade union claims to be appropriate for collective bargaining and the employees in the unit are not bound by a collective agreement, a trade union may apply at any time to the Board for certification as bargaining agent of the employees in the unit. R.S.O. 1990, c. L.2, s. 5(1), *amended.*

(2) Where a trade union has been certified as bargaining agent of the employees of an employer in a bargaining unit and has not entered into a collective agreement with the employer and no declaration has been made by the Board that the trade union no longer represents the employees in the bargaining unit, another trade union may apply to the Board for certification as bargaining agent of any of the employees in the bargaining unit determined in the certificate only after the expiration of one year from the date of the certificate. R.S.O. 1990, c. L.2, s. 5(2), *amended.*

(3) Where an employer and a trade union agree that the employer recognizes the trade union as the exclusive bargaining agent of the employees in a defined bargaining unit and the agreement is in writing signed by the parties and the parties have not entered into a collective agreement and the Board has not made a declaration under section 66, another trade union may apply to the Board for certification as bargaining agent of any of the employees in the bargaining unit defined in the recognition agreement only after the expiration of one year from the date that the recognition agreement was entered into. R.S.O. 1990, c. L.2, s. 5(3), *amended.*

(4) Where a collective agreement is for a term of not more than three years, a trade union may apply to the Board for certification as bargaining agent of any of the employees in the bargaining unit defined in the agreement only after the commencement of the last two months of its operation. R.S.O. 1990, c. L.2, s. 5(4), *amended.*

(5) Where a collective agreement is for a term of more than three years, a trade union may apply to the Board for certification as bargaining agent of any of the employees in the bargaining unit defined in the agreement only after the commencement of the 35th month of its operation and before the commencement of the 37th month of its operation and during the two-month period immediately preceding the end of each year that the agreement continues to operate thereafter or after the commencement of the last two months of its operation, as the case may be. R.S.O. 1990, c. L.2, s. 5(5), *amended.*

(6) Where a collective agreement referred to in subsection (4) or (5) provides that it will continue to operate for a further term or successive terms if either party fails to give to the other notice of termination or of its desire to bargain with a view to the renewal, with or without modifications, of the agreement or to the making of a new agreement, a trade union may apply to the Board for certification as bargaining agent of any of the employees in the bargaining unit defined in the agreement during the further term or successive terms only during the last two months of each year that it so continues to operate, or after the commencement of the last two months of its operation, as the case may be. R.S.O. 1990, c. L.2, s. 5(6), *amended.*

(7) The right of a trade union to apply for certification under this section is subject to subsection 10(3), section 67 and subsection 160(3).

(8) An application for certification may be withdrawn by the applicant upon such conditions as the Board may determine.

(9) If the trade union withdraws the application before a representation vote is taken, the Board may refuse to consider another application for certification by the trade union as the bargaining agent of the employees in the proposed bargaining unit until one year or such shorter period as the Board considers appropriate has elapsed after the application is withdrawn.

(10) If the trade union withdraws the application after the representation vote is taken, the Board shall not consider another application for

certification by the trade union as the bargaining agent of the employees in the proposed bargaining unit until one year has elapsed after the application is withdrawn.

(11) The trade union shall deliver a copy of the application for certification to the employer by such time as is required under the rules made by the Board and, if there is no rule, not later than the day on which the application is filed with the Board.

(12) The application for certification shall include a written description of the proposed bargaining unit including an estimate of the number of individuals in the unit.

(13) The application for certification shall be accompanied by a list of the names of the union members in the proposed bargaining unit and evidence of their status as union members, but the trade union shall not give this information to the employer.

(14) If the employer disagrees with the description of the proposed bargaining unit, the employer may give the Board a written description of the bargaining unit that the employer proposes and shall do so within two days (excluding Saturdays, Sundays and holidays) after the day on which the employer receives the application for certification. *New.*

8. (1) Upon receiving an application for certification, the Board may determine the voting constituency to be used for a representation vote and in doing so shall take into account,

(a) the description of the proposed bargaining unit included in the application for certification; and

(b) the description, if any, of the bargaining unit that the employer proposes.

(2) If the Board determines that 40 per cent or more of the individuals in the bargaining unit proposed in the application for certification appear to be members of the union at the time the application was filed, the Board shall direct that a representation vote be taken among the individuals in the voting constituency.

(3) The number of individuals in the proposed bargaining unit who appear to be members of the trade union shall be determined with reference only to the information provided in the application for certification and the accompanying information provided under subsection 7(13).

(4) The Board shall not hold a hearing when making a decision under subsection (1) or (2).

(5) Unless the Board directs otherwise, the representation vote shall be held within five days (excluding Saturdays, Sundays and holidays) after the day on which the application for certification is filed with the Board.

(6) The representation vote shall be by ballots cast in such a manner that individuals expressing their choice cannot be identified with the choice made.

(7) The Board may direct that one or more ballots be segregated and that the ballot box containing the ballots be sealed until such time as the Board directs.

(8) After the representation vote has been taken, the Board may hold a hearing if the Board considers it necessary in order to dispose of the application for certification.

(9) When disposing of an application for certification, the Board shall not consider any challenge to the information provided under subsection 7(13). *New.*

9. (1) Subject to subsection (2), upon an application for certification, the Board shall determine the unit of employees that is appropriate for collective bargaining, but in every case the unit shall consist of more than one employee and the Board may, before determining the unit, conduct a vote of any of the employees of the employer for the purpose of ascertaining the wishes of the employees as to the appropriateness of the unit.

(2) Where, upon an application for certification, the Board is satisfied that any dispute as to the composition of the bargaining unit cannot affect the trade union's right to certification, the Board may certify the trade union as the bargaining agent pending the final resolution of the composition of the bargaining unit.

(3) Any group of employees who exercise technical skills or who are members of a craft by reason of which they are distinguishable from the other employees and commonly bargain separately and apart from other employees through a trade union that according to established trade union practice pertains to such skills or crafts shall be deemed by the Board to be a unit appropriate for collective bargaining if the application is made by a trade union pertaining to the skills or craft, and the Board may include in the unit persons who according to established trade union practice are commonly associated in their work and bargaining with the group, but the Board shall not be required to apply this subsection where the group of employees is included in a bargaining unit represented by another bargaining agent at the time the application is made.

(4) A bargaining unit consisting solely of professional engineers shall be deemed by the Board to be a unit of employees appropriate for collective bargaining, but the Board may include professional engineers in a bargaining unit with other employees if the Board is satisfied that a majority of the professional engineers wish to be included in the bargaining unit.

(5) A bargaining unit consisting solely of dependent contractors shall be deemed by the Board to be a unit of employees appropriate for collective bargaining but the Board may include dependent contractors in a bargaining unit with other employees if the Board is satisfied that a majority of the dependent contractors wish to be included in the bargaining unit. R.S.O. 1990, c. L.2, s. 6.

Labour Relations Act of Ontario

10. (1) The Board shall certify a trade union as the bargaining agent of the employees in a bargaining unit that is determined by the Board to be appropriate for collective bargaining if more than 50 per cent of the ballots cast in the representation vote by the employees in the bargaining unit are cast in favour of the trade union.

(2) The Board shall not certify the trade union as bargaining agent and shall dismiss the application for certification if 50 per cent or less of the ballots cast in the representation vote by the employees in the bargaining unit are cast in favour of the trade union.

(3) If the Board dismisses an application for certification under this section, the Board shall not consider another application for certification by the trade union as the bargaining agent of the employees in the bargaining unit until one year has elapsed after the dismissal. *New.*

11. (1) Upon the application of a trade union, the Board may certify the trade union as the bargaining agent for the employees in a bargaining unit in the following circumstances:

1. An employer, employers' organization or person acting on behalf of an employer or employers' organization has contravened the Act.
2. The result of the contravention is that a representation vote does not or would not likely reflect the true wishes of the employees in the bargaining unit about being represented by the trade union.
3. No other remedy, including the taking of another representation vote, is sufficient to counter the effects of the contravention.
4. The trade union has membership support adequate for the purposes of collective bargaining in a bargaining unit found by the Board to be appropriate for collective bargaining.

(2) Upon the application of an interested person, the Board may dismiss an application for certification of a trade union as the bargaining agent for the employees in a bargaining unit in the following circumstances:

1. A trade union, council of trade unions or person acting on behalf of a trade union or council of trade unions has contravened the Act.
2. The result of the contravention is that a representation vote does not or would not likely reflect the true wishes of the employees in the bargaining unit about being represented by the trade union.
3. No other remedy, including the taking of another representation vote, is sufficient to counter the effects of the contravention.

(3) The Board may consider the results of a representation vote when making a decision under this section.

(4) Subsections 10 (1) and (2) do not apply with respect to a representation vote taken in the circumstances described in this section. *New.*

12. (1) Sections 7 to 15, 126 and 128 apply with necessary modifications to an application for certification by a council of trade unions, but, before the Board certifies such a council as bargaining agent for the employees of an employer in a bargaining unit, the Board shall satisfy itself that each of the trade unions that is a constituent union of the council has vested appropriate authority in the council to enable it to discharge the responsibilities of a bargaining agent.

(2) Where the Board is of opinion that appropriate authority has not been vested in the applicant, the Board may postpone disposition of the application to enable the constituent unions to vest such additional or other authority as the Board considers necessary. R.S.O. 1990, c. L.2, s. 10(1, 2).

(3) For the purposes of sections 7 and 8, a person who is a member of any constituent trade union of a council shall be deemed by the Board to be a member of the council. R.S.O. 1990, c. L.2, s. 10(3), *amended.*

13. Where employees of an employer reside on the property of the employer, or on property to which the employer has the right to control access, the employer shall, upon a direction from the Board, allow the representative of a trade union access to the property on which the employees reside for the purpose of attempting to persuade the employees to join a trade union. R.S.O. 1990, c. L.2, s. 11.

14. (1) This section applies with respect to guards who monitor other employees or who protect the property of an employer.

(2) Unless the employer notifies the Board that it objects, a trade union that admits to membership persons who are not guards or that is chartered by or affiliated with an organization that does so may be certified as the bargaining agent for a bargaining unit composed solely of guards.

(3) Unless the employer notifies the Board that it objects, a bargaining unit may include guards and persons who are not guards.

(4) If the employer objects, the trade union must satisfy the Board that no conflict of interest would result from the trade union becoming the bargaining agent or from including persons other than guards in the bargaining unit.

(5) The Board shall consider the following factors in determining whether a conflict of interest would result:

1. The extent of the guards' duties monitoring other employees of their employer or protecting their employer's property.
2. Any other duties or responsibilities of the guards that might give rise to a conflict of interest.
3. Such other factors as the Board considers relevant.

(6) If the Board is satisfied that no conflict of interest would result, the Board may certify the trade union to represent the bargaining unit. *New.*

Labour Relations Act of Ontario

15. The Board shall not certify a trade union if any employer or any employers' organization has participated in its formation or administration or has contributed financial or other support to it or if it discriminates against any person because of any ground of discrimination prohibited by the *Human Rights Code* or the *Canadian Charter of Rights and Freedoms*. R.S.O. 1990, c. L.2, s. 13.

Negotiation of Collective Agreements

16. Following certification or the voluntary recognition by the employer of the trade union as bargaining agent for the employees in the bargaining unit, the trade union shall give the employer written notice of its desire to bargain with a view to making a collective agreement. *New.*

17. The parties shall meet within 15 days from the giving of the notice or within such further period as the parties agree upon and they shall bargain in good faith and make every reasonable effort to make a collective agreement. R.S.O. 1990, c. L.2, s. 15.

18. (1) Where notice has been given under section 16 or 59, the Minister, upon the request of either party, shall appoint a conciliation officer to confer with the parties and endeavour to effect a collective agreement.
(2) Despite the failure of a trade union to give written notice under section 16 or the failure of either party to give written notice under sections 59 and 131, where the parties have met and bargained, the Minister, upon the request of either party, may appoint a conciliation officer to confer with the parties and endeavour to effect a collective agreement.
(3) Where an employer and a trade union agree that the employer recognizes the trade union as the exclusive bargaining agent of the employees in a defined bargaining unit and the agreement is in writing signed by the parties, the Minister may, upon the request of either party, appoint a conciliation officer to confer with the parties and endeavour to effect a collective agreement.
(4) Despite anything in this Act, where the Minister has appointed a conciliation officer or a mediator and the parties have failed to enter into a collective agreement within 15 months from the date of such appointment, the Minister may, upon the joint request of the parties, again appoint a conciliation officer to confer with the parties and endeavour to effect a collective agreement, and, upon the appointment being made, sections 19 to 36 and 79 to 86 apply, but the appointment is not a bar to an application for certification or for a declaration that the trade union no longer represents the employees in the bargaining unit. R.S.O. 1990, c. L.2, s.16.

19. (1) Where the Minister is required or authorized to appoint a conciliation officer, the Minister may, on the request in writing of the parties, appoint a mediator selected by them jointly before he or she has appointed a conciliation board or has informed the parties that he or she does not consider it advisable to appoint a conciliation board.

(2) Where the Minister has appointed a mediator after a conciliation officer has been appointed, the appointment of the conciliation officer is thereby terminated. R.S.O. 1990, c. L.2, s. 17.

20. (1) Where a conciliation officer is appointed, he or she shall confer with the parties and endeavour to effect a collective agreement and he or she shall, within 14 days from his or her appointment, report the result of his or her endeavour to the Minister.

(2) The period mentioned in subsection (1) may be extended by agreement of the parties or by the Minister upon the advice of the conciliation officer that a collective agreement may be made within a reasonable time if the period is extended.

(3) Where the conciliation officer reports to the Minister that the differences between the parties concerning the terms of a collective agreement have been settled, the Minister shall forthwith by notice in writing inform the parties of the report. R.S.O. 1990, c. L.2, s. 18.

21. If the conciliation officer is unable to effect a collective agreement within the time allowed under section 20,

(a) the Minister shall forthwith by notice in writing request each of the parties, within five days of the receipt of the notice, to recommend one person to be a member of a conciliation board, and upon the receipt of the recommendations or upon the expiration of the five-day period he or she shall appoint two members who in his or her opinion represent the points of view of the respective parties, and the two members so appointed may, within three days after they are appointed, jointly recommend a third person to be a member and chair of the board, and upon the receipt of the recommendation or upon the expiration of the three-day period, he or she shall appoint a third person to be a member and chair of the board; or

(b) the Minister shall forthwith by notice in writing inform each of the parties that he or she does not consider it advisable to appoint a conciliation board. R.S.O. 1990, c. L.2, s. 19.

22. No person shall act as a member of a conciliation board who has any pecuniary interest in the matters coming before it or who is acting, or has, within a period of six months preceding the date of his or her appointment, acted as solicitor, counsel or agent of either of the parties. R.S.O. 1990, c. L.2, s. 20.

23. (1) When the members of the conciliation board have been appointed, the Minister shall forthwith give notice of their names to the parties and thereupon the board shall be deemed to have been established.

(2) When notice under subsection (1) has been given, it shall be presumed conclusively that the conciliation board has been established in accordance with this Act, and no order shall be made or process entered or proceedings taken in any court, whether by way of injunction, declaratory judgment, certiorari, mandamus, prohibition, quo warranto, or otherwise, to question the establishment of the conciliation board or the appointment of any of its members, or to review, prohibit or restrain any of its proceedings. R.S.O. 1990, c. L.2, s. 21.

24. (1) If a person ceases to be a member of a conciliation board by reason of his or her resignation or death before it has completed its work, the Minister shall appoint a member in his or her place after consulting the party whose point of view was represented by the person.

(2) If in the opinion of the Minister a member of a conciliation board has failed to enter on his or her duties so as to enable it to report to the Minister within a reasonable time after its appointment, the Minister may appoint a member in his or her place after consulting the party whose point of view was represented by the person.

(3) If the chair of a conciliation board is unable to enter on his or her duties so as to enable it to report to the Minister within a reasonable time after its appointment, he or she shall advise the Minister of his or her inability and the Minister may appoint a person to act as chair in his or her place. R.S.O. 1990, c. L.2, s. 22.

25. As soon as a conciliation board has been established, the Minister shall deliver to its chair a statement of the matters referred to it and the Minister may, either before or after its report is made, amend or add to the statement. R.S.O. 1990, c. L.2, s. 23.

26. Each member of a conciliation board shall, before entering upon his or her duties, take and subscribe before a person authorized to administer oaths or before another member of the board, and file with the Minister, an oath in the following form, in English or in French:

> I do solemnly swear (or solemnly affirm) that I am not disqualified under section 22 of the *Labour Relations Act, 1995* from acting as a member of a conciliation board and that I will faithfully, truly and impartially, to the best of my knowledge, skill and ability, execute and perform the office of member (*or* chair) of the conciliation board established to
> and that I will not, except as I am legally authorized, disclose to any person any of the evidence or other matter brought before the board. So help me God. (omit this phrase in an affirmation).

R.S.O. 1990, c. L.2, s. 24.

27. As soon as a conciliation board is established, it shall endeavour to effect agreement between the parties on the matters referred to it. R.S.O. 1990, c. L.2, s. 25.

28. (1) Subject to this Act, a conciliation board shall determine its own procedure.
(2) A conciliation board shall give full opportunity to the parties to present their evidence and make their submissions. R.S.O. 1990, c. L.2, s. 26.

29. The chair of a conciliation board shall, after consultation with the other members of the board, fix the time and place of its sittings, and he or she shall notify the parties and the other members of the board of the time and place so fixed. R.S.O. 1990, c. L.2, s. 27.

30. The chair of a conciliation board shall in writing, immediately upon the conclusion of its first sitting, inform the Minister of the date on which the sitting was held. R.S.O. 1990, c. L.2, s. 28.

31. The chair and one other member of a conciliation board or, in the absence of the chair and with his or her written consent, the other two members constitute a quorum, but, in the absence of one of the members other than the chair, the other members shall not proceed unless the absent member has been given reasonable notice of the sitting. R.S.O. 1990, c. L.2, s. 29.

32. If the members of a conciliation board are unable to agree among themselves on matters of procedure or as to the admissibility of evidence, the decision of the chair governs. R.S.O. 1990, c. L.2, s. 30.

33. A conciliation board has power,
(a) to summon and enforce the attendance of witnesses and compel them to give oral or written evidence on oath, and to produce such documents and things as the board considers requisite to the full investigation and consideration of the matters referred to it in the same manner as a court of record in civil cases;
(b) to administer oaths and affirmations;
(c) to accept such oral or written evidence as it in its discretion considers proper, whether admissible in a court of law or not;
(d) to enter any premises where work is being done or has been done by the employees or in which the employer carries on business or where anything is taking place or has taken place concerning any of the matters referred to the board, and inspect and view any work, material, machinery, appliance or article therein, and interrogate any person respecting any such thing or any of such matters;

(e) to authorize any person to do anything that the board may do under clause (d) and to report to the board thereon. R.S.O. 1990, c. L.2, s. 31, *revised*.

34. (1) A conciliation board shall report its findings and recommendations to the Minister within 30 days after its first sitting.

(2) The period mentioned in subsection (1) may be extended,
    (a) for a further period not exceeding 30 days,
        (i) by the Minister at the request of the chair of the conciliation board, or
        (ii) by agreement of the parties; or
    (b) for a further period beyond the period fixed in clause (a) that the parties may agree upon and as the Minister may approve.

(3) The report of the majority constitutes the report of the conciliation board, but, where there is no majority agreement or where the board is unable to report within the time allowed under subsection (1) or (2), the chair shall notify the Minister in writing that there has been no agreement or that the board is unable to report, as the case may be, and in either case the notification constitutes the report of the board.

(4) After a conciliation board has made its report, the Minister may direct it to clarify or amplify any part of its report, and the report shall not be deemed to have been received by the Minister until it has been so clarified or amplified.

(5) On receipt of the report of the conciliation board or the mediator, the Minister shall forthwith release a copy to each of the parties. R.S.O. 1990, c. L.2, s. 32.

35. (1) Where a mediator is appointed, he or she shall confer with the parties and endeavour to effect a collective agreement.

(2) A mediator has all the powers of a conciliation board under section 33.

(3) Sections 30 and 34 apply with necessary modifications to a mediator.

(4) The report of a mediator has the same effect as the report of a conciliation board. R.S.O. 1990, c. L.2, s. 33.

36. Failure of a conciliation officer to report to the Minister within the time provided in this Act does not invalidate the proceedings of the conciliation officer. R.S.O. 1990, c. L.2, s. 34.

37. (1) The Minister may establish an industrial inquiry commission to inquire into and report to the Minister on any industrial matter or dispute that the Minister considers advisable.

(2) The industrial inquiry commission shall consist of one or more members appointed by the Minister and the commission shall have all the powers of a conciliation board under section 33.

(3) The chair and members of the commission shall be paid remuneration and expenses at the same rate as is payable to a chair and members of a conciliation board under this Act. R.S.O. 1990, c. L.2, s. 35.

38. (1) Where, at any time during the operation of a collective agreement, the Minister considers that it will promote more harmonious industrial relations between the parties, the Minister may appoint a special officer to confer with the parties and assist them in an examination and discussion of their current relationship or the resolution of anticipated bargaining problems.
(2) A special officer appointed under subsection (1) shall confer with the parties and shall report to the Minister within 30 days of his or her appointment and upon the filing of his or her report his or her appointment shall terminate unless it is extended by the Minister.
(3) Any person knowledgeable in industrial relations may be appointed a special officer, whether or not he or she is an employee of the Crown. R.S.O. 1990, c. L.2, s. 36.

39. (1) The Minister may appoint a Disputes Advisory Committee composed of one or more representatives of employers and one or more representatives of employees.
(2) At any time during the course of bargaining, either before or after the commencement of a strike or lock-out, where it appears to the Minister that the normal conciliation and mediation procedures have been exhausted, the Minister may request that the Disputes Advisory Committee be convened to confer with, advise and assist the bargaining parties. R.S.O. 1990, c. L.2, s. 37.

40. (1) Despite any other provision of this Act, the parties may at any time following the giving of notice of desire to bargain under section 16 or 59, irrevocably agree in writing to refer all matters remaining in dispute between them to an arbitrator or a board of arbitration for final and binding determination. R.S.O. 1990, c. L.2, s. 38(1).
(2) The agreement to arbitrate shall supersede all other dispute settlement provisions of this Act, including those provisions relating to conciliation, mediation, strike and lock-out, and the provisions of subsections 48 (7), (8), (11), (12) and (18) to (20) apply with necessary modifications to the proceedings before the arbitrator or board of arbitration and to its decision under this section. R.S.O. 1990, c. L.2, s. 38(2), *amended.*
(3) For the purposes of section 67 and section 132, an irrevocable agreement in writing referred to in subsection (1) shall have the same effect as a collective agreement. R.S.O. 1990, c. L.2, s. 38(3).

41. Where, at any time after the commencement of a strike or lock-out, the Minister is of the opinion that it is in the public interest that the employees in the affected bargaining unit be given the opportunity to accept or reject the offer of the employer last received by the trade union in respect of all matters remaining in dispute between the parties, the Minister may, on such terms as he or she considers necessary, direct that a vote of the employees in the bargaining unit to accept or reject the offer be held forthwith. R.S.O. 1990, c. L.2, s. 39.

42. (1) Before or after the commencement of a strike or lock-out, the employer of the employees in the affected bargaining unit may request that a vote of the employees be taken as to the acceptance or rejection of the offer of the employer last received by the trade union in respect of all matters remaining in dispute between the parties and the Minister shall, and in the construction industry the Minister may, on the terms that he or she considers necessary direct that a vote of the employees to accept or reject the offer be held and thereafter no further such request shall be made.
(2) A request for the taking of a vote, or the holding of a vote, under subsection (1) does not abridge or extend any time limits or periods provided for in this Act. R.S.O. 1990, c. L.2, s. 40.

43. (1) Where the parties are unable to effect a first collective agreement and the Minister has released a notice that it is not considered advisable to appoint a conciliation board or the Minister has released the report of a conciliation board, either party may apply to the Board to direct the settlement of a first collective agreement by arbitration.
(2) The Board shall consider and make its decision on an application under subsection (1) within 30 days of receiving the application and it shall direct the settlement of a first collective agreement by arbitration where, irrespective of whether section 17 has been contravened, it appears to the Board that the process of collective bargaining has been unsuccessful because of,

(a) the refusal of the employer to recognize the bargaining authority of the trade union;

(b) the uncompromising nature of any bargaining position adopted by the respondent without reasonable justification;

(c) the failure of the respondent to make reasonable or expeditious efforts to conclude a collective agreement; or

(d) any other reason the Board considers relevant.

(3) Where a direction is given under subsection (2), the first collective agreement between the parties shall be settled by a board of arbitration unless within seven days of the giving of the direction the parties notify the Board that they have agreed that the Board arbitrate the settlement.
(4) Where the parties give notice to the Board of their agreement that the Board arbitrate the settlement of the first collective agreement, the Board,

(a) shall appoint a date for and commence a hearing within 21 days of the giving of the notice to the Board; and

(b) shall determine all matters in dispute and release its decision within 45 days of the commencement of the hearing. R.S.O. 1990, c. L.2, s. 41(1-4).

(5) The parties to an arbitration by the Board shall jointly pay to the Board for payment into the Consolidated Revenue Fund the amount determined under the regulations for the expense of the arbitration. *New.*

(6) Where the parties do not agree that the Board arbitrate the settlement of the first collective agreement, each party, within 10 days of the giving of the direction under subsection (2), shall inform the other party of the name of its appointee to the board of arbitration referred to in subsection (3) and the appointees so selected, within five days of the appointment of the second of them, shall appoint a third person who shall be the chair.

(7) If a party fails to make appointment as required by subsection (6) or if the appointees fail to agree upon a chair within the time limited, the appointment shall be made by the Minister upon the request of either party.

(8) A board of arbitration appointed under this section shall determine its own procedure but shall give full opportunity to the parties to present their evidence and make their submissions and section 116 applies to the board of arbitration, its decision and proceedings as if it were the Board.

(9) The remuneration and expenses of the members of a board of arbitration appointed under this section shall be paid as follows:

1. A party shall pay the remuneration and expenses of the member appointed by or on behalf of the party.
2. Each party shall pay one-half of the remuneration and expenses of the chair.

(10) Subsections 6 (8), (9), (10), (12), (13), (14), (17) and (18) of the *Hospital Labour Disputes Arbitration Act* and subsections 48 (12) and (18) of this Act apply with necessary modifications to a board of arbitration established under this section.

(11) The date of the first hearing of a board of arbitration appointed under this section shall not be later than 21 days after the appointment of the chair.

(12) A board of arbitration appointed under this section shall determine all matters in dispute and release its decision within 45 days of the commencement of its hearing of the matter.

(13) The Minister may appoint a mediator to confer with the parties and endeavour to effect a settlement. R.S.O. 1990, c. L.2, s. 41 (5-12).

(14) The employees in the bargaining unit shall not strike and the employer shall not lock out the employees where a direction has been given under subsection (2) and, where the direction is made during a strike by, or a lock-out of, employees in the bargaining unit, the employees shall forthwith terminate the strike or the employer shall forthwith terminate the lock-out and the employer shall forthwith reinstate the employees in the bargaining unit in the employment they had at the time the strike or lock-out commenced,

(a) in accordance with any agreement between the employer and the trade union respecting reinstatement of the employees in the bargaining unit; or

(b) where there is no agreement respecting reinstatement of the employees in the bargaining unit, on the basis of the length of service of each employee in relation to that of the other employees in the bargaining unit employed at the time the strike or lock-out commenced, except as may be directed by an order of the Board made for the purpose of allowing the employer to resume normal operations. R.S.O. 1990, c. L.2, s. 41(13); 1993, c. 27, Sched.

(15) The requirement to reinstate employees set out in subsection (14) applies despite the fact that replacement employees may be performing the work of employees in the bargaining unit, but subsection (14) does not apply so as to require reinstatement of an employee where, because of the permanent discontinuance of all or part of the business of the employer, the employer no longer has persons engaged in performing work of the same or a similar nature to work which the employee performed before the strike or lock-out. R.S.O. 1990, c. L.2, s. 41(14).

(16) Where a direction has been given under subsection (2), the rates of wages and all other terms and conditions of employment and all rights, privileges and duties of the employer, the employees and the trade union in effect at the time notice was given under section 16 shall continue in effect, or, if altered before the giving of the direction, be restored and continued in effect until the first collective agreement is settled. R.S.O. 1990, c. L.2, s. 41(15), *revised*.

(17) Subsection (16) does not apply so as to effect any alteration in rates of wages or in any other term or condition of employment agreed to by the employer and the trade union.

(18) In arbitrating the settlement of a first collective agreement under this section, matters agreed to by the parties, in writing, shall be accepted without amendment.

(19) A first collective agreement settled under this section is effective for a period of two years from the date on which it is settled and it may provide that any of the terms of the agreement, except its term of operation, shall be retroactive to the day that the Board may fix, but not earlier than the day on which notice was given under section 16.

(20) The parties, by agreement in writing, or the Minister may extend any time limit set out in this section, despite the expiration of the time.

(21) This section does not apply to the negotiation of a first collective agreement,

(a) where one of the parties is an employers' organization accredited under section 136 as a bargaining agent for employers; or

(b) where the agreement is a provincial agreement within the meaning of section 151.

(22) This section applies to an employer and a trade union where the trade union has acquired or acquires bargaining rights for employees of the employer before or after May 26, 1986, and the bargaining rights have been acquired since January 1, 1984 and continue to exist at the time of an application under subsection (1).

(23) Despite subsection (2), where an application under subsection (1) has been filed with the Board and a final decision on the application has not been issued by it and there has also been filed with the Board, either or both,
    (a) an application for a declaration that the trade union no longer represents the employees in the bargaining unit; and
    (b) an application for certification by another trade union as bargaining agent for employees in the bargaining unit,
the Board shall consider the applications in the order that it considers appropriate and if it grants one of the applications, it shall dismiss any other application described in this section that remains unconsidered.

(24) An application for a declaration that a trade union no longer represents the employees in the bargaining unit filed with the Board after the Board has given a direction under subsection (2) is of no effect unless it is brought after the first collective agreement is settled and unless it is brought in accordance with subsection 63(2).

(25) An application for certification by another trade union as bargaining agent for employees in the bargaining unit filed with the Board after the Board has given a direction under subsection (2) is of no effect unless it is brought after the first collective agreement is settled and unless it is brought in accordance with subsections 7 (4), (5) and (6).

(26) The *Arbitration Act, 1991* does not apply to an arbitration under this section. R.S.O. 1990, c. L.2, s. 41(16-25).

44. (1) A proposed collective agreement that is entered into or memorandum of settlement that is concluded on or after the day on which this section comes into force has no effect until it is ratified as described in subsection (3).

(2) Subsection (1) does not apply with respect to a collective agreement,
    (a) imposed by order of the Board or settled by arbitration;
    (b) that reflects an offer accepted by a vote held under section 41 or subsection 42(1); or
    (c) that applies to employees in the construction industry.

(3) A proposed collective agreement or memorandum of settlement is ratified if a vote is taken in accordance with subsections 79 (7) to (9) and more than 50 per cent of those voting vote in favour of ratifying the agreement or memorandum. *New.*

Contents of Collective Agreements

45. (1) Every collective agreement shall be deemed to provide that the trade union that is a party thereto is recognized as the exclusive bargaining agent of the employees in the bargaining unit defined therein.

(2) Every collective agreement to which an accredited employers' organization is a party shall be deemed to provide that the accredited employers' organization is recognized as the exclusive bargaining agent of the employers in the unit of employers for whom the employers' organization has been accredited. R.S.O. 1990, c. L.2, s. 42.

46. Every collective agreement shall be deemed to provide that there will be no strikes or lock-outs so long as the agreement continues to operate. R.S.O. 1990, c. L.2, s. 43.

47. (1) Except in the construction industry and subject to section 52, where a trade union that is the bargaining agent for employees in a bargaining unit so requests, there shall be included in the collective agreement between the trade union and the employer of the employees a provision requiring the employer to deduct from the wages of each employee in the unit affected by the collective agreement, whether or not the employee is a member of the union, the amount of the regular union dues and to remit the amount to the trade union, forthwith.

(2) In subsection (1), "regular union dues" means,

(a) in the case of an employee who is a member of the trade union, the dues uniformly and regularly paid by a member of the trade union in accordance with the constitution and by-laws of the trade union, and

(b) in the case of an employee who is not a member of the trade union, the dues referred to in clause (a), excluding any amount in respect of pension, superannuation, sickness insurance or any other benefit available only to members of the trade union. R.S.O. 1990, c. L.2, s. 44.

48. (1) Every collective agreement shall provide for the final and binding settlement by arbitration, without stoppage of work, of all differences between the parties arising from the interpretation, application, administration or alleged violation of the agreement, including any question as to whether a matter is arbitrable. R.S.O. 1990, c. L.2, s. 45(1), *revised*.

(2) If a collective agreement does not contain a provision that is mentioned in subsection (1), it shall be deemed to contain a provision to the following effect:

> Where a difference arises between the parties relating to the interpretation, application or administration of this agreement, including any question as to whether a matter is arbitrable, or where an allegation is made that this agreement has been violated, either of the parties may after exhausting any grievance procedure established by this agreement, notify the other party in

writing of its desire to submit the difference or allegation to arbitration and the notice shall contain the name of the first party's appointee to an arbitration board. The recipient of the notice shall within five days inform the other party of the name of its appointee to the arbitration board. The two appointees so selected shall, within five days of the appointment of the second of them, appoint a third person who shall be the chair. If the recipient of the notice fails to appoint an arbitrator, or if the two appointees fail to agree upon a chair within the time limited, the appointment shall be made by the Minister of Labour for Ontario upon the request of either party. The arbitration board shall hear and determine the difference or allegation and shall issue a decision and the decision is final and binding upon the parties and upon any employee or employer affected by it. The decision of a majority is the decision of the arbitration board, but if there is no majority the decision of the chair governs.

R.S.O. 1990, c. L.2, s. 45(2), *revised.*

(3) If, in the opinion of the Board, any part of the arbitration provision, including the method of appointment of the arbitrator or arbitration board, is inadequate, or if the provision set out in subsection (2) is alleged by either party to be unsuitable, the Board may, on the request of either party, modify the provision so long as it conforms with subsection (1), but, until so modified, the arbitration provision in the collective agreement or in subsection (2), as the case may be, applies.

(4) Despite subsection (3), if there is failure to appoint an arbitrator or to constitute a board of arbitration under a collective agreement, the Minister, upon the request of either party, may appoint the arbitrator or make the appointments that are necessary to constitute the board of arbitration, as the case may be, and any person so appointed by the Minister shall be deemed to have been appointed in accordance with the collective agreement. R.S.O. 1990, c. L.2, s. 45(3, 4).

(5) On the request of either party, the Minister shall appoint a settlement officer to endeavour to effect a settlement before the arbitrator or arbitration board appointed under subsection (4) begins to hear the arbitration. However, no appointment shall be made if the other party objects. 1992, c. 21, s. 23(2).

(6) Where the Minister has appointed an arbitrator or the chair of a board of arbitration under subsection (4), each of the parties shall pay one-half the remuneration and expenses of the person appointed, and, where the Minister has appointed a member of a board of arbitration under subsection (4) on failure of one of the parties to make the appointment, that party shall pay the remuneration and expenses of the person appointed. R.S.O. 1990, c. L.2, s. 45(5).

(7) An arbitrator shall give a decision within 30 days after hearings on the matter submitted to arbitration are concluded.

(8) An arbitration board shall give a decision within 60 days after hearings on the matter submitted to arbitration are concluded.

(9) The time described in subsection (7) or (8) for giving a decision may be extended,

    (a) with the consent of the parties to the arbitration; or

    (b) in the discretion of the arbitrator or arbitration board so long as he, she or it states in the decision the reasons for extending the time.

(10) An arbitrator or arbitration board may give an oral decision and, if he, she or it does so, subsection (7) or (8) does not apply and the arbitrator or arbitration board,

    (a) shall give the decision promptly after hearings on the matter are concluded;

    (b) shall give a written decision, without reasons, promptly upon the request of either party; and

    (c) shall give written reasons for the decision within a reasonable period of time upon the request of either party.

(11) If the arbitrator or arbitration board does not give a decision within the time described in subsection (7) or (8) or does not provide written reasons within the time described in subsection (10), the Minister may,

    (a) make such orders as he or she considers necessary to ensure that the decision or reasons will be given without undue delay; and

    (b) make such orders as he or she considers appropriate respecting the remuneration and expenses of the arbitrator or arbitration board. 1992, c. 21, s. 23(3), *part.*

(12) An arbitrator or the chair of an arbitration board, as the case may be, has power,

    (a) to require any party to furnish particulars before or during a hearing;

    (b) to require any party to produce documents or things that may be relevant to the matter and to do so before or during the hearing;

    (c) to fix dates for the commencement and continuation of hearings;

    (d) to summon and enforce the attendance of witnesses and to compel them to give oral or written evidence on oath in the same manner as a court of record in civil cases, and

    (e) to administer oaths and affirmations,

and an arbitrator or an arbitration board, as the case may be, has power,

    (f) to accept the oral or written evidence as the arbitrator or the arbitration board, as the case may be, in its discretion considers proper, whether admissible in a court of law or not;

    (g) to enter any premises where work is being done or has been done by the employees or in which the employer carries on business or where anything is taking place or has taken place concerning any of the differences submitted to the arbitrator or the arbitration board, and inspect and view any work, material, machinery, appliance or article therein, and interrogate any person respecting any such thing or any of such differences;

(h) to authorize any person to do anything that the arbitrator or arbitration board may do under clause (g) and to report to the arbitrator or the arbitration board thereon;

(i) to make interim orders concerning procedural matters;

(j) to interpret and apply human rights and other employment-related statutes, despite any conflict between those statutes and the terms of the collective agreement. R.S.O. 1990, c. L.2, s.45(8); 1992, c. 21, s. 23(3), *part, amended.*

(13) An arbitrator or the chair of an arbitration board shall not make an interim order under clause (12)(i) requiring an employer to reinstate an employee in employment.

(14) An arbitrator or the chair of an arbitration board, as the case may be, may mediate the differences between the parties at any stage in the proceedings with the consent of the parties. If mediation is not successful, the arbitrator or arbitration board retains the power to determine the difference by arbitration.

(15) An arbitrator or the chair of an arbitration board, as the case may be, may enforce the written settlement of a grievance. *New.*

(16) Except where a collective agreement states that this subsection does not apply, an arbitrator or arbitration board may extend the time for the taking of any step in the grievance procedure under a collective agreement, despite the expiration of the time, where the arbitrator or arbitration board is satisfied that there are reasonable grounds for the extension and that the opposite party will not be substantially prejudiced by the extension. R.S.O. 1990, c. L.2, s. 45(6).

(17) Where an arbitrator or arbitration board determines that an employee has been discharged or otherwise disciplined by an employer for cause and the collective agreement does not contain a specific penalty for the infraction that is the subject-matter of the arbitration, the arbitrator or arbitration board may substitute such other penalty for the discharge or discipline as to the arbitrator or arbitration board seems just and reasonable in all the circumstances. R.S.O. 1990, c. L.2, s. 45(9), *revised.*

(18) The decision of an arbitrator or of an arbitration board is binding,

(a) upon the parties;

(b) in the case of a collective agreement between a trade union and an employers' organization, upon the employers covered by the agreement who are affected by the decision;

(c) in the case of a collective agreement between a council of trade unions and an employer or an employers' organization, upon the members or affiliates of the council and the employer or the employers covered by the agreement, as the case may be, who are affected by the decision; and

(d) upon the employees covered by the agreement who are affected by the decision,

and the parties, employers, trade unions and employees shall do or abstain from doing anything required of them by the decision.

(19) Where a party, employer, trade union or employee has failed to comply with any of the terms of the decision of an arbitrator or arbitration board, any party, employer, trade union or employee affected by the decision may file in the Ontario Court (General Division) a copy of the decision, exclusive of the reasons therefor, in the prescribed form, whereupon the decision shall be entered in the same way as a judgment or order of that court and is enforceable as such.

(20) The *Arbitration Act, 1991* does not apply to arbitrations under collective agreements. R.S.O. 1990, c. L.2, s. 45(10-12).

49. (1) Despite the arbitration provision in a collective agreement or deemed to be included in a collective agreement under section 48, a party to a collective agreement may request the Minister to refer to a single arbitrator, to be appointed by the Minister, any difference between the parties to the collective agreement arising from the interpretation, application, administration or alleged violation of the agreement, including any question as to whether a matter is arbitrable. R.S.O. 1990, c. L.2, s. 46(1), *revised*.

(2) Subject to subsection (3), a request under subsection (1) may be made by a party to the collective agreement in writing after the grievance procedure under the agreement has been exhausted or after 30 days have elapsed from the time at which the grievance was first brought to the attention of the other party, whichever first occurs, but no such request shall be made beyond the time, if any, stipulated in or permitted under the agreement for referring the grievance to arbitration.

(3) Despite subsection (2), where a difference between the parties to a collective agreement is a difference respecting discharge from or other termination of employment, a request under subsection (1) may be made by a party to the collective agreement in writing after the grievance procedure under the agreement has been exhausted or after 14 days have elapsed from the time at which the grievance was first brought to the attention of the other party, whichever first occurs, but no such request shall be made beyond the time, if any, stipulated in or permitted under the agreement for referring the grievance to arbitration.

(4) Where a request is received under subsection (1), the Minister shall appoint a single arbitrator who shall have exclusive jurisdiction to hear and determine the matter referred to him or her, including any question as to whether a matter is arbitrable and any question as to whether the request was timely.

(5) Where a request or more than one request concerns several differences arising under the collective agreement, the Minister may in his or

her discretion appoint an arbitrator under subsection (4) to deal with all the differences raised in the request or requests.

(6) The Minister may appoint a settlement officer to confer with the parties and endeavour to effect a settlement prior to the hearing by an arbitrator appointed under subsection (4). R.S.O. 1990, c. L.2, s. 46(2-6).

(7) An arbitrator appointed under subsection (4) shall commence to hear the matter referred to him or her within 21 days after the receipt of the request by the Minister and the provisions of subsections 48 (7) and (9) to (20) apply with all necessary modifications to the arbitrator, the parties and the decision of the arbitrator. R.S.O. 1990, c. L.2, s. 46(7), *amended*.

(8) Upon the agreement of the parties, the arbitrator shall deliver an oral decision forthwith or as soon as practicable without giving his or her reasons in writing therefor.

(9) Where the Minister has appointed an arbitrator under subsection (4), each of the parties shall pay one-half of the remuneration and expenses of the person appointed.

(10) The Minister may establish a list of approved arbitrators and, for the purpose of advising him or her with respect to persons qualified to act as arbitrators and matters relating to arbitration, the Minister may constitute a labour-management advisory committee composed of a chair to be designated by the Minister and six members, three of whom shall represent employers and three of whom shall represent trade unions, and their remuneration and expenses shall be as the Lieutenant Governor in Council determines. R.S.O. 1990, c. L.2, s. 46(8-10).

50. (1) Despite any grievance or arbitration provision in a collective agreement or deemed to be included in the collective agreement under section 48, the parties to the collective agreement may, at any time, agree to refer one or more grievances under the collective agreement to a single mediator-arbitrator for the purpose of resolving the grievances in an expeditious and informal manner.

(2) The parties shall not refer a grievance to a mediator-arbitrator unless they have agreed upon the nature of any issues in dispute.

(3) The parties may jointly request the Minister to appoint a mediator-arbitrator if they are unable to agree upon one and the Minister shall make the appointment.

(4) Subject to subsection (5), a mediator-arbitrator appointed by the Minister shall begin proceedings within 30 days after being appointed.

(5) The Minister may direct a mediator-arbitrator appointed by him or her to begin proceedings on such date as the parties jointly request.

(6) The mediator-arbitrator shall endeavour to assist the parties to settle the grievance by mediation.

(7) If the parties are unable to settle the grievance by mediation, the mediator-arbitrator shall endeavour to assist the parties to agree upon the

material facts in dispute and then shall determine the grievance by arbitration.

(8) When determining the grievance by arbitration, the mediator-arbitrator may limit the nature and extent of evidence and submissions and may impose such conditions as he or she considers appropriate.

(9) The mediator-arbitrator shall give a succinct decision within five days after completing proceedings on the grievance submitted to arbitration.

(10) Subsections 48 (12) to (19) apply with respect to a mediator-arbitrator and a settlement, determination or decision under this section. 1992, c. 21, s. 25.

51. (1) Despite anything in this Act, but subject to subsection (4), the parties to a collective agreement may include in its provisions,

(a) for requiring, as a condition of employment, membership in the trade union that is a party to or is bound by the agreement or granting a preference of employment to members of the trade union, or requiring the payment of dues or contributions to the trade union;

(b) for permitting an employee who represents the trade union that is a party to or is bound by the agreement to attend to the business of the trade union during working hours without deduction of the time so occupied in the computation of the time worked for the employer and without deduction of wages in respect of the time so occupied;

(c) for permitting the trade union that is a party to or is bound by the agreement the use of the employer's premises for the purposes of the trade union without payment therefor.

(2) No trade union that is a party to a collective agreement containing a provision mentioned in clause (1)(a) shall require the employer to discharge an employee because,

(a) the employee has been expelled or suspended from membership in the trade union; or

(b) membership in the trade union has been denied to or withheld from the employee;

for the reason that the employee,

(c) was or is a member of another trade union;

(d) has engaged in activity against the trade union or on behalf of another trade union;

(e) has engaged in reasonable dissent within the trade union;

(f) has been discriminated against by the trade union in the application of its membership rules; or

(g) has refused to pay initiation fees, dues or other assessments to the trade union which are unreasonable.

(3) Subsection (2) does not apply to an employee who has engaged in unlawful activity against the trade union mentioned in clause (1)(a) or an officer, official or agent thereof or whose activity against the trade union or

on behalf of another trade union has been instigated or procured by the employee's employer or any person acting on the employer's behalf or whose employer or a person acting on the employer's behalf has participated in such activity or contributed financial or other support to the employee in respect of the activity.

(4) A trade union and the employer of the employees concerned shall not enter into a collective agreement that includes provisions requiring, as a condition of employment, membership in the trade union that is a party to or is bound by the agreement unless the trade union has established at the time it entered into the agreement that not less than 55 per cent of the employees in the bargaining unit were members of the trade union, but this subsection does not apply,

> (a) where the trade union has been certified as the bargaining agent of the employees of the employer in the bargaining unit;
>
> (b) where the trade union has been a party to or bound by a collective agreement with the employer for at least one year;
>
> (c) where the employer becomes a member of an employer's organization that has entered into a collective agreement with the trade union or council of trade unions containing such a provision and agrees with the trade union or council of trade unions to be bound by such agreement; or
>
> (d) where the employer and the employer's employees in the bargaining unit are engaged in the construction, alteration, decoration, repair or demolition of a building, structure, road, sewer, water or gas main, pipe line, tunnel, bridge, canal, or other work at the site.

(5) Despite anything in this Act, where the parties to a collective agreement have included in it any of the provisions permitted by subsection (1), any of such provisions may be continued in effect during the period when the parties are bargaining with a view to the renewal, with or without modifications, of the agreement or to the making of a new agreement.

(6) Despite anything in this Act, where the parties to a collective agreement have included in it any of the provisions permitted by subsection (1) and the employer who was a party to or was bound by the agreement sells the employer's business within the meaning of section 69, any of the provisions that were included in the collective agreement may be continued in effect during the period when the person to whom the business was sold and the trade union that is the bargaining agent for the person's employees in the appropriate bargaining unit by reason of the sale bargain with a view to the making of a new agreement. R.S.O. 1990, c. L.2, s. 47.

52. (1) Where the Board is satisfied that an employee because of his or her religious conviction or belief,

> (a) objects to joining a trade union; or

(b) objects to the paying of dues or other assessments to a trade union, the Board may order that the provisions of a collective agreement of the type mentioned in clause 51(1)(a) do not apply to the employee and that the employee is not required to join the trade union, to be or continue to be a member of the trade union, or to pay any dues, fees or assessments to the trade union, provided that amounts equal to any initiation fees, dues or other assessments are paid by the employee to or are remitted by the employer to a charitable organization mutually agreed upon by the employee and the trade union, but if the employee and the trade union fail to so agree then to a charitable organization registered as a charitable organization in Canada under Part I of the *Income Tax Act* (Canada) that may be designated by the Board. R.S.O. 1990, c. L.2, s. 48(1).

(2) Subsection (1) applies to employees in the employ of an employer at the time a collective agreement containing a provision of the kind mentioned in subsection (1) is first entered into with that employer and only during the life of such collective agreement, and does not apply to employees whose employment commences after the entering into of the collective agreement. R.S.O. 1990, c. L.2, s. 49(2); 1993, c. 27, Sched.

Operation of Collective Agreements

53. An agreement between an employer or an employers' organization and a trade union shall be deemed not to be a collective agreement for the purposes of this Act if an employer or employers' organization participated in the formation or administration of the trade union or contributed financial or other support to the trade union. *New.*

54. A collective agreement must not discriminate against any person if the discrimination is contrary to the *Human Rights Code* or the *Canadian Charter of Rights and Freedoms.* 1992, c. 21, s. 26, *part.*

55. There shall be only one collective agreement at a time between a trade union or council of trade unions and an employer or employers' organization with respect to the employees in the bargaining unit defined in the collective agreement. R.S.O. 1990, c. L.2, s. 50.

56. A collective agreement is, subject to and for the purposes of this Act, binding upon the employer and upon the trade union that is a party to the agreement whether or not the trade union is certified and upon the employees in the bargaining unit defined in the agreement. R.S.O. 1990, c. L.2, s. 51.

57. (1) A collective agreement between an employers' organization and a trade union or council of trade unions is, subject to and for the purposes of this Act, binding upon the employers' organization and each person who was a member of the employers' organization at the time the agreement was entered into and on whose behalf the employers' organization bargained with the trade union or council of trade unions as if it was made between each of such persons and the trade union or council of trade unions and upon the employees in the bargaining unit defined in the agreement, and, if any such person ceases to be a member of the employers' organization during the term of operation of the agreement, the person shall, for the remainder of the term of operation of the agreement, be deemed to be a party to a like agreement with the trade union or council of trade unions.

(2) When an employers' organization commences to bargain with a trade union or council of trade unions, it shall deliver to the trade union, or council of trade unions a list of the names of the employers on whose behalf it is bargaining and, in default of so doing, it shall be deemed to bargain for all members of the employers' organization for whose employees the trade union or council of trade unions is entitled to bargain and to make a collective agreement at that time, except an employer who, either alone or through the employers' organization, has notified the trade union or council of trade unions in writing before the agreement was entered into that the employer will not be bound by a collective agreement between the employers' organization and the trade union or council of trade unions.

(3) A collective agreement between a certified council of trade unions and an employer is, subject to and for the purposes of this Act, binding upon each trade union that is a constituent union of such a council as if it had been made between each of such trade unions and the employer.

(4) A collective agreement between a council of trade unions, other than a certified council of trade unions, and an employer or an employers' organization is, subject to and for the purposes of this Act, binding upon the council of trade unions and each trade union that was a member of or affiliated with the council of trade unions at the time the agreement was entered into and on whose behalf the council of trade unions bargained with the employer or employers' organization as if it was made between each of such trade unions and the employer or employers' organization, and upon the employees in the bargaining unit defined in the agreement and, if any such trade union ceases to be a member of or affiliated with the council of trade unions during the term of operation of the agreement, it shall, for the remainder of the term of operation of the agreement, be deemed to be a party to a like agreement with the employer or employers' organization, as the case may be.

(5) Where a council of trade unions, other than a certified council of trade unions, commences to bargain with an employer or an employers' organization, it shall deliver to the employer or employers' organization a list of the names of the trade unions on whose behalf it is bargaining and, in default of so doing, it shall be deemed to bargain for all members or

affiliates of the council of trade unions for whose employees the respective trade unions are entitled to bargain and to make a collective agreement at that time with the employer or the employers' organization, except a trade union that, either by itself or through the council of trade unions, has notified the employer or employer's organization in writing before the agreement is entered into that it will not be bound by a collective agreement between the council of trade unions and the employer or employers' organization. R.S.O. 1990, c. L.2, s. 52.

58. (1) If a collective agreement does not provide for its term of operation or provides for its operation for an unspecified term or for a term of less than one year, it shall be deemed to provide for its operation for a term of one year from the date that it commenced to operate.

(2) Despite subsection (1), the parties may, in a collective agreement or otherwise and before or after the collective agreement has ceased to operate, agree to continue the operation of the collective agreement or any of its provisions for a period of less than one year while they are bargaining for its renewal with or without modifications or for a new agreement, but such continued operation does not bar an application for certification or for a declaration that the trade union no longer represents the employees in the bargaining unit and the continuation of the collective agreement may be terminated by either party upon 30 days notice to the other party.

(3) A collective agreement shall not be terminated by the parties before it ceases to operate in accordance with its provisions or this Act without the consent of the Board on the joint application of the parties.

(4) Despite anything in this section, when an employer joins an employers' organization that is a party to a collective agreement with a trade union or council of trade unions and the employer agrees with the trade union or council of trade unions to be bound by the collective agreement between the trade union or council of trade unions and the employers' organization, the agreement ceases to be binding upon the employer and the trade union or council of trade unions at the same time as the agreement between the employers' organization and the trade union or council of trade unions ceases to be binding.

(5) Nothing in this section prevents the revision by mutual consent of the parties at any time of any provision of a collective agreement other than a provision relating to its term of operation. R.S.O. 1990, c. L.2, s. 53.

59. (1) Either party to a collective agreement may, within the period of 90 days before the agreement ceases to operate, give notice in writing to the other party of its desire to bargain with a view to the renewal, with or without modifications, of the agreement then in operation or to the making of a new agreement.

(2) A notice given by a party to a collective agreement in accordance with provisions in the agreement relating to its termination or renewal shall be deemed to comply with subsection (1).

(3) Where notice is given by or to an employers' organization that has a collective agreement with a trade union or council of trade unions, it shall be deemed to be a notice given by or to each member of the employers' organization who is bound by the agreement or who has ceased to be a member of the employers' organization but has not notified the trade union or council of trade unions in writing that he, she or it has ceased to be a member.

(4) Where notice is given by or to a council of trade unions, other than a certified council of trade unions, that has a collective agreement with an employer or employers' organization, it shall be deemed to be a notice given by or to each member or affiliate of the council of trade unions that is bound by the agreement or that has ceased to be a member or affiliate of the council of trade unions but has not notified the employer or employers' organization in writing that it has ceased to be a member or affiliate. R.S.O. 1990, c. L.2, s. 54.

60. Sections 17 to 36 apply to the bargaining that follows the giving of a notice under section 59. R.S.O. 1990, c. L.2, s. 55.

61. (1) Where a certified council of trade unions is a party to or is bound by a collective agreement, no resolution, by-law or other action by the constituent unions of a certified council of trade unions to dissolve the council or by a constituent union of such a council to withdraw from the council, as the case may be, has effect,

    (a) unless a copy of the resolution, by-law or other action is delivered to the employer or the employers' organization and, in the case of a withdrawal, to the other constituent members and to the council at least 90 days before the collective agreement ceases to operate; and

    (b) until the collective agreement ceases to operate.

(2) Where a certified council of trade unions is not a party to or is not bound by a collective agreement, no resolution, by-law or other action by the constituent unions of a certified council of trade unions to dissolve the council or by a constituent union of such a council to withdraw from the council, as the case may be, has effect until the 90th day after the day on which a copy of such resolution, by-law or other action is delivered to the employer or the employers' organization and, in the case of a withdrawal, to the other constituent members and to the council. R.S.O. 1990, c. L.2, s. 56.

Termination of Bargaining Rights

62. (1) If the trade union that applies for certification under subsection 7 (4), (5) or (6) is certified as bargaining agent for any of the employees in the bargaining unit defined in the collective agreement, the trade union that was or is a party to the agreement, as the case may be, forthwith ceases to represent the employees in the bargaining unit determined in the certificate and the agreement ceases to operate in so far as it affects such employees.

(2) If the trade union that applies for certification under subsection 7(2) is certified as bargaining agent for any of the employees in the bargaining unit defined in the certificate issued to the trade union that was previously certified, the latter trade union forthwith ceases to represent the employees in the bargaining unit defined in the certificate issued to the former trade union. R.S.O. 1990, c. L.2, s. 57.

63. (1) If a trade union does not make a collective agreement with the employer within one year after its certification, any of the employees in the bargaining unit determined in the certificate may, subject to section 67, apply to the Board for a declaration that the trade union no longer represents the employees in the bargaining unit. R.S.O. 1990, c. L.2, s. 58(1).

(2) Any of the employees in the bargaining unit defined in a collective agreement may, subject to section 67, apply to the Board for a declaration that the trade union no longer represents the employees in the bargaining unit,

 (a) in the case of a collective agreement for a term of not more than three years, only after the commencement of the last two months of its operation;

 (b) in the case of a collective agreement for a term of more than three years, only after the commencement of the 35th month of its operation and before the commencement of the 37th month of its operation and during the two-month period immediately preceding the end of each year that the agreement continues to operate thereafter or after the commencement of the last two months of its operation, as the case may be;

 (c) in the case of a collective agreement referred to in clause (a) or (b) that provides that it will continue to operate for any further term or successive terms if either party fails to give to the other notice of termination or of its desire to bargain with a view to the renewal, with or without modifications, of the agreement or to the making of a new agreement, only during the last two months of each year that it so continues to operate or after the commencement of the last two months of its operation, as the case may be. R.S.O. 1990, c. L.2, s. 58(2), *revised*.

(3) The applicant shall deliver a copy of the application to the employer and the trade union by such time as is required under the rules made by the Board and, if there is no rule, not later than the day on which the application is filed with the Board.

(4) The application filed with the Board shall be accompanied by a list of the names of the employees in the bargaining unit who have expressed a wish not to be represented by the trade union and evidence of the wishes of those employees, but the applicant shall not give this information to the employer or trade union.

(5) If the Board determines that 40 per cent or more of the employees in the bargaining unit appear to have expressed a wish not to be represented by the trade union at the time the application was filed, the Board shall direct that a representation vote be taken among the employees in the bargaining unit.

(6) The number of employees in the bargaining unit who appear to have expressed a wish not to be represented by the trade union shall be determined with reference only to the information provided in the application and the accompanying information provided under subsection (4).

(7) The Board may consider such information as it considers appropriate to determine the number of employees in the bargaining unit.

(8) The Board shall not hold a hearing when making a decision under subsection (5).

(9) Unless the Board directs otherwise, the representation vote shall be held within five days (excluding Saturdays, Sundays and holidays) after the day on which the application is filed with the Board.

(10) The representation vote shall be by ballots cast in such a manner that individuals expressing their choice cannot be identified with the choice made.

(11) The Board may direct that one or more ballots be segregated and that the ballot box containing the ballots be sealed until such time as the Board directs.

(12) After the representation vote has been taken, the Board may hold a hearing if the Board considers it necessary in order to dispose of the application.

(13) When disposing of an application, the Board shall not consider any challenge to the information provided under subsection (4). *New.*

(14) If on the taking of the representation vote more than 50 per cent of the ballots cast are cast in opposition to the trade union, the Board shall declare that the trade union that was certified or that was or is a party to the collective agreement, as the case may be, no longer represents the employees in the bargaining unit. R.S.O. 1990, c. L.2, s. 58(4).

(15) The Board shall dismiss the application unless more than 50 per cent of the ballots cast in the representation vote by the employees in the bargaining unit are cast in opposition to the trade union.

(16) Despite subsections (5) and (14), the Board may dismiss the application if the Board is satisfied that the employer or a person acting on behalf of the employer initiated the application or engaged in threats, coercion or intimidation in connection with the application. *New.*

(17) Upon an application under subsection (1) or (2), where the trade union concerned informs the Board that it does not desire to continue to represent the employees in the bargaining unit, the Board may declare that the trade union no longer represents the employees in the bargaining unit.

(18) Upon the Board making a declaration under subsection (14) or (17), any collective agreement in operation between the trade union and the employer that is binding upon the employees in the bargaining unit ceases to operate forthwith. R.S.O. 1990, c. L.2, s. 58 (5, 6).

64. (1) If a trade union has obtained a certificate by fraud, the Board may at any time declare that the trade union no longer represents the employees in the bargaining unit and, upon the making of such a declaration, the trade union is not entitled to claim any rights or privileges flowing from certification and, if it has made a collective agreement binding upon the employees in the bargaining unit, the collective agreement is void. R.S.O. 1990, c. L.2, s. 59.

(2) Subsection 8 (9) does not apply with respect to an application for a declaration under subsection (1).

(3) If an applicant has obtained a declaration under section 63 by fraud, the Board may at any time rescind the declaration. If the declaration is rescinded, the trade union is restored as the bargaining agent for the employees in the bargaining unit and any collective agreement that, but for the declaration, would have applied with respect to the employees becomes binding as if the declaration had not been made.

(4) Subsection 63 (13) does not apply with respect to an application for the recission under subsection (3) of a declaration. *New.*

65. (1) If a trade union fails to give the employer notice under section 16 within 60 days following certification or if it fails to give notice under section 59 and no such notice is given by the employer, the Board may, upon the application of the employer or of any of the employees in the bargaining unit, and with or without a representation vote, declare that the trade union no longer represents the employees in the bargaining unit. R.S.O. 1990, c. L.2, s. 60(1); 1993, c. 27, Sched.

(2) Where a trade union that has given notice under section 16 or section 59 or that has received notice under section 59 fails to commence to bargain within 60 days from the giving of the notice or, after having commenced to bargain but before the Minister has appointed a conciliation officer or mediator, allows a period of 60 days to elapse during which it has not sought to bargain, the Board may, upon the application of the employer or of any of the employees in the bargaining unit and with or without a representation vote, declare that the trade union no longer represents the employees in the bargaining unit. R.S.O. 1990, c. L.2, s. 60(2); 1993, c. 27, Sched.

66. (1) Where an employer and a trade union that has not been certified as the bargaining agent for a bargaining unit of employees of the employer enter into a collective agreement, or a recognition agreement as provided for in subsection 18 (3), the Board may, upon the application of any employee in the bargaining unit or of a trade union representing any employee in the bargaining unit, during the first year of the period of time that the first collective agreement between them is in operation or, if no collective agreement has been entered into, within one year from the signing of such recognition agreement, declare that the trade union was not, at the time the agreement was entered into, entitled to represent the employees in the bargaining unit. R.S.O. 1990, c. L.2, s. 61(1).

(2) Before disposing of an application under subsection (1), the Board may make such inquiry, require the production of such evidence and the doing of such things, or hold such representation votes, as it considers appropriate. R.S.O. 1990, c. L.2, s. 61(2); 1993, c. 27, Sched.

(3) On an application under subsection (1), the onus of establishing that the trade union was entitled to represent the employees in the bargaining unit at the time the agreement was entered into rests on the parties to the agreement.

(4) Upon the Board making a declaration under subsection (1), the trade union forthwith ceases to represent the employees in the defined bargaining unit in the recognition agreement or collective agreement and any collective agreement in operation between the trade union and the employer ceases to operate forthwith in respect of the employees affected by the application. R.S.O. 1990, c. L.2, s. 61(3, 4).

Timeliness of Representation Applications

67. (1) Subject to subsection (3), where a trade union has not made a collective agreement within one year after its certification and the Minister has appointed a conciliation officer or a mediator under this Act, no application for certification of a bargaining agent of, or for a declaration that a trade union no longer represents, the employees in the bargaining unit determined in the certificate shall be made until,

(a) 30 days have elapsed after the Minister has released to the parties the report of a conciliation board or mediator;

(b) 30 days have elapsed after the Minister has released to the parties a notice that he or she does not consider it advisable to appoint a conciliation board; or

(c) six months have elapsed after the Minister has released to the parties a notice of a report of the conciliation officer that the differences between the parties concerning the terms of a collective agreement have been settled,

as the case may be.

(2) Where notice has been given under section 59 and the Minister has appointed a conciliation officer or a mediator, no application for certifica-

tion of a bargaining agent of any of the employees in the bargaining units as defined in the collective agreement and no application for a declaration that the trade union that was a party to the collective agreement no longer represents the employees in the bargaining unit as defined in the agreement shall be made after the date when the agreement ceased to operate or the date when the Minister appointed a conciliation officer or a mediator, whichever is later, unless following the appointment of a conciliation officer or a mediator, if no collective agreement has been made,

    (a) at least 12 months have elapsed from the date of the appointment of the conciliation officer or a mediator;

    (b) a conciliation board or a mediator has been appointed and 30 days have elapsed after the report of the conciliation board or the mediator has been released by the Minister to the parties; or

    (c) 30 days have elapsed after the Minister has informed the parties that he or she does not consider it desirable to appoint a conciliation board,

whichever is later.

(3) Where a trade union has given notice under section 16 and the employees in the bargaining unit on whose behalf the trade union was certified as bargaining agent thereafter engage in a lawful strike or the employer lawfully locks out the employees, no application for certification of a bargaining agent of, or for a declaration that the trade union no longer represents, the employees in the bargaining unit determined in the certificate shall be made,

    (a) until six months have elapsed after the strike or lock-out commenced; or

    (b) until seven months have elapsed after the Minister has released to the parties the report of the conciliation board or mediator or a notice that the Minister does not consider it advisable to appoint a conciliation board,

whichever occurs first.

(4) Subsections (1) and (3) apply with necessary modifications to an application made under subsection 7 (3). R.S.O. 1990, c. L.2, s. 62.

Successor Rights

68. (1) Where a trade union claims that by reason of a merger or amalgamation or a transfer of jurisdiction it is the successor of a trade union that at the time of the merger, amalgamation or transfer of jurisdiction was the bargaining agent of a unit of employees of an employer and any question arises in respect of its rights to act as the successor, the Board, in any proceeding before it or on the application of any person or trade union concerned, may declare that the successor has or has not, as the case may be, acquired the rights, privileges and duties under this Act of its predecessor, or the Board may dismiss the application. R.S.O. 1990, c. L.2, s. 63(1).

(2) Before issuing a declaration under subsection (1), the Board may make such inquiry, require the production of such evidence or hold such representation votes as it considers appropriate. R.S.O. 1990, c. L.2, s. 63(2); 1993, c. 27, Sched.

(3) Where the Board makes an affirmative declaration under subsection (1), the successor shall for the purposes of this Act be conclusively presumed to have acquired the rights, privileges and duties of its predecessor, whether under a collective agreement or otherwise, and the employer, the successor and the employees concerned shall recognize such status in all respects. R.S.O. 1990, c. L.2, s. 63(3).

69. (1) In this section,

"business" includes a part or parts thereof; ("entreprise")

"sells" includes leases, transfers and any other manner of disposition, and "sold" and "sale" have corresponding meanings. ("vend", "vendu", "vente")

(2) Where an employer who is bound by or is a party to a collective agreement with a trade union or council of trade unions sells his, her or its business, the person to whom the business has been sold is, until the Board otherwise declares, bound by the collective agreement as if the person had been a party thereto and, where an employer sells his, her or its business while an application for certification or termination of bargaining rights to which the employer is a party is before the Board, the person to whom the business has been sold is, until the Board otherwise declares, the employer for the purposes of the application as if the person were named as the employer in the application.

(3) Where an employer on behalf of whose employees a trade union or council of trade unions, as the case may be, has been certified as bargaining agent or has given or is entitled to give notice under section 16 or 59, sells his, her or its business, the trade union, or council of trade unions continues, until the Board otherwise declares, to be the bargaining agent for the employees of the person to whom the business was sold in the like bargaining unit in that business, and the trade union or council of trade unions is entitled to give to the person to whom the business was sold a written notice of its desire to bargain with a view to making a collective agreement or the renewal, with or without modifications, of the agreement then in operation and such notice has the same effect as a notice under section 16 or 59, as the case requires.

(4) Where a business was sold to a person and a trade union or council of trade unions was the bargaining agent of any of the employees in such business or a trade union or council of trade unions is the bargaining agent

of the employees in any business carried on by the person to whom the business was sold, and,

    (a) any question arises as to what constitutes the like bargaining unit referred to in subsection (3); or

    (b) any person, trade union or council of trade unions claims that, by virtue of the operation of subsection (2) or (3), a conflict exists between the bargaining rights of the trade union or council of trade unions that represented the employees of the predecessor employer and the trade union or council of trade unions that represents the employees of the person to whom the business was sold,

the Board may, upon the application of any person, trade union or council of trade unions concerned,

    (c) define the composition of the like bargaining unit referred to in subsection (3) with such modification, if any, as the Board considers necessary; and

    (d) amend, to such extent as the Board considers necessary, any bargaining unit in any certificate issued to any trade union or any bargaining unit defined in any collective agreement.

(5) The Board may, upon the application of any person, trade union or council of trade unions concerned, made within 60 days after the successor employer referred to in subsection (2) becomes bound by the collective agreement, or within 60 days after the trade union or council of trade unions has given a notice under subsection (3), terminate the bargaining rights of the trade union or council of trade unions bound by the collective agreement or that has given notice, as the case may be, if, in the opinion of the Board, the person to whom the business was sold has changed its character so that it is substantially different from the business of the predecessor employer.

(6) Despite subsections (2) and (3), where a business was sold to [a] person who carries on one or more other businesses and a trade union or council of trade unions is the bargaining agent of the employees in any of the businesses and the person intermingles the employees of one of the businesses with those of another of the businesses, the Board may, upon the application of any person, trade union or council of trade unions concerned,

    (a) declare that the person to whom the business was sold is no longer bound by the collective agreement referred to in subsection (2);

    (b) determine whether the employees concerned constitute one or more appropriate bargaining units;

    (c) declare which trade union, trade unions or council of trade unions, if any, shall be the bargaining agent or agents for the employees in the unit or units; and

    (d) amend, to such extent as the Board considers necessary, any certificate issued to any trade union or council of trade unions or any bargaining unit defined in any collective agreement.

(7) Where a trade union or council of trade unions is declared to be the bargaining agent under subsection (6) and it is not already bound by a collective agreement with the successor employer with respect to the employees for whom it is declared to be the bargaining agent, it is entitled to give to the employer a written notice of its desire to bargain with a view to making a collective agreement, and the notice has the same effect as a notice under section 14. R.S.O. 1990, c. L.2, s. 64(1-7).

(8) Before disposing of any application under this section, the Board may make such inquiry, may require the production of such evidence and the doing of such things, or may hold such representation votes, as it considers appropriate. R.S.O. 1990, c. L.2, s. 64(8); 1993, c. 27, Sched.

(9) Where an application is made under this section, an employer is not required, despite the fact that a notice has been given by a trade union or council of trade unions, to bargain with that trade union or council of trade unions concerning the employees to whom the application relates until the Board has disposed of the application and has declared which trade union or council of trade unions, if any, has the right to bargain with the employer on behalf of the employees concerned in the application.

(10) For the purposes of sections 7, 63, 65, 67 and 132, a notice given by a trade union or council of trade unions under subsection (3) or a declaration made by the Board under subsection (6) has the same effect as a certification under section 10.

(11) Where one or more municipalities as defined in the *Municipal Affairs Act* are erected [sic] into another municipality, or two or more such municipalities are amalgamated, united or otherwise joined together, or all or part of one such municipality is annexed, attached or added to another such municipality, the employees of the municipalities concerned shall be deemed to have been intermingled, and,

    (a) the Board may exercise the like powers as it may exercise under subsections (6) and (8) with respect to the sale of a business under this section;

    (b) the new or enlarged municipality has the like rights and obligations as a person to whom a business is sold under this section and who intermingles the employees of two of the person's businesses; and

    (c) any trade union or council of trade unions concerned has the like rights and obligations as it would have in the case of the intermingling of employees in two or more businesses under this section.

(12) Where, on any application under this section or in any other proceeding before the Board, a question arises as to whether a business has been sold by one employer to another, the Board shall determine the question and its decision is final and conclusive for the purposes of this Act.

(13) Where, on an application under this section, a trade union alleges that the sale of a business has occurred, the respondents to the application shall adduce at the hearing all facts within their knowledge that are material to the allegation. R.S.O. 1990, c. L.2, s. 64(9-13).

Labour Relations Act of Ontario

Unfair Practices

70. No employer or employers' organization and no person acting on behalf of an employer or an employers' organization shall participate in or interfere with the formation, selection or administration of a trade union or the representation of employees by a trade union or contribute financial or other support to a trade union, but nothing in this section shall be deemed to deprive an employer of the employer's freedom to express views so long as the employer does not use coercion, intimidation, threats, promises or undue influence. R.S.O. 1990, c. L.2, s. 65.

71. No trade union and no person acting on behalf of a trade union shall participate in or interfere with the formation or administration of an employers' organization or contribute financial or other support to an employers' organization. R.S.O. 1990, c. L.2, s. 66.

72. No employer, employers' organization or person acting on behalf of an employer or an employers' organization,
    (a) shall refuse to employ or to continue to employ a person, or discriminate against a person in regard to employment or any term or condition of employment because the person was or is a member of a trade union or was or is exercising any other rights under this Act;
    (b) shall impose any condition in a contract of employment or propose the imposition of any condition in a contract of employment that seeks to restrain an employee or a person seeking employment from becoming a member of a trade union or exercising any other rights under this Act; or
    (c) shall seek by threat of dismissal, or by any other kind of threat, or by the imposition of a pecuniary or other penalty, or by any other means to compel an employee to become or refrain from becoming or to continue to be or to cease to be a member or officer or representative of a trade union or to cease to exercise any other rights under this Act. R.S.O. 1990, c. L.2, s. 67, *revised*.

73. (1) No employer, employers' organization or person acting on behalf of an employer or an employers' organization shall, so long as a trade union continues to be entitled to represent the employees in a bargaining unit, bargain with or enter into a collective agreement with any person or another trade union or a council of trade unions on behalf of or purporting, designed or intended to be binding upon the employees in the bargaining unit or any of them.
    (2) No trade union council of trade unions or person acting on behalf of a trade union or council of trade unions shall, so long as another trade union continues to be entitled to represent the employees in a bargaining unit, bargain with or enter into a collective agreement with an employer

or an employers' organization on behalf of or purporting, designed or intended to be binding upon the employees in the bargaining unit or any of them. R.S.O. 1990, c. L.2, s. 68.

74. A trade union or council of trade unions, so long as it continues to be entitled to represent employees in a bargaining unit, shall not act in a manner that is arbitrary, discriminatory or in bad faith in the representation of any of the employees in the unit, whether or not members of the trade union or of any constituent union of the council of trade unions, as the case may be. R.S.O. 1990, c. L.2, s. 69.

75. Where, pursuant to a collective agreement, a trade union is engaged in the selection, referral, assignment, designation or scheduling of persons to employment, it shall not act in a manner that is arbitrary, discriminatory or in bad faith. R.S.O. 1990, c. L.2, s. 70; 1993, c. 27, Sched.

76. No person, trade union or employers' organization shall seek by intimidation or coercion to compel any person to become or refrain from becoming or to continue to be or to cease to be a member of a trade union or of an employers' organization or to refrain from exercising any other rights under this Act or from performing any obligations under this Act. R.S.O. 1990, c. L.2, s. 71.

77. Nothing in this Act authorizes any person to attempt at the place at which an employee works to persuade the employee during the employee's working hours to become or refrain from becoming or continuing to be a member of a trade union. R.S.O. 1990, c. L.2, s. 72.

78. (1) No person, employer, employers' organization or person acting on behalf of an employer or employers' organization shall engage in strike-related misconduct or retain the services of a professional strike breaker and no person shall act as a professional strike breaker.
(2) For the purposes of subsection (1),

"professional strike breaker" means a person who is not involved in a dispute whose primary object, in the Board's opinion, is to interfere with, obstruct, prevent, restrain or disrupt the exercise of any right under this Act in anticipation of, or during, a lawful strike or lock-out; ("briseur de grève professionnel")

"strike-related misconduct" means a course of conduct of incitement, intimidation, coercion, undue influence, provocation, infiltration, surveillance or any other like course of conduct intended to interfere with, obstruct, prevent, restrain or disrupt the exercise of any right under this Act in anticipation of, or during, a lawful strike or lock-out. ("inconduite liée à une grève")

(3) Nothing in this section shall be deemed to restrict or limit any right or prohibition contained in any other provision of this Act. R.S.O. 1990, c. L.2, s. 73.

79. (1) Where a collective agreement is in operation, no employee bound by the agreement shall strike and no employer bound by the agreement shall lock out such an employee.

(2) Where no collective agreement is in operation, no employee shall strike and no employer shall lock out an employee until the Minister has appointed a conciliation officer or a mediator under this Act and,

(a) seven days have elapsed after the day the Minister has released or is deemed pursuant to subsection 122 (2) to have released to the parties the report of a conciliation board or mediator; or

(b) 14 days have elapsed after the day the Minister has released or is deemed pursuant to subsection 122 (2) to have released to the parties a notice that he or she does not consider it advisable to appoint a conciliation board. R.S.O. 1990, c. L.2, s. 74(1, 2).

(3) If a collective agreement is or has been in operation, no employee shall strike unless a strike vote is taken 30 days or less before the collective agreement expires or at any time after the agreement expires and more than 50 per cent of those voting vote in favour of a strike.

(4) If no collective agreement has been in operation, no employee shall strike unless a strike vote is taken on or after the day on which a conciliation officer is appointed and more than 50 per cent of those voting vote in favour of a strike.

(5) Subsections (3) and (4) do not apply to an employee in the construction industry. *New.*

(6) No employee shall threaten an unlawful strike and no employer shall threaten an unlawful lock-out of an employee. R.S.O. 1990, c. L.2, s. 74(4).

(7) A strike vote or a vote to ratify a proposed collective agreement or memorandum of settlement taken by a trade union shall be by ballots cast in such a manner that persons expressing their choice cannot be identified with the choice expressed.

(8) All employees in a bargaining unit, whether or not the employees are members of the trade union or of any constituent union of a council of trade unions, shall be entitled to participate in a strike vote or a vote to ratify a proposed collective agreement or memorandum of settlement. *New.*

(9) Any vote mentioned in subsection (7) shall be conducted in such a manner that those entitled to vote have ample opportunity to cast their ballots. If the vote taken is otherwise than by mail, the time and place for voting must be reasonably convenient. R.S.O. 1990, c. L.2, s. 74(6), *amended.*

80. (1) Where an employee engaging in a lawful strike makes an unconditional application in writing to the employee's employer within six months from the commencement of the lawful strike to return to work, the employer shall, subject to subsection (2), reinstate the employee in the employee's former employment, on such terms as the employer and employee may agree upon, and the employer in offering terms of employment shall not discriminate against the employee for exercising or hav[ing] exercised any rights under this Act.

(2) An employer is not required to reinstate an employee who has made an application to return to work in accordance with subsection (1),

(a) where the employer no longer has persons engaged in performing work of the same or similar nature to work which the employee performed prior to the employee's cessation of work; or

(b) where there has been a suspension or discontinuance for cause of an employer's operations, or any part thereof, but, if the employer resumes such operations, the employer shall first reinstate those employees who have made an application under subsection (1). R.S.O. 1990, c. L.2, s. 75.

81. No trade union or council of trade unions shall call or authorize or threaten to call or authorize an unlawful strike and no officer, official or agent of a trade union or council of trade unions shall counsel, procure, support or encourage an unlawful strike or threaten an unlawful strike. R.S.O. 1990, c. L.2, s. 76.

82. No employer or employers' organization shall call or authorize or threaten to call or authorize an unlawful lock-out and no officer, official or agent of an employer or employers' organization shall counsel, procure, support or encourage an unlawful lock-out or threaten an unlawful lock-out. R.S.O. 1990, c. L.2, s. 77.

83. (1) No person shall do any act if the person knows or ought to know that, as a probable and reasonable consequence of the act, another person or persons will engage in an unlawful strike or an unlawful lock- out.

(2) Subsection (1) does not apply to any act done in connection with a lawful strike or lawful lock-out. R.S.O. 1990, c. L.2, s. 78.

84. Nothing in this Act prohibits any suspension or discontinuance for cause of an employer's operations or the quitting of employment for cause if the suspension, discontinuance or quitting does not constitute a lock-out or strike. R.S.O. 1990, c. L.2, s. 79.

85. No trade union shall suspend, expel or penalize in any way a member because the member has refused to engage in or to continue to engage in a strike that is unlawful under this Act. R.S.O. 1990, c. L.2, s. 80.

86. (1) Where notice has been given under section 16 or section 59 and no collective agreement is in operation, no employer shall, except with the consent of the trade union, alter the rates of wages or any other term or condition of employment or any right, privilege or duty, of the employer, the trade union or the employees, and no trade union shall, except with the consent of the employer, alter any term or condition of employment or any right, privilege or duty of the employer, the trade union or the employees,

    (a) until the Minister has appointed a conciliation officer or a mediator under this Act, and,

        (i) seven days have elapsed after the Minister has released to the parties the report of a conciliation board or mediator, or

        (ii) 14 days have elapsed after the Minister has released to the parties a notice that he or she does not consider it advisable to appoint a conciliation board,

as the case may be; or

    (b) until the right of the trade union to represent the employees has been terminated,

whichever occurs first.

(2) Where a trade union has applied for certification and notice thereof from the Board has been received by the employer, the employer shall not, except with the consent of the trade union, alter the rates of wages or any other term or condition of employment or any right, privilege or duty of the employer or the employees until,

    (a) the trade union has given notice under section 16, in which case subsection (1) applies; or

    (b) the application for certification by the trade union is dismissed or terminated by the Board or withdrawn by the trade union.

(3) Where notice has been given under section 59 and no collective agreement is in operation, any difference between the parties as to whether or not subsection (1) of this section was complied with may be referred to arbitration by either of the parties as if the collective agreement was still in operation and section 48 applies with necessary modifications thereto. R.S.O. 1990, c. L.2, s. 81.

87. (1) No employer, employers' organization or person acting on behalf of an employer or employers' organization shall,

    (a) refuse to employ or continue to employ a person;

    (b) threaten dismissal or otherwise threaten a person;

    (c) discriminate against a person in regard to employment or a term or condition of employment; or

    (d) intimidate or coerce or impose a pecuniary or other penalty on a person,

because of a belief that the person may testify in a proceeding under this Act or because the person has made or is about to make a disclosure that may be required in a proceeding under this Act or because the person has made an application or filed a complaint under this Act or has participated in or is about to participate in a proceeding under this Act.

(2) No trade union, council of trade unions or person acting on behalf of a trade union or council of trade unions shall,

    (a) discriminate against a person in regard to employment or a term or condition of employment; or

    (b) intimidate or coerce or impose a pecuniary or other penalty on a person,

because of a belief that the person may testify in a proceeding under this Act or because the person has made or is about to make a disclosure that may be required in a proceeding under this Act or because the person has made an application or filed a complaint under this Act or has participated in or is about to participate in a proceeding under this Act. R.S.O. 1990, c. L.2, s. 82.

88. No person shall wilfully destroy, mutilate, obliterate, alter, deface or remove or cause to be destroyed, mutilated, obliterated, altered, defaced or removed any notice that the Board has required to be posted during the period that the notice is required to be posted. R.S.O. 1990, c. L.2, s. 83.

Locals Under Trusteeship

89. (1) A provincial, national or international trade union that assumes supervision or control over a subordinate trade union, whereby the autonomy of such subordinate trade union, under the constitution or by-laws of the provincial, national or international trade union is suspended, shall, within 60 days after it has assumed supervision or control over the subordinate trade union, file with the Board a statement in the prescribed form, verified by the affidavit of its principal officers, setting out the terms under which supervision or control is to be exercised and it shall, upon the direction of the Board, file such additional information concerning such supervision and control as the Minister may from time to time require.

(2) Where a provincial, national or international trade union has assumed supervision or control over a subordinate trade union, such supervision or control shall not continue for more than 12 months from the date of such assumption, but such supervision or control may be continued for a further period of 12 months with the consent of the Board. R.S.O. 1990, c. L.2, s. 84.

Information

90. Each party to a collective agreement shall, forthwith after it is made, file one copy with the Minister. R.S.O. 1990, c. L.2, s. 85.

91. The Board may direct a trade union, council of trade unions or employers' organization to file with the Board within the time prescribed in the direction a copy of its constitution and by-laws and a statutory declaration of its president or secretary setting forth the names and addresses of its officers. R.S.O. 1990, c. L.2, s. 86.

92. (1) Every trade union shall upon the request of any member furnish the member, without charge, with a copy of the audited financial statement of its affairs to the end of its last fiscal year certified by its treasurer or other officer responsible for the handling and administration of its funds to be a true copy, and, upon the complaint of any member that the trade union has failed to furnish such a statement, the Board may direct the trade union to file with the Registrar of the Board, within such time as the Board may determine, a copy of the audited financial statement of its affairs to the end of its last fiscal year verified by the affidavit of its treasurer or other officer responsible for the handling and administration of its funds and to furnish a copy of the statement to the members of the trade union that the Board in its discretion may direct, and the trade union shall comply with the direction according to its terms.

(2) Where a member of a trade union complains that an audited financial statement is inadequate, the Board may inquire into the complaint and the Board may order the trade union to prepare another audited financial statement in a form and containing the particulars that the Board considers appropriate and the Board may further order that the audited financial statement, as rectified, be certified by a person licensed under the *Public Accountancy Act* or a firm whose partners are licensed under that Act. R.S.O. 1990, c. L.2, s. 87.

93. (1) In this section,

"administrator" means any trade union, trustee or person responsible for the control, management or disposition of money received or contributed to a vacation pay fund or a welfare benefit or pension plan or fund for the members of a trade union or their survivors or beneficiaries.

(2) Every administrator shall file annually with the Minister not later than June 1 in each year or at such other time or times as the Minister may direct, a copy of the audited financial statement certified by a person licensed under the *Public Accountancy Act* or a firm whose partners are licensed under that Act of a vacation pay fund, or a welfare benefit or pension plan or fund setting out its financial condition for the preceding fiscal year and disclosing,

    (a) a description of the coverage provided by the fund or plan;
    (b) the amount contributed by each employer;
    (c) the amounts contributed by the members and the trade union, if any;
    (d) a statement of the assets, specifying the total amount of each type of asset;

(e) a statement of liabilities, receipts and disbursements;

(f) a statement of salaries, fees and commissions charged to the fund or plan, to whom paid, in what amount and for what purposes; and

(g) such further information as the Minister may require.

(3) The administrator, upon the request in writing of any member of the trade union whose employer has made payments or contributions into the fund or plan, shall furnish to the member without charge a copy of the audited financial statement required to be filed by subsection (2).

(4) Where an administrator has failed to comply with subsection (2) or (3), upon a certificate of failure so to comply signed by the Minister or upon complaint by the member, the Board may direct the administrator to comply within the time that the Board may determine. R.S.O. 1990, c. L.2, s. 88.

94. (1) Every trade union and unincorporated employers' organization in Ontario that has members in Ontario shall, within 15 days after it has enrolled its first member, file with the Board a notice in the prescribed form giving the name and address of a person resident in Ontario who is authorized by the trade union or unincorporated employers' organization to accept on its behalf service of process and notices under this Act.

(2) Whenever a trade union or unincorporated employers' organization changes the authorization referred to in subsection (1), it shall file with the Board notice thereof in the prescribed form within 15 days after making such change.

(3) Service on the person named in a notice or the latest notice, as the case may be, filed under subsection (1) is good and sufficient service for the purposes of this Act on the trade union or unincorporated employers' organization that filed the notice. R.S.O. 1990, c. L.2, s. 89.

95. Every publication that deals with the relations between employers or employers' organizations and trade unions or employees shall bear the names and addresses of its printer and its publisher. R.S.O. 1990, c. L.2, s. 90.

Enforcement

96. (1) The Board may authorize a labour relations officer to inquire into any complaint alleging a contravention of this Act.

(2) The labour relations officer shall forthwith inquire into the complaint and endeavour to effect a settlement of the matter complained of.

(3) The labour relations officer shall report the results of his or her inquiry and endeavours to the Board.

(4) Where a labour relations officers is unable to effect a settlement of the matter complained of or where the Board in its discretion considers it advisable to dispense with an inquiry by a labour relations officer, the Board may inquire into the complaint of a contravention of this Act and where the

Board is satisfied that an employer, employers' organization, trade union, council of trade unions, person or employee has acted contrary to this Act it shall determine what, if anything, the employer, employers' organization, trade union, council of trade unions, person or employee shall do or refrain from doing with respect thereto and such determination, without limiting the generality of the foregoing may include, despite the provisions of any collective agreement, any one or more of,

(a) an order directing the employer, employers' organization, trade union, council of trade unions, employee or other person to cease doing the act or acts complained of;

(b) an order directing the employer, employers' organization, trade union, council of trade unions, employee or other person to rectify the act or acts complained of; or

(c) an order to reinstate in employment or hire the person or employee concerned, with or without compensation, or to compensate instead of hiring or reinstatement for loss of earnings or other employment benefits in an amount that may be assessed by the Board against the employer, employers' organization, trade union, council of trade unions, employee or other person jointly or severally. R.S.O. 1990, c. L.2, s. 91(1-4).

(5) On an inquiry by the Board into a complaint under subsection (4) that a person has been refused employment, discharged, discriminated against, threatened, coerced, intimidated or otherwise dealt with contrary to this Act as to the person's employment, opportunity for employment or conditions of employment, the burden of proof that any employer or employers' organization did not act contrary to this Act lies upon the employer or employers' organization. R.S.O. 1990, c. L.2, s. 91(5); 1993, c. 27, Sched.

(6) A trade union, council of trade unions, employer, employers' organization or person affected by the determination may file the determination, excluding the reasons, in the prescribed form in the Ontario Court (General Division) and it shall be entered in the same way as an order of that court and is enforceable as such. 1992, c. 21, s. 36(3).

(7) Where a proceeding under this Act has been settled, whether through the endeavours of the labour relations officer or otherwise, and the terms of the settlement have been put in writing and signed by the parties or their representatives, the settlement is binding upon the parties, the trade union, council of trade unions, employer, employers' organization, person or employee who have agreed to the settlement and shall be complied with according to its terms, and a complaint that the trade union, council of trade unions, employer, employers' organization, person or employee who has agreed to the settlement has not complied with the terms of the settlement shall be deemed to be a complaint under subsection (1). R.S.O. 1990, c. L.2, s. 91(7); 1992, c. 21, s. 36(4).

97. For the purposes of section 87 and any complaint made under section 96,

"person" includes any person otherwise excluded by subsection 1 (3). R.S.O. 1990, c. L.2, s. 92.

98. (1) On application in a pending proceeding, the Board may make interim orders concerning procedural matters.

(2) The Board shall not make an order under subsection (1) requiring an employer to reinstate an employee in employment. *New.*

99. (1) This section applies when the Board receives a complaint,

(a) that a trade union or council of trade unions, or an agent of either was or is requiring an employer or employers' organization to assign particular work to persons in a particular trade union or in a particular trade, craft or class rather than to persons in another;

(b) that an employer was or is assigning work to persons in a particular trade union rather than to persons in another; or

(c) that a trade union has failed to comply with its duties under section 74 or 75. 1992, c. 21, s. 38(1), *part, amended.*

(2) A complaint described in subsection (1) may be withdrawn by the complainant upon such conditions as the Board may determine. *New.*

(3) The Board is not required to hold a hearing to determine a complaint under this section.

(4) Representatives of the trade union or council of trade unions and of the employer or employers' organization or their substitutes shall promptly meet and attempt to settle the matters raised by a complaint under clause (1)(a) or (b) and shall report the outcome to the Board.

(5) The Board may make any interim or final order it considers appropriate after consulting with the parties. *New.*

(6) In an interim order or after making an interim order, the Board may order any person, employers' organization, trade union or council of trade unions to cease and desist from doing anything intended or likely to interfere with the terms of an interim order respecting the assignment of work. 1992, c. 21, s. 38(7), *part.*

(7) When making an order or at any time after doing so, the Board may alter a bargaining unit determined in a certificate or defined in a collective agreement. 1992, c. 21, s. 38(8), *part.*

(8) If a collective agreement requires the reference of any difference between the parties arising out of work assignment to a tribunal mutually selected by them, the Board may alter the bargaining unit determined in a certificate or defined in a collective agreement as it considers proper to enable the parties to conform to the decision of the tribunal. 1992, c. 21, s. 38(9), *part.*

(9) Where an employer is a party to or is bound by two or more collective agreements and it appears that the description of the bargaining unit

in one of the agreements conflicts with the description of the bargaining unit in the other or another of the agreements, the Board may, upon the application of the employer or any of the trade unions concerned, alter the description of the bargaining units in any such agreement as it considers proper, and the agreement or agreements shall be deemed to have been altered accordingly. R.S.O. 1990, c. L.2, s. 93(18).

(10) A party to an interim or final order may file it, excluding the reasons, in the prescribed form in the Ontario Court (General Division) and it shall be entered in the same way as an order of that court and is enforceable as such.

(11) An order that has been filed with the court is enforceable by a person, employers' organization, trade union or council of trade unions affected by it and is enforceable on the day after the date fixed in the order for compliance. 1993, c. 38, s. 67(5).

(12) A person, employers' organization, trade union or council of trade unions affected by an interim order made by the Board under this section shall comply with it despite any provision of this Act or of any collective agreement relating to the assignment of the work to which the order relates.

(13) A person, employers' organization, trade union or council of trade unions who is complying with an interim order made by the Board under this section is deemed not to have violated any provision of this Act or of any collective agreement. 1992, s. 21, s. 38(9).

100. Where, on the complaint of a trade union, council of trade unions, employer or employers' organization, the Board is satisfied that a trade union or council of trade unions called or authorized or threatened to call or authorize an unlawful strike or that an officer, official or agent of a trade union or council of trade unions counselled or procured or supported or encouraged an unlawful strike or threatened an unlawful strike or that employees engaged in or threatened to engage in an unlawful strike or any person has done or is threatening to do an act that the person knows or ought to know that, as a probable and reasonable consequence of the act, another person or persons will engage in an unlawful strike, the Board may so declare and it may direct what action, if any, a person, employee, employer, employers' organization, trade union or council of trade unions and their officers, officials or agents shall do or refrain from doing with respect to the unlawful strike or the threat of an unlawful strike. R.S.O. 1990, c. L.2, s. 94.

101. Where, on the complaint of a trade union, council of trade unions, employer or employers' organization, the Board is satisfied that an employer or employers' organization called or authorized or threatened to call or authorize an unlawful lock-out or locked out or threatened to lock out employees or that an officer, official or agent of an employer or employers' organization counselled or procured or supported or encouraged an unlawful lock-out or threatened an unlawful lock-out, the Board may so declare and, in addition, in its discretion, it may direct what action if any a person, employee, employer, employers' organization, trade union or council of trade unions and their officers, officials or agents shall do or refrain from doing with respect to the unlawful lock-out or the threat of an unlawful lock-out. R.S.O. 1990, c. L.2, s. 95.

102. A party to a direction made under section 100 or 101 may file it, excluding the reasons, in the prescribed form in the Ontario Court (General Division) and it shall be entered in the same way as an order of that court and is enforceable as such. 1992, c. 21, s. 39.

103. (1) Where the Board declares that a trade union or council of trade unions has called or authorized an unlawful strike or that an employer or employers' organization has called or authorized an unlawful lock-out and no collective agreement is in operation between the trade union or council of trade unions and the employer or employers' organization, as the case may be, the trade union or council of trade unions or employer or employers' organization may, within 15 days of the release of the Board's declaration, but not thereafter, notify the employer or employers' organization or trade union or council of trade unions, as the case may be, in writing of its intention to claim damages for the unlawful strike or lock-out, and the notice shall contain the name of its appointee to an arbitration board.
 (2) The recipient of the notice shall within five days inform the sender of the notice of the name of its appointee to the arbitration board.
 (3) The two appointees so selected shall, within five days of the appointment of the second of them, appoint a third person who shall be the chair.
 (4) If the recipient of the notice fails to name an appointee, or if the two appointees fail to agree upon a chair within the time limited, the appointment shall be made by the Minister upon the request of either party.
 (5) The arbitration board shall hear and determine the claim for damages including any question as to whether the claim is arbitrable and shall issue a decision and the decision is final and binding upon the parties to the arbitration, and,
   (a) in the case of a council of trade unions, upon the members of affiliates of the council who are affected by the decision; and
   (b) in the case of an employers' organization, upon the employers in the organization who are affected by the decision.
 (6) The decision of a majority is the decision of the arbitration board, but if there is no majority the decision of the chair governs.
 (7) The chair and members of the arbitration board under this section shall be paid remuneration and expenses at the same rate as is payable to a chair and members of a conciliation board under this Act, and the parties to the arbitration are jointly and severally liable for the payment of the fees and expenses. R.S.O. 1990, c. L.2, s. 97(1-7).

(8) In an arbitration under this section, subsections 48 (6), (8), (9), (11) to (13), (19) and (20) apply with necessary modifications. R.S.O. 1990, c. L.2, s. 97(8), *amended.*

104. (1) Every person, trade union, council of trade unions or employers' organization that contravenes any provision of this Act or of any decision, determination, interim order, order, direction, declaration or ruling made under this Act is guilty of an offense and on conviction is liable,
    (a) if an individual, to a fine of not more than $2,000; or
    (b) if a corporation, trade union, council of trade unions or employers' organization, to a fine of not more than $25,000.
(2) Each day that a person, trade union, council of trade unions or employers' organization contravenes any provision of this Act or of any decision, determination, interim order, order, direction, declaration or ruling made under this Act constitutes a separate offence.
(3) Every fine recovered for an offence under this Act shall be paid to the Treasurer of Ontario and shall form part of the Consolidated Revenue Fund. R.S.O. 1990, c. L.2, s. 98.

105. An information in respect of a contravention of this Act may be for one or more offences and no information, warrant, conviction or other step or procedure in any such prosecution is objectionable or insufficient by reason of the fact that it relates to two or more offences. R.S.O. 1990, c. L.2, s. 99.

106. If a corporation, trade union, council of trade unions or employers' organization is guilty of an offence under this Act, every officer, official or agent thereof who assented to the commission of the offence shall be deemed to be a party to and guilty of the offence. R.S.O. 1990, c. L.2, s. 100.

107. (1) A prosecution for an offence under this Act may be instituted against a trade union or council of trade unions or employers' organization in the name of the union, council or organization.
(2) Any act or thing done or omitted by an officer, official or agent of a trade union or council of trade unions or employers' organization within the scope of the officer, official or agent's authority to act on behalf of the union, council or organization shall be deemed to be an act or thing done or omitted by the union, council or organization. R.S.O. 1990, c. L.2, s. 101.

108. Where a trade union, a council of trade unions or an unincorporated employers' organization is affected by a determination of the Board under section 96, an interim order of the Board under section 99 or a direction of the Board under section 100, 101 or 144 or a decision of an arbitrator or arbitration board including a decision under section 103, proceedings to enforce the determination, interim order, direction or decision may be instituted in the Ontario Court (General Division) by or against the union, council or organization in the name of the union, council or organization, as the case may be. R.S.O. 1990, c. L.2, s. 102, *amended.*

109. (1) No prosecution for an offence under this Act shall be instituted except with the consent in writing of the Board.

(2) An application for consent to institute a prosecution for an offence under this Act may be made by a trade union, a council of trade unions, a corporation or an employers' organization among others, and, if the consent is given by the Board, the information may be laid by any officer, official or member of the trade union, council of trade unions, corporation or employers' organization among others. R.S.O. 1990, c. L.2, s. 103.

Selected Regulations and Forms

Regulations of the National Mediation Board —Selected Provisions
29 C.F.R. §§1201.1-1209.10

SOURCE: 11 FR 177A-922, Sept. 11, 1946, unless otherwise noted. Redesignated at 13 FR 8740, Dec. 30, 1948.

PART 1201. DEFINITIONS

§1201.1 Carrier

The term *carrier* includes any express company, sleeping car company, carrier by railroad, subject to the Interstate Commerce Act (24 Stat. 379, as amended; 49 U.S.C. et seq.), and any company which is directly or indirectly owned or controlled by or under common control with any carrier by railroad and which operates any equipment or facilities or performs any service (other than trucking service) in connection with the transportation, receipt, delivery, elevation, transfer in transit, refrigeration or icing, storage and handling of property transported by railroad, and any receiver, trustee or other individual or body, judicial or otherwise, when in the possession of the business of any such "carrier."

§1201.2 Exceptions

(a) The term "carrier" shall not include any street, interurban, or suburban electric railway, unless such railway is operating as a part of a general steam-railroad system of transportation, but shall not exclude any part of the general steam-railroad system of transportation now or hereafter operated by any other motive power.

(b) The term "carrier" shall not include any company by reason of its being engaged in the mining of coal, the supplying of coal to carrier where delivery is not beyond the tipple, and the operation of equipment or facilities therefor or any of such activities.

§1201.3 Determination as to electric lines

The Interstate Commerce Commission is hereby authorized and directed upon request of the Mediation Board or upon complaint of any part interested to determine after hearing whether any line operated by electric power falls within the terms of this part.

§1201.4 Employee

The term *employee* as used in this part includes every person in the service of a carrier (subject to its continuing authority to supervise and direct the manner of rendition of his service) who performs any work defined as that of an employee or subordinate official in the orders of the Interstate Commerce Commission now in effect, and as the same may be amended or interpreted by orders hereafter entered by the Commission pursuant to the authority which is hereby conferred upon it to enter orders amending or interpreting such existing orders: *Provided, however,* That no occupational classification made by order of the Interstate Commerce Commission shall be construed to define the crafts according to which railway employees may be organized by their voluntary action, nor shall the jurisdiction or powers of such employee organizations be regarded as in any way limited or defined by the provisions of this Act or by the orders of the Commission.

§1201.5 Exceptions

The term "employee" shall not include any individual while such individual is engaged in the physical operations consisting of the mining of coal, the preparation of coal, the handling (other than movement by rail with standard locomotives) of coal not beyond the mine tipple, or the loading of coal at the tipple.

Regulations of the National Mediation Board

§1201.6 Representatives

The term *representative* means any person or persons, labor union, organization, or corporation designated either by a carrier or group of carriers or by its or their employees, to act for it or them.

PART 1202. RULES OF PROCEDURE

§1202.1 Mediation

The mediation services of the Board may be invoked by the parties, or either party, to a dispute between an employee or group of employees and a carrier concerning changes in rates of pay, rules, or working conditions not adjusted by the parties in conference; also, concerning a dispute not referable to the National Railroad Adjustment Board or appropriate airline adjustment board, when not adjusted in conference between the parties, or where conferences are refused. The National Mediation Board may proffer its services in case any labor emergency is found by it to exist at any time.

§1202.2 Interpretation of mediation agreements

Under section 5, Second, of title I of the Railway Labor Act, in any case in which a controversy arises over the meaning or application of any agreement reached through mediation, either party to said agreement, or both, may apply to the National Mediation Board for an interpretation of the meaning or application of such agreement. Upon receipt of such request, the Board shall, after a hearing of both sides, give its interpretation within 30 days.

§1202.3 Representation disputes

If any dispute shall arise among a carrier's employees as to who are the representatives of such employees designated and authorized in accordance with the requirements of the Railway Labor Act, it is the duty of the Board, upon request of either party to the dispute, to investigate such dispute and certify to both parties, in writing, the name or names of individuals or organizations that have been designated and authorized to represent the employees involved in the dispute, and to certify the same to the carrier.

§1202.4 Secret ballot

In conducting such investigation, the Board is authorized to take a secret ballot of the employees involved, or to utilize any other appropriate method of ascertaining the names of their duly designated and authorized representatives in such manner as shall insure the choice of representatives by the employees without interference, influence, or coercion exercised by the carrier.

§1202.5 Rules to govern elections

In the conduct of a representation election, the Board shall designate who may participate in the election, which may include a public hearing on craft or class, and establish the rules to govern the election, or may appoint a committee of three neutral persons who after hearing shall within 10 days designate the employees who may participate in the election.

§1202.6 Access to carrier records

Under the Railway Labor Act the Board has access to and has power to make copies of the books and records of the carriers to obtain and utilize such information as may be necessary to fulfill its duties with respect to representatives of carrier employees.

§1202.7 Who may participate in elections

As mentioned in §1202.3, when disputes arise between parties to a representation dispute, the National Mediation Board is authorized by the Act to determine who may participate in the selection of employees [sic] representatives.

§1202.8 Hearings on craft or class

In the event the contesting parties or organizations are unable to agree on the employees eligible to participate in the selection of representatives, and either party makes application by letter for a formal hearing before the Board to determine the dispute, the Board may in its discretion hold a public hearing, at which all parties interested may present their contentions and argument, and at which the carrier concerned is usually invited to present factual information. At the conclusion of such hearings the Board customarily invites all interested parties to submit briefs supporting their views, and after considering the evidence and briefs, the Board makes a determination or finding, specifying the craft or class of employees eligible to participate in the designation of representatives.

§1202.9 Appointment of arbitrators

Section 5, Third, (a) of the Railway Labor Act provides in the event mediation of a dispute is unsuccessful, the Board endeavors to induce the parties to submit their controversy to arbitration. If the parties so agree, and the arbitrators named by the parties are unable to agree upon the neutral arbitrator or arbitrators, as provided in section 7 of the Railway Labor Act, it becomes the duty of the Board to name such neutral arbitrators and fix the compensation for such service. In performing this duty, the Board is required to appoint only those whom it deems wholly disinterested in the controversy, and to be impartial and without bias as between the parties thereto.

§1202.10 Appointment of referees

Section 3, Third, (e) title I of the act makes it the duty of the National Mediation Board to appoint and fix the compensation for service a neutral person known as a "referee" in any case where a division of the National Railroad Adjustment Board becomes deadlocked on an award, such referee to sit with the division and make an award. The National Mediation Board in appointing referees is bound by the same requirements that apply in the appointment of neutral arbitrators as outlined in §1202.9.

§1202.11 Emergency boards

Under the terms of section 10 of the Railway Labor Act, if a dispute between a carrier and its employees is not adjusted through mediation or the other procedures prescribed by the act, and should, in the judgment of the National Mediation Board, threaten to interrupt interstate commerce to a degree such as to deprive any section of the country of essential transportation service, the Board shall notify the President, who may thereupon, in his discretion, create an emergency board to investigate and report to him respecting such dispute. An emergency board may be composed of such number of persons as the President designates, and persons so designated shall not be pecuniarily or otherwise interested in any organization of employees or any carrier. The compensation of emergency board members is fixed by the President. An emergency board is created separately in each instance, and is required to investigate the facts as to the dispute and report thereon to the President within 30 days from the date of its creation.

§1202.12 National Air Transport Adjustment Board

Under section 205, title II, of the Railway Labor Act, when in the judgment of the National Mediation Board it becomes necessary to establish a permanent national board of adjustment for the air carriers subject to the act to provide for the prompt and orderly settlement of disputes between the employees and the carriers growing out of grievances, or out of the application or interpretation of working agreements, the Board is empowered by its order made, published, and served, to direct the air carriers and labor organizations, national in scope, to select and designate four representatives to constitute a Board known as the National Air Transport Adjustment Board. Two members each shall be selected by the air carriers and the labor organizations of their employees. Up to the present time, it has not been considered necessary to establish the National Air Transport Adjustment Board.

§1202.13 Air carriers

By the terms of title II of the Railway Labor Act, which was approved April 10, 1936, all of title I, except section 3, which relates to the National Railroad Adjustment Board, was extended to cover every common carrier by air engaged in interstate or foreign commerce, and every carrier by air transporting mail for or under contract with the United States Government, and to all employees or subordinate officials of such air carriers.

§1202.14 Labor members of Adjustment Board

Section 3, First, (f) of title I of the Railway Labor Act relating to the settlement of disputes among labor organizations as to the qualification of any such organization to participate in the selection of labor members of the Adjustment Board, places certain duties upon the National Mediation Board. This section of the act is quoted below:

> (f) In the event a dispute arises as to the right of any national labor organization to participate as per paragraph (c) of this section in the selection and designation of the labor members of the Adjustment Board, the Secretary of Labor shall investigate the claim of such labor organization to participate, and if such claim in the judgment of the Secretary of Labor has merit, the Secretary shall notify the Mediation Board accordingly, and within 10 days after receipt of such advice the Mediation Board shall request those national labor organizations duly qualified as per paragraph (c) of this section to participate in the selection and designation of the labor members of the Adjustment Board to select a representative. Such representatives, together with a representative

likewise designated by the claimant, and a third or neutral party designated by the Mediation Board, constituting a board of three, shall within 30 days after the appointment of the neutral member investigate the claims of the labor organization desiring participation and decide whether or not it was organized in accordance with section 2, hereof, and is otherwise properly qualified to participate in the selection of the labor members of the Adjustment Board, and the findings of such boards of three shall be final and binding.

§1202.15 Length of briefs in NMB hearing proceedings

(a) In the event briefs are authorized by the Board or the assigned Hearing Officer, principal briefs shall not exceed fifty (50) pages in length and reply briefs, if permitted, shall not exceed twenty-five (25) pages in length unless the participant desiring to submit a brief in excess of such limitation requests a waiver of such limitation from the Board which is received within five (5) days of the date on which the briefs were ordered or, in the case of a reply brief, within five (5) days of receipt of the principal brief, and in such cases the Board may require the filing of a summary of argument, suitably paragraphed which should be a succinct, but accurate and clear, condensation of the argument actually made in the brief.

(b) The page limitations provided by this section (§1202.15) are exclusive of those pages containing the table of contents, tables of citations and any copies of administrative or court decisions which have been cited in the brief. All briefs shall be submitted on standard $8\frac{1}{2} \times 11$ inch paper with double spaced type.

(c) Briefs not complying with this section (§1202.15) will be returned promptly to their initiators.

[44 FR. 10601, Feb. 22, 1979]

Part 1203. Applications for Service

§1203.1 Mediation services

Applications for the mediation services of the National Mediation Board under section 5, First, of the Railway Labor Act, may be made on printed forms N.M.B. 2, copies of which may be secured from the Board's Secretary. Such applications and all correspondence connected therewith should be submitted in duplicate. The application should show the exact nature of the dispute, the number of employees involved, name of the carrier and name of the labor organization, date of agreement between the parties, if any, date and copy of notice served by the invoking party to the other and date of final conference between the parties. Application should be signed by the highest officer of the carrier who has been designated to handle disputes under the Railway Labor Act, or by the chief executive of the labor organization, whichever party files the application. These applications, after preliminary investigation in the Board's office[s], are given docket number in series "A" and the cases are assigned for mediation to Board members or to mediators on the Board's staff.

[11 FR 177A-923, Sept. 11, 1946. Redesignated at 13 FR 8740, Dec. 30, 1948]

§1203.2 Investigation of representation disputes

Applications for the services of the National Mediation Board under section 2, [N]inth, of the Railway Labor Act to investigate representation disputes among carriers' employees may be made on printed forms NMB-3, copies of which may be secured from the Board's Executive Secretary. Such applications and all correspondence connected therewith should be filed in duplicate and the applications should be accompanied by signed authorization cards from the employees composing the craft or class involved in the dispute. The applications should show specifically the name or description of the craft or class of employees involved, the name of the invoking organization, the name of the organization currently representing the employees, if any, and the estimated number of employees in each craft or class involved. The applications should be signed by the chief executive of the invoking organization, or other authorized officer of the organization. These disputes are given docket numbers in series "R".

[43 FR 30053, July 13, 1978]

§1203.3 Interpretation of mediation agreements

(a) Applications may be filed with the Board's Secretary under section 5, Second, of the Railway Labor Act, for the interpretation of agreements reached in mediation under section 5, First. Such applications may be made by letter from either party to the mediation agreement stating the specific question on which an interpretation is desired.

(b) This function of the National Mediation Board is not intended to conflict with the provisions of section 3 of the Railway Labor Act[,] [p]roviding for interpretation of agreements by the National Railroad Adjustment Board. Many complete working agreements are revised with the aid of the Board's mediating services, and it has been the Board's policy that disputes involving the interpretation or application of such agreements should be handled by the Adjustment Board. Under this section of the law the Board

Regulations of the National Mediation Board

when called upon may only consider and render an interpretation on the specific terms of an agreement actually signed in mediation, and not for matters incident or corollary thereto.

[11 FR 177A-923, Sept. 11, 1946. Redesignated at 13 FR 8740, Dec. 30, 1948]

PART 1204. LABOR CONTRACTS

§1204.1 Making and maintaining contracts

It is the duty of all carriers, their officers, agents, and employees to exert every reasonable effort to make and maintain contracts covering rates of pay, rules, and working conditions.

§1204.2 Arbitrary changing of contracts

No carrier, its officers, or agents shall change the rates of pay, rules, or working conditions of its employees, as a class as embodied in agreements except in the manner prescribed in such agreements or in section 6 of the Railway Labor Act.

§1204.3 Filing of contracts

Section 5, Third, (e) of the Railway Labor Act requires all carriers to file with the National Mediation Board copies of all contracts in effect with organizations representing their employees, covering rates of pay, rules, and working conditions. Several thousand of such contracts are on file in the Board's Washington office and are available for inspection by interested parties.

PART 1205. NOTICES IN RE: RAILWAY LABOR ACT

§1205.1 Handling of disputes

Section 2, Eighth, of the Railway Labor Act provides that every carrier shall notify its employees by printed notices in such form and posted at such times and places as shall be specified by order of the Mediation Board and requires that all disputes between a carrier and its employees will be handled in accordance with the requirements of the act. In such notices there must be printed verbatim, in large type, the third, fourth, and fifth paragraphs of said section 2, Eighth, of the Railway Labor Act.

§1205.2 Employees' Bill of Rights

The provisions of the third, fourth, and fifth paragraphs of section 2 are by law made a part of the contract of employment between the carrier and each employee and shall be binding upon the parties regardless of any other express or implied agreements between them. Under these provisions the employees are guaranteed the right to organize without interference of management, the right to determine who shall represent them, and the right to bargain collectively through such representatives. This section makes it unlawful for any carrier to require any person seeking employment to sign any contract promising to join or not to join a labor organization. Violation of the foregoing provisions is a misdemeanor under the law and subjects the offender to punishment.

§1205.3 General Order No. 1

General Order No. 1, issued August 14, 1934, is the only order the Board has issued since its creation in 1934. This order sent to the President of each carrier coming under the act transmitted a sample copy of the Mediation Board's Form MB-1 known as "Notice in re: Railway Labor Act." The order prescribes that such notices are to be standard as to contents, dimensions of sheet, and size of type and that they shall be posted promptly and maintained continuously in readable condition on all the usual and customary bulletin boards giving information to employees and at such other places as may be necessary to make them accessible to all employees. Such notices must not be hidden by other papers or otherwise obscured from view.

§1205.4 Substantive rules

The only substantive rules issued by the National Mediation Board are those authorized under section 2, Ninth, of the Railway Labor Act to implement the procedure of determining employee representation.

[12 FR 2451, April 16, 1947. Redesignated at 13 FR 8740, Dec. 30, 1948]

PART 1206. HANDLING REPRESENTATION DISPUTES UNDER THE RAILWAY LABOR ACT

SOURCE: 12 FR 3083, May 10, 1947, unless otherwise noted. Redesignated at 13 FR 8740, Dec. 30, 1948.

§1206.1 Run-off elections

(a) If in an election among any craft or class no organization or individual receives a majority of the legal votes cast, or in the event of a tie vote, a second or run-off election shall be held forthwith: *Provided,* That a written request by an individual or organization entitled to appear on the run-off ballot is submitted to the Board within ten (10) days after the date of the report of results of the first election.

(b) In the event a run-off election is authorized by the Board, the names of the two individuals or organizations which received the highest number of votes cast in the first election shall be placed on the run-off ballot, and no blank line on which votes [sic] may write in the name of any organization or individual will be provided on the run-off ballot.

(c) Employees who were eligible to vote at the conclusion of the first election shall be eligible to vote in the runoff election except (1) those employees whose employment relationship has terminated, and (2) those employees who are no longer employed in the craft or class.

§1206.2 Percentage of valid authorizations required to determine existence of a representation dispute

(a) Where the employees involved in a representation dispute are represented by an individual or labor organization, either local or national in scope and are covered by a valid existing contract between such representative and the carrier a showing of proved authorizations (checked and verified as to date, signature, and employment status) from at least a majority of the craft or class must be made before the National Mediation Board will authorize an election or otherwise determine the representation desires of the employees under the provisions of section 2, Ninth, of the Railway Labor Act.

(b) Where the employees involved in a representation dispute are unrepresented, a showing of proved authorizations from at least thirty-five (35) percent of the employees in the craft or class must be made before the National Mediation Board will authorize an election or otherwise determine the representation desires of the employees under the provisions of section 2, Ninth, of the Railway Labor Act.

§1206.3 Age of authorization cards

Authorizations must be signed and dated in the employee's own handwriting or witnessed mark. No authorizations will be accepted by the National Mediation Board in any employee representation dispute which bear a date prior to one year before the date of the application for the investigation of such dispute.

§1206.4 Time limits on applications

Except in unusual or extraordinary circumstances, the National Mediation Board will not accept an application for investigation of a representation dispute among employees of a carrier:

(a) For a period of two (2) years from the date of a certification covering the same craft or class of employees on the same carrier, and

(b) For a period of one (1) year from the date on which:

(1) The Board dismissed a docketed application after having conducted an election among the same craft or class of employees on the same carrier and less than a majority of eligible voters participated in the election; or

(2) The Board dismissed a docketed application covering the same craft or class of employees on the same carrier because no dispute existed as defined in §1206.2 of these rules; or

(3) The Board dismissed a docketed application after the applicant withdrew an application covering the same craft or class of employees on the same carrier after the application was docketed by the Board.

[44 FR 10602, Feb. 22, 1979]

§1206.5 Necessary evidence of intervenor's interest in a representation dispute

In any representation dispute under the provisions of section 2, Ninth, of the Railway Labor Act, an intervening individual or organization must produce proved authorization from at least thirty-five (35) percent of the craft or class of employees involved to warrant placing the name of the intervenor on the ballot.

§1206.6 Eligibility of dismissed employees to vote

Dismissed employees whose requests for reinstatement [on] account of wrongful dismissal are pending before proper authorities, which includes the National Railroad Adjustment Board or other appropriate adjustment board, are eligible to participate in elections among the craft or class of employees in which they are employed at time of dismissal. This does not include dismissed employees whose guilt has been determined, and who are seeking reinstatement on a leniency basis.

§1206.7 Construction of this part

The rules and regulations in this part shall be liberally construed to effectuate the purposes and provisions of the act.

Regulations of the National Mediation Board

§1206.8 Amendment or recission of rules in this part

(a) Any rule or regulation in this part may be amended or rescinded by the Board at any time.

(b) Any interested person may petition the Board, in writing, for the issuance, amendment, or repeal of a rule or regulation in this part. An original and three copies of such petition shall be filed with the Board in Washington, DC, and shall state the rule or regulation proposed to be issued, amended, or repealed together with a statement of grounds in support of such petition.

(c) Upon the filing of such petition, the Board shall consider the same, and may thereupon either grant or deny the petition in whole or in part, conduct an appropriate hearing thereon and make other disposition of the petition. Should the petition be denied in whole or in part, prompt notice shall be given of the denial, accompanied by a simple statement of the grounds unless the denial is self-explanatory.

PART 1207. ESTABLISHMENT OF SPECIAL ADJUSTMENT BOARDS

SOURCE: 31 FR 14644, Nov. 17, 1966, unless otherwise noted.

§1207.1 Establishment of special adjustment boards (PL Boards)

Public Law 89-456 (80 Stat. 208) governs procedures to be followed by carriers and representatives of employees in the establishment and functioning of special adjustment boards, hereinafter referred to as PL Boards. Public Law 89-456 requires action by the National Mediation Board in the following circumstances:

(a) *Designation of party member of PL Board.* Public Law 89-456 provides that within thirty (30) days from the date a written request is made by an employee representative upon a carrier, or by a carrier upon an employee representative, for the establishment of a PL Board, an agreement establishing such a Board shall be made. If, however, one party fails to designate a member of the Board, the party making the request may ask the Mediation Board to designate a member on behalf of the other party. Upon receipt of such request, the Mediation Board will notify the party which failed to designate a partisan member for the establishment of a PL Board of the receipt of the request. The Mediation Board will then designate a representative on behalf of the party upon whom the request was made. This representative will be an individual associated in interest with the party he is to represent. The designee, together with the member appointed by the party requesting the establishment of the PL Board, shall constitute the Board.

(b) *Appointment of a neutral to determine matters concerning the establishment and/or jurisdiction of a PL Board.* (1) When the members of a PL Board constituted in accordance with paragraph (a) of this section, for the purpose of resolving questions concerning the establishment of the Board and/or its jurisdiction, are unable to resolve these matters, then and in that event, either party may ten (10) days thereafter request the Mediation Board to appoint a neutral member to determine these procedural issues.

(2) Upon receipt of this request, the Mediation Board will notify the other party to the PL Board. The Mediation Board will then designate a neutral member to sit with the PL Board and resolve the procedural issues in dispute. When this neutral has determined the procedural issues in dispute, he shall cease to be a member of the PL Board.

(c) *Appointment of neutral to sit with PL Boards and dispose of disputes.* (1) When the members of a PL Board constituted by agreement of the parties, or by the appointment of a party member by the Mediation Board, as described in paragraph (a) of this section, are unable within ten (10) days after their failure to agree upon an award to agree upon the selection of a neutral person, either member of the Board may request the Mediation Board to appoint such neutral person and upon receipt of such request, the Mediation Board shall promptly make such appointment.

(2) A request for the appointment of a neutral under paragraph (b) of this section or this paragraph (c) shall;

(i) Show the authority for the request—Public Law 89-456, and

(ii) Define and list the proposed specific issues or disputes to be heard.

§1207.2 Requests for Mediation Board action

(a) Requests for the National Mediation Board to appoint neutrals or party representatives should be made on NMB Form 5.

(b) Those authorized to sign request on behalf of parties:

(1) The "representative of any craft or class of employees of a carrier," as referred to in Public Law 89-456, making request for Mediation Board action, shall be either the General Chairman, Grand Lodge Officer (or corresponding officer of equivalent rank), or the Chief Executive of the representative involved. A request signed by a General Chairman or Grand Lodge Officer (or corresponding officer of equivalent rank) shall bear the approval of the Chief Executive of the employee representative.

(2) The "carrier representative" making such a request for the Mediation Board's action shall be the highest carrier officer designated to handle matters arising under the Railway Labor Act.

(c) Docketing of PL Board agreements: The National Mediation Board will docket agreements establishing PL Board, which agreements meet the requirements of coverage as specified in Public Law 89-456. No neutral will be appointed under §1207.1(c) until the agreement establishing the PL Board has been docketed by the Mediation Board.

§1207.3 Compensation of neutrals

(a) *Neutrals appointed by the National Mediation Board.* All neutral persons appointed by the National Mediation Board under the provisions of §1207.1(b) and (c) will be compensated by the Mediation Board in accordance with legislative authority. Certificates of appointment will be issued by the Mediation Board in each instance.

(b) *Neutrals selected by the parties.* (1) In cases where the party members of a PL Board created under Public Law 89-456 mutually agree upon a neutral person to be a member of the Board, the party members will jointly so notify the Mediation Board, which Board will then issue a certificate of appointment to the neutral and arrange to compensate him as under paragraph (a) of this section.

(2) The same procedure will apply in cases where carrier and employee representatives are unable to agree upon the establishment and jurisdiction of a PL Board, and mutually agree upon a procedural neutral person to sit with them as a member and determine such issues.

§1207.4 Designation of PL Boards, filing of agreements, and disposition of records

(a) *Designation of PL Boards.* All special adjustment boards created under Public Law 89-456 will be designated PL Boards, and will be numbered serially, commencing with No. 1, in the order of their docketing by the National Mediation Board.

(b) *Filing of agreements.* The original agreement creating the PL Board under Public Law 89-456 shall be filed with the National Mediation Board at the time it is executed by the parties. A copy of such agreement shall be filed by the parties with the Administrative Officer of the National Railroad Adjustment Board, Chicago, Ill.

(c) *Disposition of records.* Since the provisions of section 2(a) of Public Law 85-456 apply also to the awards of PL Boards created under this Act, two copies of all awards made by the PL Boards, together with the record of proceedings upon which such awards are based, shall be forwarded by the neutrals who are members of such Boards, or by the parties in case of disposition of disputes by PL Boards without participation of neutrals, to the Administrative Officer of the National Railroad Adjustment Board, Chicago, Ill., for filing, safekeeping, and handling under the provisions of section 2(q), as may be required.

Part 1208. Availability of Information

Source: 39 FR 1751, Jan. 14, 1974, unless otherwise noted.

§1208.1 Purpose

The purpose of this part is to set forth the basic policies of the National Mediation Board and the National Railroad Adjustment Board in regard to the availability and disclosure of information in the possession of the NMB and the NRAB.

§1208.2 Production or disclosure of material or information

(a) *Requests for identifiable records and copies.* (1) All requests for National Mediation Board records shall be filed in writing by mailing the request or delivering it to the Executive Secretary, National Mediation Board, Washington, DC 20572, except that requests for records of the National Railroad Adjustment Board shall be in writing and addressed to the Administrative Officer, National Railroad Adjustment Board, 220 South State Street, Chicago, Illinois 60604.

(2) The request shall reasonably describe the records being sought in a manner which permits identification and location of the records.

(i) If the description is insufficient to locate the records, the National Mediation Board will so notify the person making the request and indicate the additional information needed to identify the records requested.

(ii) Every reasonable effort shall be made by the Board to assist in the identification and location of the records sought.

(3) Upon receipt of a request for records the Executive Secretary shall maintain records in reference thereto which shall include the date and time received, the name and address of the requester, the nature of the records requested, the action taken, the date the determination letter is sent to the requester, appeals and action thereon, the date any records are subsequently furnished, the number of staff hours and grade levels of persons who spent time responding to the request and the payment requested and received.

(4) All time limitations established pursuant to this section with respect to processing initial requests and appeals shall commence at the time a written request for records is received at the Board's offices in Washington, DC, except for requests directed to the National Railroad Adjustment Board pursuant to §1208.2(a)(1) in which case the time limit shall commence when the request is received at the NRAB's office in Chicago.

(i) An oral request for records shall not begin any time requirement.

(b) *Processing the initial request.* (1) Time limitations. Within 10 working days (excepting Saturdays, Sundays, and working holidays) after a request for records is received, the Executive Secretary shall determine and inform the requester by letter whether or the extent to which the request will be complied with, unless an extension is taken under paragraph (b)(3) of this section.

(2) Such reply letter shall include:

(i) A reference to the specific exemption or exemptions under the Freedom of Information Act authorizing the withholding of the record, a brief explanation of how the exemption applies to the record withheld.

(ii) The name or names and positions of the person or persons, other than the Executive Secretary, responsible for the denial.

(iii) A statement that the denial may be appealed within thirty days by writing to the Chairman, National Mediation Board, Washington, DC 20572, and that judicial review will thereafter be available in the district in which the requester resides, or has his principal place of business, or the district in which the agency records are situated, or the District of Columbia.

(3) *Extension of time.* In unusual circumstances as specified in this paragraph, the Executive Secretary may extend the time for initial determination on requests up to a total of ten days (excluding Saturdays, Sundays, and legal public holidays). Extensions shall be granted in increments of five days or less and shall be made by written notice to the requester which sets forth the reason for the extension and the date on which a determination is expected to be dispatched. As used in this paragraph "unusual circumstances" means, but only to the extent necessary to the proper processing of the request:

(i) The need to search for and collect the requested records from field facilities or other establishments that are separate from the office processing the request;

(ii) The need to search for, collect, and appropriately examine a voluminous amount of separate and distinct records which are demanded in a single request; or

(iii) The need for consultation, which shall be conducted with all practicable speed, with another agency or another division having substantial interest in the determination of the request, or the need for consultation among components of the agency having substantial subject matter interest therein.

(4) *Treatment of delay as a denial.* If no determination has been dispatched at the end of the ten-day period, or the last extension thereof, the requester may deem his request denied, and exercise a right of appeal, in accordance with §1208.2(c). When no determination can be

dispatched within the applicable time limit, the responsible official shall nevertheless continue to process the request; on expiration of the time limit he shall inform the requester of the reason for the delay, of the date on which a determination may be expected to be dispatched, and of his right to treat the delay as a denial and to appeal to the Chairman of the Board in accordance with §1208.2(c) and he may ask the requester to forego appeal until a determination is made.

(c) *Appeals to the Chairman of the Board.* (1) When a request for records has been denied in whole or in part by the Executive Secretary or other person authorized to deny requests, the requester may, within thirty days of its receipt, appeal the denial to the Chairman of the Board. Appeals to the Chairman shall be in writing, addressed to the Chairman, National Mediation Board, Washington, DC 20572.

(2) The Chairman of the Board will act upon the appeal within twenty working days (excluding Saturdays, Sundays and legal public holidays) of its receipt unless an extension is made under paragraph (c)(3) of this section.

(3) In unusual circumstances as specified in this paragraph, the time for action on an appeal may be extended up to ten days (excluding Saturdays, Sundays and legal public holidays) minus any extension granted at the initial request level pursuant to §1208.2(b)(3). Such extension shall be made by written notice to the requester which sets forth the reason for the extension and the date on which a determination is expected to be dispatched. As used in this paragraph "unusual circumstances" means, but only to the extent necessary to the proper processing of the appeal:

(i) The need to search for and collect the requested records from field facilities or other establishments that are separate from the office processing the request;

(ii) The need to search for, collect, and appropriately examine a voluminous amount of separate and distinct records which are demanded in a single request; or

(iii) The need for consultation, which shall be conducted with all practicable speed, with another agency or another division having substantial interest in the determination of the request or the need for consultation among components of the agency having substantial subject matter interest therein.

(4) *Treatment of delay as a denial.* If no determination on the appeal has been dispatched at the end of the twenty-day period or the last extension thereof, the requester is deemed to have exhausted his administrative remedies, giving rise to a right of review in a district court of the United States as specified in 5 U.S.C. 552(a)(4). When no determination can be dispatched within the applicable time limit, the appeal will nevertheless continue to be processed; on expiration of the time limit the requester shall be informed of the reason for the delay, of the date on which a

determination may be expected to be dispatched, and of his right to seek judicial review in the United States district court in the district in which he resides or has his principal place of business, [or] the district in which the Board records are situated or the District of Columbia. The requester may be asked to forego judicial review until determination of the appeal.

(d) *Indexes of certain records.* (1) The National Mediation Board at its office in Washington, DC will maintain, make available for public inspection and copying, and publish quarterly (unless the Board determines by order published in the FEDERAL REGISTER that such publication would be unnecessary or impracticable) a current index of the materials available at the Board offices which are required to be indexed by 5 U.S.C. 552(a)(2).

 (i) A copy of such index shall be available at cost from the National Mediation Board, Washington, DC 20572.

 (ii) [Reserved]

(2) The National Railroad Adjustment Board at its offices in Chicago, Illinois will maintain, make available for public inspection and copying, and publish quarterly (unless the Board determines by order published in the FEDERAL REGISTER that such publication would be unnecessary or impracticable) a current index of the materials available at the Board offices which are required to be indexed by 5 U.S.C. 552(a)(2).

[42 FR 43627, Aug. 30, 1977]

§1208.3 General policy

(a) Public policy and the successful effectuation of the NMB's mission require that Board members and the employees of the NMB maintain a reputation for impartiality and integrity. Labor and management and other interested parties participating in mediation efforts must have assurance, as must labor organizations and individuals involved in questions of representation, that confidential information disclosed to Board members and employees of the NMB will not be divulged, voluntarily or by compulsion.

(b) Notwithstanding this general policy, the Board will under all circumstances endeavor to make public as much information as can be allowed.

§1208.4 Material relating to representation function

(a) The documents constituting the record of a case, such as the notices of hearing, motions, rulings, orders, stenographic reports of the hearings, briefs, exhibits, findings upon investigation, determinations of craft or class, interpretations, dismissals, withdrawals, and certifications, are matters of official record and are available for inspection and examination during the usual business hours at the Board's offices in Washington.

(b) This part notwithstanding, the Board will treat as confidential the evidence submitted in connection with a representation dispute and the investigatory file pertaining to the representation function.

§1208.5 Material relating to mediation function—confidential

(a) All files, reports, letters, memoranda, documents, and papers (hereinafter referred to as confidential documents) relating to the mediation function of the NMB, in the custody of the NMB or its employees relating to or acquired in their mediatory capacity under any applicable section of the Railway Labor Act of 1926, as amended, are hereby declared to be confidential. No such confidential documents or the material contained therein shall be disclosed to any unauthorized person, or be taken or withdrawn, copied or removed from the custody of the NMB or its employees by any person or by any agent of such person or his representative without the explicit consent of the NMB.

(b) However, the following specific documents: Invocation or proffer of mediation, the reply or replies of the parties, the proffer of arbitration and replies thereto, and the notice of failure of mediatory efforts in cases under section 5, First, of the Railway Labor Act, as amended, are matters of official record and are available for inspection and examination.

(c) Interpretations of mediation agreements by the NMB, arising out of section 5, Second, of the Railway Labor Act, as amended, are public records and are therefore open for public inspection and examination.

§1208.6 Fees—duplication costs and search

(a)(1) Unless waived in accordance with the provisions of §1208.62, the following fees shall be imposed for the reproduction of any record disclosed pursuant to this part.

(i) *Copying of records.* Fifteen cents per copy of each page.

(ii) *Copying of microfilm.* Fifty cents per microfilm frame.

(iii) *Clerical searches.* $1.80 for each one quarter hour spent by clerical personnel searching for and producing a requested record, including time spent copying any record.

(iv) *Non-clerical searches.* $4.10 for each one quarter hour spent by professional or managerial personnel searching for and producing a requested record, including time spent copying any record.

(v) *Certification or authentication of records.* $1.00 per certification or authentication.

(vi) *Forwarding material to destination.* Postage, insurance and special fees will be charged on an actual cost basis.

Regulations of the National Mediation Board

(2)(i) No charge shall be assessed for time spent in resolving legal or policy questions relating to the documents or in examining records for the purpose of deleting nondisclosable portions thereof.

(ii) No charge shall be assessed for time spent in monitoring an individual who examines documents at the Board's offices.

(3) Payment shall be made by check or money order payable to "United States Treasury."

(b)(1) No fee shall be charged for disclosure of records pursuant to this part where:

(i) The cost of providing the records is less than $5.00.

(ii) The records are requested by a congressional committee or subcommittee, a Federal court, a Federal department or agency, or the General Accounting Office.

(2)(i) The Executive Secretary may waive payment of fees, in whole or in part, when he determines that the person making the request is indigent.

(ii) A person seeking such a determination shall petition the Executive Secretary in writing stating the reasons therefore.

(iii) Determinations made pursuant to this provision will be made within the discretion of the agency.

(3)(i) The Executive Secretary may reduce or waive payment of fees in whole or in part when he determines that such reduction or waiver is in the public interest because furnishing the information can be considered as primarily benefiting the general public.

(ii) Determinations pursuant to this provision shall be made within the discretion of the agency.

(4) No fee shall be charged if a record requested is not found or for any record that is determined to be totally exempt from disclosure.

[42 FR 43628, Aug. 30, 1977]

§1208.7 Compliance with subpoenas

(a) No person connected in any official way with the NMB shall produce or present any confidential records of the Board or testify on behalf of any party to any cause pending in any court, or before any board, commission, committee, tribunal, investigatory body, or administrative agency of the U.S. Government, or any State or Territory of the United States, or the District of Columbia, or any municipality with respect to matters coming to his knowledge in his official capacity or with respect to any information contained in confidential documents of the NMB, whether in answer to any order, subpoena, subpoena duces tecum, or otherwise without the express written consent of the Board.

(b) Whenever any subpoena or subpoena duces tecum calling for confidential documents, or the information contained therein, or testimony as described above shall have been served on any such person, he will appear in answer thereto, and unless otherwise expressly permitted by the Board, respectfully decline, by reason of this section, to produce or present such confidential documents or to give such testimony.

PART 1209. PUBLIC OBSERVATION OF NATIONAL MEDIATION BOARD MEETINGS

SOURCE: 42 FR 60739, Nov. 29, 1977, unless otherwise noted.

§1209.01 Scope and purpose

(a) The provisions of this part are intended to implement the requirements of section 3(a) of the Government in the Sunshine Act, 5 U.S.C. 552b.

(b) It is the policy of the National Mediation Board that the public is entitled to the fullest practicable information regarding its decisionmaking processes. It is the purpose of this part to provide the public with such information while protecting the rights of individuals and the ability of the agency to carry out its responsibilities.

§1209.02 Definitions

For purposes of this part:

(a) The terms *Board* or *Agency* mean the National Mediation Board, a collegial body composed of three members appointed by the President with the advice and consent of the Senate.

(b) The term *meeting* means the deliberations of at least two members of the Board where such deliberations determine or result in the joint conduct or disposition of official agency business, but does not include deliberations required or permitted or with respect to any information proposed to be withheld under by [sic] 5 U.S.C. 552b(d) or (e)/[sic] 5 U.S.C. 552b(c).

§1209.03 Conduct of National Mediation Board business

Members shall not jointly conduct or dispose of agency business other than in accordance with this part.

Regulations of the National Mediation Board

§1209.04 Open meetings

Every portion of every Board meeting shall be open to public observation except as otherwise provided by §1209.05 of this part.

§1209.05 Closing of meetings; reasons therefor

(a) Except where the Board determines that the public interest requires otherwise, meetings, or portions thereof, shall not be open to public observation where the deliberations concern the issuance of a subpoena, the Board's participation in a civil action or proceeding or an arbitration, or the initiation, conduct or disposition by the Board of any matter involving a determination on the record after opportunity for a hearing, or any court proceeding collateral or ancillary thereto.

(b) Except where the Board determines that the public interest requires otherwise, the Board also may close meetings, or portions thereof, when the deliberations concern matters or information falling within the scope of 5 U.S.C. 552b(c)(1) (secret matters concerning national defense or foreign policy); (c)(2) (internal personnel rules and practices); (c)(3) (matters specifically exempted from disclosure by statute); (c)(4) (trade secrets and commercial or financial information obtained from a person and privileged or confidential); (c)(5) (matters of alleged criminal conduct or formal censure); (c)(6) (personal information where disclosure would cause a clearly unwarranted invasion of personal privacy); (c)(7) (certain materials or information from investigatory files compiled for law enforcement purposes); or (c)(9)(B) (disclosure would significantly frustrate implementation of a proposed agency action).

§1209.06 Action necessary to close meetings; record of votes

A meeting shall be closed to public observation under §1209.05, only when a majority of the members of the Board who will participate in the meeting vote to take such action.

(a) When the meeting deliberations concern matters specified in §1209.05(a), the Board members shall vote at the beginning of the meeting, or portion thereof, on whether to close such meeting, or portion thereof, to public observation, and on whether the public interest requires that a meeting which may properly be closed should nevertheless be open to public observation. A record of such vote, reflecting the vote of each member of the Board, shall be kept and made available to the public at the earliest practicable time.

(b) When the meeting deliberations concerns matters specified in §1209.05(b), the Board shall vote on whether to close such meeting, or portion thereof, to public observation, and on whether the public interest requires that a meeting which may properly be closed should nevertheless be open to public observation. The vote shall be taken at a time sufficient to permit inclusion of information concerning the open or closed status of the meeting in the public announcement thereof. A single vote may be taken with respect to a series of meetings at which the deliberations will concern the same particular matters where subsequent meetings in the series are scheduled to be held within one day after the vote is taken.

(c) Whenever any person whose interests may be directly affected by deliberations during a meeting, or a portion thereof, requests that the Board close that meeting, or portion thereof, to public observation for any of the reasons specified in 5 U.S.C. 552b(c)(5) (matters of alleged criminal conduct or formal censure), (c)(6) (personal information where disclosure would cause a clearly unwarranted invasion of personal privacy), or (c)(7) (certain materials or information from investigatory files compiled for law enforcement purposes), the Board members participating in the meeting upon request of any one member of the Board, shall vote on whether to close such meeting, or any portion thereof, for that reason. A record of such vote, reflecting the vote of each member of the Board participating in the meeting, shall be kept and made available to the public within one day after the vote is taken.

(d) After public announcement of a meeting as provided in §1209.07 of this part, a meeting, or portion thereof, announced as closed may be opened or a meeting, or portion thereof, announced as open may be closed, only if a majority of the members of the Board who will participate in the meeting determine by a recorded vote that Board business so requires and that an earlier announcement of the change was not possible. The change made and the vote of each member on the change shall be announced publicly at the earliest practicable time.

(e) Before a meeting may be closed pursuant to §1209.05 the General Counsel of the Board shall certify that in his or her opinion the meeting may properly be closed to public observation. The certification shall set forth each applicable exemptive provision for such closing. The certification shall be retained by the agency and made publicly available as soon as practicable.

§1209.07 Notice of meetings; public announcement and publication

(a) A public announcement setting forth the time, place and subject matter of meetings or portions thereof closed to public observation pursuant to the provisions of §1209.05(a) of this part, shall be made at the earliest practicable time.

(b) Except for meetings closed to public observation pursuant to the provisions of §1209.05(a) of this part, the agency shall make public announcement of each meeting at least 7 days before the scheduled date of

Regulations of the National Mediation Board

the meeting. The announcement shall specify the time, place and subject matter of the meeting, whether it is to be open to public observation or closed, and the name, address and phone number of an agency official designated to respond to requests for information about the meeting. The 7 day period for advance notice may be shortened only upon a determination by a majority of the members of the Board who will participate in the meeting that agency business requires that such meeting be called at an earlier date, in which event the public announcement shall be made at the earliest practicable time. A record of the vote to schedule a meeting at an earlier date shall be kept and made available to the public.

(c) Within one day after a vote to close a meeting, or any portion thereof, pursuant to the provisions of §1209.05(b) of this part, the agency shall make publicly available a full written explanation of its action closing the meeting, or portion thereof, together with a list of all persons expected to attend the meeting and their affiliation.

(d) If after a public announcement required by paragraph (b) of this section has been made, the time and place of the meeting are changed, a public announcement of such changes shall be made at the earliest practicable time. The subject matter of the meeting may be changed after public announcement thereof only if a majority of the members of the Board who will participate in the meeting determine that agency business so requires and that no earlier announcement of the change was possible. When such a change in subject matter is approved a public announcement of the change shall be made at the earliest practicable time. A record of the vote to change the subject matter of the meeting shall be kept and made available to the public.

(e) All announcements or changes thereof issued pursuant to the provisions of paragraphs (b) and (d) of this section, or pursuant to the provisions of §1209.06(d), shall be submitted for publication in the FEDERAL REGISTER immediately following their release to the public.

(f) Announcement of meeting made pursuant to the provisions of this section shall be posted on a bulletin board maintained for such purpose at the Board's offices, 1425 K Street, NW., Washington, DC. Interested individuals or organizations may request the Executive Secretary, National Mediation Board, Washington, DC 20572 to place them on a mailing list for receipt of such announcements.

§1209.08 Transcripts, recordings or minutes of closed meetings; retention; public availability

(a) For every meeting or portion thereof closed under the provisions of §1209.05, the presiding officer shall prepare a statement setting forth the time and place of the meeting and the persons present, which statement shall be retained by the agency. For each such meeting or portion thereof there also shall be maintained a complete transcript or electronic recording of the proceedings, except that for meetings closed pursuant to §1209.05(a) the Board may, in lieu of a transcript or electronic recording, maintain a set of minutes fully and accurately summarizing any action taken, the reason therefor and views thereof, documents considered, and the members' vote on each roll call vote.

(b) The agency shall maintain a complete verbatim transcript, a complete electronic recording, or a complete set of minutes for each meeting or portion thereof closed to public observation, for a period of at least one year after the close of the agency proceeding of which the meeting was a part, but in no event for a period of less than two years after such meeting.

(c) The agency shall make promptly available to the public copies of transcripts, electronic recordings or minutes maintained as provided in paragraphs (a) and (b) of this section, except to the extent the items therein contain information which the agency determines may be withheld pursuant to the provisions of 5 U.S.C. 552b(c).

(d) Upon request in accordance with the provisions of this paragraph and except to the extent they contain information which the agency determines may be withheld pursuant to the provisions of 5 U.S.C. 552b(c), copies of transcripts or minutes, or transcriptions of electronic recordings including the identification of speakers, shall be furnished subject to the payment of duplication costs in accordance with the schedule of fees set forth in §1208.06 of the Board's Rules, and the actual cost of transcription. Requests for copies of transcripts or minutes, or transcriptions of electronic recordings of Board meetings shall be directed to the Executive Secretary, National Mediation Board, Washington, DC 20572. Such requests shall reasonably identify the records sought and include a statement that whatever costs are involved in furnishing the records will be acceptable or, alternatively, that costs will be acceptable up to a specified amount. The Board may determine to require prepayment of such costs.

§1209.09 Requests for records under Freedom of Information Act

Requests to review or obtain copies of agency records other than notices or records prepared under this part may be pursued in accordance with the Freedom of Information Act (5 U.S.C. 552). Part 1208 of the Board's Rules addresses the requisite procedures under that Act.

§1209.10 Capacity of public observers

The public may attend open Board meetings for the sole purpose of observation. Observers may not participate in meetings unless expressly invited or otherwise interfere with the conduct and disposition of agency

Forms of the National Mediation Board

business. When a portion of a meeting is closed to the public, observers will leave the meeting room upon request to enable discussion of the exempt matter therein under consideration.

Forms of the National Mediation Board

Form NMB-2   Application for Mediation Services
Form NMB-3   Application for Investigation of Representation Dispute

Form NMB-2
(Revised 6-94)

OMB No. 3140-0001

NATIONAL MEDIATION BOARD

APPLICATION FOR MEDIATION SERVICES

TO THE NATIONAL MEDIATION BOARD
Washington, D.C. 20572

A dispute has arisen between the parties shown below which has not been adjusted between them, and the services of the National Mediation Board under Section 5, First, of the Railway Labor Act, are hereby invoked on specific questions set forth below. **The approximate number of employees involved is** _____ **in the craft or class of** _____.

THE SPECIFIC QUESTION IN DISPUTE

_____

_____

(if necessary extend question on additional sheet or attach exhibit)

PARTIES TO DISPUTE

_____   _____
(Name of Carrier)   (Name of Organization or Individual)

_____   _____
(Labor Relations Officer)   (Organization Official)

_____   _____
(Address)   (Address)

_____   _____
(City, State and Zip)   (City, State and Zip)

WORKING AGREEMENT

If an agreement governing rates of pay, rules, or working conditions is in effect, give name of parties thereto and date thereof. If there is no such agreement, so state _____.

COMPLIANCE WITH RAILWAY LABOR ACT

1. If this dispute involves change in the above-mentioned agreement, attach copy of the 30-day notice served by party desiring change and insert date of notice here _____.

2. If this dispute involves the negotiation of a new or supplemental agreement, attach copy of request made by party desiring same and insert date of request here _____.

3. If there has been a refusal to confer, so state and give reason; otherwise, give date of last conference here _____.

Signed at .... this .... day of ...., 19....

Name.............................   Name.............................
(Signature of Carrier Official)   (Signature of Organization Official)

Title............................   Title............................

(File this application in duplicate)
(If necessary, use and attach additional sheets)

Forms of the National Mediation Board

Form NMB-3
(Revised 6-94)

NATIONAL MEDIATION BOARD

OMB No. 3140-0002

APPLICATION FOR INVESTIGATION OF REPRESENTATION DISPUTE

TO THE NATIONAL MEDIATION BOARD
Washington, D.C. 20572

A dispute has arisen among the employees of ....
(Name of Carrier)

....
(Address of Carrier)

....
(City, State and Zip)

as to who are the representatives of these employees designated and authorized in accordance with the requirements of the Railway Labor Act. The undersigned, one of the parties to the dispute, hereby requests the National Mediation Board to investigate this dispute, and to certify the name or names of the individuals or organizations authorized to represent the employees involved in accordance with Section 2, Ninth, of the Act.

....
(Petitioning organization or representative)

Parties to Dispute
.... Date ......
(Organization holding existing agreement, if any, and date thereof)

....
(Other organizations or representatives involved in dispute)

If more than one craft or class, list separately	Estimated Number of Employees
1.	....
2.	....
3.	....
4.	....
5.	....
6.	....
7.	....

Craft or class of employees involved

Use separate line for each craft or class

Evidence of representation

This application is supported by (check applicable box):
☐ At least a majority, if the employees are represented and there is a valid collective bargaining agreement.
☐ At least 35%, if the employees are unrepresented.

Signed at .... this .... day of ...., 19....

Name ....
(Signature of applicant)

Title ....

....
(Address)

....
(City, State and Zip)

(File this application in duplicate)
(If necessary, use and attach additional sheets)

Regulations of the National Labor Relations Board — Selected Provisions
29 C.F.R. §§102.9-102.88, 102.94-102.97

SUBPART B. PROCEDURE UNDER SECTION 10(a) TO (i) OF THE ACT FOR THE PREVENTION OF UNFAIR LABOR PRACTICES[1]

Charge

§102.9 Who may file; withdrawal and dismissal

A charge that any person has engaged in or is engaging in any unfair labor practice affecting commerce may be made by any person. Any such charge may be withdrawn, prior to the hearing, only with the consent of the regional director with whom such charge was filed; at the hearing and until the case has been transferred to the Board pursuant to §102.45, upon motion, with the consent of the administrative law judge designated to conduct the hearing; and after the case has been transferred to the Board pursuant to §102.45, upon motion, with the consent of the Board. Upon withdrawal of any charge, any complaint based thereon shall be dismissed by the regional director issuing the complaint, the administrative law judge designated to conduct the hearing, or the Board.

§102.10 Where to file

Except as provided in §102.33 such charge shall be filed with the regional director for the region in which the alleged unfair labor practice has occurred or is occurring. A charge alleging that an unfair labor practice has occurred or is occurring in two or more regions may be filed with the regional director for any of such regions.

§102.11 Forms; jurat; or declaration

Such charge shall be in writing and signed, and either shall be sworn to before a notary public, Board agent, or other person duly authorized by law to administer oaths and take acknowledgments or shall contain a declaration by the person signing it, under the penalties of the Criminal Code, that its

---

1. Procedure under sec. 10(j) to (*l*) of the Act is governed by subparts F and G of this part. Procedure for unfair labor practice cases and representation cases under sec. 8(b)(7) of the Act is governed by subpart D of this part.

contents are true and correct to the best of his knowledge and belief. Three additional copies of such charge shall be filed together with one additional copy for each named party respondent.[2]

§102.12 Contents

Such charge shall contain the following:
(a) The full name and address of the person making the charge.
(b) If the charge is filed by a labor organization, the full name and address of any national or international labor organization of which it is an affiliate or constituent unit.
(c) The full name and address of the person against whom the charge is made (hereinafter referred to as the "respondent").
(d) A clear and concise statement of the facts constituting the alleged unfair labor practices affecting commerce.

§102.13 [Reserved]

§102.14 Service of charge

Upon the filing of a charge, the charging party shall be responsible for the timely and proper service of a copy thereof upon the person against whom such charge is made. The regional director will, as a matter of course, cause a copy of such charge to be served upon the person against whom the charge is made, but he shall not be deemed to assume responsibility for such service.

Complaint

§102.15 When and by whom issued; contents; service

After a charge has been filed, if it appears to the regional director that formal proceedings in respect thereto should be instituted, he shall issue and cause to be served on all other parties a formal complaint in the name of the Board stating the unfair labor practices and containing a notice of hearing before an administrative law judge at a place therein fixed and at a time not less than 14 days after the service of the complaint. The complaint shall contain:

---

2. A blank form for making a charge will be supplied by the regional director upon request.

(a) A clear and concise statement of the facts upon which assertion of jurisdiction by the Board is predicated, and

(b) A clear and concise description of the acts which are claimed to constitute unfair labor practices, where known, the approximate dates and places of such acts and the names of respondent's agents or other representatives by whom committed.

[51 FR 23745, July 1, 1986]

§102.16 Hearing; change of date or place

(a) Upon his own motion or upon proper cause shown by any other party, the Regional Director issuing the complaint may extend the date of such hearing or may change the place at which it is to be held, except that the authority of the Regional Director to extend the date of a hearing shall be limited to the following circumstances:

(1) Where all parties agree or no party objects to extension of the date of hearing;

(2) Where a new charge or charges have been filed which, if meritorious, might be appropriate for consolidation with the pending complaint;

(3) Where negotiations which could lead to settlement of all or a portion of the complaint are in progress;

(4) Where issues related to the complaint are pending before the General Counsel's Division of Advice or Office of Appeals; or

(5) Where more than 21 days remain before the scheduled date of hearing.

(b) In circumstances other than those set forth in subsection (a) of this section, motions to reschedule the hearing should be filed with the Division of Judges in accordance with §102.24(a). When a motion to reschedule has been granted, the Regional Director issuing the complaint shall retain the authority to order a new date for hearing and retain the responsibility to make the necessary arrangements for conducting such hearing, including its location and the transcription of the proceedings.

[54 FR 51197, Dec. 13, 1989; 54 FR 52506, Dec. 21, 1989]

§102.17 Amendment

Any such complaint may be amended upon such terms as may be deemed just, prior to the hearing, by the regional director issuing the complaint; at the hearing and until the case has been transferred to the Board pursuant to §102.45 upon motion, by the administrative law judge designated to conduct the hearing; and after the case has been transferred to the Board pursuant to §102.45, at any time prior to the issuance of an order based thereon, upon motion, by the Board.

§102.18 Withdrawal

Any such complaint may be withdrawn before the hearing by the regional director on his own motion.

§102.19 Appeal to the general counsel from refusal to issue or reissue

(a) If, after the charge has been filed, the regional director declines to issue a complaint or, having withdrawn a complaint pursuant to §102.18, refuses to reissue it, the regional director shall so advise the parties in writing, accompanied by a simple statement of the procedural or other grounds for his action. The person making the charge may obtain a review of such action by filing an appeal with the general counsel in Washington, DC, and filing a copy of the appeal with the regional director, within 14 days from the service of the notice of such refusal to issue or reissue by the regional director, except as a shorter period is provided by §102.81. If an appeal is taken the person doing so should notify all other parties of his action, but any failure to give such notice shall not affect the validity of the appeal. The appeal shall contain a complete statement setting forth the facts and reasons upon which it is based. A request for an extension of time to file an appeal shall be in writing and be received by the general counsel, and a copy of such request filed with the regional director, prior to the expiration of the filing period. Copies of the acknowledgment of the filing of an appeal and of any ruling on a request for an extension of time for the filing of an appeal shall be served on all parties. Consideration of an appeal untimely filed is within the discretion of the general counsel upon good cause shown.

(b) Oral presentation in Washington, DC, of the appeal issues may be permitted a party on written request made within 4 days after service of acknowledgment of the filing of an appeal. In the event such request is granted, the other parties shall be notified and afforded, without additional request, a like opportunity at another appropriate time.

(c) The general counsel may sustain the regional director's refusal to issue or reissue a complaint, stating the grounds of his affirmance, or may direct the regional director to take further action; the general counsel's decision shall be served on all the parties. A motion for reconsideration of the decision must be filed within 14 days of service of the decision, except as hereinafter provided, and shall state with particularity the error requiring reconsideration. A motion for reconsideration based upon newly discovered evidence which has become available only since the decision on appeal shall be filed promptly on discovery of such evidence. Motions for reconsideration of a decision previously reconsidered will not be entertained, except in unusual situations where the moving party can establish that new evidence has been discovered which could not have been discovered by diligent inquiry prior to the first reconsideration.

[32 FR 9548, July 1, 1967, as amended at 51 FR 23746, July 1, 1986]

Answer

§102.20 Answer to complaint; time for filing; contents; allegations not denied deemed admitted

The respondent shall, within 14 days from the service of the complaint, file an answer thereto. The respondent shall specifically admit, deny, or explain each of the facts alleged in the complaint, unless the respondent is without knowledge, in which case the respondent shall so state, such statement operating as a denial. All allegations in the complaint, if no answer is filed, or any allegation in the complaint not specifically denied or explained in an answer filed, unless the respondent shall state in the answer that he is without knowledge, shall be deemed to be admitted to be true and be so found by the Board, unless good cause to the contrary is shown.

[51 FR 23746, July 1, 1986]

§102.21 Where to file; service upon the parties; form

An original and four copies of the answer shall be filed with the regional director issuing the complaint. Immediately upon the filing of his answer, respondent shall serve a copy thereof on each of the other parties. An answer of a party represented by counsel shall be signed by at least one attorney of record in his individual name, whose address shall be stated. A party who is not represented by an attorney shall sign his answer and state his address. Except when otherwise specifically provided by rule or statute, an answer need not be verified or accompanied by affidavit. The signature of an attorney constitutes a certificate by him that he has read the answer; that to the best of his knowledge, information, and belief there is good ground to support it; and that it is not interposed for delay. If an answer is not signed or is signed with intent to defeat the purpose of this rule, it may be stricken as sham and false and the action may proceed as though the answer had not been served. For a willful violation of this rule an attorney may be subjected to appropriate disciplinary action. Similar action may be taken if scandalous or indecent matter is inserted.

§102.22 Extension of time for filing

Upon his own motion or upon proper cause shown by any other party the regional director issuing the complaint may by written order extend the time within which the answer shall be filed.

§102.23 Amendment

The respondent may amend his answer at any time prior to the hearing. During the hearing or subsequent thereto, he may amend his answer in any case where the complaint has been amended, within such period as may be fixed by the administrative law judge or the Board. Whether or not the complaint has been amended, the answer may, in the discretion of the administrative law judge or the Board, upon motion, be amended upon such terms and within such periods as may be fixed by the administrative law judge or the Board.

Motions

(49 Stat. 449; 29 U.S.C. 151-166, as amended by (61 Stat. 136; 29 U.S.C. Sup. 151-167), (65 Stat. 601; 29 U.S.C. 158, 159, 168), (73 Stat. 519; 29 U.S.C. 141-168), (88 Stat. 395-397; 29 U.S.C. 152, 158, 169, 183))

§102.24 Motions; where to file; contents; service on other parties; promptness in filing and response; summary judgment procedures

(a) All motions under §102.22 and 102.29 made prior to the hearing shall be filed in writing with the Regional Director issuing the complaint. All motions for summary judgment or dismissal made prior to the hearing shall be filed in writing with the Board pursuant to the provisions of §102.50. All other motions made prior to the hearing, including motions to reschedule the hearing under circumstances other than those set forth in §102.16(a), shall be filed in writing with the chief administrative law judge in Washington, DC, with the deputy chief judge in San Francisco,

California, with the associate chief judge in New York, New York, or with the associate chief judge in Atlanta, Georgia, as the case may be. All motions made at the hearing shall be made in writing to the administrative law judge or stated orally on the record. All motions filed subsequent to the hearing, but before the transfer of the case to the Board pursuant to §102.45, shall be filed with the administrative law judge, care of the chief administrative law judge in Washington, DC, the deputy chief judge in San Francisco, California, the associate chief judge in New York, New York, or the associate chief judge in Atlanta, Georgia, as the case may be. Motions shall briefly state the order or relief applied for and the grounds therefor. All motions filed with a Regional Director or an administrative law judge as set forth above shall be filed therewith by transmitting three copies thereof together with an affidavit of service on the parties. All motions filed with the Board, including motions for summary judgment or dismissal, shall be filed with the Executive Secretary of the Board in Washington, DC, by transmitting eight copies thereof together with an affidavit of service on the parties. Unless otherwise provided in these rules, motions and responses thereto shall be filed promptly and within such time as not to delay the proceeding.

(b) All motions for summary judgment or dismissal shall be filed with the Board no later than 28 days prior to the scheduled hearing. Where no hearing is scheduled, or where the hearing is scheduled less than 28 days after the date for filing an answer to the complaint or compliance specification, whichever is applicable, the motion shall be filed promptly. Upon receipt of the motion, the Board may deny the motion or issue a notice to show cause why the motion should not be granted. If a notice to show cause is issued, the hearing, if scheduled, will normally be postponed indefinitely. If a party desires to file an opposition to the motion prior to issuance of the notice to show cause in order to prevent postponement of the hearing, it may do so; *Provided however,* That any such opposition shall be filed no later than 21 days prior to the hearing. If a notice to show cause is issued, an opposing party may file a response thereto notwithstanding any opposition it may have filed prior to issuance of the notice. The time for filing the response shall be fixed in the notice to show cause. It is not required that either the opposition or the response be supported by affidavits or other documentary evidence showing that there is a genuine issue for hearing. The Board in its discretion may deny the motion where the motion itself fails to establish the absence of a genuine issue, or where the opposing party's pleadings, opposition and/or response indicate on their face that a genuine issue may exist. If the opposing party files no opposition or response, the Board may treat the motion as conceded, and summary judgment or dismissal, if appropriate, shall be entered.

[54 FR 38516, Sept. 19, 1989, as amended at 54 FR 51197, Dec. 13, 1989]

Regulations of the National Labor Relations Board 249

§102.25 Ruling on motions

An administrative law judge designated by the chief administrative law judge, by the deputy chief judge in San Francisco, California, by the associate chief judge in New York, New York, or by the associate chief judge in Atlanta, Georgia, as the case may be, shall rule on all prehearing motions (except as provided in §§102.16, 102.22, 102.29, and 102.50), and all such rulings and orders shall be issued in writing and a copy served on each of the parties. The administrative law judge designated to conduct the hearing shall rule on all motions after opening of the hearing (except as provided in §102.47), and any orders in connection therewith, if announced at the hearing, shall be stated orally on the record; in all other cases the administrative law judge shall issue such rulings and orders in writing and shall cause a copy of the same to be served on each of the parties, or shall make his ruling in his decision. Whenever the administrative law judge has reserved his ruling on any motion, and the proceeding is thereafter transferred to and continued before the Board pursuant to §102.50, the Board shall rule on such motion.

(49 Stat. 449; 29 U.S.C. 151-166, as amended by (61 Stat. 136; 29 U.S.C. Sup. 151-167), (65 Stat. 601; 29 U.S.C. 158, 159, 168), (73 Stat. 519; 29 U.S.C. 141-168), (88 Stat. 395-397; 29 U.S.C. 152, 158, 169, 183))

[45 FR 51193, Aug. 1, 1980]

§102.26 Motions, rulings, and orders part of the record; rulings not to be appealed directly to the Board without special permission; requests for special permission to appeal

All motions, rulings, and orders shall become a part of the record, except that rulings on motions to revoke subpenas shall become a part of the record only upon the request of the party aggrieved thereby as provided in §102.31. Unless expressly authorized by the Rules and Regulations, rulings by the regional director or by the administrative law judge on motions and/or by the administrative law judge on objections, and orders in connection therewith, shall not be appealed directly to the Board except by special permission of the Board, but shall be considered by the Board in reviewing the record if exception to the ruling or order is included in the statement of exceptions filed with the Board pursuant to §102.46. Requests to the Board for special permission to appeal from a ruling of the regional director or of the administrative law judge, together with the appeal from such ruling, shall be filed promptly, in writing, and shall briefly state the reasons special permission should be granted and the grounds relied on for the appeal. The moving party shall immediately serve a copy of the request for special permission and of the appeal on the other parties and, if the request involves a ruling by an administrative law judge, on the administrative law judge. Any statement in opposition or other response to the request and/or to the appeal shall be filed promptly, in writing, and shall be served immediately on the other parties and on the administrative law judge, if any. If the Board grants the request for special permission to appeal, it may proceed forthwith to rule on the appeal.

[47 FR 40770, Sept. 15, 1982]

§102.27 Review of granting of motion to dismiss entire complaint; reopening of the record

If any motion in the nature of a motion to dismiss the complaint in its entirety is granted by the administrative law judge before filing his decision, any party may obtain a review of such action by filing a request therefor with the Board in Washington, DC, stating the grounds for review, and immediately on such filing shall serve a copy thereof on the regional director and on the other parties. Unless such request for review is filed within 28 days from the date of the order of dismissal, the case shall be closed.

[51 FR 23746, July 1, 1986]

§102.28 Filing of answer or other participation in proceedings not a waiver of rights

The right to make motions or to make objections to rulings upon motions shall not be deemed waived by the filing of an answer or by other participation in the proceedings before the administrative law judge or the Board.

[45 FR 51192, Aug. 1, 1980]

Intervention

§102.29 Intervention; requisites; rulings on motions to intervene

Any person desiring to intervene in any proceeding shall file a motion in writing or, if made at the hearing, may move orally on the record, stating the grounds upon which such person claims an interest. Prior to the hearing, such a motion shall be filed with the regional director issuing the complaint; during the hearing such motion shall be made to the administrative

Regulations of the National Labor Relations Board

law judge. An original and four copies of written motions shall be filed. Immediately upon filing such motion, the moving party shall serve a copy thereof upon each of the other parties. The regional director shall rule upon all such motions filed prior to the hearing, and shall cause a copy of said rulings to be served upon each of the other parties, or may refer the motion to the administrative law judge for ruling. The administrative law judge shall rule upon all such motions made at the hearing or referred to him by the regional director, in the manner set forth in §102.25. The regional director or the administrative law judge, as the case may be, may by order permit intervention in person or by counsel or other representative to such extent and upon such terms as he may deem proper.

Witnesses, Depositions, and Subpenas

§102.30 Examination of witnesses; deposition

Witnesses shall be examined orally under oath, except that for good cause shown after the issuance of a complaint, testimony may be taken by deposition.

(a) Applications to take depositions shall be in writing setting forth the reasons why such depositions should be taken, the name and post office address of the witness, the matters concerning which it is expected the witness will testify, and the time and place proposed for the taking of the deposition, together with the name and address of the person before whom it is desired that the deposition be taken (for the purposes of this section hereinafter referred to as the "officer"). Such application shall be made to the regional director prior to the hearing, and to the administrative law judge during and subsequent to the hearing but before transfer of the case to the Board pursuant to §102.45 or §102.50. Such application shall be served upon the regional director or the administrative law judge, as the case may be, and upon all other parties, not less than 7 days (when the deposition is to be taken within the continental United States) and 15 days (if the deposition is to be taken elsewhere) prior to the time when it is desired that the deposition be taken. The regional director or administrative law judge, as the case may be, shall upon receipt of the application, if in his discretion good cause has been shown, make and serve upon the parties an order which will specify the name of the witness whose deposition is to be taken and the time, the place, and the designation of the officer before whom the witness is to testify, who may or may not be the same officer as that specified in the application. Such order shall be served upon all the other parties by the regional director or upon all parties by the administrative law judge.

(b) Such deposition may be taken before any officer authorized to administer oaths by the laws of the United States or of the place where the examination is held, including any agent of the Board authorized to administer oaths. If the examination is held in a foreign country, it may be taken before any secretary of embassy or legation, consul general, consul, vice consul, or consular agent of the United States.

(c) At the time and place specified in said order the officer designated to take such deposition shall permit the witness to be examined and cross-examined under oath by all the parties appearing, and his testimony shall be reduced to typewriting by the officer or under his direction. All objections to questions or evidence shall be deemed waived unless made at the examination. The officer shall not have power to rule upon any objections but he shall note them upon the deposition. The testimony shall be subscribed by the witness in the presence of the officer who shall attach his certificate stating that the witness was duly sworn by him, that the deposition is a true record of the testimony and exhibits given by the witness, and that said officer is not of counsel or attorney to any of the parties nor interested in the event of the proceeding or investigation. If the deposition is not signed by the witness because he is ill, dead, cannot be found, or refuses to sign it, such fact shall be included in the certificate of the officer and the deposition may then be used as fully as though signed. The officer shall immediately deliver an original and two copies of said transcript, together with his certificate, in person or by registered or certified mail to the regional director or the administrative law judge, care of the chief administrative law judge in Washington, DC, the deputy chief judge, in San Francisco, California, the associate chief judge in New York, New York, or the associate chief judge in Atlanta, Georgia, as the case may be.

(d) The administrative law judge shall rule upon the admissibility of the deposition or any part thereof.

(e) All errors or irregularities in compliance with the provisions of this section shall be deemed waived unless a motion to suppress the deposition or some part thereof is made with reasonable promptness after such defect is or, with due diligence, might have been ascertained.

(f) If the parties so stipulate in writing, depositions may be taken before any person at any time or place, upon any notice and in any manner, and when so taken may be used like other depositions.

(National Labor Relations Act approved July 5, 1935, 49 Stat. 449; 29 U.S.C. 151-166, as amended by Act of June 23, 1947 (61 Stat. 136; 29 U.S.C. Sup. 151-167), Act of Oct. 22, 1951 (65 Stat. 601; 29 U.S.C. 158, 159, 168), Act of Sept. 14, 1959 (73 Stat. 519; 29 U.S.C. 141-168), and Act of July 26, 1974 (88 Stat. 395-397; 29 U.S.C. 152, 158, 169, 183))

[24 FR 9102, Nov. 7, 1959, as amended at 45 FR 37425, June 3, 1980; 45 FR 51193, Aug. 1, 1980]

§102.31 Issuance of subpenas; petitions to revoke subpenas; rulings on claim of privilege against self-incrimination; subpena enforcement proceedings; right to inspect and copy data

(a) Any member of the Board shall, on the written application of any party, forthwith issue subpenas requiring the attendance and testimony of witnesses and the production of any evidence, including books, records, correspondence, or documents, in their possession or under their control. Applications for subpenas, if filed prior to the hearing, shall be filed with the regional director. Applications for subpenas filed during the hearing shall be filed with the administrative law judge. Either the regional director or the administrative law judge, as the case may be, shall grant the application, on behalf of any member of the Board. Applications for subpenas may be made ex parte. The subpena shall show on its face the name and address of the party at whose request the subpena was issued.

(b) Any person, served with a subpena, whether ad testificandum or duces tecum, if he does not intend to comply with the subpena, shall, within 5 days after the date of service of the subpena upon him, petition in writing to revoke the subpena. All petitions to revoke subpenas shall be served upon the party at whose request the subpena was issued. Such petition to revoke, if made prior to the hearing, shall be filed with the regional director and the regional director shall refer the petition to the administrative law judge or the Board for ruling. Petitions to revoke subpenas filed during the hearing shall be filed with the administrative law judge. Notice of the filing of petitions to revoke shall be promptly given by the regional director or the administrative law judge, as the case may be, to the party at whose request the subpena was issued. The administrative law judge or the Board, as the case may be, shall revoke the subpena if in its opinion the evidence whose production is required does not relate to any matter under investigation or in question in the proceedings or the subpena does not describe with sufficient particularity the evidence whose production is required, or if for any other reason sufficient in law the subpena is otherwise invalid. The administrative law judge or the Board, as the case may be, shall make a simple statement of procedural or other grounds for the ruling on the petition to revoke. The petition to revoke, any answer filed thereto, and any ruling thereon shall not become part of the official record except upon the request of the party aggrieved by the ruling.

(c) With the approval of the Attorney General of the United States, the Board may issue an order requiring any individual to give testimony or provide other information at any proceeding before the Board if, in the judgment of the Board, (1) the testimony or other information from such individual may be necessary to the public interest, and (2) such individual has refused or is likely to refuse to testify or provide other information on the basis of his privilege against self-incrimination. Requests for the issuance of such an order by the Board may be made by any party. Prior to hearing, and after transfer of the proceeding to the Board, such requests shall be made to the Board in Washington, DC, and the Board shall take such action thereon as it deems appropriate. During the hearing, and thereafter while the proceeding is pending before the administrative law judge, such requests shall be made to the administrative law judge. If the administrative law judge denies the request, his ruling shall be subject to appeal to the Board in Washington, DC, in the manner and to the extent provided in §102.26 with respect to rulings and orders by an administrative law judge, except that requests for permission to appeal in this instance shall be filed within 24 hours of the administrative law judge's ruling. If no appeal is sought within such time, or the appeal is denied, the ruling of the administrative law judge shall become final and his denial shall become the ruling of the Board. If the administrative law judge deems the request appropriate, he shall recommend that the Board seek the approval of the Attorney General for the issuance of the order, and the Board shall take such action on the administrative law judge's recommendation as it deems appropriate. Until the Board has issued the requested order no individual who claims the privilege against self-incrimination shall be required, or permitted, to testify or to give other information respecting the subject matter of the claim.

(d) Upon the failure of any person to comply with a subpena issued upon the request of a private party, the general counsel shall, in the name of the Board but on relation of such private party, institute proceedings in the appropriate district court for the enforcement thereof, unless in the judgment of the Board the enforcement of such subpena would be inconsistent with law and with the policies of the act. Neither the general counsel nor the Board shall be deemed thereby to have assumed responsibility for the effective prosecution of the same before the court.

(e) Persons compelled to submit data or evidence at a public proceeding are entitled to retain or, on payment of lawfully prescribed costs, to procure copies or transcripts of the data or evidence submitted by them. Persons compelled to submit data or evidence in the nonpublic investigative stages of proceedings may, for good cause, be limited by the regional director to inspection of the official transcript of their testimony, but shall be entitled to make copies of documentary evidence or exhibits which they have produced.

[24 FR 9102, Nov. 7, 1959, as amended at 35 FR 18797, Dec. 11, 1970]

§102.32 Payment of witness fees and mileage; fees of persons taking depositions

Witnesses summoned before the trial examiner shall be paid the same fees and mileage that are paid witnesses in the courts of the United

States, and witnesses whose depositions are taken and the persons taking the same shall severally be entitled to the same fees as are paid for like services in the courts of the United States. Witness fees and mileage shall be paid by the party at whose instance the witnesses appear and the person taking the deposition shall be paid by the party at whose instance the deposition is taken.

Transfer, Consolidation, and Severance

§102.33 Transfer of charge and proceeding from region to region; consolidation of proceedings in same region; severance

(a) Whenever the general counsel deems it necessary in order to effectuate the purposes of the Act or to avoid unnecessary costs or delay, he may permit a charge to be filed with him in Washington, DC, or may, at any time after a charge has been filed with a regional director pursuant to §102.10, order that such charge and any proceeding which may have been initiated with respect thereto:

(1) Be transferred to and continued before him for the purpose of investigation or consolidation with any other proceeding which may have been instituted in a regional office or with him; or

(2) Be consolidated with any other proceeding which may have been instituted in the same region; or

(3) Be transferred to and continued in any other region for the purpose of investigation or consolidation with any proceeding which may have been instituted in or transferred to such other region; or

(4) Be severed from any other proceeding with which it may have been consolidated pursuant to this section.

(b) The provisions of §§102.9 to 102.32, inclusive, shall, insofar as applicable, govern proceedings before the general counsel pursuant to this section, and the powers granted to regional directors in such provisions shall, for the purpose of this section, be reserved to and exercised by the general counsel. After the transfer of any charge and any proceeding which may have been instituted with respect thereto from one region to another pursuant to this section, the provisions of this subpart shall, insofar as applicable, govern such charge and such proceeding as if the charge had originally been filed in the region to which the transfer is made.

(c) The regional director may, prior to hearing, exercise the powers in paragraph (a)(2) and (4) of this section with respect to proceedings pending in his region.

(d) Motions to consolidate or sever proceedings after issuance of complaint shall be filed as provided in §102.34 and ruled upon as provided in §102.25, except that the regional director may consolidate or sever proceedings prior to hearing upon his own motion. Rulings by the administrative law judge upon motions to consolidate or sever may be appealed to the Board as provided in §102.26.

[32 FR 9549, July 1, 1967, as amended at 36 FR 9132, May 20, 1971]

Hearings

§102.34 Who shall conduct; to be public unless otherwise ordered

The hearing for the purpose of taking evidence upon a complaint shall be conducted by an administrative law judge designated by the chief administrative law judge in Washington, DC, or by the deputy chief judge, San Francisco, California, by the associate chief judge in New York, New York, or by the associate chief judge in Atlanta, Georgia, as the case may be, unless the Board or any member thereof presides. At any time an administrative law judge may be designated to take the place of the administrative law judge previously designated to conduct the hearing. Such hearing shall be public unless otherwise ordered by the Board or the administrative law judge.

(49 Stat. 449; 29 U.S.C. 151-166, as amended by (61 Stat. 136; 29 U.S.C. Sup. 151-167), (65 Stat. 601; 29 U.S.C. 158, 159, 168), (73 Stat. 519; 29 U.S.C. 141-168), (88 Stat. 395-397; 29 U.S.C. 152, 158, 169, 183))

[45 FR 51193, Aug. 1, 1980]

§102.35 Duties and powers of administrative law judges; assignment and powers of settlement judges

(a) It shall be the duty of the administrative law judge to inquire fully into the facts as to whether the respondent has engaged in or is engaging in an unfair labor practice affecting commerce as set forth in the complaint or amended complaint. The administrative law judge shall have authority, with respect to cases assigned to him, between the time he is designated and transfer of the case to the Board, subject to the Rules and Regulations of the Board and within its powers:
    (1) To administer oaths and affirmations;
    (2) To grant applications for subpoenas;
    (3) To rule upon petitions to revoke subpoenas;
    (4) To rule upon offers of proof and receive relevant evidence;
    (5) To take or cause depositions to be taken whenever the ends of justice would be served thereby;

(6) To regulate the course of the hearing and, if appropriate or necessary, to exclude persons or counsel from the hearing for contemptuous conduct and to strike all related testimony of witnesses refusing to answer any proper questions;

(7) To hold conferences for the settlement or simplification of the issues by consent of the parties, but not to adjust cases;

(8) To dispose of procedural requests, motions, or similar matters, including motions referred to the administrative law judge by the Regional Director and motions for summary judgment or to amend pleadings; also to dismiss complaints or portions thereof; to order hearings reopened; and upon motion order proceedings consolidated or severed prior to issuance of administrative law judge decisions;

(9) To approve a stipulation voluntarily entered into by all parties to the case which will dispense with a verbatim written transcript of record of the oral testimony adduced at the hearing, and which will also provide for the waiver by the respective parties of their right to file with the Board exceptions to the findings of fact (but not to conclusions of law or recommended orders) which the administrative law judge shall make in his decisions;

(10) To make and file decisions, including bench decisions delivered within 72 hours after conclusion of oral argument, in conformity with Public Law 89-554, 5 U.S.C. 557;

(11) To call, examine, and cross-examine witnesses and to introduce into the record documentary or other evidence;

(12) To request the parties at any time during the hearing to state their respective positions concerning any issue in the case or theory in support thereof;

(13) To take any other action necessary under the foregoing and authorized by the published Rules and Regulations of the Board.

(b) Upon the request of any party or the judge assigned to hear a case, or on his or her own motion, the chief administrative law judge in Washington, DC, the deputy chief judge in San Francisco, the associate chief judge in Atlanta, or the associate chief judge in New York may assign a judge who shall be other than the trial judge to conduct settlement negotiations. In exercising his or her discretion, the chief, deputy chief, or associate chief judge making the assignment will consider, among other factors, whether there is reason to believe that resolution of the dispute is likely, the request for assignment of a settlement judge is made in good faith, and the assignment is otherwise feasible. *Provided*, however, that no such assignment shall be made absent the agreement of all parties to the use of this procedure.

(1) The settlement judge shall convene and preside over conferences and settlement negotiations between the parties, assess the practicalities of a potential settlement, and report to the chief, deputy, or

associate the status of settlement negotiations, recommending continuation or termination of the settlement negotiations. Where feasible, settlement conferences shall be held in person.

(2) The settlement judge may require that the attorney or other representative for each party be present at settlement conferences and that the parties or agents with full settlement authority also be present or available by telephone.

(3) Participation of the settlement judge shall terminate upon the order of the chief, deputy, or associates issued after consultation with the settlement judge. The conduct of settlement negotiations shall not unduly delay the hearing.

(4) All discussions between the parties and the settlement judge shall be confidential. The settlement judge shall not discuss any aspect of the case with the trial judge, and no evidence regarding statements, conduct, offers of settlement, and concessions of the parties made in proceedings before the settlement judge shall be admissible in any proceeding before the Board, except by stipulation of the parties. Documents disclosed in the settlement process may not be used in litigation unless voluntarily produced or obtained pursuant to subpoena.

(5) No decision of a chief, deputy, or associate concerning the assignment of a settlement judge or the termination of a settlement judge's assignment shall be appealable to the Board.

(6) Any settlement reached under the auspices of a settlement judge shall be subject to approval in accordance with the provisions of §101.9 of the Board's Statements of Procedure.

[59 FR 65944, Dec. 22, 1994]

EFFECTIVE DATE NOTE: At 59 FR 65944, Dec. 22, 1994, §102.35 was revised effective February 1, 1995, through January 31, 1996.

§102.36 Unavailability of administrative law judge

In the event the administrative law judge designated to conduct the hearing becomes unavailable to the Board after the hearing has been opened, the chief administrative law judge, in Washington, DC, the deputy chief judge, in San Francisco, California, the associate chief judge in New York, New York, or the associate chief judge in Atlanta, Georgia, as the case may be, may designate another administrative law judge for the purpose of further hearing or other appropriate action.

(49 Stat. 449; 29 U.S.C. 151-166, as amended by (61 Stat. 136; 29 U.S.C. Sup. 151-167), (65 Stat. 601; 29 U.S.C. 158, 159, 168), (73 Stat. 519; 29 U.S.C. 141-168), (88 Stat. 395-397; 29 U.S.C. 152, 158, 169, 183))

[45 FR 51193, Aug. 1, 1980]

§102.37 Disqualification of administrative law judge

An administrative law judge may withdraw from a proceeding whenever he deems himself disqualified. Any party may request the administrative law judge, at any time following his designation and before filing of his decision, to withdraw on ground of personal bias or disqualification, by filing with him promptly upon the discovery of the alleged facts a timely affidavit setting forth in detail the matters alleged to constitute grounds for disqualification. If, in the opinion of the administrative law judge, such affidavit is filed with due diligence and is sufficient on its face, he shall forthwith disqualify himself and withdraw from the proceeding. If the administrative law judge does not disqualify himself and withdraw from the proceeding, he shall so rule upon the record, stating the grounds for his ruling and proceed with the hearing, or, if the hearing has closed, he shall proceed with issuance of his decision, and the provisions of §102.26, with respect to review of rulings of administrative law judges, shall thereupon apply.

(49 Stat. 449; 29 U.S.C. 151-166, as amended by (61 Stat. 136; 29 U.S.C. Sup. 151-167), (65 Stat. 601; 29 U.S.C. 158, 159, 168), (73 Stat. 519; 29 U.S.C. 141-168), (88 Stat. 395-397; 29 U.S.C. 152, 158, 169, 183)))

[45 FR 51193, Aug. 1, 1980]

§102.38 Rights of parties

Any party shall have the right to appear at such hearing in person, by counsel, or by other representative, to call, examine, and cross-examine witnesses, and to introduce into the record documentary or other evidence, except that the participation of any party shall be limited to the extent permitted by the administrative law judge: *And provided further,* That documentary evidence shall be submitted in duplicate.

§102.39 Rules of evidence controlling so far as practicable

Any such proceeding shall, so far as practicable, be conducted in accordance with the rules of evidence applicable in the district courts of the United States under the rules of civil procedure for the district courts of the United States, adopted by the Supreme Court of the United States pursuant to the Act of June 19, 1934, (title 28 U.S.C., secs. 723-B, 723-C).

§102.40 Stipulations of fact admissible

In any such proceeding stipulations of fact may be introduced in evidence with respect to any issue.

§102.41 Objection to conduct of hearing; how made; objections not waived by further participation

Any objection with respect to the conduct of the hearing, including any objection to the introduction of evidence, may be stated orally or in writing, accompanied by a short statement of the grounds of such objection, and included in the record. No such objection shall be deemed waived by further participation in the hearing.

§102.42 Filings of briefs and proposed findings with the administrative law judge and oral argument at the hearing

Any party shall be entitled, upon request, to a reasonable period at the close of the hearing for oral argument, which may include presentation of proposed findings and conclusions, and shall be included in the stenographic report of the hearing. In the discretion of the administrative law judge, any party may, upon request made before the close of the hearing, file a brief or proposed findings and conclusions, or both, with the administrative law judge, who may fix a reasonable time for such filing, but not in excess of 35 days from the close of the hearing. Requests for further extensions of time shall be made to the chief administrative law judge in Washington, D.C., to the deputy chief judge in San Francisco, California, to the associate chief judge in New York, New York, or to the associate chief judge in Atlanta, Georgia, as the case may be. Notice of the request for any extension shall be immediately served on all other parties, and proof of service shall be furnished. Three copies of the brief or proposed findings and conclusions shall be filed with the administrative law judge, and copies shall be served on the other parties, and a statement of such service shall be furnished. In any case in which the administrative law judge believes that written briefs or proposed findings of fact and conclusions may not be necessary, he or she shall notify the parties at the opening of the hearing or as soon thereafter as practicable that he or she may wish to hear oral argument in lieu of briefs.

[59 FR 65945, Dec. 22, 1994]

EFFECTIVE DATE NOTE: At 59 FR 65945, Dec. 22, 1994, §102.42 was revised effective February 1, 1995, through January 31, 1996.

§102.43 Continuance and adjournment

In the discretion of the administrative law judge, the hearing may be continued from day to day, or adjourned to a later date or to a different place, by announcement thereof at the hearings by the administrative law judge, or by other appropriate notice.

§102.44 Misconduct at hearing before an administrative law judge or the Board; refusal of witness to answer questions

(a) Misconduct at any hearing before an administrative law judge or before the Board shall be ground for summary exclusion from the hearing.

(b) Such misconduct of an aggravated character, when engaged in by an attorney or other representative of a party, shall be ground for suspension or disbarment by the Board from further practice before it after due notice and hearing.

(c) The refusal of a witness at any such hearing to answer any question which has been ruled to be proper shall, in the discretion of the administrative law judge, be ground for striking all testimony previously given by such witness on related matters.

Administrative Law Judge's Decision and Transfer of Case to the Board

§102.45 Administrative Law Judge's decision; contents; service; transfer of the case to the Board; contents of record in case

(a) After hearing for the purpose of taking evidence upon a complaint, the administrative law judge shall prepare a decision. Such decision shall contain findings of fact, conclusions, and the reasons or basis therefor, upon all material issues of fact, law, or discretion presented on the record, and shall contain recommendations as to what disposition of the case should be made, which may include, if it be found that the respondent has engaged in or is engaging in the alleged unfair labor practices, a recommendation for such affirmative action by the respondent as will effectuate the policies of the Act. The administrative law judge shall file the original of his decision with the Board and cause a copy thereof to be served on each of the parties. If the administrative law judge delivers a bench decision, promptly upon receiving the transcript the judge shall certify the accuracy of the pages of the transcript containing the decision; file with the Board a certified copy of those pages together with any supplementary matter the judge may deem necessary to complete the decision; and cause a copy thereof to be served on each of the parties. Upon the filing of the decision, the Board shall enter an order transferring the case to the Board and shall serve copies of the order, setting forth the date of such transfer, on all the parties. Service of the administrative law judge's decision and of the order transferring the case to the Board shall be complete upon mailing.

(b) The charge upon which the complaint was issued and any amendments thereto, the complaint and any amendments thereto, notice of hearing, answer and any amendments thereto, motions, rulings, orders, the stenographic report of the hearing, stipulations, exhibits, documentary evidence, and depositions, together with the administrative law judge's decision and exceptions, and any cross-exceptions or answering briefs as provided in §102.46, shall constitute the record in the case.

[28 FR 7973, Aug. 6, 1963, as amended at 59 FR 65945, Dec. 22, 1994]

EFFECTIVE DATE NOTE: At 59 FR 65945, Dec. 22, 1994, in §102.45, paragraph (a) was revised effective February 1, 1995, through January 31, 1996.

Exceptions to the Record and Proceedings

§102.46 Exceptions, cross-exceptions, briefs, answering briefs; time for filing; where to file; service on the parties; extension of time; effect of failure to include matter in exceptions; reply briefs; oral arguments

(a) Within 28 days. or within such further period as the Board may allow, from the date of the service of the order transferring the case to the Board, pursuant to §102.45, any party may (in accordance with section 10(c) of the Act and §§102.111 and 102.112 of these rules) file with the Board in Washington, DC, exceptions to the administrative law judge's decision or to any other part of the record or proceedings (including rulings upon all motions or objections), together with a brief in support of said exceptions. Any party may, within the same period, file a brief in support of the administrative law judge's decision. The filing of such exceptions and briefs is subject to the provisions of paragraph (j) of this section. Requests for extension of time to file exceptions or briefs shall be in writing and copies thereof shall be served promptly on the other parties.

(b)(1) Each exception (i) shall set forth specifically the questions of procedure, fact, law, or policy to which exception is taken; (ii) shall identify that part of the administrative law judge's decision to which objection is made; (iii) shall designate by precise citation of page the portions of the record relied on; and (iv) shall concisely state the grounds for the exception. If a supporting brief is filed the exceptions document shall not contain any argument or citation of authority in support of the exceptions, but such matters shall be set forth only in the brief. If no supporting brief is filed the exceptions document shall also include the citation of authorities and argument in support of the exceptions, in which event the exceptions document shall be subject to the 50-page limit as for briefs set forth in §102.46(j).

(2) Any exception to a ruling, finding, conclusion, or recommendation which is not specifically urged shall be deemed to have been waived.

Any exception which fails to comply with the foregoing requirements may be disregarded.

(c) Any brief in support of exceptions shall contain no matter not included within the scope of the exceptions and shall contain, in the order indicated, the following:

    (1) A clear and concise statement of the case containing all that is material to the consideration of the questions presented.

    (2) A specification of the questions involved and to be argued, together with a reference to the specific exceptions to which they relate.

    (3) The argument, presenting clearly the points of fact and law relied on in support of the position taken on each question, with specific page reference to the record and the legal or other material relied on.

(d)(1) Within 14 days, or such further period as the Board may allow, from the last date on which exceptions and any supporting brief may be filed, a party opposing the exceptions may file an answering brief to the exceptions, in accordance with the provisions of paragraph (j) of this section.

    (2) The answering brief to the exceptions shall be limited to the questions raised in the exceptions and in the brief in support thereof. It shall present clearly the points of fact and law relied on in support of the position taken on each question. Where exception has been taken to a factual finding of the administrative law judge and it is proposed to support that finding, the answering brief should specify those pages of the record which, in the view of the party filing the brief, support the administrative law judge's finding.

    (3) Requests for extension of time to file an answering brief to the exceptions shall be in writing and copies thereof shall be served promptly on the other parties.

(e) Any party who has not previously filed exceptions may, within 14 days, or such further period as the Board may allow, from the last date on which exceptions and any supporting brief may be filed, file cross-exceptions to any portion of the administrative law judge's decision, together with a supporting brief, in accordance with the provisions of paragraphs (b) and (j) of this section.

(f)(1) Within 14 days, or such further period as the Board may allow, from the last date on which cross-exceptions and any supporting brief may be filed, any other party may file an answering brief to such cross-exceptions in accordance with the provisions of paragraphs (c) and (j) of this section. Such answering brief shall be limited to the questions raised in the cross-exceptions.

    (2) Requests for extension of time to file cross-exceptions, or answering brief to cross-exceptions, shall be in writing and copies thereof shall be served promptly on the other parties.

(g) No matter not included in exceptions or cross-exceptions may thereafter be urged before the Board, or in any further proceeding.

(h) Within 14 days from the last date on which an answering brief may be filed pursuant to paragraph (d) or (f) of this section, any party may file a reply brief to any such answering brief. Any reply brief filed pursuant to this subsection shall be limited to matters raised in the brief to which it is replying, and shall not exceed 10 pages. No extensions of time shall be granted for the filing of reply briefs, nor shall permission be granted to exceed the 10 page length limitation. Eight copies of any reply brief shall be filed with the Board, copies shall be served on the other parties, and a statement of such service shall be furnished. No further briefs shall be filed except by special leave of the Board. Requests for such leave shall be in writing and copies thereof shall be served promptly on the other parties.

(i) Should any party desire permission to argue orally before the Board, request therefor must be made in writing to the Board simultaneously with the statement of any exceptions or cross-exceptions filed pursuant to the provisions of this section with a statement of service on the other parties. The Board shall notify the parties of the time and place of oral argument, if such permission is granted. Oral arguments are limited to 30 minutes for each party entitled to participate. No request for additional time will be granted unless timely application is made in advance of oral argument.

(j) Exceptions to administrative law judges' decisions, or to the record, and briefs shall be printed or otherwise legibly duplicated. Carbon copies of typewritten matter will not be accepted. Eight copies of such documents shall be filed with the Board in Washington, DC, and copies shall also be served promptly on the other parties. All documents filed pursuant to this section shall be double spaced on $8\frac{1}{2}$ by 11-inch paper. Any brief filed pursuant to this section shall not be combined with any other brief, and except for reply briefs whose length is governed by paragraph (h) of this section, shall not exceed 50 pages in length, exclusive of subject index and table of cases and other authorities cited, unless permission to exceed that limit is obtained from the Board by motion, setting forth the reasons therefor, filed not less than 10 days prior to the date the brief is due. Where any brief filed pursuant to this section exceeds 20 pages, it shall contain a subject index with page references and an alphabetical table of cases and other authorities cited.

[56 FR 49142, Sept. 27, 1991]

§102.47 Filing of motion after transfer of case to Board

All motions filed after the case has been transferred to the Board pursuant to §102.45 shall be filed with the Board in Washington, DC, by transmitting eight copies thereof, together with an affidavit of service on the parties. Such motions shall be printed or otherwise legibly duplicated:

Provided, however, That carbon copies of typewritten matter shall not be filed and if submitted will not be accepted.

[29 FR 15919, Nov. 28, 1964]

Procedure Before the Board

§102.48 Action of the Board upon expiration of time to file exceptions to the administrative law judge's decision; decisions by the Board; extraordinary postdecision motions

(a) In the event no timely or proper exceptions are filed as herein provided, the findings, conclusions, and recommendations of the administrative law judge as contained in his decision shall, pursuant to section 10(c) of the Act, automatically become the decision and order of the Board and become its findings, conclusions, and order, and all objections and exceptions thereto shall be deemed waived for all purposes.

(b) Upon the filing of timely and proper exceptions, and any cross-exceptions, or answering briefs, as provided in §102.46, the Board may decide the matter forthwith upon the record, or after oral argument, or may reopen the record and receive further evidence before a member of the Board or other Board agent or agency, or may make other disposition of the case.

(c) Where exception is taken to a factual finding of the administrative law judge, the Board, in determining whether the finding is contrary to a preponderance of the evidence, may limit its consideration to such portions of the record as are specified in the exceptions, the supporting brief, and the answering brief.

(d)(1)A party to a proceeding before the Board may, because of extraordinary circumstances, move for reconsideration, rehearing, or reopening of the record after the Board decision or order. A motion for reconsideration shall state with particularity the material error claimed and with respect to any finding of material fact shall specify the page of the record relied on. A motion for rehearing shall specify the error alleged to require a hearing de novo and the prejudice to the movant alleged to result from such error. A motion to reopen the record shall state briefly the additional evidence sought to be adduced, why it was not presented previously, and that, if adduced and credited, it would require a different result. Only newly discovered evidence, evidence which has become available only since the close of the hearing, or evidence which the Board believes should have been taken at the hearing will be taken at any further hearing.

(2) Any motion pursuant to this section shall be filed within 28 days, or such further period as the Board may allow, after the service of the Board's decision or order, except that a motion for leave to adduce additional

evidence shall be filed promptly on discovery of such evidence. Copies of any request for an extension of time shall be served promptly on the other parties.

(3) The filing and pendency of a motion under this provision shall not operate to stay the effectiveness of the action of the Board unless so ordered. A motion for reconsideration or for rehearing need not be filed to exhaust administrative remedies.

[28 FR 7974, Aug. 6, 1963, as amended at 34 FR 14432, Sept. 16, 1969; 51 FR 23746, July 1, 1986; 56 FR 49143, Sept. 27, 1991]

§102.49 Modification or setting aside of order of Board before record filed in court; action thereafter

Within the limitations of the provisions of section 10(c) of the Act, and §102.48, until a transcript of the record in a case shall have been filed in a court, within the meaning of section 10 of the Act, the Board may at any time upon reasonable notice modify or set aside, in whole or in part, any findings of fact, conclusions of law, or order made or issued by it. Thereafter, the Board may proceed pursuant to §102.50, insofar as applicable.

§102.50 Hearings before Board or member thereof

Whenever the Board deems it necessary in order to effectuate the purpose of the act or to avoid unnecessary costs or delay, it may, at any time after a complaint has issued pursuant to §102.15 or §102.33, order that such complaint and any proceeding which may have been instituted with respect thereto be transferred to and continued before it or any member of the Board. The provisions of this subpart shall, insofar as applicable, govern proceedings before the Board or any member pursuant to this section, and the powers granted to administrative law judges in such provisions shall, for the purpose of this section, be reserved to and exercised by the Board or the member thereof who shall preside.

§102.51 Settlement or adjustment of issues

At any stage of a proceeding prior to hearing, where time, the nature of the proceeding, and the public interest permit, all interested parties shall have opportunity to submit to the regional director, with whom the charge was filed, for consideration facts, arguments, offers of settlement, or proposals of adjustment.

§102.52 Compliance with Board order; notification of compliance determination

After entry of a Board order directing remedial action, or the entry of a court judgment enforcing such order, the Regional Director shall seek compliance from all persons having obligations thereunder. The Regional Director shall make a compliance determination as appropriate and shall notify the parties of the compliance determination. A charging party adversely affected by a monetary, make-whole, reinstatement, or other compliance determination will be provided, on request, with a written statement of the basis for that determination.

[53 FR 37755, Sept. 28, 1988]

§102.53 Review by the General Counsel of compliance determination; appeal to the Board of the General Counsel's decision

(a) The charging party may appeal such determination to the General Counsel in Washington, DC, within 14 days of the written statement of compliance determination provided as set forth in §102.52. The appeal shall contain a complete statement setting forth the facts and reasons upon which it is based and shall identify with particularity the error claimed in the Regional Director's determination. The charging party shall serve a copy of the appeal on all other parties and on the Regional Director. The General Counsel may for good cause shown extend the time for filing an appeal.

(b) The General Counsel may affirm or modify the determination of the Regional Director, or may take such other action deemed appropriate, stating the grounds for the decision.

(c) Within 14 days after service of the General Counsel's decision, the charging party may file a request for review of that decision with the Board in Washington, DC. The request for review shall contain a complete statement of the facts and reasons upon which it is based and shall identify with particularity the error claimed in the General Counsel's decision. A copy of the request for review shall be served on the General Counsel and on the Regional Director.

(d) The Board may affirm or modify the decision of the General Counsel, or make such other disposition of the matter as it deems appropriate. The denial of the request for review will constitute an affirmance of the decision of the General Counsel.

[53 FR 37755, Sept. 28, 1988]

§102.54 Initiation of formal compliance proceedings; issuance of compliance specification and notice of hearing

(a) If it appears that controversy exists with respect to compliance with an order of the Board which cannot be resolved without a formal proceeding, the Regional Director may issue and serve on all parties a compliance specification in the name of the Board. The specification shall contain or be accompanied by a notice of hearing before an administrative law judge at a place therein fixed and at a time not less than 21 days after the service of the specification.

(b) Whenever the Regional Director deems it necessary in order to effectuate the purposes and policies of the Act or to avoid unnecessary costs or delay, the Regional Director may consolidate with a complaint and notice of hearing issued pursuant to §102.15 a compliance specification based on that complaint. After opening of the hearing, consolidation shall be subject to the approval of the Board or the administrative law judge, as appropriate. Issuance of a compliance specification shall not be a prerequisite or bar to Board initiation of proceedings in any administrative or judicial forum which the Board or the Regional Director determines to be appropriate for obtaining compliance with a Board order.

[53 FR 37755, Sept. 28, 1988]

§102.55 Contents of compliance specification

(a) *Contents of specification with respect to allegations concerning the amount of backpay due.* With respect to allegations concerning the amount of backpay due, the specification shall specifically and in detail show, for each employee, the backpay periods broken down by calendar quarters, the specific figures and basis of computation of gross backpay and interim earrings, the expenses for each quarter, the net backpay due, and any other pertinent information.

(b) *Contents of specification with respect to allegations other than the amount of backpay due.* With respect to allegations other than the amount of backpay due, the specification shall contain a clear and concise description of the respects in which the respondent has failed to comply with a Board or court order, including the remedial acts claimed to be necessary for compliance by the respondent and, where known, the approximate dates, places, and names of the respondent's agents or other representatives described in the specification.

(c) *Amendments to specification.* After the issuance of the notice of compliance hearing but prior to the opening of the hearing, the Regional Director may amend the specification. After the opening of the hearing, the specification may be amended upon leave of the administrative law judge or the Board, as the case may be, upon good cause shown.

[53 FR 37756, Sept. 28, 1988]

§102.56 Answer to compliance specification

(a) *Filing and service of answer; form.* Each respondent alleged in the specification to have compliance obligations shall, within 21 days from the service of the specification, file an original and four copies of an answer thereto with the Regional Director issuing the specification, and shall immediately serve a copy thereof on the other parties. The answer to the specification shall be in writing, the original being signed and sworn to by the respondent or by a duly authorized agent with appropriate power of attorney affixed, and shall contain the mailing address of the respondent.

(b) *Contents of answer to specification.* The answer shall specifically admit, deny, or explain each and every allegation of the specification, unless the respondent is without knowledge, in which case the respondent shall so state, such statement operating as a denial. Denials shall fairly meet the substance of the allegations of the specification at issue. When a respondent intends to deny only a part of an allegation, the respondent shall specify so much of it as is true and shall deny only the remainder. As to all matters within the knowledge of the respondent, including but not limited to the various factors entering into the computation of gross backpay, a general denial shall not suffice. As to such matters, if the respondent disputes either the accuracy of the figures in the specification or the premises on which they are based, the answer shall specifically state the basis for such disagreement, setting forth in detail the respondent's position as to the applicable premises and furnishing the appropriate supporting figures.

(c) *Effect of failure to answer or to plead specifically and in detail to backpay allegations of specification.* If the respondent fails to file any answer to the specification within the time prescribed by this section, the Board may, either with or without taking evidence in support of the allegations of the specification and without further notice to the respondent, find the specification to be true and enter such order as may be appropriate. If the respondent files an answer to the specification but fails to deny any allegation of the specification in the manner required by paragraph (b) of this section, and the failure so to deny is not adequately explained, such allegation shall be deemed to be admitted to be true, and may be so found by the Board without the taking of evidence supporting such allegation, and the respondent shall be precluded from introducing any evidence controverting the allegation.

(d) *Extension of time for filing answer to specification.* Upon the Regional Director's own motion or upon proper cause shown by any respondent, the Regional Director issuing the compliance specification and notice of hearing may by written order extend the time within which the answer to the specification shall be filed.

(e) *Amendment to answer.* Following the amendment of the specification by the Regional Director, any respondent affected by the amendment may amend its answer thereto.

[53 FR 37756, Sept. 28, 1988]

§102.57 Extension of date of hearing

Upon the Regional Director's own motion or upon proper cause shown, the Regional Director issuing the compliance specification and notice of hearing may extend the date of the hearing.

[53 FR 37756, Sept. 28, 1988]

§102.58 Withdrawal

Any compliance specification and notice of hearing may be withdrawn before the hearing by the Regional Director upon his or her own motion.

[53 FR 37756, Sept. 28, 1988]

§102.59 Hearing; posthearing procedure

After the issuance of a compliance specification and notice of hearing, the procedures provided in §§102.24 to 102.51 shall be followed insofar as applicable.

[53 FR 37756, Sept. 28, 1988]

SUBPART C. PROCEDURE UNDER SECTION 9(c) OF THE ACT FOR THE DETERMINATION OF QUESTIONS CONCERNING REPRESENTATION OF EMPLOYEES[3] AND FOR CLARIFICATION OF BARGAINING UNITS AND FOR AMENDMENT OF CERTIFICATIONS UNDER SECTION 9(b) OF THE ACT

§102.60 Petitions

(a) *Petition for certification or decertification; who may file; where to file; withdrawal.* A petition for investigation of a question concerning representation of employees under paragraphs (1)(A)(i) and (1)(B) of section 9(c) of the Act (hereinafter called a petition for certification) may be filed by an employee or group of employees or any individual or labor organization acting in their behalf or by an employer. A petition under paragraph (1)(A)(ii) of section 9(c) of the Act, alleging that the individual or labor organization which has been certified or is being currently recognized as the bargaining representative is no longer such representative (hereinafter called a petition for decer-

---

[3]. Procedure under the first proviso to sec. 8(b)(7)(C) of the Act is governed by subpart D.

tification), may be filed by any employee or group of employees or any individual or labor organization acting in their behalf. Petitions under this section shall be in writing and signed,[4] and either shall be sworn to before a notary public, Board agent, or other person duly authorized by law to administer oaths and take acknowledgments or shall contain a declaration by the person signing it, under the penalties of the Criminal Code, that its contents are true and correct to the best of his knowledge and belief. Four copies of the petition shall be filed. Except as provided in §102.72, such petitions shall be filed with the regional director for the regions wherein the bargaining unit exists, or, if the bargaining unit exists in two or more regions, with the regional director for any such regions. Prior to the transfer of the case to the Board, pursuant to §102.67, the petition may be withdrawn only with the consent of the regional director with whom such petition was filed. After the transfer of the case to the Board, the petition may be withdrawn only with the consent of the Board. Whenever the regional director or the Board, as the case may be, approves the withdrawal of any petition, the case shall be closed.

(b) *Petition for clarification of bargaining unit or petition for amendment of certification under section 9(b) of the Act; who may file; where to file; withdrawal.* A petition for clarification of an existing bargaining unit or a petition for amendment of certification, in the absence of a question concerning representation, may be filed by a labor organization or by an employer. Where applicable the same procedures set forth in paragraph (a) of this section shall be followed.

[29 FR 15919, Nov. 28, 1964]

§102.61 Contents of petition for certification; contents of petition for decertification; contents of petition for clarification of bargaining unit; contents of petition for amendment of certification

(a) A petition for certification, when filed by an employee or group of employees or an individual or labor organization acting in their behalf, shall contain the following:

(1) The name of the employer.

(2) The address of the establishments involved.

(3) The general nature of the employer's business.

(4) A description of the bargaining unit which the petitioner claims to be appropriate.

(5) The names and addresses of any other persons or labor organizations who claim to represent any employees in the alleged appropriate

---

4. Blank forms for filing such petitions will be supplied by the regional office upon request.

unit, and brief descriptions of the contracts, if any, covering the employees in such unit.

(6) The number of employees in the alleged appropriate unit.

(7) A statement that the employer declines to recognize the petitioner as the representative within the meaning of section 9(a) of the Act or that the labor organization is currently recognized but desires certification under the act.

(8) The name, affiliation, if any, and address of the petitioner.

(9) Whether a strike or picketing is in progress at the establishment involved and, if so, the approximate number of employees participating, and the date such strike or picketing commenced.

(10) Any other relevant facts.

(b) A petition for certification, when filed by an employer, shall contain the following:

(1) The name and address of the petitioner.

(2) The general nature of the petitioner's business.

(3) A brief statement setting forth that one or more individuals or labor organizations have presented to the petitioner a claim to be recognized as the exclusive representative of all employees in the unit claimed to be appropriate; a description of such unit; and the number of employees in the unit.

(4) The name or names, affiliation, if any, and addresses of the individuals or labor organizations making such claim for recognition.

(5) A statement whether the petitioner has contracts with any labor organization or other representatives of employees and, if so, their expiration date.

(6) Whether a strike or picketing is in progress at the establishment involved and, if so, the approximate number of employees participating, and the date such strike or picketing commenced.

(7) Any other relevant facts.

(c) Petitions for decertification shall contain the following:

(1) The name of the employer.

(2) The address of the establishments and a description of the bargaining unit involved.

(3) The general nature of the employer's business.

(4) Name and address of the petitioner and affiliation, if any.

(5) Name or names of the individuals or labor organizations who have been certified or are being currently recognized by the employer and who claim to represent any employees in the unit involved, and the expiration date of any contracts covering such employees.

(6) An allegation that the individuals or labor organizations who have been certified or are currently recognized by the employer are no longer the representative in the appropriate unit as defined in section 9(a) of the Act.

(7) The number of employees in the unit.

(8) Whether a strike or picketing is in progress at the establishment involved and, if so, the approximate number of employees participating, and the date such strike or picketing commenced.

(9) Any other relevant facts.

(d) A petition for clarification shall contain the following:

(1) The name of the employer and the name of the recognized or certified bargaining representative.

(2) The address of the establishment involved.

(3) The general nature of the employer's business.

(4) A description of the present bargaining unit, and, if the bargaining unit is certified, an identification of the existing certification.

(5) A description of the proposed clarification.

(6) The names and addresses of any other persons or labor organizations who claim to represent any employees affected by the proposed clarifications, and brief descriptions of the contracts, if any, covering any such employees.

(7) The number of employees in the present bargaining unit and in the unit as proposed under the clarification.

(8) The job classifications of employees as to whom the issue is raised, and the number of employees in each classification.

(9) A statement by petitioner setting forth reasons why petitioner desires clarification of unit.

(10) The name, the affiliation, if any, and the address of the petitioner.

(11) Any other relevant facts.

(e) A petition for amendment of certification shall contain the following:

(1) The name of the employer and the name of the certified union involved.

(2) The address of the establishment involved.

(3) The general nature of the employer's business.

(4) Identification and description of the existing certification.

(5) A statement by petitioner setting forth the details of the desired amendment and reasons therefor.

(6) The names and addresses of any other persons or labor organizations who claim to represent any employees in the unit covered by the certification and brief descriptions of the contracts, if any, covering the employees in such unit.

(7) The name, the affiliation, if any, and the address of the petitioner.

(8) Any other relevant facts.

[26 FR 3887, May 4, 1961, as amended at 29 FR 15919, Nov. 28, 1964]

§102.62 Consent-election agreements

(a) Where a petition has been duly filed, the employer and any individuals or labor organizations representing a substantial number of employees involved may, with the approval of the regional director, enter into a consent election agreement leading to a determination by the regional director of the facts ascertained after such consent election. Such agreement shall include a description of the appropriate unit, the time and place of holding the election, and the payroll period to be used in determining what employees within the appropriate unit shall be eligible to vote. Such consent election shall be conducted under the direction and supervision of the regional director. The method of conducting such consent election shall be consistent with the method followed by the regional director in conducting elections pursuant to §§102.69 and 102.70 except that the rulings and determinations by the regional director of the results thereof shall be final, and the regional director shall issue to the parties a certification of the results of the election, including certification of representatives where appropriate, with the same force and effect as if issued by the Board, provided further that rulings or determinations by the regional director in respect to any amendment of such certification shall also be final.

(b) Where a petition has been duly filed, the employer and any individuals or labor organizations representing a substantial number of the employees involved may, with the approval of the regional director, enter into an agreement providing for a waiver of hearing and a consent election leading to a determination by the Board of the facts ascertained after such consent election, if such a determination is necessary. Such agreement shall also include a description of the appropriate bargaining unit, the time and place of holding the election, and the payroll period to be used in determining which employees within the appropriate unit shall be eligible to vote. Such consent election shall be conducted under the direction and supervision of the regional director. The method of conducting such election and the post election procedure shall be consistent with that followed by the regional director in conducting elections pursuant to §§102.69 and 102.70.

[26 FR 3887, May 4, 1961]

§102.63 Investigation of petition by regional director; notice of hearing; service of notice; withdrawal of notice

(a) After a petition has been filed under §102.61 (a), (b), or (c), if no agreement such as that provided in §102.62 is entered into and if it appears to the regional director that there is reasonable cause to believe that a question of representation affecting commerce exists, that the policies of the act will be effectuated, and that an election will reflect the free choice of employees in the appropriate unit, the Regional Director shall prepare and cause to be served upon the parties and upon any known individuals or labor organizations purporting to act as representatives of any employees directly affected by such investigation, a notice of hearing before a hearing officer at a time and place fixed therein. A copy of the petition shall be served with such notice of hearing. Any such notice of hearing may be amended or withdrawn before the close of the hearing by the regional director on his own motion.

(b) After a petition has been filed under §102.61(d) or (e), the regional director shall conduct an investigation and, as appropriate, he may issue a decision without a hearing; or prepare and cause to be served upon the parties and upon any known individuals or labor organizations purporting to act as representatives of any employees directly affected by such investigation, a notice of hearing before a hearing officer at a time and place fixed therein; or take other appropriate action. If a notice of hearing is served, it shall be accompanied by a copy of the petition. Any such notice of hearing may be amended or withdrawn before the close of the hearing by the regional director on his own motion. All hearing and posthearing procedure under this paragraph (b) shall be in conformance with §§102.64 through 102.68 whenever applicable, except where the unit or certification involved arises out of an agreement as provided in §102.62(a), the regional director's action shall be final, and the provisions for review of regional director's decisions by the Board shall not apply. Dismissals of petitions without a hearing shall not be governed by §102.71. The regional director's dismissal shall be by decision, and a request for review therefrom may be obtained under §102.67, except where an agreement under §102.62(a) is involved.

[29 FR 15919, Nov. 28, 1964]

§102.64 Conduct of hearing

(a) Hearings shall be conducted by a hearing officer and shall be open to the public unless otherwise ordered by the hearing officer. At any time, a hearing officer may be substituted for the hearing officer previously presiding. It shall be the duty of the hearing officer to inquire fully into all matters and issues necessary to obtain a full and complete record upon which the Board or the regional director may discharge *their* duties under section 9(c) of the Act.

(b) The hearing officer may, in his discretion, continue the hearing from day to day, or adjourn it to a later date or to a different place, by announcement thereof at the hearing or by other appropriate notice.

[26 FR 3888, May 4, 1961]

§102.65 Motions; intervention

(a) All motions, including motions for intervention pursuant to paragraphs (b) and (e) of this section, shall be in writing or, if made at the hearing, may be stated orally on the record and shall briefly state the order or relief sought and the grounds for such motion. An original and two copies of written motions shall be filed and a copy thereof immediately shall be served on the other parties to the proceeding. Motions made prior to the transfer of the case to the Board shall be filed with the regional director, except that motions made during the hearing shall be filed with the hearing officer. After the transfer of the case to the Board, all motions shall be filed with the Board. Such motions shall be printed or otherwise legibly duplicated: *Provided, however,* That carbon copies of typewritten matter shall not be filed and if submitted will not be accepted. Eight copies of such motions shall be filed with the Board. The regional director may rule upon all motions filed with him, causing a copy of said ruling to be served on the parties, or he may refer the motion to the hearing officer: *Provided,* That if the regional director prior to the close of the hearing grants a motion to dismiss the petition, the petitioner may obtain a review of such ruling in the manner prescribed in §102.71. The hearing officer shall rule, either orally on the record or in writing, upon all motions filed at the hearing or referred to him as hereinabove provided, except that all motions to dismiss petitions shall be referred for appropriate action at such time as the entire record is considered by the regional director or the Board, as the case may be.

(b) Any person desiring to intervene in any proceeding shall make a motion for intervention, stating the grounds upon which such person claims to have an interest in the proceeding. The regional director or the hearing officer, as the case may be, may by order permit intervention in person or by counsel or other representative to such extent and upon such terms as he may deem proper, and such intervenor shall thereupon become a party to the proceeding.

(c) All motions, rulings, and orders shall become a part of the record, except that rulings on motions to revoke subpenas shall become a part of the record only upon the request of the party aggrieved thereby as provided in §102.66(c). Unless expressly authorized by the Rules and Regulations, rulings by the regional director or by the hearing officer shall not be appealed directly to the Board, but shall be considered by the Board on appropriate appeal pursuant to §102.67(b), (c), and (d) or whenever the case is transferred to it for decision: *Provided, however,* That if the regional director has issued an order transferring the case to the Board for decision such rulings may be appealed directly to the Board by special permission of the Board. Nor shall rulings by the hearing officer be appealed directly to the regional director unless expressly authorized by the Rules and Regulations, except by special permission of the regional director, but shall be considered by the regional director when he reviews the entire record. Requests to the regional director, or to the Board in appropriate cases, for special permission to appeal from a ruling of the hearing officer, together with the appeal from such ruling, shall be filed promptly, in writing, and shall briefly state (1) the reasons special permission should be granted and (2) the grounds relied on for the appeal. The moving party shall immediately serve a copy of the request for special permission and of the appeal on the other parties and on the regional director. Any statement in opposition or other response to the request and/or to the appeal shall be filed promptly, in writing, and shall be served immediately on the other parties and on the regional director. If the Board or the regional director, as the case may be, grants the request for special permission to appeal, the Board or the regional director may proceed forthwith to rule on the appeal.

(d) The right to make motions or to make objections to rulings on motions shall not be deemed waived by participation in the proceeding.

(e)(1) A party to a proceeding may, because of extraordinary circumstances, move after the close of the hearing for reopening of the record, or move after the decision or report for reconsideration, for rehearing, or to reopen the record, but no such motion shall stay the time for filing a request for review of a decision or exceptions to a report. No motion for reconsideration, for rehearing, or to reopen the record will be entertained by the Board or by any regional director with respect to any matter which could have been but was not raised pursuant to any other section of these rules: *Provided, however,* That the regional director may treat a request for review of a decision or exceptions to a report as a motion for reconsideration. A motion for reconsideration shall state with particularity the material error claimed and with respect to any finding of material fact shall specify the page of the record relied on for the motion. A motion for rehearing or to reopen the record shall specify briefly the error alleged to require a rehearing or hearing de novo, the prejudice to the movant alleged to result from such error, the additional evidence sought to be adduced, why it was not presented previously, and what result it would require if adduced and credited. Only newly discovered evidence—evidence which has become available only since the close of the hearing—or evidence which the regional director or the Board believes should have been taken at the hearing will be taken at any further hearing.

(2) Any motion for reconsideration or for rehearing pursuant to this paragraph shall be filed within 14 days, or such further period as may be allowed, after the service of the decision or report. Any request for an extension of time to file such a motion shall be served promptly on the other parties. A motion to reopen the record shall be filed promptly on discovery of the evidence sought to be adduced.

(3) The filing and pendency of a motion under this provision shall not unless so ordered operate to stay the effectiveness of any action taken

or directed to be taken, except that, if the motion states with particularity that the granting thereof will affect the eligibility to vote of specific employees, the ballots of such employees shall be challenged and impounded in any election conducted while such motion is pending. A motion for reconsideration, for rehearing, or to reopen the record need not be filed to exhaust administrative remedies.

[26 FR 3888, May 4, 1961, as amended at 36 FR 9133, May 20, 1971; 47 FR 40771, Sept. 15, 1982; 57 FR 12876, Apr. 14, 1992]

§102.66 Introduction of evidence: rights of parties at hearing; subpenas

(a) Any party shall have the right to appear at any hearing in person, by counsel, or by other representative, and any party and the hearing officer shall have power to call, examine, and cross-examine witnesses and to introduce into the record documentary and other evidence. Witnesses shall be examined orally under oath. The rules of evidence prevailing in courts of law or equity shall not be controlling. Stipulations of fact may be introduced in evidence with respect to any issue.

(b) Any objection with respect to the conduct of the hearing, including any objection to the introduction of evidence, may be stated orally or in writing, accompanied by a short statement of the grounds of such objection, and included in the record. No such objection shall be deemed waived by further participation in the hearing.

(c) Any party may file applications for subpenas in writing with the regional director if made prior to hearing, or with the hearing officer if made at the hearing. Applications for subpenas may be made ex parte. The regional director or the hearing officer, as the case may be, shall forthwith grant the subpenas requested. Any person served with a subpena, whether ad testificandum or duces tecum, if he does not intend to comply with the subpena, shall, within 5 days after the date of service of the subpena, petition in writing to revoke the subpena. Such petition shall be filed with the regional director who may either rule upon it or refer it for ruling to the hearing officer: *Provided, however,* That if the evidence called for is to be produced at a hearing and the hearing has opened, the petition to revoke shall be filed with the hearing officer. Notice of the filing of petitions to revoke shall be promptly given by the regional director or hearing officer, as the case may be, to the party at whose request the subpena was issued. The regional director or the hearing officer, as the case may be, shall revoke the subpena if, in his opinion, the evidence whose production is required does not relate to any matter under investigation or in question in the proceedings or the subpena does not describe with sufficient particularity the evidence whose production is required, or if for any other reason sufficient in law the subpena is otherwise invalid. The regional director or the hearing officer, as the case may be, shall make a simple statement of procedural or other grounds for his ruling. The petition to revoke, any answer filed thereto, and any ruling thereon shall not become part of the record except upon the request of the party aggrieved by the ruling. Persons compelled to submit data or evidence are entitled to retain or, on payment of lawfully prescribed costs, to procure copies or transcripts of the data or evidence submitted by them.

(d)(1) Misconduct at any hearing before a hearing officer or before the regional director or the Board shall be ground for summary exclusion from the hearing.

(2) Such misconduct of an aggravated character, when engaged in by an attorney or other representative of a party, shall be ground for suspension or disbarment by the Board from further practice before it after due notice and hearing.

(3) The refusal of a witness at any such hearing to answer any question which has been ruled to be proper shall, in the discretion of the hearing officer, be ground for striking all testimony previously given by such witness on related matters.

(e) Any party shall be entitled, upon request, to a reasonable period at the close of the hearing for oral argument, which shall be included in the stenographic report of the hearing.

(f) The hearing officer may submit an analysis of the record to the regional director or the Board but he shall make no recommendations.

(g) Witness fees and mileage shall be paid by the party at whose instance the witness appears.

[26 FR 3888, May 4, 1961]

§102.67 Proceedings before the regional director; further hearing; briefs; action by the regional director; appeals from action by the regional director; statement in opposition to appeal; transfer of case to the Board; proceedings before the Board; Board action

(a) The regional director may proceed, either forthwith upon the record or after oral argument, the submission of briefs, or further hearing, as he may deem proper, to determine the unit appropriate for the purpose of collective bargaining, to determine whether a question concerning representation exists, and to direct an election, dismiss the petition, or make other disposition of the matter. Any party desiring to submit a brief to the regional director shall file the original and one copy thereof, which may be a typed carbon copy, within 7 days after the close of the hearing: *Provided, however,* That prior to the close of the hearing and for good cause the hearing officer may grant an extension of time not to exceed an additional 14 days.

Copies of the brief shall be served on all other parties to the proceeding and a statement of such service shall be filed with the regional director together with the brief. No reply brief may be filed except upon special leave of the regional director.

(b) A decision by the regional director upon the record shall set forth his findings, conclusions, and order or direction. The decision of the regional director shall be final: *Provided, however,* That within 14 days after service thereof any party may file a request for review with the Board in Washington, DC. The regional director shall schedule and conduct any election directed by the decision notwithstanding that a request for review has been filed with or granted by the Board. The filing of such a request shall not, unless otherwise ordered by the Board, operate as a stay of the election or any action taken or directed by the regional director: *Provided, however,* That if a pending request for review has not been ruled upon or has been granted ballots whose validity might be affected by the final Board decision shall be segregated in an appropriate manner, and all ballots shall be impounded and remain unopened pending such decision.

(c) The Board will grant a request for review only where compelling reasons exist therefor. Accordingly, a request for review may be granted only upon one or more of the following grounds:

(1) That a substantial question of law or policy is raised because of (i) the absence of, or (ii) a departure from, officially reported Board precedent.

(2) That the regional director's decision on a substantial factual issue is clearly erroneous on the record and such error prejudicially affects the rights of a party.

(3) That the conduct of the hearing or any ruling made in connection with the proceeding has resulted in prejudicial error.

(4) That there are compelling reasons for reconsideration of an important Board rule or policy.

(d) Any request for review must be a self-contained document enabling the Board to rule on the basis of its contents without the necessity or recourse to the record; however, the Board may, in its discretion, examine the record in evaluating the request. With respect to ground (2), and other grounds where appropriate, said request must contain a summary of all evidence or rulings bearing on the issues together with page citations from the transcript and a summary of argument. But such request may not raise any issue or allege any facts not timely presented to the regional director.

(e) Any party may, within 7 days after the last day on which the request for review must be filed, file with the Board a statement in opposition thereto, which shall be served in accordance with the requirements of paragraph (k) of this section. A statement of such service of opposition shall be filed simultaneously with the Board. The Board may deny the request for review without awaiting a statement in opposition thereto.

(f) The parties may, at any time, waive their right to request review. Failure to request review shall preclude such parties from relitigating, in any related subsequent unfair labor practice proceeding, any issue which was, or could have been, raised in the representation proceeding. Denial of a request for review shall constitute an affirmance of the regional director's action which shall also preclude relitigating any such issues in any related subsequent unfair labor practice proceeding.

(g) The granting of a request for review shall not stay the regional director's decision unless otherwise ordered by the Board. Except where the Board rules upon the issues on review in the order granting review, the appellants and other parties may, within 14 days after issuance of an order granting review, file briefs with the Board. Such briefs may be reproductions of those previously filed with the regional director and/or other briefs which shall be limited to the issues raised in the request for review. Where review has been granted, the Board will consider the entire record in the light of the grounds relied on for review. Any request for review may be withdrawn with the permission of the Board at any time prior to the issuance of the decision of the Board thereon.

(h) In any case in which it appears to the regional director that the proceeding raises questions which should be decided by the Board, he may, at any time, issue an order, to be effective after the close of the hearing and before decision, transferring the case to the Board for decision. Such an order may be served on the parties upon the record of the hearing.

(i) If any case is transferred to the Board for decision after the parties have filed briefs with the regional director, the parties may, within such time after service of the order transferring the case as is fixed by the regional director, file with the Board the brief previously filed with the regional director. No further briefs shall be permitted except by special permission of the Board. If the case is transferred to the Board before the time expires for the filing of briefs with the regional director and before the parties have filed briefs, such briefs shall be filed as set forth above and served in accordance with the requirements of paragraph (k) of this section within the time set by the regional director. If the order transferring the case is served on the parties during the hearing, the hearing officer may, prior to the close of the hearing and for good cause, grant an extension of time within which to file a brief with the Board for a period not to exceed an additional 14 days. No reply brief may be filed except upon special leave of the Board.

(j) Upon transfer of the case to the Board, the Board shall proceed, either forthwith upon the record, or after oral argument or the submission of briefs or further hearing, as it may determine, to decide the issues referred to it or to review the decision of the regional director and shall direct a secret ballot of the employees or the appropriate action to be taken on impounded ballots of an election already conducted, dismiss the petition, affirm or reverse the regional director's order in whole or in part, or make such other disposition of the matter as it deems appropriate.

(k)(1) All documents filed with the Board under the provisions of this section shall be filed in eight copies, double spaced, on $8\frac{1}{2}$- by 11-inch paper, and shall be printed or otherwise legibly duplicated. Carbon copies of typewritten materials will not be accepted. Requests for review, including briefs in support thereof; statements in opposition thereto; and briefs on review shall not exceed 50 pages in length, exclusive of subject index and table of cases and other authorities cited, unless permission to exceed that limit is obtained from the Board by motion, setting forth the reasons therefor, filed not less than 5 days, including Saturdays, Sundays, and holidays, prior to the date the document is due. Where any brief filed pursuant to this section exceeds 20 pages, it shall contain a subject index with page authorities cited.

(2) The party filing with the Board a request for review, a statement in opposition to a request for review, or a brief on review shall serve a copy thereof on the other parties and shall file a copy with the regional director. A statement of such service shall be filed with the Board together with the document.

(3) Requests for extensions of time to file requests for review, statements in opposition to a request for review, or briefs, as permitted by this section, shall be filed with the Board or the Regional Director, as the case may be. The party filing the request for an extension of time shall serve a copy thereof on the other parties and, if filed with the Board, on the Regional Director. A statement of such service shall be filed with the document.

[26 FR 3889, May 4, 1961, as amended at 42 FR 41117, Aug. 15, 1977; 47 FR 40771, Sept. 15, 1982; 51 FR 23747, July 1, 1986, 56 FR 49143, Sept. 27, 1991]

§102.68 Record; what constitutes; transmission to Board

The record in a proceeding conducted pursuant to the foregoing section shall consist of: the petition, notice of hearing with affidavit of service thereof, motions, rulings, orders, the stenographic report of the hearing and of any oral argument before the regional director, stipulations, exhibits, affidavits of service, and any briefs or other legal memoranda submitted by the parties to the regional director or to the Board, and the decision of the regional director, if any. Immediately upon issuance by the regional director of an order transferring the case to the Board, or upon issuance of an order granting a request for review by the Board, the regional director shall transmit the record to the Board.

[46 FR 45922, Sept. 15, 1981]

§102.69 Election procedure; tally of ballots; objections; certification by the regional director; report on challenged ballots; report on objections; exceptions; action of the Board; hearing

(a) Unless otherwise directed by the Board, all elections shall be conducted under the supervision of the regional director in whose region the proceeding is pending. All elections shall be by secret ballot. Whenever two or more labor organizations are included as choices in an election, either participant may, upon its prompt request to and approval thereof by the regional director, whose decision shall be final, have its name removed from the ballot: *Provided, however,* That in a proceeding involving an employer-filed petition or a petition for decertification the labor organization certified, currently recognized, or found to be seeking recognition may not have its name removed from the ballot without giving timely notice in writing to all parties and the regional director, disclaiming any representation interest among the employees in the unit. Any party may be represented by observers of his own selection, subject to such limitations as the regional director may prescribe. Any party and Board agents may challenge, for good cause, the eligibility of any person to participate in the election. The ballots of such challenged persons shall be impounded. Upon the conclusion of the election the ballots will be counted and a tally of ballots prepared and immediately made available to the parties. Within 7 days after the tally of ballots has been prepared, any party may file with the regional director an original and five copies of objections to the conduct of the election or to conduct affecting the results of the election, which shall contain a short statement of the reasons therefor. Such filing must be timely whether or not the challenged ballots are sufficient in number to affect the results of the election. The regional director will cause a copy of the objections to be served on each of the other parties to the proceeding. Within 7 days after the filing of objections, or such additional time as the regional director may allow, the party filing objections shall furnish to the regional director the evidence available to it to support the objections.

(b) If no objections are filed within the time set forth above, if the challenged ballots are insufficient in number to affect the results of the election, and if no runoff election is to be held pursuant to §102.70, the regional director shall forthwith issue to the parties a certification of the results of the election, including certification of representative where appropriate, with the same force and effect as if issued by the Board, and the proceeding will thereupon be closed.

(c)(1) If timely objections are filed to the conduct of the election or to conduct affecting the results of the election, or if the challenged ballots are sufficient in number to affect the results of the election, the regional director shall, consistent with the provisions of §102.69(d), initiate an investigation, as required, of such objections or challenges.

(2) If a consent election has been held pursuant to §102.62(b), the regional director shall prepare and cause to be served on the parties a report on challenged ballots or on objections, or on both, including his recommendations, which report, together with the tally of ballots, he shall forward to the Board in Washington, DC. Within 14 days from the date of issuance of the report on challenged ballots or on objections, or on both, any party may file with the Board in Washington, DC, exceptions to such report, with supporting documents as permitted by §102.69(g)(3) and/or a supporting brief if desired. Within 7 days from the last date on which exceptions and any supporting documents and/or supporting brief may be filed, or such further period as the Board may allow, a party opposing the exceptions may file an answering brief, with supporting documents as permitted by §102.69(g)(3) if desired, with the Board in Washington, DC. If no exceptions are filed to such report, the Board, upon the expiration of the period for filing such exceptions, may decide the matter forthwith upon the record or may make other disposition of the case. The report on challenged ballots may be consolidated with the report on objections in appropriate cases.

(3) If the election has been conducted pursuant to a direction of election issued following any proceeding under §102.67, the regional director may (i) issue a report on objections or on challenged ballots, or on both, as in the case of a consent election pursuant to paragraph (b) of §102.62, or (ii) exercise his authority to decide the case and issue a decision disposing of the issues, and directing appropriate action or certifying the results of the election.

(4) If the regional director issues a report on objections and challenges, the parties shall have the rights set forth in paragraph (c)(2) of this section and in §102.69(f); if the regional director issues a decision, the parties shall have the rights set forth in §102.67 to the extent consistent herewith, including the right to submit documents supporting the request for review or opposition thereto as permitted by §102.69(g)(3).

(d) In issuing a report on objections or challenged ballots, or both, following proceedings under §§102.62(b) or 102.67, or in issuing a decision on objections or challenged ballots, or both, following proceedings under §102.67, the regional director may act on the basis of an administrative investigation or upon the record of a hearing before a hearing officer. Such hearing shall be conducted with respect to those objections or challenges which the regional director concludes raise substantial and material factual issues.

(e) Any hearing pursuant to this section shall be conducted in accordance with the provisions of §§102.64, 102.65, and 102.66, insofar as applicable, except that, upon the close of such hearing, the hearing officer shall, if directed by the regional director, prepare and cause to be served on the parties a report resolving questions of credibility and containing findings of fact and recommendations as to the disposition of the issues. In any case in which the regional director has directed that a report be prepared and served, any party may, within 14 days from the date of issuance of such report, file with the regional director the original and one copy, which may be a carbon copy, of exceptions to such report, with supporting brief if desired. A copy of such exceptions, together with a copy of any brief filed, shall immediately be served on the other parties and a statement of service filed with the regional director. Within 7 days from the last date on which exceptions and any supporting brief may be filed, or such further time as the regional director may allow, a party opposing the exceptions may file an answering brief with the regional director. An original and one copy, which may be a carbon copy, shall be submitted. A copy of such answering brief shall immediately be served on the other parties and a statement of service filed with the regional director. If no exceptions are filed to such report, the regional director, upon the expiration of the period for filing such exceptions, may decide the matter forthwith upon the record or may make other disposition of the case.

(f) In a case involving a consent election held pursuant to §102.62(b), if exceptions are filed, either to the report on challenged ballots or on objections, or on both if it be a consolidated report, and it appears to the Board that such exceptions do not raise substantial and material issues with respect to the conduct or results of the election, the Board may decide the matter forthwith upon the record or may make other disposition of the case. If it appears to the Board that such exceptions raise substantial and material factual issues, the Board may direct the regional director or other agent of the Board to issue and cause to be served on the parties a notice of hearing on said exceptions before a hearing officer. The hearing shall be conducted in accordance with the provisions of §§102.64, 102.65, and 102.66 insofar as applicable. Upon the close of the hearing the agent conducting the hearing, if directed by the Board, shall prepare and cause to be served on the parties a report resolving questions of credibility and containing findings of fact and recommendations to the Board as to the disposition of the challenges or objections, or both if it be a consolidated report. In any case in which the Board has directed that a report be prepared and served, any party may within 14 days from the date of issuance of the report on challenged ballots or on objections, or on both, file with the Board in Washington, DC, exceptions to such report, with supporting brief if desired. Within 7 days from the last date on which exceptions and any supporting brief may be filed, or such further period as the Board may allow, a party opposing the exceptions may file an answering brief with the Board in Washington, DC. If no exceptions are filed to such report, the Board, upon the expiration of the period for filing such exceptions, may decide the matter forthwith upon the record or may make other disposition of the case. The Board shall thereupon proceed pursuant to §102.67: *Provided, however,*

That in any with [sic] an unfair labor practice case for purposes of hearing the provisions of §102.46 of these rules shall govern with respect to the filing of exceptions or an answering brief to the exceptions to the administrative law judge's decision.

(g)(1)(i) In a proceeding pursuant to this section in which a hearing is held, the record in the case shall consist of the notice of hearing, motions, rulings, orders, stenographic report of the hearing, stipulations, exhibits, together with the objections to the conduct of the election or to conduct affecting the results of the election, any report on such objections, any report on challenged ballots, exceptions to any such report, any briefs or other legal memoranda submitted by the parties, the decision of the regional director, if any, and the record previously made as defined in §102.68. Materials other than those set out above shall not be a part of the record.

(ii) In a proceeding pursuant to this section in which no hearing is held, the record shall consist of the objections to the conduct of the election or to conduct affecting the results of the election, any report on objections or on challenged ballots and any exceptions to such a report, any regional director's decision on objections or challenged ballots and any request for review of such a decision, any documentary evidence, excluding statements of witnesses, relied upon by the regional director in his decision or report, any briefs or other legal memoranda submitted by the parties, and any other motions, rulings or orders of the regional director. Materials other than those set out above shall not be a part of the record, except as provided in paragraph (g)(3) of this section.

(2) Immediately upon issuance of report on objections or challenges, or both, upon issuance by the regional director of an order transferring the case to the Board, or upon issuance of an order granting a request for a review by the Board, the regional director shall transmit to the Board the record of the proceeding as defined in paragraph (g)(1) of this section.

(3) In a proceeding pursuant to this section in which no hearing is held, a party filing exceptions to a regional director's report on objections or challenges, a request for review of a regional director's decision on objections or challenges, or any opposition thereto, may support its submission to the Board by appending thereto copies of documentary evidence, including copies of any affidavits, it has timely submitted to the regional director and which were not included in the report or decision. Documentary evidence so appended shall there upon become part of the record in the proceeding. Failure to timely submit such documentary evidence to the regional director, or to append that evidence to its submission to the Board in the representation proceeding as provided above,

shall preclude a party from replying on such evidence in any subsequent related unfair labor proceeding.

(h) In any such case in which the regional director or the Board, upon a ruling on challenged ballots, has directed that such ballots be opened and counted and a revised tally of ballots issued, and no objection to such revised tally is filed by any party within 7 days after the revised tally of ballots has been made available, the regional director shall forthwith issue to the parties certification of the results of the election, including certifications of representative where appropriate, with the same force and effect as if issued by the Board. The proceeding shall thereupon be closed.

(i)(1) The action of the regional director in issuing a notice of hearing on objections or challenged ballots, or both, following proceedings under §102.62(b) shall constitute a transfer of the case to the Board, and the provisions of §102.65(c) shall apply with respect to special permission to appeal to the Board from any such direction of hearing.

(2) Exceptions, if any, to the hearing officer's report or to the administrative law judge's decision, and any answering brief to such exceptions shall be filed with the Board in Washington, DC, in accordance with paragraph (f) of this section.

(j)(1) All documents filed with the Board under the provisions of this section shall be filed in eight copies, double spaced, on $8\frac{1}{2}$- by 11-inch paper, and shall be printed or otherwise legibly duplicated. Carbon copies of typewritten materials will not be accepted. Briefs in support of exceptions or answering briefs shall not exceed 50 pages in length, exclusive of subject index and table of cases and other authorities cited, unless permission to exceed that limit is obtained from the Board by motion, setting forth the reasons therefor, filed not less than 5 days, including Saturdays, Sundays, and holidays, prior to the date the brief is due. Where any brief filed pursuant to this section exceeds 20 pages, it shall contain a subject index with page references and an alphabetical table of cases and other authorities cited.

(2) The party filing with the Board exceptions to a report, a supporting brief, or an answering brief shall serve a copy thereof on the other parties and shall file a copy with the regional director. A statement of such service shall be filed with the Board together with the document.

(3) Requests for extensions of time to file exceptions to a report, supporting briefs, or answering briefs, as permitted by this section, shall be filed with the Board on the Regional Director, as the case may be. The party filing the request for an extension of time shall serve a copy thereof on the other parties and, if filed with the Board, or the Regional Director. A statement of such service shall be filed with the document.

[38 FR 3961, Feb. 8, 1973, as amended at 46 FR 45923, Sept. 15, 1981; 47 FR 40772, Sept. 15, 1982; 47 FR 42569, Sept. 28, 1982; 51 FR 23747, July 1, 1986; 51 FR 32919, Sept. 17, 1986; 56 FR 49144, Sept. 27, 1991]

§102.70 Runoff election

(a) The regional director shall conduct a runoff election, without further order of the Board, when an election in which the ballot provided for not less than three choices (i.e., at least two representatives and "neither") results in no choice receiving a majority of the valid ballots cast and no objections are filed as provided in §102.69. Only one runoff shall be held pursuant to this section.

(b) Employees who were eligible to vote in the election and who are in an eligible category on the date of the runoff election shall be eligible to vote in the runoff election.

(c) The ballot in the runoff election shall provide for a selection between the two choices receiving the largest and second largest number of votes.

(d) In the event the number of votes cast in an inconclusive election in which the ballot provided for a choice among two or more representatives and "neither" or "none" is equally divided among the several choices; or in the event the number of ballots cast for one choice in such election is equal to the number cast for another of the choices but less than the number cast for the third choice, the regional director shall declare the first election a nullity and shall conduct another election, providing for a selection from among the three choices afforded in the original ballot; and he shall thereafter proceed in accordance with paragraphs (a), (b), and (c) of this section. In the event two or more choices receive the same number of ballots and another choice receives no ballots and there are no challenged ballots that would affect the results of the election, and if all eligible voters have cast valid ballots, there shall be no runoff election and a certification of results of election shall be issued. Only one such further election pursuant to this paragraph may be held.

(e) Upon the conclusion of the runoff election, the provisions of §102.69 shall govern, insofar as applicable.

[26 FR 3891, May 4, 1961]

§102.71 Dismissal of petition; refusal to proceed with petition; requests for review by the Board of action of the regional director

(a) If, after a petition has been filed and at any time prior to the close of hearing, it shall appear to the regional director that no further proceedings are warranted, the regional director may dismiss the petition by administrative action and shall so advise the petitioner in writing, setting forth a simple statement of the procedural or other grounds for the dismissal, with copies to the other parties to the proceeding. Any party may obtain a review of such action by filing a request therefor with the Board in Washington,

DC, in accordance with the provisions of paragraph (c) of this section. A request for review from an action of a regional director pursuant to this subsection may be granted only upon one or more of the following grounds:

(1) That a substantial question of labor policy is raised because of (i) the absence of, or (ii) a departure from, officially reported Board precedent.

(2) There are compelling reasons for reconsideration of an important Board rule or policy.

(3) The request for review is accompanied by documentary evidence previously submitted to the regional director raising serious doubts as to the regional director's factual findings, thus indicating that there are factual issues which can best be resolved upon the basis of a record developed at a hearing.

(4) The regional director's action is, on its face, arbitrary or capricious.

(5) The petition raises issues which can best be resolved upon the basis of a record developed at a hearing.

(b) Where the regional director dismisses a petition or directs that the proceeding on the petition be held in abeyance, and such action is taken because of the pendency of concurrent unresolved charges of unfair labor practices, and the regional director, upon request, has so notified the parties in writing, any party may obtain a review of the regional director's action by filing a request therefor with the Board in Washington, DC, in accordance with the provisions of paragraph (c) of this section. A review of an action of a regional director pursuant to this subsection may be granted only upon one or more of the following grounds:

(1) That a substantial question of law or policy is raised because of (i) the absence of, or (ii) a departure from, officially reported Board precedent.

(2) There are compelling reasons for reconsideration of an important Board rule or policy.

(3) The regional director's action is, on its face, arbitrary or capricious.

(c) A request for review must be filed with the Board in Washington, DC, and a copy filed with the regional director and copies served on all the other parties within 14 days of service of the notice of dismissal or notification that the petition is to be held in abeyance. The request shall be submitted in eight copies and shall contain a complete statement setting forth facts and reasons upon which the request is based. Such request shall be printed or otherwise legibly duplicated: *Provided, however,* That carbon copies of typewritten materials will not be accepted. Requests for an extension of time within which to file the request for review shall be filed with the Board in Washington, DC, and a statement of service shall accompany such request.

[39 FR 4080, Feb. 1, 1974, as amended at 40 FR 6204, Feb. 10, 1975; 51 FR 23748, July 1, 1986]

§102.72 **Filing petition with general counsel; investigation upon motion of general counsel; transfer of petition and proceeding from region to general counsel or to another region; consolidation of proceedings in same region; severance; procedure before general counsel in cases over which he has assumed jurisdiction**

(a) Whenever it appears necessary in order to effectuate the purposes of the Act, or to avoid unnecessary costs of delay, the general counsel may permit a petition to be filed with him in Washington, DC, or may, at any time after a petition has been filed with a regional director pursuant to §102.60, order that such petition and any proceeding that may have been instituted with respect thereto:

(1) Be transferred to and continued before him, for the purpose of investigation or consolidation with any other proceeding which may have been instituted in a regional office or with him; or

(2) Be consolidated with any other proceeding which may have been instituted in the same region; or

(3) Be transferred to and continued in any other region, for the purpose of investigation or consolidation with any proceeding which may have been instituted in or transferred to such region; or

(4) Be severed from any other proceeding with which it may have been consolidated pursuant to this section.

(b) The provisions of §§102.60 to 102.71, inclusive, shall, insofar as applicable, apply to proceedings before the general counsel pursuant to this section, and the powers granted to regional directors in such provisions shall, for the purpose of this section, be reserved to and exercised by the general counsel. After the transfer of any petition and any proceeding which may have been instituted in respect thereto from one region to another pursuant to this section, the provisions of this subpart shall, insofar as applicable, govern such petition and such proceedings as if the petition has originally been filed in the region to which the transfer was made.

(c) The regional director may exercise the powers in paragraph (a)(2) and (4) of this section with respect to proceedings pending in his region.

[32 FR 9550, July 1, 1967]

Subpart D. Procedure for Unfair Labor Practice and Representation Cases Under Sections 8(b)(7) and 9(c) of the Act

§102.73 Initiation of proceedings

Whenever it is charged that any person has engaged in an unfair labor practice within the meaning of section 8(b)(7) of the Act, the regional

Regulations of the National Labor Relations Board

director shall investigate such charges, giving it the priority specified in subpart G of this part.

§102.74 Complaint and formal proceedings

If it appears to the regional director that the charge has merit, formal proceedings in respect thereto shall be instituted in accordance with the procedures described in §§102.15 to 102.51, inclusive, insofar as they are applicable, and insofar as they are not inconsistent with the provisions of this subpart. If it appears to the regional director that issuance of a complaint is not warranted, he shall decline to issue a complaint, and the provisions of §102.19, including the provisions for appeal to the general counsel, shall be applicable unless an election has been directed under §§102.77 and 102.78, in which event the provisions of §102.81 shall be applicable.

§102.75 Suspension of proceedings on the charge where timely petition is filed

If it appears to the regional director that issuance of a complaint may be warranted but for the pendency of a petition under section 9(c) of the Act, which has been filed by any proper party within a reasonable time not to exceed 30 days from the commencement of picketing, the regional director shall suspend proceedings on the charge and shall proceed to investigate the petition under the expedited procedure provided below, pursuant to the first proviso to subparagraph (C) of section 8(b)(7) of the Act.

§102.76 Petition; who may file; where to file; contents

When picketing of an employer has been conducted for an object proscribed by section 8(b)(7) of the Act, a petition for the determination of a question concerning representation of the employees of such employer may be filed in accordance with the provisions of §§102.60 and 102.61, insofar as applicable: *Provided, however,* That if a charge under §102.73 has been filed against the labor organization on whose behalf picketing has been conducted, the petition shall not be required to contain a statement that the employer declines to recognize the petitioner as the representative within the meaning of section 9(a) of the Act; or that the labor organization is currently recognized but desires certification under the act; or that the individuals or labor organizations who have been certified or are currently recognized by the employer are no longer the representative; or, if the petitioner is an employer, that one or more individuals or labor organizations have presented to the petitioner a claim to be recognized as the exclusive representative of the employees in the unit claimed to be appropriate.

§102.77 Investigation of petition by regional director; directed election

(a) Where a petition has been filed pursuant to §102.76 the regional director shall make an investigation of the matters and allegations set forth therein. Any party, and any individual or labor organization purporting to act as representative of the employees involved and any labor organization on whose behalf picketing has been conducted as described in section 8(b)(7)(C) of the Act may present documentary and other evidence relating to the matters and allegations set forth in the petition.

(b) If after the investigation of such petition or any petition filed under subpart C of these rules, and after the investigation of the charge filed pursuant to §102.73, it appears to the regional director that an expedited election under section 8(b)(7)(C) is warranted, and that the policies of the act would be effectuated thereby, he shall forthwith proceed to conduct an election by secret ballot of the employees in an appropriate unit, or make other disposition of the matter: *Provided, however,* That in any case in which it appears to the regional director that the proceeding raises questions which cannot be decided without a hearing, he may issue and cause to be served on the parties, individuals, and labor organizations involved a notice of hearing before a hearing officer at a time and place fixed therein. In this event, the method of conducting the hearing and the procedure following, including transfer of the case to the Board, shall be governed insofar as applicable by §§102.63 to 102.68, inclusive, except that the parties shall not file briefs without special permission of the regional director or the Board, as the case may be, but shall, however, state their respective legal positions upon the record at the close of the hearing, and except that any request for review of a decision of the regional director shall be filed promptly after the issuance of such decision.

[24 FR 9102, Nov. 7, 1959, as amended at 26 FR 3892, May 4, 1961]

§102.78 Election procedure; method of conducting balloting; postballoting procedure

If no agreement such as that provided in §102.79 has been made, the regional director shall fix the time and place of the election, eligibility requirements for voting, and other arrangements for the balloting. The method of conducting the balloting and the postballoting procedure shall be governed, insofar as applicable, by the provisions of §§102.69 and 102.70 except that the labor organization on whose behalf picketing has been conducted may not have its name removed from the ballot without the consent of the regional director and except that the regional director's rulings on any objections or challenged ballots shall be final unless the Board grants special permission to appeal from the regional director's rulings. Any request for such permission shall be filed promptly, in writing, and shall briefly state the grounds relied upon. The party requesting review shall immediately serve a copy thereof on each other party. A request for review shall not operate as a stay of the regional director's rulings unless so ordered by the Board.

§102.79 Consent-election agreements

Where a petition has been duly filed, the parties involved may, subject to the approval of the regional director, enter into an agreement governing the method of conducting the election as provided for in §102.62(a), insofar as applicable.

§102.80 Dismissal of petition; refusal to process petition under expedited procedure

(a) If, after a petition has been filed pursuant to the provisions of §102.76, and prior to the close of the hearing, it shall appear to the regional director that further proceedings in respect thereto in accordance with the provisions of §102.77 are not warranted, he may dismiss the petition by administrative action, and the action of the regional director shall be final, subject to a prompt appeal to the Board on special permission which may be granted by the Board. Upon such appeal the provisions of §102.71 shall govern insofar as applicable. Such appeal shall not operate as a stay unless specifically ordered by the Board.

(b) If it shall appear to the regional director that an expedited election is not warranted but that proceedings under subpart C of this part are warranted, he shall so notify the parties in writing with a simple statement of the grounds for his decision.

(c) Where the regional director, pursuant to §§102.77 and 102.78, has determined that a hearing prior to election is not required to resolve the issues raised by the petition and has directed an expedited election, any party aggrieved may file a request with the Board for special permission to appeal from such determination. Such request shall be filed promptly, in writing, and shall briefly state the grounds relied upon. The party requesting such appeal shall immediately serve a copy thereof on each other party. Should the Board grant the requested permission to appeal, such action shall not, unless specifically ordered by the Board, operate as a stay of any action by the regional director.

[24 FR 9102, Nov. 7, 1959, as amended at 26 FR 3892, May 4, 1961]

§102.81 Review by the general counsel of refusal to proceed on charge; resumption of proceedings upon charge held during pendency of petition; review by the general counsel of refusal to proceed on related charge

(a) Where an election has been directed by the regional director or the Board in accordance with the provisions of §§102.77 and 102.78, the regional director shall decline to issue a complaint on the charge, and he shall so advise the parties in writing, accompanied by a simple statement of the procedural or other grounds for his action. The person making the charge may obtain a review of such action by filing an appeal with the general counsel in Washington, DC, and filing a copy of the appeal with the regional director, within 7 days from the service of the notice of such refusal by the regional director. In all other respects the appeal shall be subject to the provisions of §102.19. Such appeal shall not operate as a stay of any action by the regional director.

(b) Where an election has not been directed and the petition has been dismissed in accordance with the provisions of §102.80, the regional director shall resume investigation of the charge and shall proceed in accordance with §102.74.

(c) If in connection with an 8(b)(7) proceeding, unfair labor practice charges under other sections of the act have been filed and the regional director upon investigation has declined to issue a complaint upon such charges, he shall so advise the parties in writing, accompanied by a simple statement of the procedural or other grounds for his action. The person making such charges may obtain a review of such action by filing an appeal with the general counsel in Washington, DC, and filing a copy of the appeal with the regional director, within 7 days from the service of the notice of such refusal by the regional director. In all other respects the appeal shall be subject to the provisions of §102.19.

[32 FR 9550, July 1, 1967, as amended at 51 FR 23749, July 1, 1986]

§102.82 Transfer, consolidation, and severance

The provisions of §§102.33 and 102.72, respecting the filing of a charge or petition with the general counsel and the transfer, consolidation, and severance of proceedings, shall apply to proceedings under this subpart, except that the provisions of §§102.73 to 102.81, inclusive, shall govern proceedings before the general counsel.

Subpart E. Procedure for Referendum Under Section 9(e) of the Act

§102.83 Petition for referendum under section 9(e)(1) of the Act; who may file; where to file; withdrawal

A petition to rescind the authority of a labor organization to make an agreement requiring as a condition of employment membership in such labor organization may be filed by an employee or group of employees on behalf of 30 percent or more of the employees in a bargaining unit covered by such an agreement. The petition shall be in writing and signed, and either shall be sworn to before a notary public, Board agent, or other person duly authorized by law to administer oaths and take acknowledgments or shall contain a declaration by the person signing it, under the penalties of the Criminal Code, that its contents are true and correct to the best of his knowledge and belief.[5] Four copies of the petition shall be filed with the regional director wherein the bargaining unit exists or, if the unit exists in two or more regions, with the regional director for any of such regions. The petition may be withdrawn only with the approval of the regional director with whom such petition was filed, except that if the proceeding has been transferred to the Board, pursuant to §102.67, the petition may be withdrawn only with the consent of the Board. Upon approval of the withdrawal of any petition the case shall be closed.

§102.84 Contents of petition to rescind authority

(a) The name of the employer.
(b) The address of the establishments involved.
(c) The general nature of the employer's business.
(d) A description of the bargaining unit involved.
(e) The name and address of the labor organization whose authority it is desired to rescind.
(f) The number of employees in the unit.
(g) Whether there is a strike or picketing in progress at the establishment involved and, if so, the approximate number of employees participating, and the date such strike or picketing commenced.
(h) The date of execution and of expiration of any contract in effect covering the unit involved.
(i) The name and address of the person designated to accept service of documents for petitioners.
(j) Any other relevant facts.

---

[5]. Forms for filing such petitions will be supplied by the regional office upon request.

§102.85 Investigation of petition by regional director; consent referendum; directed referendum

Where a petition has been filed pursuant to §102.83 and it appears to the regional director that the petitioner has made an appropriate showing, in such form as the regional director may determine, that 30 percent or more of the employees within a unit covered by an agreement between their employer and a labor organization requiring membership in such labor organization desire to rescind the authority of such labor organization to make such an agreement, he shall proceed to conduct a secret ballot of the employees involved on the question whether they desire to rescind the authority of the labor organization to make such an agreement with their employer: *Provided, however,* That in any case in which it appears to the regional director that the proceeding raises questions which cannot be decided without a hearing, he may issue and cause to be served on the parties a notice of hearing before a hearing officer at a time and place fixed therein. The regional director shall fix the time and place of the election, eligibility requirements for voting, and other arrangements of the balloting, but the parties may enter into an agreement, subject to the approval of the regional director, fixing such arrangements. In any such consent agreements, provision may be made for final determination of all questions arising with respect to the balloting by the regional director or by the Board.

[26 FR 3892, May 4, 1961]

§102.86 Hearing; posthearing procedure

The method of conducting the hearing and the procedure following the hearing, including transfer of the case to the Board, shall be governed, insofar as applicable, by §§102.63 to 102.68, inclusive.

§102.87 Method of conducting balloting; postballoting procedure

The method of conducting the balloting and the postballoting procedure shall be governed by the provisions of §102.69, insofar as applicable.

§102.88 Refusal to conduct referendum; appeal to Board

If, after a petition has been filed, and prior to the close of the hearing, it shall appear to the regional director that no referendum should be conducted, he shall dismiss the petition by administrative action. Such dismissal shall be in writing and accompanied by a simple statement of the procedural or other grounds. The petitioner may obtain a review of such action

Regulations of the National Labor Relations Board 297

by filing a request therefor with the Board in Washington, DC, and filing a copy of such request with the regional director and the other parties within 14 days from the service of notice of such dismissal. The request shall contain a complete statement setting forth the facts and reasons upon which the request is based.

[51 FR 30636, Aug. 28, 1986]

SUBPART G. PROCEDURE IN CASES UNDER SECTION 10(j), (l), AND (m) OF THE ACT

§102.94 Expeditious processing of section 10(j) cases

(a) Whenever temporary relief or a restraining order pursuant to section 10(j) of the Act has been procured by the Board, the complaint which has been the basis for such temporary relief or restraining order shall be heard expeditiously and the case shall be given priority by the Board in its successive steps following the issuance of the complaint (until ultimate enforcement or dismissal by the appropriate circuit court of appeals) over all other cases except cases of like character and cases under section 10(l) and (m) of the Act.

(b) In the event the trial examiner hearing a complaint, concerning which the Board has procured temporary relief or a restraining order pursuant to section 10(j), recommends a dismissal in whole or in part of such complaint, the chief law officer shall forthwith suggest to the district court which issued such temporary relief or restraining order the possible change in circumstances arising out of the findings and recommendations of the trial examiner.

§102.95 Priority of cases pursuant to section 10(l) and (m) of the Act

(a) Whenever a charge is filed alleging the commission of an unfair labor practice within the meaning of paragraph (4)(A), (B), (C), or (7) of section 8(b) of the Act or section 8(e) of the Act, the regional office in which such charge is filed or to which it is referred shall give it priority over all other cases in the office except cases of like character and cases under paragraph (4)(D) of section 8(b) of the Act in which it is deemed appropriate to seek injunctive relief of a district court pursuant to section 10(l) of the Act.

(b) Whenever a charge is filed alleging the commission of an unfair labor practice within the meaning of subsection (a)(3) or (b)(2) of section 8 of the Act, the regional office in which such charge is filed or to which it

§102.96 Issuance of complaint promptly

Whenever the regional attorney or other Board officer to whom the matter may be referred seeks injunctive relief of a district court pursuant to action 10(l) of the Act, a complaint against the party or parties sought to be enjoined, covering the same subject matter as such application for injunctive relief, shall be issued promptly normally within 5 days of the date upon which such injunctive relief is first sought, except in those cases under section 10(l) of the Act in which the procedure set forth in §§102.90 to 102.92, inclusive, is deemed applicable.

§102.97 Expeditious processing of section 10(l) and (m) cases in successive stages

(a) Any complaint issued pursuant to §102.95(a) or, in a case in which it is deemed appropriate to seek injunctive relief of a district court pursuant to section 10(l) of the Act, any complaint issued pursuant to §102.93 or notice of hearing issued pursuant to §102.90 shall be heard expeditiously and the case shall be given priority in such successive steps following its issuance (until ultimate enforcement or dismissal by the appropriate circuit court of appeals) over all cases except cases of like character.

(b) Any complaint issued pursuant to §102.95(b) shall be heard expeditiously and the case shall be given priority in its successive steps following its issuance (until ultimate enforcement or dismissal by the appropriate circuit court of appeals) over all cases except cases of like character and cases under section 10(l) of the Act.

Forms of the National Labor Relations Board

Form NLRB-501   Charge Against Employer
Form NLRB-502   Petition
Form NLRB-508   Charge Against Labor Organization or Its Agents

Forms of the National Labor Relations Board

FORM NLRB-501
(11-88)

FORM EXEMPT UNDER 44 U.S.C. 3512

UNITED STATES OF AMERICA
NATIONAL LABOR RELATIONS BOARD
CHARGE AGAINST EMPLOYER

DO NOT WRITE IN THIS SPACE

Case	Date Filed

INSTRUCTIONS:
File an original and 4 copies of this charge with NLRB Regional Director for the region in which the alleged unfair labor practice occurred or is occurring.

1. EMPLOYER AGAINST WHOM CHARGE IS BROUGHT

a. Name of Employer		b. Number of workers employed
c. Address (street, city, state, ZIP code)	d. Employer Representative	e. Telephone No.
f. Type of Establishment (factory, mine, wholesaler, etc.)	g. Identify principal product or service	

h. The above-named employer has engaged in and is engaging in unfair labor practices within the meaning of section 8(a), subsections (1) and (list subsections) _____ of the National Labor Relations Act, and these unfair labor practices are unfair practices affecting commerce within the meaning of the Act.

2. Basis of the Charge (set forth a clear and concise statement of the facts constituting the alleged unfair labor practices)

By the above and other acts, the above-named employer has interfered with, restrained, and coerced employees in the exercise of the rights guaranteed in Section 7 of the Act

3. Full name of party filing charge (if labor organization, give full name, including local name and number)

4a. Address (street and number, city, state, and ZIP code)	4b. Telephone No.

5. Full name of national or international labor organization of which it is an affiliate or constituent unit (to be filled in when charge is filed by a labor organization)

6. DECLARATION
I declare that I have read the above charge and that the statements are true to the best of my knowledge and belief.

By _____   _____
(signature of representative or person making charge)   (title if any)

Address _____
                                                     (Telephone No.)   (date)

WILLFUL FALSE STATEMENTS ON THIS CHARGE CAN BE PUNISHED BY FINE AND IMPRISONMENT (U. S. CODE, TITLE 18, SECTION 1001)

FORM NLRB-502
(5-85)

UNITED STATES GOVERNMENT
NATIONAL LABOR RELATIONS BOARD
PETITION

FORM EXEMPT UNDER 44 U.S.C. 3512

DO NOT WRITE IN THIS SPACE	
Case No.	Date Filed

INSTRUCTIONS: Submit an original and 4 copies of this Petition to the NLRB Regional Office in the Region in which the employer concerned is located. If more space is required for any one item, attach additional sheets, numbering item accordingly.

The Petitioner alleges that the following circumstances exist and requests that the National Labor Relations Board proceed under its proper authority pursuant to Section 9 of the National Labor Relations Act.

1. PURPOSE OF THIS PETITION (If box RC, RM, or RD is checked and a charge under Section 8(b)(7) of the Act has been filed involving the Employer named herein, the statement following the description of the type of petition shall not be deemed made.) **(Check One)**

   ☐ **RC-CERTIFICATION OF REPRESENTATIVE** - A substantial number of employees wish to be represented for purposes of collective bargaining by Petitioner and Petitioner desires to be certified as representative of the employees.

   ☐ **RM-REPRESENTATION (EMPLOYER PETITION)** - One or more individuals or labor organizations have presented a claim to Petitioner to be recognized as the representative of employees of Petitioner.

   ☐ **RD-DECERTIFICATION** - A substantial number of employees assert that the certified or currently recognized bargaining representative is no longer their representative.

   ☐ **UD-WITHDRAWAL OF UNION SHOP AUTHORITY** - Thirty percent (30%) or more of employees in a bargaining unit covered by an agreement between their employer and a labor organization desire that such authority be rescinded.

   ☐ **UC-UNIT CLARIFICATION** - A labor organization is currently recognized by Employer, but Petitioner seeks clarification of placement of certain employees: (Check one) ☐ In unit not previously certified. ☐ In unit previously certified in Case No. _____.

   ☐ **AC-AMENDMENT OF CERTIFICATION** - Petitioner seeks amendment of certification issued in Case No. _____ Attach statement describing the specific amendment sought.

2. Name of Employer	Employer Representative to contact	Telephone Number

3. Address(es) of Establishment(s) involved (Street and number, city, State, ZIP code)

4a. Type of Establishment (Factory, mine, wholesaler, etc.)	4b. Identify principal product or service

5. Unit Involved (In UC petition, describe **present** bargaining unit and attach description of proposed clarification.)	6a. Number of Employees in Unit:
Included	Present
	Proposed (By UC/AC)
Excluded	6b. Is this petition supported by 30% or more of the employees in the unit? * ___ Yes ___ No *Not applicable in RM, UC, and AC

(If you have checked box RC in 1 above, check and complete EITHER item 7a or 7b, whichever is applicable)

7a. ☐ Request for recognition as Bargaining Representative was made on (Date) _____ and Employer declined recognition on or about (Date) _____ (If no reply received, so state).

7b. ☐ Petitioner is currently recognized as Bargaining Representative and desires certification under the Act.

8. Name of Recognized or Certified Bargaining Agent (If none, so state)	Affiliation
Address and Telephone Number	Date of Recognition or Certification

9. Expiration Date of Current Contract, If any (Month, Day, Year)	10. If you have checked box UD in 1 above, show here the date of execution of agreement granting union shop (Month, Day, and Year)

11a. Is there now a strike or picketing at the Employer's establishment(s) Involved? Yes ___ No ___	11b. If so, approximately how many employees are participating?

11c. The Employer has been picketed by or on behalf of (Insert Name) _____, a labor organization, of (Insert Address) _____ Since (Month, Day, Year) _____.

12. Organizations or individuals other than Petitioner (and other than those named in items 8 and 11c), which have claimed recognition as representatives and other organizations and individuals known to have a representative interest in any employees in unit described in item 5 above. (If none, so state)

Name	Affilation	Address	Date of Claim (Required only if Petition is filed by Employer)

I declare that I have read the above petition and that the statements are true to the best of my knowledge and belief.

_____
(Name of Petitioner and Affilation, if any)

By _____   _____
   (Signature of Representative or person filing petition)   (Title, if any)

Address _____   _____
        (Street and number, city, State, and ZIP Code)   (Telephone Number)

Forms of the National Labor Relations Board

FORM NLRB-508
(6-90)

FORM EXEMPT UNDER 44 U.S.C. 3512

UNITED STATES OF AMERICA
NATIONAL LABOR RELATIONS BOARD

CHARGE AGAINST LABOR ORGANIZATION OR ITS AGENTS

DO NOT WRITE IN THIS SPACE	
Case	Date Filed

INSTRUCTIONS: File an original and 4 copies of this charge and an additional copy for each organization, each local, and each individual named in Item 1 with the NLRB Regional Director of the region in which the alleged unfair labor practice occurred or is occurring.

1. LABOR ORGANIZATION OR ITS AGENTS AGAINST WHICH CHARGE IS BROUGHT

a. Name

b. Union Representative to contact

c. Telephone No.

d. Address *(street, city, state and ZIP code)*

e. The above-named organization(s) or its agents has *(have)* engaged in and is *(are)* engaging in unfair labor practices within the meaning of section 8(b), subsection(s) *(list subsections)* _____ of the National Labor Relations Act, and these unfair labor practices are unfair practices affecting commerce within the meaning of the Act.

2. Basis of the Charge *(set forth a clear and concise statement of the facts constituting the alleged unfair labor practices)*

By these and other acts, the above-named labor organization has restrained and coerced employees in the exercise of the rights guaranteed in Section 7 of the Act.

3. Name of Employer	4. Telephone No.
5. Location of plant involved *(street, city, state and ZIP code)*	6. Employer representative to contact
7. Type of establishment *(factory, mine, wholesaler, etc.)*	8. Identify principal product or service	9. Number of workers employed

10. Full name of party filing charge

11. Address of party filing charge *(street, city, state and ZIP code)*

12. Telephone No.

13. DECLARATION
I declare that I have read the above charge and that the statements therein are true to the best of my knowledge and belief.

By _____   _____
   (signature of representative or person making charge)   *(title or office, if any)*

Address _____
   (Telephone No.)   *(date)*

WILLFUL FALSE STATEMENTS ON THIS CHARGE CAN BE PUNISHED BY FINE AND IMPRISONMENT (U. S. CODE, TITLE 18, SECTION 1001)

Selected Agreements

1994-1997 Collective Bargaining Agreement
Between General Electric Company and the
International Union of Electronic, Electrical, Salaried,
Machine and Furniture Workers (AFL-CIO)

Article I. Union Recognition

1. The Company agrees to recognize the Union on behalf of and in conjunction with its Locals for those bargaining units of Company employees for which the Union or any of its Locals, through National Labor Relations Board certifications, is designated as the exclusive collective bargaining representative of employees within such units for the purpose of collective bargaining in respect to rates of pay, wages, hours of employment and other conditions of employment.

2. Where the Union or any of its Locals through National Labor Relations Board certifications shall have been lawfully designated as the exclusive collective bargaining representative for any additional bargaining units of Company employees, such certified representative shall be recognized as provided above and become a party hereto, and the terms of this National Agreement shall thereupon be applicable to the employees within such unit.

Article II. Union Security

1. *Agency Shop*
(a) Subject to applicable law, all employees who, as of the date of this Agreement are members of the Union in good standing in accordance with

the constitution and bylaws of the Union or who become members of the Union following the effective date of this Agreement, shall, as a condition of employment, remain members of the Union in good standing insofar as the payment of an amount equal to the periodic dues and initiation fees, uniformly required, is concerned.

(b) Subject to applicable law, all present employees who are not members of the Union and all individuals hired after the effective date of this agreement, shall, beginning on the thirtieth (30th) day following the effective date of this agreement or the thirtieth (30th) day following employment, whichever is later, as a condition of employment, either become and remain members of the Union in good standing insofar as the payment of an amount equal to the periodic dues and initiation fees, uniformly required, is concerned, or, in lieu of such Union membership, pay to the Union an equivalent service charge.

2. *Union Dues or Service Charge Deduction Authorization*

(a) The Company, for each of its employees included within the bargaining units recognized by the Company pursuant to Article I hereof, who individually, in writing, duly authorizes his Company Paymaster to do so, will deduct from the earnings payable to such employee on the second pay day of each month, the monthly dues (including initiation fee, if any) for such employee's membership in the Local, or the equivalent service charge, and shall remit promptly to the Local all such deductions. Local unions and local management are authorized to negotiate variations from this checkoff procedure with respect to the frequency of dues deductions (including weekly dues deductions), or the equivalent service charge, and to modify checkoff authorization forms in accordance with any such local agreements.

(b) Subject to applicable law, individual authorizations executed after the effective date of this Agreement shall be signed cards in the form agreed to by the Company and the Union.

Article III. Working Conditions

1. The Company will continue to provide systematic safety inspections, safety devices, guards, and medical service to minimize accidents and health hazards on its premises.

Article IV. Discrimination and Coercion

1. Neither the Company nor any of its Foremen, Superintendents, or other agents or representatives, shall discriminate against any employee because such employee is a member, Steward, Officer, or other agent or representative of the Union or of any Local.

2. Neither the Union nor any Local, nor any Steward, Officer, or other

agent or representative of either, shall intimidate or coerce any employee, nor solicit members or funds in the plant during working hours.

3. (a) The Company, the Union and its IUE Locals shall not discriminate against any employee on account of race, color, sex, creed, marital status, age or national origin.

(b) The Company, the Union and its IUE Locals shall not discriminate against any employee because of physical or mental **disability*** or because he or she is a disabled veteran or veteran of the Vietnam era in regard to any position for which the employee is qualified.

Article V. Working Hours: Straight Time — Overtime

1. (a) *Workweek.* The regular working week for both salaried and hourly rated employees shall be 40 hours per week, 8 hours per day, 5-day week, from Monday to Friday inclusive. The workweek on multiple shifts may be less than 40 hours.

An employee's workday is the twenty-four hour period beginning with his regularly assigned starting time of his workshift, and his day of rest starts at the same time on the day or days he is not scheduled to work. His workweek starts with the start of his regularly assigned work period on Monday of that workweek, except on continuous operations. Upon commencing work on Monday at a newly assigned starting time which is earlier than his starting time during the preceding week, the workday immediately preceding such Monday shall end provided the employee has had a 24-hour period of rest prior to the newly assigned starting time.

Variations in hours of work and schedules of hours of the several shifts, including multiple shifts where the workweek starts late Sunday night and where such hours on Sunday are considered as part of the Monday workday, are subjects for local negotiations.

(b) *Continuous Operations.* Special schedules of hours and overtime will apply (1) on jobs which require continuous operation such as powerhouse attendants and on jobs requiring continuous manufacturing processes such as those which, for reasons of protection of equipment and material, must be run on a 24-hour day and a week-by-week basis, or (2) on process oriented jobs which cannot readily be operated on a non-continuous basis such as chemical, plastic, silicone and glass operations. Existing jobs or processes described in (2), but not currently on continuous operations as of July 1, 1973, may be designated as continuous operations by negotiation and agreement between local management and the Local Union. In the case of jobs described in (2), where new operations or processes are developed or established after July 1, 1973, the Local will be given thirty (30) calendar days notice prior to the designation of such jobs as continuous operations.

---

*Boldface appears as in the original.— Eds.

(c) When a change is made in the hours of work or working schedules of substantially all employees of a plant or a department thereof, local management will notify the employees and the Locals respectively affected at least one week in advance of the effective date of such change. When a change is made in the hours of work or working schedules of various individuals or smaller groups of employees, the Foreman will give the affected employees and their Union Steward as much notice as possible.

Any grievance resulting from the establishment of a new working schedule will be handled through the regular grievance procedure.

2. *Overtime—Regular Workweek*

The Company will pay an hourly rated or salaried employee on a nonexempt job for overtime as follows:

(a) At the rate of time and one-half for hours worked either

(1) In excess of 8 hours in any single workday; or

(2) In excess of 40 hours in any given workweek; or

(3) In excess of 8 hours in any continuous 24 hours beginning at the starting time of the employee's shift; or

(4) After working his regular schedule, if on multiple shifts of less than 8 hours each; or

(5) On his Saturday.

(b) At the rate of double time for hours worked either

(1) On his Sunday; or

(2) On his "observed" holiday; or

(3) In excess of 12 hours in his workday; provided that an employee who shall have worked in excess of 12 hours in any single workday, and who shall be required to continue at work beyond that workday, shall continue to be paid at the double time rate for hours worked until he shall have been relieved from work; or

(4) Outside the employee's regularly scheduled shift on a calendar Sunday or calendar observed holiday.

(c) At the rate of double time and one-half for hours worked either

(1) On his holidays listed in Article VII as paid holidays; or

(2) Outside the employee's regularly scheduled shift on any of the calendar holidays listed in Article VII as paid holidays; or

(3) For salaried employees only, for hours worked on an observed holiday or outside the employee's regularly scheduled shift on any calendar observed holiday.

(d) An employee who is transferred from his regular established shift to another and who is thereafter returned to his original shift during the same week, or during the immediately succeeding week, shall be paid at the rate of time and one-half for the first 8 hours worked following the first such transfer, except where either or both such transfers (i) results from the failure of another employee or employees to report for work; or (ii) is made in connection with a lack of work situation; or (iii) is made at the employee's request; or (iv) results from an emergency breakdown of equipment or machinery; or (v) is made in connection with an established program of shift rotation.

3. *Continuous Operations*
(a) *Workday - Workweek*
(1) When any employee on continuous operations has a scheduled workweek of 5 days at work and 2 days off, his first scheduled day off shall be considered as the 6th day of his workweek, and his second scheduled day off whether or not successive, as the 7th day of his workweek. When such working schedule contains a regularly recurring workweek of 6 days at work and one day off, such scheduled day off shall be considered as the 7th day of his workweek and the day immediately preceding as the 6th day of his workweek.

4. *Overtime — Continuous Operations*
The Company will pay an hourly rated or salaried employee on a nonexempt job for overtime as follows:
(a) At the rate of time and one-half for hours worked either
(1) In excess of 8 hours in any single workday; or
(2) In excess of 40 hours in any given workweek; or
(3) In excess of 8 hours in any continuous 24 hours beginning at the starting time of the employee's shift; or
(4) On his Saturdays or Sundays if either day is not his 7th day of his workweek; or
(5) On employee's 7th day of his workweek if such day is neither his Saturday, Sunday or observed holiday; or
(6) On his Saturdays and Sundays (as a minimum if employee is on a special schedule other than that outlined in 3(a)(1) above).
(b) At the rate of double time for hours worked either
(1) On the employee's 7th day of his workweek, if such day is his Saturday, Sunday or observed holiday; or
(2) On the employee's 6th day of the workweek if falling on an observed holiday; or
(3) In excess of 12 hours in his workday; provided that an employee who shall have worked in excess of 12 hours in any single workday, and who shall be required to continue at work beyond that workday, shall continue to be paid at the double time rate for hours worked until he shall have been relieved from work.
(c) At the rate of double time and one-half for hours worked on the holidays listed in Article VII as paid holidays.

5. *General*

(a) Listed holidays referred to above shall mean those holidays listed in Article VII of this Agreement.

(b) Each Local shall be furnished a list of the observed holidays referred to above.

(c) Computation of overtime shall be in accordance with the day as defined in 1(a) above and shall be allowed under only one of these overtime provisions for any given hours.

(d) All salaried employees if absent for personal reasons other than vacation shall be paid in accordance with the established plan.

(e) In cases where the Company instructs employees to report ahead of schedule and/or remain after the regular schedule to change clothes, etc., employees involved will be paid for such additional time.

6. *Night Shift Differential*

Hourly rated and salaried employees assigned to recognized second and third shift operations shall have 10% added to their regularly determined earnings for all work performed on such shifts except that employees hired after **August 5, 1991** who have no record of prior GE service shall have sixty cents ($.60) added to their regular hourly rate for all work performed on such shifts until they have accumulated **three (3)** years of continuous service after which they will receive the 10% night shift differential. Employees hired after **August 1, 1994**, who have no record of prior GE service, shall have sixty cents ($.60) added to their regular hourly rate for all work performed on such shifts until they have accumulated **five (5)** years of continuous service after which they will receive the 10% night shift differential. Recognized second and third shifts shall in all cases be those beginning between 12 noon and 3:30 a.m. In exceptional cases the starting time for a recognized second shift may be earlier by mutual agreement between the Local and local management.

7. *Other Special Payments*

(a) *Early Reporting and Call-In*

(1) Employees who are called in outside of their regular schedule of hours will be paid at the applicable premium rate, but not less than the equivalent of four hours pay at their straight-time rate. The straight-time rate for qualified pieceworkers will be not less than their AER* and for learners on piecework will be the lower of their average earnings or their AER.

(2) Day shift employees who are called back after the end of their regular day shift (or told to report prior to their regular starting time) will be paid at the rate of time and one-half for hours worked outside their regular schedule, up to midnight and at the rate of double time for hours worked after midnight and up to the beginning of the regular day shift.

(3) Employees on the second and third shifts who are called back

---

*Anticipated earned rate.—EDS.

after the end of their regular shift (or told to report prior to their regular starting time) will be paid at the rate of time and one-half for hours worked up to the beginning of their regular shift.

(4) Subsections (1), (2) and (3) above are not applicable where an employee continues to work into the next shift following his normal quitting time.

(b) *Report-in Time.* Employees who report for work in accordance with their regular schedules, and, without previous notice thereof, neither their regularly assigned nor any reasonably comparable work is available, will receive not less than four hours pay at the rate applicable had they worked. This Subsection (b) shall not be applicable where the inability of the Company to supply work is the result of fire, snowstorm, flood, power failure or work stoppage by employees in the same Company location. Qualified pieceworkers will be paid at least their anticipated earned rate. Learners on piecework will be paid their average earnings if less than the anticipated earned rate.

(c) *Dispensary Time.* Employees will be paid at their applicable rate for time spent in attending the Company dispensary for examination or treatment of any injuries arising out of and in the course of their employment, whenever such time would otherwise have been spent by the injured employee on the work assigned to him. Qualified pieceworkers will be paid at least their anticipated earned rate. Learners on piecework will be paid their average earnings if less than the anticipated earned rate. Employees who are directed not to return to work as a result of their injury shall be paid at their straight-time rate to the end of their scheduled work shift.

8. *Division of Overtime*

Overtime shall be divided as equally as proficient operations permit among the employees who are performing similar work in the group. A record of overtime worked by employees (or credited to them) will be maintained by the **immediate supervisor of the group** and will be available for examination by the appropriate Union Steward upon request.

ARTICLE VI. WAGE RATES

1. Any question which affects hourly rates, piecework rates or salary rates of individuals or groups shall be subject to negotiation between the Local and the local management.

2. The Company shall furnish the respective Locals concerned with information concerning all hourly and salaried job classifications, definitions, rates and progression schedules, including the anticipated earned rate, if any, for piecework jobs, and changes therein, for all jobs included within the bargaining units respectively represented by such Locals. Such Locals will also be informed of those piecework jobs within such bargaining units for which

there is no anticipated earned rate. It is understood that the job classifications and definitions referred to above are merely for purposes of identification and general description and do not purport to be all-inclusive or exhaustive of the actual requirements of any job so classified or defined. In addition, upon request of any Local, the Company will furnish to such Local a copy of the currently applicable wage structure for the plant or location.

3. When an employee is hired or transferred through the Company Personnel Department, he will be given a card showing his job classification, starting rate, rate of progression or progression schedule, if any, job rate and anticipated earned rate and sharing rate, if any, applicable to the job for which he is hired or to which transferred.

4. *Piece Prices—Hourly Rated Piecework Employees*

(a) Piece prices are classified as standard, temporary or special and all piecework vouchers will indicate the classification.

(1) A Standard Piece Price is one set where the manufacturing method has become established.

(2) A Temporary Piece Price is one set where the manufacturing method is under development or has been changed, or the average pieceworker on the job has not yet attained normal performance.

(3) A Special Piece Price is one set on work which usually repeats infrequently or is in small quantities or has some special feature or purpose.

(b) There will be no change in a standard price except where there is a change in manufacturing method.

Where such a change in manufacturing method is made, the price may be adjusted. However, such adjustment shall be limited to those parts of the job affected by the change.

In order that the operator will be able to make the same hourly earnings under a new price where a change in manufacturing method is made which does not reduce the job value on which the original price was computed, the adjusted price will be in direct proportion to the change in allowed time for the part of the job affected by the new method. When a price is reduced on such jobs, the employee and his representative will be given at least one week's notice that the price is to be changed.

(c) Subject to the foregoing, the Company will replace a temporary price with a standard price within six months if reasonably possible under the circumstances.

(d) A piecework employee temporarily taken off his regular job by the Company to perform another job, when he would otherwise have continued working on his regular job, shall be paid no less than his average straight-time earning rate on his regular job.

In cases of machine breakdowns, faulty materials, lack of material, or other unusual conditions, generally of short duration and not the fault of the operator, the employee will be paid for such conditions in accordance with the present local practice, provided the employee notifies his Foreman or other designated supervisor at the time the condition occurs.

(e) When a Company representative makes a time study of any job, the employee and his Steward will be notified and advised of its purpose. On jobs where the piece price is in dispute between the Company and the Local, and is scheduled to be retimed, the Steward may be present during this retiming and observe the conditions under which it is made. If the Steward requests, the Foreman will explain to him the data used in making up the piece price from the time study and/or applicable tables.

5. *Step Rates and Progression Schedules*

The Union and the Locals recognize that starting rates, progression rates, and job rates for hourly rated and salaried employees will vary, depending on the job, its location, and its surrounding circumstances.

The following provisions of this Section 5 are applicable to all hourly rated and salaried employees except draftsmen, apprentices and other trainees participating in an entry-type training program; provided that hourly rated employees who are hired after July 1, 1985 on any job with a job rate at or below the top of the one month progression schedule, will not begin progression toward job rates until they have accumulated six (6) months of service credits with the Company. This proviso shall not apply to subsequent upgrades to jobs above the top of the one month progression schedule. Also, provided that hourly rated and salaried employees hired after June 26, 1988 who have no record of prior GE service, shall be placed on starting rates and progression schedules in accordance with the provisions contained in Section 8 of this Article.

(a) *Hourly Rated Employees on Daywork*

(1) All starting, progression and job rates for hourly rated employees will be on steps in accordance with the applicable local wage structure.

(2) The minimum starting rates for all hourly rated jobs will be as follows:

(a) On jobs with a job rate which is not more than two (2) steps below the top of the one month progression schedule:

Four (4) steps below job rate; provided that this minimum starting rate shall be six (6) steps below job rate for employees who are hired after July 1, 1985 on any job with a job rate at or below the top of the one month progression schedule. This proviso shall not apply to subsequent upgradings to jobs above the top of the one month progression schedule or after the employees have completed their initial progression to job rate.

(b) On jobs with a job rate which is not more than five (5) steps, nor less than three (3) steps below the top of the one month progression schedule:

Three (3) steps below job rate; provided that this minimum starting rate shall be five (5) steps below job rate for employees who are hired after July 1, 1985 on any job with a job rate at or below the top of the one month progression schedule. This proviso shall not apply to subsequent upgradings to jobs above the top of the one month progression schedule or after the employees have completed their initial progression to job rate.

(c) On jobs with a job rate which is more than five (5) steps below the top of the one month progression schedule:

Two (2) steps below job rate; provided that this minimum starting rate shall be four (4) steps below job rate for employees who are hired after July 1, 1985 on any job with a job rate at or below the top of the one month progression schedule. This proviso shall not apply to subsequent upgradings to jobs above the top of the one month progression schedule or after the employees have completed their initial progression to job rate.

(3) Applicants fully experienced on jobs of the kind for which hired will begin at a rate not less than two steps below the job rate and will be increased to the job rate in accordance with the applicable progression schedule set forth in paragraph 4 below, except that when the applicant is hired for a job to which the six month progression schedule is applicable, the job rate must be paid at the end of six months.

(4) Each hourly rated employee will progress on steps from starting rate to the job rate of his job in accordance with the following progression schedules:

(a) ONE MONTH PROGRESSION SCHEDULE

Step rates up to, and including, the top of the One Month Progression Schedule in effect at each local plant on October 26, 1969:

One (1) step at the end of each one month period.

(b) THREE MONTH PROGRESSION SCHEDULE

Step rates from one to three steps (inclusive) above the top of the One Month Progression Schedule:

One (1) step at the end of each three month period.

(c) SIX MONTH PROGRESSION SCHEDULE

Step rates more than three steps above the top of the One Month Progression Schedule:

One (1) step at the end of each six month period.

(5) The above progression schedules are mandatory for employees on the job.

(b) *Salaried Employees*

(1) All starting, progression and job rates for salaried employees will be on steps in accordance with the applicable local salaried structure.

(2) The minimum starting rates for all salaried jobs will be as follows:

(a) On jobs with a job rate of Grade No. 8 or higher:

Four (4) steps below job rate.

(b) On jobs with a job rate of Grade Nos. 4 through 7:

Three (3) steps below job rate.

(c) On jobs with a job rate of Grade No. 3 or lower:

Two (2) steps below job rate.

(3) Each salaried employee will progress on steps, from the starting rate to the job rate established for that employee's particular job, or to the top of the progression schedule (the Grade No. 11 rate), whichever is less as follows:

(a) THREE MONTH PROGRESSION SCHEDULE

Step rates up to and including Grade No. 6:

One (1) step at the end of each three month period.

(b) SIX MONTH PROGRESSION SCHEDULE

Step rates from Grade No. 6 up to and including Grade No. 11:

One (1) step at the end of each six month period.

(4) The above progression schedules are mandatory for employees on the job.

(5) Any further increase in rate for any salaried employee above the top of the progression schedule, up to the job rate for the employee's job will also be on steps but shall be based solely on the employee's performance on the job. In addition, each such employee will be reviewed at least once each year.

(6) Applicants fully experienced on jobs of the kind for which hired will begin at a rate not less than two steps below the job rate and will be increased to the job rate within six months for normal performance.

(7) Subject to the foregoing provisions of this Section 5(b), the job rate shall be paid for normal performance.

(c) *Hourly Rated Employees*

New incentive prices will be set on the basis of the established step rate plan for incentive workers in those locations which have such plans in effect.

(d) *Group Leaders and Instructors*

(1) Group leaders of dayworker groups shall be paid two steps above the highest job rate in the group. If individuals in any group have

a preferential rate above the job rate, the leader may be assigned a rate up to two steps above such preferential rate if negotiated locally.

(2) Group leaders who are leading pieceworkers who are on individual piecework shall be paid at least two steps above the highest AER in the group. Rates in excess of this minimum shall be paid in accordance with job requirements and paragraph [sic] will progress to the job rate of their assigned job in accordance with the schedules contained herein; the other provisions of this Article and Article X, Transfers, notwithstanding. After completing the initial progression schedule and reaching job rate of the assigned job the other provisions of this Article and Article X will be applicable to subsequent transfers.

Article VII. Holidays

1. *Listed Holidays*

New Year's Day	Thanksgiving Day
Memorial Day	The day before Christmas
Independence Day	Day
Election Day	Christmas Day
Labor Day	

George Washington's Birthday (in any bargaining unit where the local union (a) chose an eighth paid holiday under the holiday-vacation option in 1960 or 1963 or (b) notified local management in writing prior to September 30, 1968, of its election of an eighth paid holiday under the 1966 holiday option.)

An additional listed holiday (negotiated in 1966) to be designated by each location. (This holiday will be mutually selected by the local union and local management prior to December 31 of the year preceding the year in which the holiday will occur. In the absence of mutual agreement by such December 31, the holiday will be designated by local management.)

2. *Hourly Rated Employees*

(a) An hourly rated employee not on continuous operations will be paid, for each of the above listed holidays not worked, up to eight hours at his average straight-time hourly rate as taken from the last periodic statistics available at the time his holiday occurs (current rate for dayworkers), for a number of hours equal to his regular daily working schedule during such week, providing each of the following conditions are met:

(1) Such employee has been employed at least 30 days prior to any such holiday.

(2) Such employee works his last scheduled workday prior to and his

next scheduled workday after such holiday within his scheduled workweeks. This condition shall not prevent payment of holiday pay to:

(i) an employee who has been absent from work because of verified personal illness for not more than three months prior to the week in which the holiday occurs and who works or reports for the Company's physical examination the next scheduled workday following the holiday; or

(ii) an employee who has been continuously absent from work for not more than two weeks prior to the week in which the holiday occurs and who is not at work either or both such workdays due to approved absences for personal illness or emergency illness at home, death in his family, layoff or union activity; or

(iii) an employee who is not at work on either or both such workdays solely due to military encampment or jury duty; or

(iv) an employee who is absent from work on either the last scheduled workday prior to double consecutive holidays (when such double consecutive holidays have been arranged under the provisions of Section 4 thereof) or his next scheduled workday after such double consecutive holidays (in such case, the employee will be entitled to holiday pay only for the first of such double consecutive holidays if he works the last scheduled workday prior to that holiday, but not the next scheduled workday after the second holiday; and he will be entitled to holiday pay only for the second of such double consecutive holidays if he fails to work the last scheduled workday prior to the first of such double consecutive holidays but works the next scheduled workday after the second of such double consecutive holidays).

(b) Hourly rated employees on continuous operations will be paid for the above-listed holidays under the above conditions if the holiday falls within their scheduled workweek and they are not scheduled to work on the holiday. If such employee fails to work as scheduled, he will not be paid for the holiday. If, however, such failure to work on the holiday is due to verified personal illness, death in family, jury duty, or emergency illness at home, the employee will be paid for the holiday if he is otherwise eligible in accordance with all the provisions of Section 2(a) above.

(c) Hourly rated employees who are receiving the night shift differential pursuant to Article V, 6 shall have the same added to any holiday pay received by them under this article.

3. Any of the above-listed holidays falling on Sunday shall be treated for all purposes under this Agreement as falling on the following Monday and shall for such purposes be observed on that Monday only. In like manner, any of the above-listed holidays falling on Saturday shall be treated for all purposes under this Agreement (including the purposes of Section 2(c) of Article V) as falling on the preceding Friday and shall for such purposes be

observed on that Friday only. However, local plant management and a local union may, by local agreement in writing, substitute a day other than the preceding Friday for any such holiday which falls on Saturday.

For an employee on continuous operations, when a holiday falls on his scheduled day off, his next non-premium scheduled workday shall be deemed to be his holiday. In no event will an employee receive the holiday pay or premium more than once for a holiday.

4. Local management and the local union at each plant may agree in writing to substitute a different holiday in place of any of the above-listed holidays for all purposes.

ARTICLE VIII. CONTINUITY OF SERVICE—SERVICE CREDITS

1. *Definition of Terms*
(a) "Continuity of service" designates the status of an employee who has service credits totaling 52 or more weeks.
(b) "Continuous service" designates the length of each employee's continuity of service and shall equal the total service credits of an employee who has "continuity of service."
(c) "Service credits" are credits for periods during which the employee is actually at work for the Company or for periods of absence for which credit is granted. (As provided in Section 3.)
(d) "Absence" is the period an employee is absent from work either with or without pay (except a paid vacation period), computed by subtracting the date following the last day worked from the date the employee returns to work. Each separate continuous period away from work shall be treated as a single absence from work.
(e) "Illness" shall include pregnancy, whenever the Foreman or other immediate supervisor is notified prior to absence from work.

2. *Loss of Service Credits and Continuity of Service*
(a) Service credits previously accumulated and continuity of service, if any, will be lost whenever the employee:
   (1) Quits, dies, resigns, retires or is discharged.
   (2) Is absent from work for more than two consecutive weeks without satisfactory explanation.
   (3) Is absent from work because of personal illness or accident and fails to keep the Company notified monthly, stating the probable date of his return to work.
   (4) Is notified within a year from date of layoff that he may return but fails to return or to give satisfactory explanation within two weeks.
   (5) Is absent from work without satisfactory explanation beyond the period of any leave of absence granted him by the Company.

(6) Is absent from work for a continuous period of more than one year for any reason, other than (a) a leave of absence granted in advance, or (b) an absence due to a compensable accident (up to 18 months) or compensable illness (up to 18 months).

(b) Individuals who at the time of layoff had one (1) year of continuous service shall, despite loss of service as a result of such layoff, be retained on the recall list and be eligible for reemployment in accordance with the applicable local procedure for a period of sixty (60) months following layoff or until retirement, whichever occurs first. Similarly, in the case of individuals with the required service absent due to illness or injury, the same extended recall arrangement will be made only if:

(1) The individual reports promptly to the Personnel Office for employment upon recovery.

(2) The individual is otherwise eligible in which case he will promptly thereafter have his name added to the recall list.

Actual recall will be predicated upon the individual meeting the Company health requirements.

(c) If the Company reemploys an employee who has lost service credits and continuity of service because of layoff due to lack of work for more than one year, because of absence due to illness or injury for more than one year, or because of termination for transfer to a successor employer, such employee shall have such service credits and continuity of service automatically restored if his continuous service at the time of his layoff, termination for transfer to a successor employer, or first day of illness was greater than the total length of such absence or if the employee has recall rights under Section 2(b) of this Article.

(d) The service record of each employee laid off and reemployed after layoff or reemployed following illness or injury, will be reviewed by the Company at the time of his reemployment and in each case, such employee will be notified as to his service credits and continuity of service, if any.

(e) If the Company reemploys, on or after June 27, 1988, a former employee who had continuity of service at the time of a previous termination of Company employment {and the employee is not eligible for automatic service restoration under Section 2(c)}, the Company shall restore such continuity of service after the employee has completed three years of continuous service following reemployment. **An employee in the process of service restoration under this section who is laid off and again rehired or recalled shall have all service credits earned following reemployment on or after June 27, 1988 accumulated for the purpose of service restoration under this Section 2(e).**

(f) For employees reemployed prior to June 27, 1988 who do not have restoration rights under prior National Agreements, the Company shall restore the employee's prior unrestored continuity of service when such employee has three years of continuous service (effective January 1, 1990), provided, however, that if the employee is absent on the date the restoration would otherwise occur, such service restoration will occur when the employee returns to work with continuity of service.

(g) Service restoration provided for in this Section 2 will be contingent upon the employee's full repayment of **any of the following lump sum benefits paid under Article XXII:** Income Extension Aid **under Section 4(b)(1)(iii), Special Voluntary Layoff Bonus under Section 4(c), Special Retirement Bonus under Section 3(b), or severance pay due to** a plant closing termination which occurred within six months prior to the date of reemployment. **Such repayment must be made within a reasonable time after rehire. No such repayment is required of benefits paid if the reemployment date is more than one year from the date of the prior termination.**

3. *Service Credits*

Service credits for each employee shall be granted for periods during which the employee is actually at work for the Company, and service credits for absences shall be added to an employee's service, after reemployment with continuity of service or with prior service credits, as follows:

(a) Employees when reemployed with prior service credits or continuity of service following absence due to illness, accident, layoff, leave of absence granted by the Company, because of termination for transfer to a successor employer, or due to plant closing, will receive service credits for up to a total of the first twelve months of such absence. Where the absence of an employee, with continuity of service, is due to a compensable accident or compensable illness, and the employee is reemployed without loss of continuity of service, service credits will be granted for the period of his absence in excess of twelve months up to a maximum of six additional months.

(b) For all other absences of two weeks or less, such employees will receive service credits, but, if the absence is longer than two weeks, no service credits will be allowed for any part of such absence.

If an employee who has lost prior service credits or continuity of service is reemployed, he shall be considered a new employee and will not receive service credits (unless all or part of prior service credits are restored) for any time prior to the date of such reemployment.

Article IX. Vacations

1. *Paid Vacation Periods*

Vacations with pay will be granted in each calendar year (hereinafter called the "vacation year") to eligible hourly rated and nonexempt salaried employees as follows:

(a) *Salaried Employees*

Years of Continuous Service	Vacation
1	2 weeks
5	2½ weeks
7	3 weeks
15	4 weeks
20	5 weeks
30	6 weeks

(b) *Hourly Rated Employees*

Years of Continuous Service	Vacation
1	1 week
2	2 weeks
5	2½ weeks
7	3 weeks
15	4 weeks
20	5 weeks
30	6 weeks

2. Eligibility Requirements

An employee whose continuity of service is unbroken as of December 31 or his last scheduled workday in the last week of the year immediately preceding the vacation year shall qualify for a vacation or vacation allowance under the provisions of this Article if he:

(a) Actually performs work as an active employee of the Company during the last full calendar week of the year immediately preceding the vacation year; or

(b) Receives earnings from the Company directly applicable to all or part of such week.

If an employee has not qualified under (a) and (b) above, but returns to work without loss of continuity of service during the vacation year, he will become entitled to a vacation or vacation allowance in the vacation year after he shall have worked in the vacation year for one month or for a period equal to that of his absence if his absence was less than one month. Any such employee reemployed too late to work for one month in the vacation year will be paid his vacation allowance and may have a portion of the time out considered as the vacation to which he is otherwise eligible.

3. *Determination of Paid Vacations*

(a) *Basic or Guaranteed Vacations.* The basic vacation period of an eligible employee shall be based upon his length of continuous service as of December 31 of the year immediately preceding the vacation year.

(b) *Additional (or Initial) Vacation.* An eligible employee whose continuing accumulation of service credits during a vacation year entitles him to an additional vacation under the provisions of Section 1 (or who completes his first year of continuous service during the vacation year) will receive such additional vacation (or his initial vacation), provided that an employee shall not be entitled to any such vacation in a vacation year unless he shall actually perform work as an active employee of the Company during such vacation year after having qualified for such vacation. EXCEPTION: Where a plant shutdown is scheduled for the last week of the year employees who would have qualified for vacation payment during this shutdown will receive such payment if they return to work (or report for physical examination and are approved for employment) the first scheduled workday following the shutdown or were at work the last scheduled workday immediately preceding the shutdown.

4. *Termination of Employment*

An employee who quits, is discharged, dies or retires will promptly thereafter receive the full vacation allowance to which he may then be entitled. In the case of employees who died, vacation allowances will be treated as wages owing the employee, and payment made accordingly.

5. *Use of Vacation Time for Absences of Employees*

(a) *Leave of Absence.* An employee who is granted a leave of absence may have the first portion of such leave designated as the period of any vacation to which he may then be entitled, if the Manager shall approve.

(b) *Extended Illness, Accident or Layoff.* An employee who is absent because of illness or accident, or because he is laid off for lack of work, may (except in a plant or part thereof which is scheduled for an annual shutdown) have the first portion of such absence designated as the period of any vacation to which he may then be entitled, if the Manager shall approve.

(c) *Incidental Absences.* An employee whose absence is excused because of personal illness, personal business, holidays that are unpaid, temporary lack of work, or short workweeks (of ½ day or longer) may (with the Manager's approval) utilize extra vacation time to which he is entitled in excess of the scheduled Shutdown or in excess of two weeks in locations where there is no shutdown for such absences in the form of vacation days. This time may be paid out in units of no less than ½ day periods.

(d) *Other Absences.* An employee who is absent from work for any reason other than those reasons listed above will not be entitled either to have his vacation scheduled or to receive a vacation allowance during the period of such absence.

(e) *Vacation Payment Guarantee.* An employee whose absence from work continues beyond the end of a vacation year and who did not receive in such vacation year the full vacation pay for which he had qualified, shall receive at the end of such absence or upon prior termination of service, a vacation allowance in lieu of any vacation to which he was still entitled at the end of the vacation year.

6. *Computation of Vacation Pay*

(a) *Basic Formulas.* Vacation pay for each week of vacation to which an employee is entitled will be computed by multiplying the appropriate weekly hour-multiplier as determined by Subsection (b) below, by the appropriate rate-multiplier as determined by Subsection (c) below. (Vacation pay for any extra day or half day of vacation to which an employee may be entitled will be determined by (i) dividing by five or ten respectively the weekly hour-multiplier determined for him under Subsection (b) below and (ii) multiplying such daily equivalent by the appropriate rate-multiplier determined by Subsection (c) below.)

(b) *Determination of Weekly Hour-Multiplier.* The weekly hour-multiplier for vacation pay computations for all employees will be 40 hours except as noted in the following paragraphs of this Subsection (b).

(i) *Short Schedules.* The weekly hour-multiplier of an employee whose regular weekly schedule at the time his vacation begins is less than 40 hours will be the greater of either (A) his scheduled hours per week at the time the vacation begins, or (B) his scheduled hours per week during the last fiscal week, as determined by the GE fiscal calendar, worked by him during the year preceding the vacation year, but in any event will not be greater than 40 hours.

(ii) *Multiple-Shift Short Schedule.* Notwithstanding the provisions of (i) above, the weekly hour-multiplier for an employee who is on a multiple shift operation and whose regular weekly schedule of hours is not less than 37½ hours shall be not less than 40 hours.

(iii) *Extended Schedules.* The weekly hour-multiplier of an employee who shall have worked an average of more than 40 hours per week during the weeks paid in the calendar year which immediately precedes the vacation year will be determined in accordance with the following schedule:

Average Weekly Hours		Weekly Hour-Multiplier
40	but less than 42	40
42	but less than 42.5	42
42.5	but less than 43.5	43
43.5	but less than 44.5	44
44.5	but less than 45.5	45
45.5	but less than 46.5	46
46.5	but less than 47.5	47
47.5	and higher	48 (maximum)

NOTE: For the purposes of the foregoing schedule, average weekly hours will be computed by dividing the total number of hours actually worked by the employee during the weeks paid in said year by the number of weeks in such year, except that the following listed types of time lost from work will be counted as time worked:

(A) Time spent on union activity;
(B) A listed or observed holiday;
(C) Jury duty service;
(D) Military Service for which service credits are granted under Article XXIII;
(E) Annual shutdowns and vacation periods;
(F) Employees' personal absences for which pay is granted;
(G) Time paid for death-in-family absence;
(H) Time lost due to a compensable accident or compensable illness.

(iv) *Continuous Operation.* The weekly hour-multiplier of an employee who is, at the time of his vacation, regularly assigned to work on a continuous operation schedule will be the greater of either (a) the number of hours per week he would have been paid, up to a maximum of 48 hours, including premium hours for Saturday and/or Sunday, had he worked forty (40) hours on his established regular schedule including Saturday and/or Sunday, on the week or weeks scheduled for vacation or (b) the hours provided by the application of Section 6(b)(iii) above.

(c) *Determination of Rate-Multiplier.* The rate-multiplier for various types of employees will be as follows:

Rate-Multiplier
The greater of:

Type of employee	*Current Rate (including night-shift bonus for employees who are regularly scheduled on a night shift)*	*Year End Rate (including night-shift bonus for employees who are regularly scheduled on a night shift)*
Hourly employee on incentive	His average earnings (exclusive of overtime premium) obtained from the last periodic statistics available at the time his vacation begins (except that when an employee's job and rate are changed within one month before his vacation period, the new	His average earnings (exclusive of overtime premium) obtained from the last periodic statistics applicable to time worked by him during year preceding vacation year.

Collective Bargaining Agreement: General Electric

		rate of earnings will be used in place of the last regular periodic statistics).
Hourly employee on daywork	Regular hourly daywork rate in effect at the time his vacation begins.	Regular hourly daywork rate in effect during the last full calendar [week] worked by him during year preceding vacation year.
Salaried employee	Hourly equivalent of employee's actual straight time salary rate in effect at time vacation begins.	Hourly equivalent of employee's actual straight time salary rate for last week worked by him during year preceding vacation year.

(d) *Payments for Incidental Absences.* The payments described in Section 5(c) will be paid on the same basis as outlined above.

7. *Scheduling of Vacations*

(a) *Scheduling.* In the event of one or more shutdowns scheduled in any plant within the vacation year, one of such shutdowns will be of no less than two (2) weeks duration and during such Shutdown, the vacation for eligible employees shall be considered to run concurrently. **Provided written notice is given to the Local union prior to April 1, this Shutdown may be split into two periods of not less than one (1) week duration, but in no case shall the combined split periods exceed three weeks. In such cases, local management and the Local may also agree on special rules dealing with vacation eligibility for the subsequent year where one of the mandatory Shutdown periods extends into the last calendar week of the year.** Exceptions for certain departments or individuals by reason of the requirements of the business shall be at management's discretion. With respect to other scheduled shutdown periods, employees entitled to vacation time in excess of two (2) weeks, may elect to take the time off without pay as though on temporary layoff for lack of work and take his remaining vacation time off at some earlier or later date including the week immediately preceding or following the Shutdown period. Vacations taken at times other than during shutdown periods will be scheduled to conform to the requirements of the business at the Manager's discretion. For any part of a Shutdown period for which an employee is not eligible or does not become eligible for vacation pay during the vacation year, and during which he has no work available, he will be deemed to be on temporary layoff for lack of work.

(b) *Postponement or Division of Vacation.* It will not be permissible to postpone vacations from one year to another, or to omit vacations and draw vacation pay allowances in lieu thereof, except with the written approval of the Manager. No vacation shall be divided unless it is of two weeks or more duration, in which case it may, with the consent of the Manager, be divided.

8. *Time of Vacation Payment*

Except as otherwise provided in this Article, vacation allowances for full weeks shall be paid to an employee on or about the last day worked by him prior to the beginning of the vacation scheduled for him (except payments under 5(c)). An employee who takes his vacation prior to the date upon which he becomes eligible, will receive payment (computed in accordance with Section 6 above) after he becomes eligible. Additional day or days for which an employee may qualify later in the year may be taken at the time of the regular vacation and payment for such time (computed in accordance with Section 6 above) will be made after the employee has qualified.

9. *Holiday in Vacation Period*

When the vacation period of any employee includes one of the holidays listed in Article VII, an additional day of vacation will be granted with pay, if the holiday occurs during the scheduled workweek of the employee. When the vacation period of a salaried employee includes an observed holiday, an additional day of vacation will be granted with pay, if the holiday occurs during the scheduled workweek of the employee. In either case, the extra day must be taken immediately before or after as an extension of the vacation.

Article X. Transfers

1. *Hourly and Salaried Employees*

(a) In the case of employees who are laid off from their regular jobs for lack of work, every effort will be made to transfer them to related jobs having an equal rate or to available openings on jobs having a higher rate.

(b) Employees permanently transferred to lower rated jobs will receive either one week's advance notice of such transfer, or payment for the first week's work after transfer at their rate immediately prior to transfer. For pieceworkers such payment shall be at the rate of their immediately preceding average straight time earnings.

(c) An employee who desires a transfer to another shift may so advise his Foreman in writing with a copy to the Personnel Department. As openings occur in his department on work for which he is presently qualified, consideration will be given his request along with others in accordance with his relative seniority. Such transfers, however, shall not take precedence over the normal upgrading of qualified longer service employees. Exceptions to the above may be made in certain special cases by mutual consent.

This does not supersede any existing local agreement.

Collective Bargaining Agreement: General Electric

2. *Hourly Rated Daywork Employees*
An hourly rated employee on daywork when permanently transferred
(a) To a higher rated daywork job will be transferred at a rate commensurate with his qualifications to perform the job to which transferred, but not less than the rate he was paid on the job from which transferred.
(b) To an equal or lower rated daywork job will be transferred at the lower of the daywork rate he was paid on the job from which transferred or the job rate of the job to which transferred.
(c) To a piecework job will be paid for three weeks the lower of the daywork rate he was paid on the job from which transferred or the AER of the job to which transferred, except that he will be paid his piecework earnings on the new job if they are higher.

3. *Hourly Rated Piecework Employees*
An hourly rated employee on piecework when permanently transferred
(a) To a higher rated daywork job will be transferred at a rate commensurate with his qualifications to perform the job to which transferred, but not less than his immediately preceding average earnings or two steps below the job rate of the job to which transferred, whichever is lower; however, an employee transferred to a related daywork job where the training time is incidental will receive the job rate of the new job.
(b) To an equal or lower rated daywork job will be transferred at the job rate of the job to which transferred.
(c) To a piecework job will be paid for three weeks the lower of the AER of the job from which transferred or the AER of the job to which transferred, except that he will be paid his piecework earnings on the new job if they are higher.

4. Sections (2) and (3) above notwithstanding, an employee who is transferred to a daywork job that he formerly held on a permanent basis will be transferred at not less than the step rate he was paid at the time he held such job.

5. *Salaried Employees*
A salaried employee when permanently transferred
(a) To a higher rated salaried job will be transferred at a rate commensurate with that employee's qualifications to perform the job to which transferred, but not less than the rate that employee was paid on the job from which transferred.
(b) To an equal or lower rated salaried job will be paid the lower of the rate that employee was paid on the job from which transferred or the job rate of the new job.

6. *Minimum Starting Rate*
In any case where the transfer rate as provided above is less than the minimum starting rate of the job to which transferred, the minimum starting rate will be paid.

7. Progression to Job Rate

If after transfer, an employee is on a progression schedule and receiving less than the job rate of the job to which transferred, he will progress to job rate in accordance with the provisions of Article VI.

Article XI. Reduction or Increase in Forces

1. Whenever there is a reduction in the working force or employees are laid off from their regular jobs, total length of **seniority**, applied on a plant, department, or other basis as negotiated locally, shall be the major factor determining the employees to be laid off or transferred (exclusive of upgrading or transfers to higher rated jobs). However, ability will be given consideration.

Similarly, in all cases of rehiring after layoff, total length of **seniority**, applied on a plant, department, or other basis as negotiated locally, shall be the major factor covering such rehiring if the employee is able to do the available work in a satisfactory manner after a minimum amount of training.

Where employees have accumulated six months or more of service credits, but have not established continuity of service, **seniority** will be considered in the above cases.

2. Since the number of employees in the individual bargaining units covered under this Agreement varies from less than 50 to more than 10,000, each Local shall negotiate with local management a written agreement covering the layoff and rehiring procedure of the employees represented by the Local.

3. Employees who have been or who may be transferred to jobs outside the bargaining units, may be returned to their former classification in the bargaining unit in accordance with their total length of continuous service.

Employees who, after October 3, 1966, are transferred to jobs outside the bargaining units may be returned to their former classification in the bargaining unit in accordance with their total length of continuous service at the time they left the unit plus the number of years outside the unit up to a maximum of five such years outside the unit.

Employees who, after June 30, 1985, are transferred to exempt management jobs outside the bargaining units may be returned to their former classification in the bargaining unit in accordance with their total length of continuous service during the period up to twenty-four (24) months following the first such transfer to a job outside the unit.

Employees who, after June 30, 1991, are transferred to jobs outside the bargaining units may be returned to their former classification in the bargaining unit in accordance with their total length of continuous service during the period up to six (6) months following the first such transfer to a job outside the unit.

4. An employee who retires at his or her option as provided in the Company Pension Plan shall cease to have any rights under the provisions of this Agreement. (However, this Agreement shall continue to be applicable to retired employees returned to active employment by the Company.)

5. Employees will be given at least one week's notice and one week's work at the prevailing schedule before layoffs are made due to decreasing forces.

6. An employee with continuity of service out due to illness for a period not exceeding one (1) year, **or in the case of a work-related injury or illness, not exceeding eighteen (18) months,** who returns to work shall be reemployed on his former job providing he is able to perform the job and normal seniority provisions permit.

ARTICLE XII. UNION AND LOCAL REPRESENTATIVES AND STEWARDS

1. *Layoff Deferment*

(a) An employee who is an official of any Local, and who has accumulated six months or more of service credits shall, on written request of the Local, be deferred from layoff (except temporary layoffs) so long as work for which he is qualified is available and so long as the official's duties would permit such layoff deferment under applicable law. Such employee shall displace an employee with less actual seniority on work for which the employee who is a Local official is qualified or, in the event such employee does not have actual seniority to displace any employee, then the employee shall to the extent necessary to defer him from such layoff be deemed to have greater seniority than the shortest service employee in the bargaining unit on work for which the employee who is a Local official is qualified. Such deferral from layoff will continue only so long as the employee retains his position as an official of any Local. This provision shall apply to a minimum of four and a maximum of twelve such officials, dependent on the number of employees within such units as follows:

Employees	*Union Officials*
500 or less	4
501-2000	6
2001-5000	8
Over 5000	12

(b) An employee who is a Steward of such Local and who has accumulated six months or more of service credits shall, upon written request of the Local, and if a majority of the group of employees he represents assents as certified in writing by the Local, be deferred from layoff (except temporary layoffs) so long as work for which he is qualified is available among the group of employees he represents. In the event of a layoff affecting the group of employees represented by the employee who is a Steward, such employee shall, in accordance with the applicable local supplement or the local procedures on layoff and displacement, displace an employee within the group who has less actual seniority on work for which the Steward is qualified. In the event the Steward does not have sufficient actual seniority to displace any employee within the group, in accordance with the applicable local supplement or the local procedures on layoff, then such Steward shall be deemed to have sufficient seniority to retain his job classification and wage rate within the group. Such deferral from layoff will continue only so long as the employee retains his position as a Steward. This provision shall, in general, apply to a maximum of one Steward for each Company Foreman.

(c) Paragraph (a) and (b) hereof shall apply only to those officials whose names, titles and order of precedence, and to those Stewards whose names and sections, have been furnished in writing to the Company prior to the giving of notice of layoff by the Company and shall not apply to any such officials or Stewards who are on leave of absence pursuant to the provisions of Section 2 hereof.

2. *Leave of Absence*

Upon written request of the Union or any Local:

(a) Employees who are officials of the Union or officers of such a Local, who have at least one year of continuous service, and who represent the Union in its relations with the Company, shall be granted one year's leave of absence by the Company, without forfeiture of prior accumulated continuous service. This provision shall be limited at any one time to not more than 12 officials of the National Union and not more than 6 officers of any Local.

(b) If made at the end of such leave of absence

(1) such leave of absence may be extended yearly.

(2) such employees will be reemployed in work of the same or a similar character in the same or other divisions of the same plant, if qualified therefor, and if entitled thereto on the basis of their prior accumulated continuous service. In the case of employees who are officials of the Union or officers of a Local and who are granted a leave of absence after the effective date of this Agreement, such employees will be entitled (solely for determining their relative seniority for purposes of layoff and rehire under Article XI) to add to their prior accumulated continuous service the total period of any such leave of absence.

3. *Payment for Time on Local Union Activities*

(a) Unless otherwise provided by local written agreement, employees not on leave of absence pursuant to the provisions of Section 2 hereof will be paid by the Company at their respective rates then prevailing for absences from work while engaged in the following activities on Company premises:

(1) During each fiscal month, the number of weeks in such General Electric fiscal month multiplied by 1½ hours per week for those Stewards whose names and sections have been furnished to the Company pursuant to the provisions of Section 1(c) hereof, while engaged in processing grievances at Foreman level pursuant to the provisions of Article XIII, Section 2(a).

Where any plant is regularly scheduled on a forty-eight hour per week basis, the above allowances will be based on 2 hours per week.

Payment to Stewards will be made on a weekly basis within the above limits.

(2) Up to a total of eight hours per week (exclusive of time payable under Section 1 hereof) for members of Local Executive Board or for Negotiating Committee members while engaged in processing grievances with representatives of local management pursuant to the provisions of Article XIII, Section 2(b). Such Committee members or Executive Board representatives shall be limited at any one meeting concerning a bargaining unit of less than 5000 employees to six representatives and shall not exceed twelve for any large bargaining unit, unless the number is increased by mutual agreement of the Local and local management. This does not limit the number of Executive Board members and does not prevent meeting of the full Executive Board with local management when such meetings are arranged in advance.

(b)(1) Local management and the Local may negotiate a local agreement with respect to payment to local Stewards in excess of the limits provided in (a)(1) above.

(2) In those plant locations where the number of employees in the bargaining unit is 5000 employees or more or where more than one product department is located, local management and the Local may negotiate a local agreement with respect to payment to Local Executive Boards or Negotiating Committee members in excess of the limits provided in (a)(2) above.

(c) Employees requesting payment pursuant to the provisions of Paragraph (a) hereof, shall report all time spent on the handling of grievances to their respective Foremen or other immediate supervisors.

Chief Stewards or Executive Committee members in Works where they act as Chief Stewards, will be permitted to contact Stewards in their respective divisions when the officers of the Local deem such contact necessary. They will advise their own Foremen before leaving their departments and also contact the Foreman in the department which they are visiting before they contact the Steward.

The Company shall report their names, rates of pay and time absent from work to their respective Locals, and shall in no event be required to make any payments pursuant to Paragraph (a) hereof, except to the extent that such reports are approved by such Locals, and such Paragraph (a) is otherwise applicable.

(d) Whenever an OSHA inspection shall occur in a work area that includes employees represented by a Local Union listed in the Preamble, an employee designated by the Union who accompanies the OSHA inspector as the employees' representative will be paid for time lost from work during such inspection.

ARTICLE XIII. GRIEVANCE PROCEDURE

1. Grievances may be filed by an employee or group of employees, a Steward or the Local. Grievances of a general nature filed by the Local shall be initiated at the second step of the grievance procedure.

2. *Steps.* Grievances other than those of a general nature may be processed only by recourse to the following successive steps:

(a) *Step One (Foreman Level)*

(1) Within a reasonable time after the occurrence or knowledge of the situation, condition or action of Management giving rise to the grievance, the employee affected thereby or his Steward may present the grievance to the employee's Foreman or other immediate supervisor. (If presented by the employee, he may also have his Steward present.)

(2) Within one working day after such presentation, such Foreman or other immediate supervisor shall give to such employee and Steward his decision with respect to such grievance, or shall advise them that additional time for such decision is needed, in which event he shall give them such decision within one week thereafter.

(3) A Steward who submits a written grievance to his Foreman shall receive, upon request, a written reply.

(4) If a settlement is not reached between the Steward and his immediate supervisor, the Local may refer the grievance to two representatives of the Local for discussion in the department with representatives of local management for settlement, if possible.

(b) *Step Two (Management Level)*

(1) If a settlement is not reached at Step One, the designated Local official may present to a representative designated by local management, a written statement of such grievance within thirty (30) days of the Company answer at Step One of the grievance procedure giving all pertinent information relative to the grievance and indicating the relief requested, provided, however, that the designated Local official may advise local management that additional time is needed, in which case the Local shall have an additional one week to process the grievance to Step Two. The time limit between Step One and Step Two may be extended by mutual agreement.

(2) Meetings between representatives of the Local and local management shall be arranged at mutually agreeable times for the purpose of discussing such grievances. In those cases where it is mutually agreed by Management and Local representatives that an inspection of the job would be helpful in settling the case, a subcommittee of the Local with Management representatives shall be allowed to make an inspection of the job. Local representatives may include the Business Agent or his assistant or officers of the Local.

Grievances referred to Step Two will be scheduled and discussed as expeditiously as possible but not later than forty-five (45) days after the grievance has been presented to Step Two. Such time limits may be extended by mutual agreement.

(3) Upon request, local management will give the Local a written reply, **such reply generally to be issued within two weeks following discussion of the grievance on the merits at the Second Step. Any extension necessary to issue a written reply shall be limited to two weeks.**

(c) *Step Three (Headquarters Level)*

Any grievance, having been processed through Step Two without satisfactory settlement, may be referred to the National Officers of the Union for submission to an Executive Officer of the Company or his designated representative, who shall arrange meetings for the purpose of discussing such grievances.

Such grievances shall be submitted to the Company not less than two weeks prior to the date of any discussion and not more than three months after the completion of discussions and the final decision of local management at Step Two.

When the Union requests an emergency meeting on a particular grievance or grievances, such a meeting shall take place within one week after the Company receives the request for such an emergency meeting.

The Company shall give its final decision to the Union in writing within a reasonable time after the completion of discussion on any grievance.

The discussions provided for above may, by mutual agreement, be held at the plant location of the Local submitting the grievance, if requested by the Union.

3. *Discipline Based on Warning Notices*

Before imposing a disciplinary penalty or discharge which is based upon the cumulative effect of written warning notices, the Company will notify the employee concerned one week in advance. The matter may be made a subject for grievance discussions, but such discussions shall not prevent imposition of the penalty pending their final outcome, and in the event it is determined that an employee has been improperly penalized, he will be reimbursed for any loss of wages sustained as a result of the imposition of the penalty.

Article XIV. Strikes and Lockouts

1. There shall be no strike, sitdown, slowdown, employee demonstration or any other organized or concerted interference with work of any kind in connection with any matter subject to the grievance procedure, and no such interference with work shall be directly or indirectly authorized or sanctioned by a Local or the Union, or their respective Officers or Stewards, unless and until all of the respective provisions of the successive steps of the grievance procedure set forth in Article XIII shall have been complied with by the Local and the Union. The foregoing exception will not apply if (a) the matter is submitted to arbitration as provided in Article XV, or (b) 12 months shall have elapsed after receipt by the Union of the Company's final decision on the grievance at Step Three, or (c) the Company shall not have received written or telegraphic notice of such strike from the Local more than 24 hours prior to the commencement of such strike, which notice will specify the exhausted grievance over which the strike is being called. Upon receipt by the Company of such a strike notice, the Company and the Union will meet immediately to discuss the dispute and the contemplated action so that management may assess the situation.

2. The Company will not lock out any employee or transfer any job under dispute from the Local Works, nor will the local management take similar action while a disputed job is under discussion at any of the steps of the grievance procedure set forth in Article XIII, or if the matter is submitted to arbitration as provided in Article XV.

Article XV. Arbitration

1. Any grievance which remains unsettled after having been fully processed pursuant to the provisions of Article XIII, and which involves either,

(a) the interpretation or application of a provision of the Agreement, or

(b) a disciplinary penalty (including discharge) imposed on or after the effective date of this Agreement, which is alleged to have been imposed without just cause, or

(c) a nondisciplinary termination occurring after the effective date of this agreement,

may be submitted to arbitration upon written request of either the Union or the Company, provided such request is made within 60 days after the final decision of the Company has been given to the Union pursuant to Article XIII, Section 2(c). For the purpose of proceedings within the scope of (b) above, the standard to be applied by an arbitrator to cases involving disciplinary penalties (including discharge) is that such penalties shall be imposed only for just cause.

2.(a) A request for arbitration shall state in reasonable detail the nature of the dispute and the remedy requested. A copy of the request shall be sent to the American Arbitration Association.

(b) Within 30 days after receipt of a request to arbitrate, the receiving party will give its response thereto in writing, with a copy to the Association, stating whether or not it believes the stated dispute to be arbitrable. If the receiving party believes the dispute not to be arbitrable, it will state its reasons in reasonable detail.

(c) If the response agrees to the arbitrability of the dispute, the Association will proceed to process the request in accordance with Section 3.

(d) If a response to a request for arbitration disagrees as to arbitrability of the dispute, either party may request a conference to discuss the arbitrability of the dispute, and to seek to resolve the differences between the parties.

3.(a) When a request for arbitration involves only relief from a disciplinary penalty or discharge alleged to have been imposed without just cause, or involves a dispute which the Company admits to be arbitrable, or when a final court judgment shall have ordered arbitration of a request, the Association shall submit the appropriate matter promptly to one of the Contract Arbitrators listed below for scheduling of a hearing thereon.

The Contract Arbitrators shall serve for the duration of this Agreement. The Association will assign each arbitration case in rotation, in the order of Contract Arbitrators listed below. If a Contract Arbitrator states that he is unable to accept a case, it will be referred to the next Contract Arbitrator in line.

Whenever the number of unresolved arbitration requests assigned to a Contract Arbitrator shall exceed three, any additional requests which would otherwise be assigned him in order of rotation shall be referred to the next Contract Arbitrator in line.

CONTRACT ARBITRATORS

Timothy L. Bornstein	Richard Mittenthal
Leroy D. Clark	Craig E. Overton
Robert L. Gibson	Joan W. Parker
Lawrence T. Holden, Jr.	Frank E.A. Sander
Wayne Howard	Eric J. Schmertz
Charles F. Ipavec	Anthony Sinicropi
Mark L. Irvings	Joseph P. Sirefman
James E. Jones	Janet M. Spencer
Robert F. Koretz	Theodore St. Antoine
Bertram T. Kupsinel	Robert L. Stutz
Robert E. Light	Jeffrey B. Tener
Anne Harmon Miller	Joseph F. Wildebush

In all discharge and upgrading cases, the Association shall expedite the handling of such cases as follows:

(i) Request from the Contract Arbitrator, at the time of appointment, two or three proposed alternative hearing dates for hearing days within sixty (60) days of appointment.

(ii) Communicate proposed alternative hearing dates to designated representatives of the parties promptly and secure a firm commitment on a hearing date.

(iii) Schedule agreed upon hearing date in accordance with regular procedure.

(b) Only one request shall be scheduled for the same arbitration hearing, except by mutual agreement of the parties.

(c) In the conduct of an arbitration hearing, the applicable provisions of the Voluntary Labor Arbitration Rules of the Association shall control, except that either party may, if it desires, be represented by counsel.

(d) The dispute as stated in the request for arbitration shall constitute the sole and entire subject matter to be heard by the arbitrator, unless the parties agree to modify the scope of the hearing.

4.(a) In the event the receiving party has asserted that the dispute contained in a request for arbitration is not arbitrable, the Association shall have authority to process the request for arbitration and appoint an arbitrator in accordance with the procedure set forth in Section 3 above only after a final judgment of a court has determined that the grievance upon which arbitration has been requested raises arbitrable issues and has directed arbitration of such issues. The foregoing part of this section shall not be applicable if the request for arbitration involves only relief from a disciplinary penalty or discharge alleged to have been imposed without just cause.

(b) In the consideration and decision of any question involving arbitrability (including any application to a court for an order directing arbitration), it is the specific agreement of the parties that:

(i) Some types of grievance disputes which may arise during the term of this Agreement shall be subject to arbitration as a matter of right, enforceable in court, at the demand of either party. (See Section 6 below.)

(ii) Other types of disputes shall be subject only to voluntary arbitration, i.e., can be arbitrated only if both parties agree in writing, in the case of each dispute, to do so. (See Section 7 below.)

(iii) This Agreement sets out expressly all the restrictions and obligations assumed by the respective parties, and no implied restrictions or obligations [are] inherent in this Agreement or were assumed by the parties in entering into this Agreement.

(iv) In the consideration of whether a matter is subject to arbitration as a matter of right, a fundamental principle shall be that the Company retains all its rights to manage the business, including (but not limited to) the right to determine the methods and means by which its operations are to be carried on, to direct the work force and to conduct its operations in a safe and effective manner, subject only to the express limitations set forth in this National Agreement, Local Seniority Supplements executed under the provisions of Article XI thereof, and Local Understandings executed in accordance with Section 3 of Article XXI thereof; and it is understood that the parties have not agreed to arbitrate demands which challenge action taken by the Company in the exercise of any such rights, except where such challenge is based upon a violation of any such express limitations (other than those set out in Section 7 below).

(v) No matter will be considered arbitrable unless it is found that the parties clearly agreed that the subject involved would be arbitrable in light of the principles of arbitrability set forth in this Article and no court or arbitrator shall or may proceed under any presumption that a request to arbitrate is arbitrable.

(c) If a final judgment of a court has determined that a request raises arbitrable issues, the court's decision shall specify in reasonable detail the issues as to which arbitration is directed. The arbitration shall thereafter proceed only upon the issues specified in such final court judgment and the arbitrator shall have no authority or jurisdiction to consider issues other than those specified.

5. The powers of an arbitrator shall include the authority to render a final and binding decision with respect to any dispute brought before him including the right to modify or reduce or rescind any disciplinary action taken by the Company but excluding the right to amend, modify or alter the terms of this Agreement, or any Local Understanding.

The expense of the arbitration will be borne equally by both parties.

Individuals who are covered by this Agreement do not have the right to invoke the arbitration procedure on their own initiative. The arbitration procedure can only be invoked by the Company on its behalf or the Union on behalf of the employees.

6.(a) Arbitration as a matter of right includes only requests to arbitrate which involve:

(i) Disciplinary action (including discharge) or nondisciplinary terminations but with certain exceptions spelled out in this article;

(ii) The claimed violation of a specific provision or provisions of the National Agreement (with the limitations and exceptions set out in this Article);

(iii) The claimed violation of a provision or provisions of a signed Local Seniority Supplement entered into in accordance with Article XI, Section 2 of this National Agreement or of a provision or provisions of a Local Understanding entered into in accordance with Article XXI, Section 3 of this National Agreement.

(b) A request for arbitration, in order to be subject to arbitration as a matter of right under the provisions of Subsections (a)(ii) and (a)(iii) above, must allege a direct violation of the express purpose of the contractual provision in question, rather than of an indirect or implied purpose. For example, a request which claims incorrect application of the method of computing overtime pay under the provisions of Section 2 of Article V would be arbitrable as a matter of right, whereas a request which questioned the right of the Company to require the performance of reasonable overtime work, on the claimed ground that Article V contains an implied limitation of that right, would be subject only to voluntary arbitration. A request that Article XI and the appropriate Local Seniority Supplement had been violated by the layoff of a senior employee in preference to a junior employee would be arbitrable as a matter of right but a request that subcontracting of work in the plant while bargaining unit employees are on layoff violated a claimed implied limitation of Article XI and the applicable Local Seniority Supplement would be subject only to voluntary arbitration.

7. All requests for arbitration which are not subject to arbitration as a matter of right under the provisions of Section 6 above, are subject only to voluntary arbitration. In particular, it is specifically agreed that arbitration requests shall be subject only to voluntary arbitration, by mutual agreement, if they

(a) Involve the existence or alleged violation of any agreement other than those described in 6(a) above.

(b) Involve issues which were discussed at national level negotiations, but which are not expressly covered in this National Agreement.

(c) Involve claims that an allegedly implied or assumed obligation of this National Agreement has been violated.

(d) Involve claims that Article I, or Section 3 of Article IV of this National Agreement has been violated; provided, however, that grievances which claim that a disciplinary action, discharge, upgrading action or transfer action violates Section 3 of Article IV will be subject to arbitration as a matter of right.

(e) Would require an arbitrator to consider, rule on or decide the appropriate hourly, salary or incentive rate at which an employee shall be paid, or the method (day, salary or incentive) by which his pay shall be determined. (See footnote*)

(f) Would require an arbitrator to consider, rule on or decide any of the following:

(i) The elements of an employee's job assignment;

---

*Subsections e, f, and g reflect the fact that this National Agreement does not set out specific rates or classifications for jobs, and are designed to confirm the intent of Article VI, Section 1 and Article VI, Section 5 (first sentence) that disputes over individual job classifications, rates of pay, incentive standards, etc., are assigned by the parties to local negotiations and not to arbitration.

(ii) The level, title or other designation of an employee's job classification;

(iii) The right of management to assign or reassign work or elements of work. (See footnote [on page 336])

(g) Would require an arbitrator to determine the method or data to be used by the Company in setting an incentive price or standard. (See footnote [on page 336])

(h) Involve claims of violation of Sections 1 and 2 of Article XI, in locations in which a Local Seniority Supplement has not been signed in accordance with Section 2 of Article XI.

(i) Pertain in any way to the establishment, administration, interpretation or application of Insurance, Pension or Savings Plans, or other Benefit plans in which employees covered by this Agreement are eligible to participate.

(j) Involve discipline or discharge imposed on employees having less than six months of service credits with the Company, provided that if by Local Understanding a period of less than six months has been agreed upon as the probationary period for new employees, and such Local Understanding is applicable to the particular employee involved, such agreed upon shorter period of time shall be substituted for "six months" in the foregoing; and provided further that nothing in this subsection shall limit the authority of an arbitrator with respect to disciplinary penalties or discharges imposed in violation of Section 1 of Article IV.

(k) Pertain in any way to Article XXII of this Agreement or its interpretation or application.

(l) Pertain in any way to the provisions of any local agreement covering a retraining program under the provisions of Article XXIV hereof, or the interpretation or application thereof.

8.(a) The parties shall refrain from requesting transcripts for those hearings where the submission to arbitration meets the following criteria:

(i) The interpretation of one or more provisions of the collective bargaining agreement is not involved; and

(ii) There is [sic] no "procedural" questions such as arbitrability or due process; and

(iii) There is no claim alleging discrimination in violation of Section 3 of Article IV of this Agreement; and

(iv) The only issue in a discharge or discipline case is whether the discharge or discipline was imposed for just cause.

(b) An arbitrator shall give his Award without an Opinion in certain arbitration cases in accordance with the following:

(i) An Award without an Opinion shall consist of a summary statement by an arbitrator of no more than two pages which briefly sets forth the basis of the Award.

(ii) An Award without an Opinion shall be given in all discipline or discharge cases meeting the criteria in Section 8(a), above, under the following procedure:

(1) If the party requesting arbitration believes the grievance meets the criteria, that party would so indicate in its written request for arbitration.

(2) If the party requesting arbitration does not indicate in its written request for arbitration that it believes the case meets the criteria, the other party may indicate that it believes the grievance meets the criteria in its written agreement to arbitrate.

(3) If the party requesting arbitration indicates that it believes the grievance meets the criteria in 8(a), above, in its request for arbitration, or if the other party so indicates in its written agreement to arbitrate, the Association will instruct the designated arbitrator to issue an Award without an Opinion subject to the discretion given the arbitrator in (4) below.

(4) If either party disagrees with the indication of the other party (provided for in (1) and (2), above) that the grievance meets the criteria set forth in 8(a), above, that party may request a written Opinion from the arbitrator so long as such request is made before the hearing is closed. When such a request is made by either party, the arbitrator shall rule whether a written Opinion is waived under the criteria set forth in 8(a) above.

(5) If evidence is admitted during the hearing at the instance of either party which, in the judgment of the other party, would change the case from one meeting the criteria in 8(a), above, to a case not meeting the criteria, the other party may then demand a written Opinion so long as such demand is made before the oral hearing is closed—notwithstanding prior agreement to waive the Opinion. This provision, however, should not be interpreted in any way to imply that either party would agree to the introduction of evidence at the hearing which would change the nature of the case.

9. Any arbitration case between the Company and the Union which is limited to a disciplinary penalty other than discharge is covered by the supplemental arbitration procedure set forth below:

(a) The following rules shall apply in cases covered by this section:

(i) The only issue before the arbitrator shall be whether the discipline was imposed for just cause.

(ii) There shall be no transcript of the hearing.

(iii) There shall be no post-hearing briefs or other written arguments by the parties.

(iv) If either party so requests, there shall be a thirty (30) minute recess before any closing oral argument by the parties.

(v) The arbitrator shall render an Award without an Opinion no more than twenty-four (24) hours after the closing of the oral hearing.

(b) The compensation for an arbitrator for hearing a case under this procedure shall be a fee of $450.00 for each case. The arbitrator shall also be entitled to travel expenses in accordance with the regular procedures of the American Arbitration Association.

(c) A special panel of arbitrators shall be established to hear cases under this procedure by mutual agreement of the parties.

(d) Whenever a request for arbitration meets the criteria set forth above, the Association shall designate an arbitrator from the special panel of arbitrators, as provided for herein, to hear the case instead of a regular Contract Arbitrator, as provided for in Section 3(a) of this Article, as follows:

 (i) Assignments will be made by the American Arbitration Association based on the arbitrators' geographical proximity, the availability of the arbitrators, and the number of cases assigned particular arbitrators at given locations. No arbitrator will be assigned to more than 25% of the cases at a given location under this procedure without the mutual consent of the parties.

 (ii) A date for a hearing shall be scheduled within sixty (60) days of the appointment of the arbitrator.

Article XVI. Posting

The Company will make bulletin boards available for the use of the Locals for the posting of notices. All notices shall be subject to the Manager's approval and he will also arrange for posting.

Article XVII. Notification and Publicity

1. The Company agrees to notify the Local and the National Officers of any matter affecting employees generally and concerning which the Union or the Local is the certified bargaining representative and not covered by this Agreement as soon as the Foremen are notified.

2. On any grievance or other matter which has been negotiated between the Company and the Union or the Local, the Company will notify the Union or Local of any decision or determination before it notifies the employees affected.

Article XVIII. Financial Support

The Company shall not give financial aid to or otherwise support any labor organization. This, however, shall not prevent both parties to this contract from cooperating and exchanging such information essential for the furtherance of agreeable relations.

Article XIX. Information

1. *New Employees-Reengaged Employees*

The Company will provide each Local, from information of record, with a monthly list of newly hired and reengaged employees; the information will consist of name, home address, seniority date, occupation, department, Foreman, and checkoff status.

2. *Laid Off Employees*

The Company will provide each Local, on a monthly basis, with information on employees laid off for lack of work after notification has been given to the employees; the information will consist of the name, home address of record, continuous service date, occupation, department, and Foreman. The Foreman will give to the Steward information on extended layoffs, whenever possible one week before the employee is laid off.

3. *Transfers*

The Company will provide each Local with information on transfers which are made through the Personnel Office.

4. *Master List of Employees*

Semiannually, the Company, from information of record, will provide the Local with a compete list of all employees then in the bargaining unit and showing the name, home address, continuous service date, seniority date, occupation, department, job rate, paid rate/average earnings, clock card number, and checkoff status of each employee on such list.

Article XX. Traveling Time and Expenses

Hourly rated and salaried employees traveling at the request and with the prior approval of the Company will receive:

1. Payment at the rates applicable had they worked for all time spent in such travel; provided, however, that where transportation with sleeping accommodations is used, an additional one hour's pay at such rates for trip preparation shall be allowed, but no payment shall be made for traveling time between the hours of 6:00 p.m. and 6:00 a.m., or in excess of eight hours in any one day.

2. Reasonable expenses for transportation, meals, and hotels wherever necessary. Where travel is by automobile not owned by the Company, such transportation expense shall be at the rate of **twenty-nine (29)** cents per mile or as negotiated locally, provided use of such automobile has been specifically approved in advance by the Company. (Apparatus Service Centers are covered by a separate supplement.)

3. Traveling time and expenses shall be itemized and submitted to Management for approval.

Article XXI. Local Understandings

1. The provisions of this Agreement are subject to all present local understandings, and such understandings will remain in effect unless changed in the manner provided in the following section.

2. After the effective date of this Agreement, new local understandings will be recognized and made effective only where set forth in writing and signed by local management and the Local, and approved by the Company and the Union.

3. The existence of, or any alleged violation of, a local understanding shall not be the basis of any arbitration proceeding, unless such understanding is in writing and signed by the Company and Union.

Article XXII. Job and Income Security

1. *Definitions*
(a) The terms "plant closing" and "to close a plant" mean the announcement and carrying out of a plan to terminate and discontinue either all Company operations at any plant, service shop, or other facility, or those Company operations which would result in the termination of all employees represented by the Union at that location when those employees do not have displacement rights.

Such terms do not refer to the termination and discontinuance of only part of the Company's operations at any plant, service shop, or other facility (except as specifically provided in the paragraph above) nor to the termination or discontinuance of all of its former operations coupled with the announced intention to commence there either larger or smaller other operations. Any employees released by such later changes will be considered as out for lack of work and will be subject to provisions applicable to those on layoff.

Also, such terms do not refer to the transfer or sale of such operations to a successor employer who offers continued employment to Company employees. Company employees who are not offered continued employment by the Company or by the successor employer will be considered as out for lack of work and will be subject to provisions applicable to those on layoff.

(b) The term "plant closing date" means the day when benefits for and terminations of represented employees begin because of a plant closing.

(c) The terms "transfer of work," "to transfer work," and "work transfer" mean the discontinuance of ongoing work at one location coupled with the assignment of the same work to a different location, including subcontracting the same work to another employer, if such assignment of work would directly cause a decrease in the number of represented employees performing such work at the first location.

(d) The term "robot" means a programmable, multifunction manipulator designed to move materials, parts, tools, or specialized devices through variable programmed motions for the performance of a variety of tasks.

(e) The term "automated manufacturing machine" means a device for doing work which has programmable controllers (PC), numerical controls (NC), computer numerical controls (CNC) or direct numerical controls (DNC).

(f) The term "automated office machine" means a device for doing office work which is computer-based and which includes word processing, data processing, image processing, electronic mail or business and engineering graphics devices.

(g) The term "week's pay" as used in this Article XXII, for a salaried employee shall be the higher of (a) the employee's normal straight-time weekly salary (including any night shift bonus) for the last full week worked by him or (b) the employee's normal straight-time weekly salary (including any night shift bonus) in effect during the last full calendar week worked by him during the calendar year preceding the year in which his current layoff began. A "week's pay" for an hourly employee on daywork shall be calculated by multiplying the higher of (a) his straight-time hourly rate (including any night shift bonus) which he was paid during the last week worked by him or (b) his straight-time hourly rate (including any night shift bonus) which he was paid during the last full calendar week worked by him during the calendar year preceding the year in which his current layoff began, times the number of hours in the employee's normal workweek, up to 40 hours. A "week's pay" for an hourly employee on incentive shall be calculated by multiplying the higher of (a) his average straight-time earning rate (including any night shift bonus) obtained from the last available periodic statistics applicable to time worked by him during his last week worked or (b) his average straight-time earning rate (including any night shift bonus) obtained from the last available periodic statistics applicable to time worked by him during the calendar year preceding the year in which his current layoff began, times the number of hours in the employee's normal work week, up to 40 hours.

(h) The term "Special Early Retirement Option Offset" includes the present value of the difference between the pension benefits the employee would be eligible to receive absent exercise of the Special Early Retirement Option or the Plant Closing Pension Option, and the benefits to be received under the Special Early Retirement Option or the Plant Closing Pension Option, including the present value of any Pension Plan Supplements payable as a result of a permanent job loss event as defined in the GE Pension Plan. This difference shall be measured from the date of termination for retirement to the date the individual would be otherwise able to receive an unreduced pension. For the purpose of determining present value, the interest rate discount assumption will be that used (as of the beginning of the calendar year in which the employee retires) by the Pension Benefit Guaranty Corporation in determining the present value of immediate annuities for terminating single employer trusteed plans.

This Special Early Retirement Option Offset shall also include an amount attributable to health benefits payable as a result of a permanent job loss event as defined in the GE Pension Plan. This amount will be calculated by multiplying $3,000 times the number of whole years between the date of termination for retirement and the date when first eligible for Medicare. The resulting number shall be reduced by a factor equivalent to the percent of employee contributions toward the average value of health coverage at the time of the Special Early Retirement Option or Plant Closing Pension Option election. The $3,000 figure shall be adjusted annually based on annual increases in the medical component of the Consumer Price Index for all-urban consumers. The annual adjustment will be made at the end of the calendar year based on the year over year increases of the October index figures.

2. *Plant Closing*
(a) *General*
   (1) Whenever the Company decides to close a plant, the Company shall give notice of its decision to the Union, the Local or Locals involved, and the employees concerned. Thereafter, as the Company, in the course of such plant closing, no longer has need for the work then being done by an employee, his employment by the Company may be terminated, subject to compliance with the provisions of this Section 2.
   (2) Each employee shall be given at least one week's advance notice of the specific date of his termination.
(b) *Severance Pay*
   (1) An eligible employee whose employment is terminated because of plant closing shall be entitled to Severance Pay in a lump sum, for which he is eligible as described below and the full vacation allowance for which he might have qualified for the calendar year in which his employment is terminated and any other accumulated allowances due him, provided that **after** the announcement of **intent to close a** plant **he:**
      (i) continues regularly at work **at** the **closing location** until the specific date of his termination, or
      (ii) **fails** to continue regularly at work until the specific date of his termination due to verified personal illness, leave of absence, or layoff. **An eligible employee will be similarly eligible for Severance Pay and his full vacation allowance if he was laid off or was placed on an approved illness or injury absence prior to the Company's announcement of intent to close a plant** and continues on layoff **with protected service, or on illness or injury absence with protected service, until the location's plant closing date.**

(2) Such employee may request that his date of termination be advanced so that he can accept other employment and the local management will give due regard to this request.

(3) Notwithstanding the provisions of this Section 2, an employee who is affected by plant closing may elect, prior to the specific date of his termination for plant closing, to be placed on lack of work status. In such event, the employee will be paid benefits under Section 4 below, in lieu of any and all of the benefits set forth in this Section 2.

(4) *Computation of Severance Pay*

(i) An employee with **one** or more but less than fifteen years of continuous service will, in accordance with the provisions set forth above, be eligible for Severance Pay computed on the basis of one and ½ week's pay for each of the employee's full years of continuous service plus ⅜ of a week's pay for each additional 3 months of continuous service at the time of termination; provided that the amount of the Severance Pay benefit as computed under this paragraph shall be subject to a minimum benefit equal to 4 weeks' pay.

(ii) An employee with fifteen or more years of continuous service will, in accordance with the provisions set forth above, be eligible for Severance Pay computed on the basis of two weeks' pay for each of the employee's full years of continuous service plus ½ of a week's pay for each additional 3 months of continuous service at the time of termination.

(5) *Deferral Election.* An employee who elects to receive Severance Pay in a lump sum may elect to defer payment of half or all of the lump sum until the first month of the year following his termination because of a plant closing. Once made, such election will be irrevocable. **Payment shall be made to the estate of any employee electing to defer payment under this Section 2(b)(5) if such employee dies before payment has been made.**

(c) *Employment Assistance Program.* To assist employees terminated because of a plant closing to find new jobs and to learn new skills, local management will establish an Employment Assistance Program following announcement of a decision to close a plant. The Employment Assistance Program will include job placement assistance and education and retraining assistance.

(1) *Job Placement Assistance*

(i) Job Placement Assistance will include job counselling as well as job information services. Examples of such services are counselling in job search and interviewing techniques, identification and assessment of skills, and employment application and resume preparation as well as providing employees information on placement opportunities.

(ii) Local Union involvement will be encouraged in these activities and local management may also use the expertise and resources of public and private agencies in providing these services.

(iii) Two (2) employee representatives designated by the Local (one such representative in a plant of less than 300 represented employees) will each be paid by the Company at their respective rate then prevailing, for approved absences from work up to a total of eight (8) hours per week to work with local management in the establishment and operation of the Employment Assistance Program.

(2) *Education and Retraining Assistance*

(i) An employee with **one** or more years of continuous service who is terminated as a result of a plant closing will be eligible to receive Education and Retraining Assistance for courses approved by the Company which contribute to or enhance the employee's ability to obtain other employment provided that the employee begins the approved course within one year following termination. Approved courses will normally be given at schools which are accredited by recognized regional or state accrediting agencies and may include:

- Occupational or vocational skill development;
- Fundamental reading or numerical skill improvement;
- High school diploma or equivalency achievement; and
- College level career oriented courses.

(ii) An employee will be reimbursed up to a maximum of five thousand ($5,000) for authorized expenses which are incurred within three years following termination provided a passing grade is received in the course. Authorized expenses include verified tuition, registration and other compulsory fees, costs of necessary books, and other required supplies. However, if tuition or other authorized expenses are covered by government benefits, other employers, or scholarships, the Company reimbursement will not apply to that portion covered by such other plan.

(iii) An employee who elects to receive benefits under the Income Extension Aid layoff option in lieu of benefits under the Plant Closing section of this Article will not be eligible for Education and Retraining Assistance.

(d) *Preferential Hiring*

(1) *Election.* An hourly rated or nonexempt salaried employee eligible for Severance Pay under this Section 2 may elect, prior to the employee's termination for plant closing or within thirty (30) days following the employee's scheduled termination date for plant closing, to be placed in a Preferential Hiring status. During this period, the employee will be considered eligible for IEA* benefits provided he otherwise meets the requirements in Section 4(b)(1)(i). If at the end of the thirty (30) day period the affected employee does not elect to participate in Preferential Hiring, the amount of Severance Pay available under this

---

*Income extension aid (see page 351).—EDS.

Section 2, less any amount paid in IEA benefits, will be paid in lump sum and the employee will terminate service. When making this election, the employee shall designate up to three (3) domestic General Electric Company manufacturing plant, service shop or distribution center locations. Up to three location substitutions to those designated will be permitted during the three year eligibility period. Locations which are opened or closed during an eligibility period may be added or eliminated from the designated locations and shall not be considered one of the three substitutions, provided however that no more than three locations may be designated at any one time. The election shall be effective for three years. Election of Preferential Hiring status will not affect an individual's continuity of service.

(2) *Procedure.* Individuals who have made this election for Preferential Hiring will be placed in a Preferential Hiring status on their designated termination date for plant closing. Individuals in a Preferential Hiring status will be given preference, to the extent practical, over new hires for job openings at the locations designated by them in order of their length of continuity of service when such individuals with the necessary qualifications are available. **Individuals who accept a job offer under Preferential Hiring status and who fail to report as scheduled without satisfactory explanation shall forfeit their right to remain in this status.**

(3) *Layoff Benefits.* While in a Preferential Hiring status, an eligible employee will be paid IEA-type layoff benefits under the procedures set forth in Section 4(b)(1)(i) of this Article up to the amount of the employee's eligibility for Severance Pay under Section 2(b)(4) of this Article in lieu of any and all other benefits set forth in this Section 2; **provided, however, that an eligible employee may receive reimbursement for authorized expenses incurred pursuant to Section 2(c)(2) respecting courses registered for within one year, and completed within three years, of the employee's scheduled plant closing date.** If reemployed from Preferential Hiring status, IEA-type layoff benefits must be repaid in order to restore eligibility for IEA benefits based on prior service for future layoffs under Section 4(a)(2) of this Article. **This repayment obligation shall be reduced by the weekly amounts the employee earned under Section 2(b)(4), based on years of continuous service, for each year of continuous service or seniority previously acquired at the employee's prior work location which the local union has agreed to recognize.**

(4) *Seniority.* Individuals reemployed under this Section 2(d) will have seniority for the purpose of subsequent layoff, recall, upgrading and other seniority purposes at their new locations based upon the established seniority procedures and practices at their new location.

(5) *Relocation Assistance.* If an individual employee who elected Preferential Hiring is reemployed under this Section 2(d) within three

(3) years from that individual's designated date of termination for plant closing, that employee shall be eligible for reimbursement for substantiated reasonable and necessary relocation expenses to the new location up to **a maximum** of **$1,500** for individual employees without dependents or **$3,000** for employees with dependents living in the employee's home (as verified by federal income tax returns). **An eligible employee who has elected Preferential Hiring is eligible for reimbursement of documented expenses up to $100 per interview incurred for the purpose of attending approved placement interviews at selected locations.**

(6) *Severance Pay.* If an individual employee who elected Preferential Hiring is not reemployed by the Company within one year from that individual's designated date of termination for plant closing, that individual will then be deemed to have been terminated as of that individual's designated date of termination for plant closing and paid the Severance Pay the individual would have received under this Section 2(b)(4) if the Preferential Hiring option had not been elected, less any layoff benefit paid under (3) of this Section 2(d) while in the Preferential Hiring status.

(7) *Limited Pre-Closing Election.* **Employees on active payroll at a location which the Company has announced its decision to close, may be afforded a limited, advanced opportunity to elect Preferential Hiring. Such election must be in writing and, upon management approval, will entitle the employee to be considered for placement under Preferential Hiring at up to three (3) domestic General Electric Company locations prior to the employee's designated termination date for plant closing. If the employee so electing is hired under Preferential Hiring prior to his plant closing date, the employee will be eligible for relocation and job interview assistance under Section 2(d)(5). The electing employee shall not be eligible for any other benefits available under Article XXII or the GE Pension Plan prior to his designated termination date for plant closing. If, on or before his designated termination date for plant closing, the employee electing Preferential Hiring under this paragraph has not been hired at a selected location, Preferential Hiring status under this paragraph shall automatically terminate unless renewed in writing by the employee. In either case, the benefits available to the employee, provided he otherwise qualifies under Section 2, shall be those benefits available to employees eligible for Plant Closing benefits under Section 2, without regard to the employee's pre-Plant Closing election under this paragraph. In the case of renewal of Preferential Hiring Status, such status shall continue for three years from the employee's designated termination date for plant closing.**

(e) *Optional Local Plant Closing Termination Agreement.* Because the circumstances in a plant closing will vary in terms of employment, location and timing, as well as other local considerations, the Local Union and local management may negotiate a Special Local Agreement covering the plant closing termination procedure for employees represented by the Local. Any such agreement shall be in writing and approved in accordance with Article XXI, Section 2, of this National Agreement.

3. *Retraining and Readjustment Assistance*

(a) *Rate Guarantee.* An hourly rated or nonexempt salaried employee whose job is directly eliminated by a transfer of work, the discontinuance of a discrete, unreplaced product line, the introduction of a robot, or the introduction of an automated manufacturing or office machine shall be paid on any job to which transferred or recalled in the plant at a rate not less than the regular hourly daywork rate (average earnings exclusive of overtime premium in the case of incentive workers and actual straight time salary rate in the case of nonexempt salaried employees) of the job eliminated for up to seventy-eight (78) weeks immediately following the original transfer or layoff.

(b) *Special Retirement Bonus*

(1) *Election.* An hourly rated or nonexempt salaried employee who is age sixty (60) or older with fifteen (15) or more years of continuous service and is assigned to a job classification which the Company has announced is expected to be directly adversely affected by a transfer of work, the discontinuance of a discrete, unreplaced product line, the introduction of a robot, or the introduction of an automated manufacturing or office machine may elect to be considered for termination with a Special Retirement Bonus. This election shall be made within fifteen (15) days following the Company announcement of its decision involving the transfer of work, the discontinuance of a discrete, unreplaced product line, introduction of a robot, or introduction of an automated manufacturing or office machine which is expected to result in the elimination of certain jobs.

(2) *Procedure.* Eligible employees electing this option will be designated by their seniority for a Special Retirement Bonus. A termination under this option will be effective and the Special Retirement Bonus will be paid when a job in the particular job classification to which the eligible employee is assigned is directly eliminated by the previously announced transfer of work, the discontinuance of a discrete, unreplaced product line, introduction of a robot, or introduction of an automated manufacturing or office machine, which directly results in a net reduction in the total number of employees working in that same job classification.

(3) *Special Payment.* This Special Retirement Bonus shall be **$10,000.**

(4) *Indirect Bonus Eligibility.* In the event that the number of eligible employees electing this option is less than the number of employees directly adversely affected by the Company's announced action, opportunities to elect Special Voluntary Layoff Bonus under Section 4(c) shall

arise, up to the number of positions directly adversely affected by the transfer of work, the discontinuance of a discrete, unreplaced product line, or the introduction of an automated manufacturing or office machine. To be eligible an employee must be in a classification that is reduced due to displacement as a result of an announced Company action described above, and otherwise meets the criteria established in Section 4(c). Such displacement is hereby deemed to be a reduction of force of indefinite duration.

(c) *Special Placement Procedure*

(1) *Election.* An hourly rated employee whose job is directly eliminated by a transfer of work, the discontinuance of a discrete, unreplaced product line, the introduction of a robot, or the introduction of an automated manufacturing machine may request a Special Placement from the eliminated job in lieu of placement, displacement or layoff under the regular local layoff and rehiring procedure. The Special Placement request must be made within two (2) working days following notification to the employee of the regular placement, displacement or layoff.

(2) *Placement*

(i) If a timely request is made, an eligible employee shall be placed, or displace with seniority, on an available equal or lower rated job classification if the employee has the necessary minimum qualifications for the job; provided the Special Placement would be on a higher rated job than that provided by the regular placement.

(ii) If an eligible employee who has made a timely request is unable to be placed under Section 3(c)(2)(i) above, such employee shall be placed, or displaced with seniority, on an equal or lower rated job up to the top of the one month progression schedule without regard to the regular minimum qualifications for the job; provided the Special Placement would be on a higher rated job than that provided by the regular placement.

(iii) An employee placed under this Section 3(c) is required to achieve normal performance within the time period of the regular progression schedule.

(d) *Optional Local Retraining and Placement Agreement.* Whenever the Company announces a transfer of work, the discontinuance of a discrete, unreplaced product line, the introduction of a robot, or the introduction of an automated manufacturing or office machine, the Local Union and local management may negotiate a Local Retraining and Placement Agreement.

(e) *Special Preferential Hiring*

(1) *Election.* An hourly rated or nonexempt salaried employee eligible for Income Extension Aid who is given notice under the local layoff procedure of being displaced and subject to layoff in the immediate chain of displacements resulting when a job is directly eliminated by a transfer of work, the discontinuance of a discrete, unreplaced product

line, the introduction of a robot, or the introduction of an automated manufacturing or office machine may elect, prior to the day of the employee's scheduled layoff because of such Company action, or within thirty (30) days following such layoff if weekly IEA payments have been elected to be placed in a Special Preferential Hiring status. When making this election, an employee shall designate up to three (3) domestic General Electric Company manufacturing plant, service shop or distribution center locations. Up to three location substitutions to those designated will be permitted during the three year eligibility period. Locations which are opened or closed during an eligibility period may be added or deleted from the designated locations and shall not be considered a substitution, provided however that not more than three locations may be designated at any one time. The election shall be effective for three years. Election of Special Preferential Hiring status will not affect an individual's continuity of service.

(2) *Procedure.* Individuals who have made this election for a Special Preferential Hiring status will be placed in a Special Preferential Hiring status at the time of layoff. Individuals in the Special Preferential Hiring status will be given preference, to the extent practical, over new hires for job openings at the locations designated by them in order of their length of continuity of service when such individuals with the necessary qualifications are available. An employee so electing may request that his layoff date be advanced so that he can accept other employment with the Company and local management will give due regard to this request. **Individuals who accept a job offer under Special Preferential Hiring status and who fail to report as scheduled without satisfactory explanation shall forfeit their right to remain in this status.**

(3) *Layoff Benefits.* While in a Special Preferential Hiring status, an eligible employee will be paid IEA layoff benefits under the procedures set forth in Section 4(b)(1)(i) of this Article up to the amount of the employee's eligibility for IEA under Section 4(a)(1) of this Article in lieu of any and all other benefits set forth in this Section. **An eligible employee electing Special Preferential Hiring status is eligible to participate in the Individual Development Program.** If reemployed from Special Preferential Hiring status, IEA benefits must be repaid in order to restore eligibility for IEA benefits based on prior service for future layoffs under Section 4(a)(2) of this Article. **This repayment obligation shall be reduced by the weekly amounts the employee earned under Section 4(a)(1), based on years of continuous service, for each year of continuous service or seniority previously acquired at the employee's prior work location which the local union has agreed to recognize.**

(4) *Seniority.* Individuals reemployed under this Section 3(e) will have seniority for the purpose of subsequent layoff, recall, upgrading and other seniority purposes at their new locations based upon the estab-

lished seniority procedures and practices at their new location. While reemployed at the new location as a result of Special Preferential Hiring, an employee will not be eligible for recall at the old location.

(5) *Relocation Assistance.* If an individual employee who elected Special Preferential Hiring is reemployed under this Section 3(e) within three years from that individual's placement in the Special Preferential Hiring status, that employee shall be eligible for reimbursement for substantiated reasonable and necessary relocation expenses to the new location up to **a maximum** of **$1,500** for individual employees without dependents or **$3,000** for employees with dependents living in the employee's home (as verified by federal income tax returns). **An eligible employee who has elected Special Preferential Hiring is eligible for reimbursement of documented expenses up to $100 per interview incurred for the purpose of attending approved placement interviews at selected locations.**

(6) *Income Extension Aid.* If an individual employee who elected Special Preferential Hiring is not reemployed by the Company within one year from that individual's placement in the Special Preferential Hiring status, that individual will have continuity of service broken and be paid any remaining Income Extension Aid available under Section 4(a)(1), less any layoff benefits paid under (3) of this Section 3(e) while in the Special Preferential Hiring status.

4. *Income Extension Aid*
(a) *Computation of Income Extension Aid*

(1) An employee with **one** or more years of continuous service will, in accordance with the provisions hereinafter set forth, have available Income Extension Aid computed on the basis of one week's pay for each of the employee's full years of continuous service plus ¼ of a week's pay for each additional 3 months of continuous service at the time of layoff.

(2) If the amount of Income Extension Aid available to any employee as computed in Subsection (a)(1) has been reduced by payments under any of the options below, then, providing he has returned to work from layoff, the total amount available as described in Subsection (a)(1) shall be automatically restored. This Subsection (2) shall not apply where payments have been made under Section 4(b)(1)(iii) or under Plant Closing Section 2 where the employee is rehired within 6 months of termination or under Preferential Hiring Section 2(d), except, that when an employee makes repayment of benefits paid under such Section 4(b)(1)(iii) or Section 2, this Subsection (a)(2) shall apply when he returns to work with respect to a subsequent layoff.

(3) *Minimum Benefit.* The amount of the Income Extension Aid benefit as computed under Section 4(a)(1) shall be subject to a minimum benefit equal to 4 weeks' pay. **An employee laid off while in the process**

of service restoration under Article VIII, Section 2(e) shall qualify for the minimum benefit so long as his or her total service credits (including credits not yet restored) equal 24 months.

(b) *Benefits Available at Layoff*

(1) An eligible employee laid off for lack of work may elect from the following:

(i) The employee, while on layoff from the Company and so long as he is unemployed, may elect to receive a weekly payment from the Income Extension Aid payable to him, in such amounts and upon such conditions as set forth in this subsection. Payment may begin only after a one week waiting period following the commencement of layoff.

Prior to the exhaustion of his entitlements to federal and state unemployment compensation benefits, the weekly payment shall be in that amount (if any) which, when added to the total federal and state unemployment compensation benefits received for that week, equals **seventy** percent of his weekly pay as defined in Section 1(g), provided, however, that payment shall be made only if the employee has applied for and received unemployment compensation benefits for that week and only if he has provided the Company with satisfactory proof of the total of such benefits received for the week. In the event an employee seeking benefits under this Section 4 is denied unemployment compensation payment in whole or in part, solely because of a disability arising more than 31 days following layoff rendering the employee unable to work, or due to the receipt of public or private retirement income, because of insufficient earnings to establish unemployment compensation eligibility or because unemployment compensation benefits have been exhausted for the base year, that employee shall be entitled to weekly IEA payment as though there had been no such unemployment compensation disqualification.

After exhaustion of his entitlements to federal and state unemployment compensation benefits, the weekly payment shall be in that amount which equals **seventy** percent of his weekly pay as defined in Section 1(g). Payments shall be made only if the employee certifies that he is still unemployed and they shall continue only until the full amount for which the employee qualifies under Section 4(a) is paid.

Payments (in such amount and upon such conditions as set forth above) may also be made to an employee on layoff while he is unemployed and attending a recognized trade or professional school or training course under the GE Individual Development Program, attendance at which makes him ineligible for state or federal unemployment compensation benefits. **Percentage changes referenced in this Section 4(b)(1)(i) shall be effective 10/1/94.**

(ii) In any event, at the end of one year on layoff, or upon termination of continuity of service due to voluntary retirement, any balance in the Income Extension Aid available to him not theretofore paid will be paid in a lump sum to the employee.

(iii) As a special option, an employee may, with the approval of local management, which approval shall not be unreasonably withheld, elect to receive the total amount of Income Extension Aid and any vacation or other accumulated allowances due, and at the time of such payment, terminate employment and thus forego recall rights.

(2) Income Extension payments made under Subsections (b)(1)(i) and (ii), above, shall not affect service credits previously accumulated, continuity of service, and recall rights. It will not be necessary for an employee to repay any Income Extension Aid payable under said Subsections (b)(1)(i) and (ii) above.

(3) In the event an employee elects, as provided for in Section 7(a) of Article IX of this Agreement with respect to a scheduled shutdown period, to take the time off without pay as though on a temporary layoff, the employee shall not be eligible for Income Extension Aid for that scheduled shutdown period.

(c) *Special Voluntary Layoff Bonus.* Whenever the Company announces an indefinite reduction in force, a Special Voluntary Layoff Bonus opportunity will exist. To be eligible an employee must be age sixty (60) or older, have fifteen (15) years of continuous service, be in a specific job classification directly adversely affected, and must have filed a request to be considered at least fifteen (15) days in advance of the announcement of the indefinite reduction in force. To the extent such requests exceed the number of affected jobs in each classification, selection will be on the basis of seniority. **Alternatively, in the event that the number of eligible employees electing this option is less than the number of employees directly adversely affected, secondary opportunities, up to the total number of positions directly adversely affected, shall be available to eligible employees in classifications affected by displacements resulting from the indefinite reduction in force.** Employees selected for a Special Voluntary Layoff Bonus must confirm their acceptance immediately following the Company's offer of the Special Voluntary Layoff Bonus. Employees accepting a Special Voluntary Layoff Bonus will receive a lump sum payment of **$10,000** in lieu of any other payment under this Article and will terminate service with the Company.

5. *Notice, Bargaining and Information Requirements*

This Section sets forth the full obligations of the Company with regard to notice, bargaining with and information to the Union concerning plant closing, work transfer, subcontracting and the installation of robots or automated manufacturing or office machines.

(a) *Plant Closing*

(1) *Notice.* The Company will give notice of its intent to close a manufacturing plant, service shop or distribution center a minimum of six (6)

months in advance of the plant closing date to the Union, the Local involved and to employees concerned. Such notice will include identification of the plant to be closed, the Local involved and the date when terminations of represented employees because of the plant closing are expected to begin.

(2) *Bargaining.* If the Local requests decision bargaining within ten (10) working days following a Company notice of intent to close a manufacturing plant, service shop, or distribution center, the Company will be available to meet with the Local within five (5) working days of such request and the bargaining period shall continue for up to forty-five (45) calendar days from the date of the Company notice of intent to close the plant unless this period is extended by mutual agreement. The Company will make a decision whether or not to close the plant after this bargaining period.

(3) *Information.* If information is requested by the Local for bargaining provided for in Section 5(a)(2) of this Article, the Company will promptly make the following information available to the Local for such bargaining. This information will specifically include the express reason(s) for intending to close the plant and, where employment cost is a significant factor, the related wages, payroll allowances and employee benefits expenses of represented employees at the plant intended to be closed. This information will be treated as confidential by the Local.

(b) *Transfer of Ongoing Production Work*

(1) *Notice.* The Company will give notice of its intent to transfer ongoing production work a minimum of six (6) months in advance of the effective date of the work transfer to the Local involved. Such notice will include identification of the work to be transferred, the expected decrease in the number of represented employees as a direct consequence of the transfer of work and the anticipated date of the transfer of work.

(2) *Bargaining.* If the Local requests decision bargaining within ten (10) working days following a Company notice of intent to transfer ongoing production work, the Company will be available to meet with the Local within five (5) working days of such request and the bargaining period shall continue for up to forty-five (45) calendar days from the date of the Company notice of intent to transfer the work unless the period is extended by mutual agreement. The Company will make a decision whether or not to transfer such work after this bargaining period.

(3) *Information.* If information is requested by the Local for bargaining provided for in Section 5(b)(2) of this Article, the Company will promptly make the following information available to the Local for such bargaining. The information will specifically include the express reason(s) for intending to transfer the work and, where employment cost is a significant factor, comparative related wages, payroll allowances and employee benefits expenses of represented employees for the work intended to be

transferred and of their counterparts who would be assigned the work. This information will be treated as confidential by the Local.

(c) *Transfer of Nonproduction Work*

(1) *Notice.* The Company will give notice of its intent to transfer nonproduction work, or subcontract nonproduction work at the same plant location **or elsewhere** if such subcontracting of work would directly cause a decrease in the number of represented employees performing such work, a minimum of sixty (60) calendar days in advance of the effective date of the work transfer or subcontracting to the Local involved. Such notice will include identification of the work to be transferred or subcontracted, the expected decrease in the number of represented employees as a direct consequence of the transfer of work or subcontracting and the anticipated date of the transfer of work or subcontracting.

(2) *Bargaining.* If the Local requests decision bargaining within ten (10) working days following a Company notice of intent to subcontract or transfer nonproduction work, the Company will be available to meet with the Local within five (5) working days of such request and the bargaining period shall continue for up to forty-five (45) calendar days from the date of the Company notice of intent to subcontract or transfer the work unless this period is extended by mutual agreement. The Company will make a decision whether or not to subcontract or transfer such work after this bargaining period.

(3) *Information.* If information is requested by the Local for bargaining provided for in Section 5(c)(2) of this Article, the Company will promptly make the following information available to the Local for such bargaining. The information will specifically include the express reason(s) for intending to subcontract or transfer the work and, where employment cost is a significant factor, comparative related wages, payroll allowances and employee benefits expenses of represented employees for the work intended to be subcontracted or transferred and of their counterparts who would be assigned the work. This information will be treated as confidential by the Local.

(d) *Subcontracting of Trades Work at Plant Location*

(1) *Notice.* The Company will give notice to the Local of its intent to subcontract **trades** work, where the work will be done by a subcontractor at the same plant location or elsewhere **and there is no decrease in the number of represented employees performing such trades work,** before finalization of the proposed action provided that the work is of a nature that is normally performed by trades workers (maintenance, tool & die, and other similar classifications). Notice will not be required in emergency situations.

(2) *Bargaining.* If the Local requests bargaining concerning such subcontracting, the Company will promptly meet and discuss its plans with the Local. However, in no event will the Company be obligated to

withhold the effectuation of the proposed subcontracting for more than **twenty-one (21) calendar** days from the date of the notification to the Local.

(3) *Information.* If information is requested by the Local for bargaining provided for in Section 5(d)(2) of this Article, the Company will promptly make the following information available to the Local for such bargaining. This information will specifically include the express reason(s) for intending to subcontract the work and, where employment cost is a significant factor, comparative related wages, payroll allowances and employee benefits expenses of represented employees for the work intended to be subcontracted and of their counterparts who would be assigned the work. This bargaining information will be treated as confidential by the Local.

(e) *Installation of Robots or Automated Manufacturing or Office Machines.* With respect to the installation of robots or automated manufacturing or office machines, the Company will give a minimum of sixty (60) days' notice to the Local involved before the use of a robot or an automated manufacturing or office machine in a work area. Such notice will include a description of the function of the device, identification of the work involved, the expected decrease in the number of represented employees as a direct consequence of the use of the device and the anticipated date of the use of the device.

6. *Vested Rights Under Pension Plan*

The receipt of Income Extension Aid, Severance Pay, or a rate guarantee will not affect any rights the employee may have under the Vesting Provision of the Pension Plan.

7. *Lump Sum Payments*

Service credits previously accumulated, continuity of service, and recall rights will be lost upon receipt by the employee of an Income Extension Aid payment in lump sum under Section 4(b)(1)(iii), special termination payments under this Article, or payment of Severance Pay under the Plant Closing Section 2. However, an employee eligible for such a payment, who is within one year of reaching optional retirement at age 60 under the GE Pension Plan, shall retain such previously accumulated service credits and continuity of service until such employee reaches optional retirement age notwithstanding the receipt of such a payment unless the employee retires before electing optional retirement at age 60.

In the event of a subsequent rehire as a "new" employee within a period of time which does not exceed the length of prior service, service credits, and recall rights previously lost shall be **automatically** restored provided repayment of the Income Extension Aid is made by the employee within a reasonable time after rehire. **No such repayment, however, shall be required if the rehire date is more than one year from the date of termination which resulted from the election of a lump sum payment under Section 4(b)(1)(iii) or the special termination payments under Section 3(b) or Section 4(c).**

Service credits, continuity of service, and recall rights lost at termination upon receipt of payments under Plant Closing Section 2, shall be restored automatically without repayment in the event of subsequent rehire more than 6 months after such termination. An employee who having received payments under Plant Closing Section 2, is rehired 6 months or less after his termination and who has made arrangements satisfactory to the Company providing for repayment shall, during such time as he is not in default of such arrangements and for the purpose only of layoff and recall, be deemed to possess the service credits, continuity of service, and recall rights to be restored to him upon full repayment.

8. *Non-Duplication*

If any part of an employee's continuous service is used as the basis for an actual payment under any of the options of the Income Extension Aid or Severance Pay arrangement, that part of his continuous service may not be used again for such purpose, either during that period of layoff or any subsequent period of layoff or plant closing, unless repayment has been made as provided in Section 7, above.

Where an indefinite reduction in force triggers eligibility for benefits under this Article, the designation of individuals who may exercise the benefits under this Article will be based on the integrated order of their seniority so that the number of employees electing benefits does not exceed the net number of positions eliminated.

Employees, eligible for a benefit under this Article either by designation or by election, may exercise only one severance or layoff benefit. Employees who have exercised the Special Early Retirement Option or Plant Closing Pension Option under the Pension Plan shall have the Special Early Retirement Option Offset deducted from any severance or layoff benefit otherwise due under this Article.

9. *Other*

The provisions of this article shall not be applicable where the Company decides to close a plant or lay off an employee because of the Company's inability to secure production, or carry on its operations, as a consequence of a strike, slowdown, or other interference with or interruption with work participated in by employees in a Company plant, service shop, or other facility. However, the operation of this section shall not affect the rights or benefits already provided hereunder to an employee laid off for lack of work prior to the commencement of any such strike, interference, or interruption.

10. A grievance arising under this article may be processed in accordance with the grievance procedure set forth in Article XIII. However, no matter or controversy concerning the provisions of this article or the interpretation or application thereof shall be subject to arbitration under the provisions of Article XV hereof, except by mutual agreement.

Article XXIII. Military Pay Differential

An employee with 30 days or more of service credits attending annual encampments of or training duty in the Armed Forces, State or National Guard or U.S. Reserves shall be granted a military pay differential, computed as set forth below, for a period of up to 17 days of such military service, during each calendar year. The employee shall be granted service credits for such 17 day period or portion thereof during which he is absent. Such military pay differential shall be the amount by which the employee's normal straight time wages or salary, calculated on the basis of a workweek up to a maximum of 40 hours, which the employee has lost by virtue of such absence, exceeds any pay received for such absence from the Federal or State Government, recalculated to exclude the Government pay applicable to Saturdays and Sundays. Saturdays and Sundays shall be counted in computing the 17 day period. Such items as subsistence, rental, and travel allowance shall not be included in determining pay received from the Government.

An employee with 30 days or more of service credits who does not exhaust the 17 calendar day period during the calendar year for his annual encampment or training duty and who is required during the same calendar year to attend a weekend period of training shall be granted a military pay differential provided that the 17 calendar day period of military service in the same calendar year is not exceeded. Such military pay differential shall be the amount by which the employee's normal straight time pay, calculated on the basis of a nonpremium workday, up to a maximum of eight (8) hours, which the employee has lost by virtue of such absence, exceeds any pay received for such day or days of absence from the Federal or State Government, recalculated to exclude the Government pay applicable to Saturdays and Sundays. Saturdays and Sundays shall be counted for the purpose of determining the extent to which the 17 calendar days of military service have been utilized in the same manner as annual encampment or training duty.

An employee with 30 days or more of service credits, who is called out by the National Guard or the U.S. Reserves to perform temporary emergency duty (other than duty under an order by the President or Congress activating members or units of the Reserves or National Guard) due to a fire, flood, or domestic civil disturbance, or other such disaster will be paid a military differential calculated as described above, for the pay lost by reason of such emergency duty, for a period not to exceed **eight** weeks in any calendar year and shall be granted service credits for such absence up to **eight** weeks.

An employee who has less than 30 days of service credits may also be absent for the reasons and periods set forth above without deduction of service credits for such absence, but shall not be eligible for the military pay differential.

Employees will be permitted to take a vacation and attend a military encampment at separate times and be granted both a vacation pay allowance and a military pay differential. However, an employee may not receive a vacation pay allowance and a military pay differential for the same period. An employee may, however, receive a military pay differential for the period, if any, by which the time spent in such encampment exceeds such vacation, but not exceeding the maximums specified above.

Article XXIV. Retraining Program

1. Retraining Programs as appropriate for employees represented by each Local are subject to negotiations between the Local and local management. Any written agreements covering such Retraining Programs are subject to approval by the Union and the Company.

2. No matter or controversy concerning the provisions of this article or any local retraining agreement shall be arbitrable except by mutual agreement.

Article XXV. Jury Duty

1. When an hourly-paid employee is called for service as a juror, he will be paid **upon proof of service** the amount of straight-time earnings lost by him by reason of such service, up to a limit of 8 hours per day and 40 hours per week.

2. When a salaried employee is called for service as a juror, he will continue to be paid his normal straight-time salary during the period of such service.

3. Similar makeup pay as specified in Sections 1 and 2 will be granted to an employee who loses time from work because of his appearance in court pursuant to proper subpoena, except when he is either a plaintiff, defendant, or other party to the court proceeding.

Article XXVI. Absence for Death in Family

An hourly paid employee with 30 days or more of service credits who is absent from work solely because of the death and funeral of his or her spouse, child, stepchild, **stepbrother, stepsister,** foster child (if living in the employee's home), grandchild, son-in-law, daughter-in-law, parent, stepparent, grandparent, grandparent-in-law, brother, brother-in-law, sister, sister-in-law, mother-in-law, or father-in-law, will be compensated, on the basis of his average straight-time earnings, for the time lost by him from his regular schedule by reason of such absence, for three days for each such absence and up to eight hours per day. In the event of death of the employee's spouse, child, stepchild or foster child, an additional two days absence (up to eight hours per day) shall be allowed.

Article XXVII. Sick and ÏPay

1. An hourly employee with one or more years of continuous service, absent because of (a) personal business, **or** (b) personal illness for which weekly disability benefits are not payable under the General Electric Insurance Plan, or under Workmen's Compensation, will **be paid** Sick and Personal Pay for each absence of **an hour** or longer, up to the number of **hours** applicable in accordance with the following schedule:

Continuous Service	*Maximum* **Hours** *of Sick and Personal Pay for Each Calendar Year*
1 through 9 years	**16 Hours**
10 through 14 years	**24 Hours**
15 through 24 years	**32 Hours**
25 years and over	**40 Hours**

Sick and Personal Pay **for absences of an hour or longer shall be calculated based on** the actual scheduled hours of work during which **the employee** was absent. In no event will the payment for hours absent exceed the number of hours in the employee's established regular daily schedule.

An employee **may seek approval from his Manager to utilize Sick and Personal Pay for absences due to an observed holiday or temporary layoff.** Management approval, as provided herein, will not be unreasonably withheld. **An employee is expected to notify his Manager in advance of the absence whenever possible, in order that the Manager may have an opportunity to arrange for a replacement or to reschedule the work.**

2. *Accumulation of Sick and Personal Pay*

An employee who has any unused Sick and Personal Pay remaining at the end of a calendar year **may elect during November of each year to accumulate** such unused Sick and Personal Pay, up to a maximum of thirty (30) days, **and have such pay** carried forward to the following calendar year for use in the event of approved absences. **Absent such an election, all unused Sick and Personal Pay attributable to the current year will be paid as an allowance during the last pay period of the calendar year at rates specified under Section 3. Notwithstanding anything to the contrary in Section 1, effective 7/1/95, an employee who is otherwise eligible for Short Term Disability benefits under the GE Life, Disability and Medical Plan may be retained at full pay during an extended absence due to illness or injury, to** the extent possible, by combining any accumulated pay under this Section with Short Term Disability benefits.

3. *Rate of Pay*

The rate of pay applicable to absences covered under this article will be current normal straight-time hourly earnings in effect when last at work prior to the absence, including night shift bonus for employees who are regularly scheduled on a night shift. (In cases of pieceworkers, the normal straight-time hourly wages as determined for the last periodic earnings statistics will be used.)

4. *Half-Day Definition*

A half-day is defined as half of the number of hours in the employee's established regular daily schedule, or the entire segment of the employee's workday either preceding or following the employee's established lunch period.

5. *Maximum Hours*

(a) The maximum Sick and Personal Pay hours payable for any one day of approved absence will be the number of hours in the employee's established regular daily schedule in effect when last at work prior to the absence.

(b) The maximum hours of Sick and Personal Pay payable to an employee in a calendar year will be the **maximum** number of Sick and Personal Pay **hours** based on the employee's continuous service **as stated in Section 1.**

In addition, any unused Sick and Personal Pay up to a maximum of thirty (30) days carried over from the preceding calendar year, will be available for payment of approved absences. Such thirty (30) day maximum will be converted to hours on the basis of the employee's established regular daily schedule of work hours (up to a maximum daily rate of eight (8) hours) in effect at the end of such preceding calendar year.

When the hours of an employee's established regular daily schedule are changed during the course of a calendar year, the maximum Sick and Personal Pay hours payable to such employee for that calendar year will be adjusted by determining the proportion of the maximum Sick and Personal Pay hours used by the employee prior to such change (based on the regular daily schedule of work hours in effect before the change) and then reducing by the same proportion the employee's revised maximum hours based on the regular daily schedule of work hours in effect after the change.

6. *Sick and Personal Pay Allowance*

When an employee is terminated because of a plant closing or the sale of a business to a successor employer and the successor employer does not have a similar sick and/or personal pay benefit, the employee will receive an allowance in lieu of any unused sick and/or personal days. Similarly, an allowance in lieu of any unused sick and/or personal days will be paid if an employee retires, **dies or breaks continuity of service due to layoff.**

Article XXVIII. Upgrading and Job Posting

1. *Standard for Filling Open Jobs and Upgrading*

The Company will, to the extent practical, give first consideration for job openings and upgrading to present employees, when employees with the necessary qualifications are available. In upgrading employees to higher rated jobs, the Company will take into consideration as an important factor, the relative length of **seniority** of the employees who it finds are qualified for such upgrading; provided, however, that in upgrading employees to job openings with job rates within the one-month progression schedule, as provided for in Article VI, Section 5(a)(4)(a) of this Agreement, the relative seniority of those employees found qualified for such upgrading shall be the controlling factor.

When filling a job opening by upgrading, a request for the open job by an employee in a different, equal rated job classification or a higher rated job classification shall be treated as though it were a request to be considered for a higher rated job classification if the job opening affords the employee with an immediate or future higher earnings opportunity; provided that the employee has not previously so transferred during the same calendar year.

2. *Local Negotiations*

Because the product mix, organization complexity, and other circumstances vary in the plant locations covered by this agreement and to improve the opportunity for upward mobility of all employees represented by the Union and to continue to assure an equal opportunity for such employees to express their interests in and be considered for upgrading to job openings without regard to race, color, sex, creed, marital status, age, or national origin, local management and the Local Union shall negotiate a written upgrading agreement for each of the locations listed in the Preamble. In order to implement the provisions of Section 1, above, it is the intent of the parties that such agreement would provide for advance notice of job openings which are to be filled by upgrading where practical. Such agreement shall be approved in accordance with Article XXI, Section 2, of this National Agreement and shall not alter any obligation or right not to fill an opening by upgrading nor shall it limit any right an employee or the Union may have under Article XIII, XIV, and XV of this National Agreement to protest a selection.

Article XXIX. Responsibility of the Parties

The parties recognize that, under this Agreement, each of them has responsibilities for the welfare and security of the employees:

(a) The Company recognizes that it is the responsibility of the Union to represent the employees effectively and fairly;

(b) Subject only to any limitations stated in this Agreement, or in any other agreement between the Company and the Union or a Local, the Union and the Locals recognize that the Company retains the exclusive right to manage its business, including (but not limited to) the right to determine the methods and means by which its operations are to be carried on, to direct the work force, and to conduct its operations in a safe and effective manner.

This article does not modify or limit the rights of the parties, or of the employees, under any other provisions of this Agreement or under any other agreement between the Company and the Union or the Locals, nor will it operate to deprive employees of any wage or other benefits to which they have been or will become entitled by virtue of an existing or future agreement between the Company and the Union or a Local.

ARTICLE XXX. ISSUES OF GENERAL APPLICATION

This Agreement, the **1994-1997** Settlement Agreement, the **1994-1997** Wage Agreement, and the **1994-1997** Pension and Insurance Agreement between the parties are intended to be and shall be in full settlement of all issues which were the subject of collective bargaining between the parties in national level collective bargaining negotiations in **1994.** Consequently, it is agreed that none of such issues shall be subject to collective bargaining during the term of this Agreement and there shall be no strike or lockout in connection with any such issue or issues; provided, however, that this provision shall not be construed to limit or modify the rights of the parties hereto under Article VI, Section 1, and Article XIV of this Agreement.

ARTICLE XXXI. DURATION OF AGREEMENT

This National Agreement shall be effective as of **June 27, 1994,** between the Company, the Union, and each of the IUE (AFL-CIO) Locals now certified as the representative of Company employees, as set forth in the Preamble to this Agreement, and shall continue in full force and effect to and including the **29th day of June, 1997,** and from year to year thereafter unless modified or terminated as hereinafter provided.

ARTICLE XXXII. MODIFICATION AND TERMINATION

(a) Either the Company or the Union may terminate this National Agreement by written notice to the other not more than ninety days and not less than sixty days prior to **June 29, 1997,** or prior to **June 29** of any subsequent year. Not more than 15 days following receipt of such notice, collective bargaining negotiations shall commence between the parties for the purpose of considering the terms of a new agreement, and a proposal for revision of wages which may be submitted by either the Company or the Union.

(b) If either the Company or the Union desires to modify this National Agreement, it shall, not more than ninety days and not less than sixty days prior to **June 29, 1997,** or prior to **June 29** of any subsequent year, so notify the other in writing. Not more than 15 days following receipt of such notice, collective bargaining negotiations shall commence between the parties for the purpose of considering changes in this National Agreement, and a proposal for revision of wages which may be submitted by either the Company or the Union.

If settlement is not reached by **June 29, 1997,** or prior to **June 29** of any subsequent year, this National Agreement shall continue in full force and effect until the tenth day following written notice given by either the Company or the Union of its intention to terminate such Agreement, during which time there shall be no strike or lockout.

Article XXXIII. Notices

All notices given under the provisions of this Agreement shall be in writing and shall be sufficient if sent by mail addressed, if to the Union, to the International Union of Electronic, Electrical, Salaried, Machine and Furniture Workers (AFL-CIO), 1126 16th Street, N.W., Washington, D.C. 20036, or to such other address the Union shall furnish the Company in writing; and if to the Company, to General Electric Company, Fairfield, Connecticut 06431, or to such other address the Company shall furnish the Union in writing.

Dated: July 29, 1994

> **1994 Memorandum of Agreement Between Saturn Corporation and the International Union, United Automobile, Aerospace and Agricultural Implement Workers of America (AFL-CIO)**

1. Preamble

This Memorandum of Agreement (Agreement) is entered into between Saturn Corporation (Saturn), a wholly-owned subsidiary of General Motors Corporation (GM) and the International Union, United Automobile, Aerospace and Agricultural Implement Workers of American (Union).

Memorandum of Agreement: Saturn Corporation

Saturn and the Union have long recognized the need for a new approach to Union/Management relations and the more effective use of human resources in the manufacture of small cars in the United States. Since GM and the Union first met and authorized the establishment of a study center and the creation of the Corporation, the parties recognize that the global competitiveness in the auto industry has significantly increased. GM and the Union further recognize the necessity of further developing this innovative approach to Union/Management relations and the necessary staffing to accomplish our mutual objectives. General Motors, Saturn Corporation and the Union understand fully the necessity to successfully forge a renewed commitment to a cooperative problem solving relationship and demonstrate that a competitive, world class, quality vehicle will be developed and manufactured in the United States with a represented work force. It is in this renewed spirit of mutual respect and recognition of each other's stakes and equities that this Agreement is entered into and agreed upon.

2. Recognition

From the outset, Saturn has been and is, a joint effort of both Union and Management. The success of Saturn is fully dependent on its people. Hiring and retention of experienced, dedicated personnel is essential. It is recognized that the best source of such trained automotive workers is found in the existing GM-UAW workforce. Therefore, to insure a fully qualified workforce, a majority of the full initial complement of operating and skilled technicians in Saturn will come from GM-UAW units throughout the United States.

The UAW is recognized as the bargaining agent for the operating and skilled technicians within Saturn.

3. Union Representation During Bridging Period

During any bridging period, the Vice President of the GM Department, UAW, will appoint representatives to work jointly with the Saturn organization. The International Union will charter separate Union locals to represent Saturn members.

4. Union Membership and Check-off

To the extent permitted by law, within ten (10) days after the thirtieth (30th) day following hire by Saturn, all bargaining unit members shall become and shall remain members of the Union to the extent of paying an initiation fee and membership dues specified by the International Union.

Saturn will agree to provide for check-off of union dues and initiation fees. The Union will agree to indemnify Saturn with respect to any claims arising out of the check-off provisions.

5. Current GM-UAW National Agreement

This separate, free-standing, Agreement will cover bargaining unit Saturn members. The provisions of the current or any subsequent GM-UAW National Agreement will have no bearing on Saturn unless adopted by agreement between Saturn and the Union.

6. Saturn People Philosophy Summary Statement

We believe that all people want to be involved in decisions that affect them, care about their jobs and each other, take pride in themselves and in their contributions and want to share in the success of their efforts.

7. Saturn Corporation Philosophy

Fundamental to the Saturn philosophy is the shared belief that meeting the needs of people, customers, Saturn members, suppliers, retailers and neighbors is fundamental to fulfilling the Saturn mission.

8. Mission

The mission of Saturn is to market vehicles developed and manufactured in the United States that are world leaders in quality, cost and customer enthusiasm through the integration of people, technology and business systems.

Consistent with being quality and cost competitive, a goal of Saturn is to utilize American-made components in assembly of its vehicles.

9. Symbols

Saturn believes that symbols should be positive to promote our philosophy and culture. Saturn and the Union will strive to achieve positive symbols that minimize the differentiation between people in the elements of a successful organization, such as methods of pay, purchase of GM products, common cafeterias, parking, identification, entrances, lack of time clocks, etc. To the degree possible, recognizing the need to remain competitive, consistency of treatment for everyone (represented and non-represented) will be an important objective for Saturn.

10. STRUCTURE AND DECISION-MAKING PROCESS

The structure of Saturn reflects certain basic principles, e.g., recognition of the stakes and equities of everyone in the organization; full participation by the Union; use of a consensus decision-making process; placement of authority and decision-making in the most appropriate part of the organization, with emphasis on the Work Unit; and, free flow of information and clear definition of the decision-making process.

As guided by these principles, the organization will be structured in the following way:

Structure:

WORK UNIT MEMBER
   The individual Saturn member.

WORK UNIT
   An integrated group of approximately 6-15 Work Unit members.

WORK UNIT MODULE
   A grouping of Work Units interrelated as to geography, product or technology.

BUSINESS UNITS
   An integrated group of Work Units and Work Unit Modules representing common areas.

MANUFACTURING ACTION COUNCIL (MAC)
   An integrated group of Business Units comprising the entire manufacturing and assembly complex, at a given site location.

TECHNICAL DEVELOPMENT ACTION COUNCIL (TDAC)
   An Integrated Business Unit comprising the Advanced product and Manufacturing Engineering Functions, at a given site location.

STRATEGIC ACTION COUNCIL (SAC)
   Will have particular concern for long range goals and health of Saturn, with particular emphasis on planning and outside interested parties, including retailers, suppliers, communities, stockholders, etc. Composition of the SAC will be determined with appropriate input from Saturn and the Union.

The Structure also provides for:

UAW WORK UNIT COUNSELOR
 Will be elected by the members in the Unit or jointly selected by the Parties and will represent the Union and Saturn in the Work Unit; the current manner and process for such election will remain in effect until a mutually agreed upon selection process is established by the Parties. The Counselor is a working member of the Work Unit.

UAW CREW COORDINATOR
 Will be elected; the manner and process determined by the Union. The UAW Crew Coordinator will serve as administrator of the Agreement on behalf of and for the Union.

UAW SKILLED TRADES ADVISOR
 Will be elected; the manner and process determined by the Union. The UAW Skilled Trades Advisor will serve as administrator of the Agreement on behalf of and for the Union.

UAW BUSINESS UNIT ADVISOR
 Will be elected at large; the manner and process for such election to be determined by the Union. The UAW Business Unit Advisor will serve as administrator of the Agreement on behalf of and for the Union.

UAW MAC ADVISOR
 Will be elected at large; the manner and process for such election to be determined by the Union. The UAW MAC Advisor represents the Union and its members as part of the MAC consensus decision-making body. The UAW MAC Advisor serves as the highest local administrator of the Agreement, and as a communication link with the UAW SAC Advisor.

UAW TDAC ADVISOR
 Will be elected at large; the manner and process for such election to be determined by the Union. The UAW TDAC Advisor represents the Union and its members as part of the TDAC consensus decision-making body. The UAW TDAC Advisor serves as the highest Local administrator of the Agreement, and as a communication link with the UAW SAC Advisor.

UAW SAC ADVISOR
 There will be Union representation on the SAC selected by the Union. The manner and process of such selection will be determined by the Union.

Function

Saturn will be unique in the manner in which the basic building blocks, the Work Units, will operate. Consensus decision-making will be utilized with a strong focus on both current and near term decisions. These Work Units will be self-managed, integrated horizontally and reflect synergistic group growth. These Units will have responsibilities to manage such functions as producing to schedule, producing a quality product, performing to budget, housekeeping, health, safety and ergonomics, maintenance of equipment, material and inventory control, training, job assignment, repairs, scrap control and absenteeism. They will hold meetings, obtain supplies, keep records, seek resources as needed, and be responsible for their job preparation. They will constantly seek improvement in quality, cost and work environment.

The Work Unit will also be responsible for the planning and the scheduling of the work and communications within and outside the group.

The Module will be responsible for selection decisions for acceptance into the Work Units. Appropriate criteria will be used in making such decisions by utilizing a hiring team consisting of both represented and non-represented module leadership and elected union representation.

The Business Unit will do advanced planning for resources both short and near term. The Business Units will be composed of all Work Unit Advisors. The Business Units will determine the resources needed by the Work Units, including administration, engineering, materials, financial, etc.

The Manufacturing Action Council (MAC) will be responsible for living the Saturn philosophy to insure success of the mission. It will provide the resources needed by the Business Units on a timely and cost effective basis.

In addition, the MAC will represent and protect the interests, stakes and equities of the Business Units and the Work Unit members, coordinate the activities of and provide information to the Business Units, appraise the performance of the entire organization, and serve as a link to Saturn as a whole.

The Technical Development Action Council (TDAC) will be responsible for living the Saturn philosophy to insure success of the mission. It will provide the resources needed by the Business Unit on a timely and cost effective basis.

In addition, the TDAC will represent and protect the interests, stakes, and equities of the Business Unit and the Work Unit members, coordinate the activities of and provide information to the Business Unit, appraise the performance of the entire organization, and serve as a link to Saturn as a whole.

The Strategic Action Council (SAC) will undertake the strategic business planning necessary to assure the long-term viability of the enterprise, and will be responsive to the needs of the marketplace relative to quality, cost and timing. The SAC will obtain, maintain and replace the resources necessary to meet the mission in concert with the philosophy. It is charged with creating the environment, facilities, tools, education and support systems which will enable Saturn members to perform their responsibilities.

11. Consensus Guidelines

The structure described in Section 10 is intended to make the Union a full partner in Saturn.

The consensus technique is the basic support methodology for Saturn decision-making and conflict resolution processes.

The parties agree that the consensus process, as outlined below, is the primary method for making decisions and resolving disagreements.

In the context of Saturn's philosophy and mission, decisions and disagreements will be resolved within the following guidelines:

- Resolution is achieved through the joint efforts of the parties in discovering the "best" solution.
- The solution must provide a high level of acceptance for all parties.
- Once agreement is reached, the parties must be totally committed to the solution.
- Any of the parties may block a potential decision. However, the party blocking the decision must search for alternatives.
- In the event an alternative solution is not forthcoming, the blocking party must reevaluate the position in the context of the philosophy and mission.
- Voting, "trading" and compromise are not part of this process.
- The joint effort is aimed at discovering the best decision/resolution within the context of Saturn's philosophy and mission while, at the same time, satisfying the stakes and equities of all major stakeholders.

12. Saturn Conflict Resolution Procedure

There is a four-step problem solving procedure, the last step of which involves final and binding arbitration. Conflicts may be reinstated in those instances where the International Union, UAW, by its Executive Board, Public Review Board, or Constitutional Convention Appeals Committee finds the conflict was improperly resolved by the Union or the Union representative.

SATURN CONFLICT RESOLUTION PROCEDURE

Step	Participants	Process
STEP 1	• MEMBER • WORK UNIT • WORK UNIT COUNSELOR • MODULE ADVISOR	• Discuss • Seek consensus using conflict resolution model • Obtain resource assistance as required • Discuss with other advisors as necessary
STEP 2	**MANAGEMENT:** PEOPLE SYSTEMS ADVISOR (BUSINESS UNIT OR TDAC) **UAW:** UAW CREW COORDINATOR, UAW SKILLED TRADES ADVISOR, UAW BUSINESS UNIT ADVISOR, UAW TDAC ADVISOR	• Timely meeting • Seek consensus using conflict resolution model • Obtain resource as required • If unresolved issue put in writing by UAW Crew coordinator, UAW Skilled Trades Advisor or UAW Business Unit Advisor or UAW TDAC Advisor • If unresolved–Mgmt. issues written answer
STEP 3	**MANAGEMENT:** PEOPLE SYSTEMS ADVISOR (BUSINESS UNIT OR TDAC), PEOPLE SYSTEMS ADVISOR (MAC) **UAW:** • UAW BUSINESS UNIT ADVISOR • UAW TDAC ADVISOR • UAW MAC ADVISOR • UAW REGIONAL REP	• Timely meeting • Obtain resources as req'd • Seek consensus using conflict resolution model • If unsolved–both parties issue written positions
STEP 4	UAW/GM DEPT UMPIRE STAFF	• Impartial Umpire Selected • Cost Shared • Issue Presented • Decision Final and binding

13. Equal Employment Opportunity

The philosophy and mission of Saturn are designed to be in full and complete compliance with the legal and moral principles of equal opportunity in employment. Accordingly, Saturn, the Union, and each and every member of Saturn pledge to treat all persons equally without regard to their race, color, religion, age, sex, national origin or handicap.

14. Recruitment and Selection

The Saturn organization will require people who can fully commit to the philosophy and effectively contribute to its mission. Both parties recognize the critical importance of a process for recruitment and selection which accurately and objectively assesses candidate qualifications. The complexity of such a process supports the establishment of a joint team to work on the development and ultimate implementation of such a process in accordance with guidelines to be established by the parties.

In this regard, because of the qualifications and experience of the current GM-UAW workforce, they will be the primary source of the initial complement, up to full capacity, of operating and skilled trades technicians. The parties will actively recruit GM-UAW employees (active and inactive), including communications emphasizing the exciting and unique opportunities available in the Saturn culture. It is understood that Saturn membership is conditional on meeting established recruitment and selection criteria.

The Saturn philosophy requires a dedicated and committed workforce. Accordingly, no active or inactive UAW-represented GM employee will be required to become a Saturn applicant, nor will such employee's refusal of an offer of employment by Saturn impact the employee's benefits under the GM-UAW National Agreement.

15. Orientation

The Saturn organization will jointly develop and administer the pre-hire and post-hire orientation programs for prospective and selected members.

16. Training

The success of Saturn in meeting its mission in an internationally competitive environment is dependent upon the continuous development and implementation of new tools, methods, and cutting edge technology. Training and education provide the tools necessary for all Saturn team members to meet these ongoing challenges, and programs to meet these goals will be jointly developed and administered. To help assure Saturn's long-term viability, jointly developed competency-based training of all Saturn members is mandatory.

17. Job Design

In keeping with the Saturn mission and culture, each Work Unit will have the responsibility and authority to produce quality products to schedule at competitive costs. The Units will have responsibility for both direct and indirect work, including training, housekeeping, provision for relief, etc. Individual jobs will be designed with the appropriate resources to develop the optimum balance between people and technology, taking into account health, safety and ergonomic issues, with ongoing responsibility to determine methods to become more competitive.

Memorandum of Agreement: Saturn Corporation

18. Planning and Relief

Job content within the Work Units will be designed to include both direct work and indirect work. Therefore, it is expected that Work Units will be able to handle the personal relief needs of individual Saturn members.

19. Classifications

Saturn will have a job classification structure for represented members that has the classification of "Operating Technician" to which other than skilled trades members will be assigned, and six additional classifications to which all skilled trades members will be assigned as identified below:

- Tool & Die
- Machine Repair
- Electrical
- Stationary Engineer
- Assembly Layout (TDAC only)
- Model maker (TDAC only)

20. Length of Service

New Saturn members will establish a Length of Service date by site location effective with their date of hire. Length of service will be used as a tie-breaker in those unusual situations where competing members are equal in all respects; and, as a trigger point for compensation progression or specifically negotiated benefit coverage.

21. Job Security

Saturn recognizes that people are the most valuable asset of the organization. It is people who develop new technologies and systems, and people who make these systems work in order to meet Saturn's mission. Accordingly, those Saturn members who are eligible for job security, as defined below, shall not be laid off except in situations which the SAC determines are due to unforeseen or catastrophic events or severe economic conditions. In the event former GM employees (active or laid off) who are required to quit to become Saturn members are laid off because of such events or conditions, the parties will discuss the matter in an attempt to effect an equitable solution, such as separation payments, return to General Motors or reinstatement of GM recall or rehire rights.

A Saturn member will have permanent job security eligibility if either of the following applies to that member:

a. The member quit while an active GM-UAW employee or was hired while on layoff with recall or rehire rights from a GM-UAW unit in the U.S. to join Saturn as part of the full initial complement of operating and skilled technicians in Saturn; or
b. The member is, at any point in time, among the 80% of Saturn members with the longest Saturn Length of Service by site location.

Saturn recognizes the desirability of regular employment and will attempt to avoid laying off members not eligible for job security. In the unlikely event of a layoff at a site location, members will be laid off and recalled by Saturn Length of Service.

22. REWARD SYSTEM

The reward system in Saturn will recognize certain critical elements including the mission and philosophy, the necessity that Saturn be profitable and the principle of risk and reward.

Three basic elements are recognized: base compensation, risk/reward and benefits.

Base Compensation

Saturn members' base compensation is established on an annual salary basis and they will be paid semi-monthly on the 15th of the month and the last day of the month.

The base compensation for Saturn members was adjusted to 90% of straight time wages (base plus COLA) of UAW/GM compensation rates. Base compensation will remain at this level until the complete phase-in of risk/reward. Thereafter, base compensation may be adjusted periodically based on such factors as the general state of the economy, inflation, the competitive situation, etc., by approval of the SAC.

Quarterly Payments

In addition, during the phase-in of risk/reward, a sum will be calculated quarterly reflecting the remaining economics received by a comparable GM/UAW employee including COLA. The total sum generated through this calculation will be distributed to members on a quarterly basis.

Memorandum of Agreement: Saturn Corporation

Risk/Reward

In addition to the base rate, a risk/reward system will be phased-in by increments of 5% up to 20% total risk, and will be based on factors such as:

a. Performance to Objectives of Saturn and Individual Business and Work Units;
b. Achievement of specific objective productivity targets;
c. Saturn sharing formula through which profits will be shared above a specified level of return to Saturn;
d. Quality bonus based on World Class Levels.

The risk/reward system will be designed to provide attainable goals which, if met, will provide compensation equivalent to that earned by comparable employees in GM. Performance above or below those goals would provide greater or lesser compensation than comparable employees in GM.

Hire Rates and Progression Operating Technicians

Former GM employees who were hired while on layoff with recall or rehire rights at any GM plant(s) or quit to become Saturn members shall receive an initial base rate at the same relative position to the maximum base rate the employee had attained under the GM-UAW National Agreement. Thereafter, they will progress in accordance with the Hire Rate and Progression Chart (Attachment #1).

Former GM employees who did not possess recall or rehire rights at any GM plant as of the date they become Saturn members and new members who have not previously worked for GM will hire in and progress as reflected in Attachment #1.

23. Working Hours

To fulfill the objectives of the Saturn philosophy and mission, it will be necessary to have flexible hours of work that meet the needs of the individual as well as Saturn.

24. Holidays

Saturn will observe the following paid holidays and other holidays as determined by the SAC:

Martin Luther King Day
Good Friday
Monday after Easter
Memorial Day
Independence Day
Labor Day
Thanksgiving Day
Friday after Thanksgiving
Christmas Holiday Period

25. Vacations

Vacation with pay will be based on combined Saturn and GM Length of service.

Length of Service	Vacation Entitlement
Less than three years	80 hrs.
Three but less than five years	100 hrs.
Five but less than ten years	120 hrs.
Ten but less than fifteen years	140 hrs.
Fifteen but less than twenty years	160 hrs.
Twenty or more years	200 hrs.

Vacation schedules must be planned ahead and coordinated within each Work Unit.

Vacation entitlement must be used each year. Unused vacation balances of 40 hours or less will be paid in lieu. Unused vacation balances in excess of 40 hours will be forfeited.

Saturn may schedule a shutdown of operations for vacation purposes. Saturn members entitled to vacation must schedule their vacation during this shutdown period. It is understood that necessary members may be scheduled to work during the shutdown.

26. Shift Assignments in Saturn

The Saturn philosophy emphasizes equality among all members and the shared sense of belonging to a successful operation in which everyone has common needs and goals. Accordingly the rotating shift approach has been implemented by the parties. The feasibility of introducing fixed shifts or other options will be examined by the parties and presented for consideration by the appropriate Action Council.

27. Personal Absence/Leaves of Absence

Absenteeism affects the commitment to Saturn and places an unnecessary burden on fellow team members. Accordingly, programs will be developed to discourage absenteeism and to encourage regular attendance. Provision will be made for both paid and unpaid leaves of absence.

28. Code of Conduct

The code of conduct for Saturn is established in its mission and philosophy statements, which set forth the basic operating principles of the organization. Actions or behavior that are contrary to these principles may be subject to the Saturn Consultation Process, which will be established by the parties and set out in the Agreement. If counselling and attempts to modify behavior prove ineffective or in instances of severe misconduct, Saturn may initiate disciplinary action or discharge. Complaints concerning discipline or discharge must be filed within three (3) working days of the action to be valid.

29. Saturn Consultation Process

The Consultation Process will include three formal stages: (1) Amber Zone, (2) Red Zone, (3) Decision Day. Members in the Consultation Process will be offered Union Representation to ensure a fair and equitable process. In situations where any member's conduct or attitude is adversely affecting the Work Unit, initial corrective action will concentrate on consultation, guidance and review. Such assistance does not affect the basic principle that the individual member is responsible for his/her behavior. The parties agree to work toward a variety of approaches to be followed in the attempt to encourage the member to become a full participant in the unit.

30. Strikes, Stoppages and Lockouts

The philosophy and mission of Saturn and the unique culture created in the work environment are opposed to unauthorized lockouts, strikes, work stoppages, sit-downs, slow-downs, curtailment of work, restriction or interference with production or facilities, picketing, or similar activities. Further, the parties hereby pledge that no lockouts or strikes will be authorized without full and complete compliance with the Procedure to Modify the Agreement contained herein.

31. BENEFITS HSMD

The basic approach to HSMD will be provision for a closed panel, either HMO or PPO. Medical, dental, vision, hearing and prescription drugs will be provided at HMO or PPO levels comparable to similar provisions in the current GM-UAW Agreement.

Saturn will negotiate coverage with providers to assure quality care at reasonable cost. There will be a careful review to determine the feasibility of establishing an on-site or adjacent medical/wellness clinic as a provider to deliver services such as:

- In-plant medical service;
- Routine service for Saturn members and dependents;
- Employee/dependent physicals;
- Wellness/rehabilitation programs.

All Saturn members would be provided coverage at date of hire.

Retirement Plan

Saturn members will participate in a retirement plan under which individual Saturn Accounts will be maintained for each member. The value of such individual accounts will be determined by the earnings on funds invested by Saturn for each individual member. Saturn will guarantee a minimum return on earnings each investment year at 4% above the inflation rate up to age 55 phasing down to 2% above the inflation rate by age 60. The funding of such retirement accounts will be at the rate of 8% of base compensation.

Saturn contributions, and earnings thereon, will vest in 5 years. Combined GM and Saturn credited service will be taken into account for purposes of determining vesting.

At retirement, Saturn members would be given the choice of receiving their Saturn Account balance in a single cash payment or in the form of a lifetime monthly retirement benefit.

Former GM employees will receive benefits under the GM plan for credited service at the time of transfer to Saturn. Benefits under the GM plan would be based on pension rates in effect at the time of retirement from Saturn.

Individual Savings Plan

An individual savings plan will be offered under which any Saturn member can contribute up to [sic].

Memorandum of Agreement: Saturn Corporation

S&A – Extended Disability Benefits

All Saturn members will be eligible for Sickness and Accident benefits the first day after disability commences. Full base compensation will be paid for the first 30 days of the same disability; 80% of base compensation will be paid for the next 30 days of the same disability; and, 60% of base compensation will be paid thereafter for up to one year from the initial date of disability. In no event will disability pay exceed Length of Service.

Extended Disability Benefits will be paid at a rate of 60% of base compensation for a period equal to combined GM and Saturn length of service for Saturn members with combined length of service of less than 10 years. Saturn members with 10 or more years of combined service will be eligible for 60% of base compensation until they reach eligibility for un-reduced social security benefits.

Life Insurance Benefits

Saturn believes it is important to plan for the security of survivors, a responsibility that is shared through the insurance plan. In the case of death, the beneficiary named by the Saturn member will receive benefits from the plan according to the level of coverage as follows:

a. Saturn will provide 2.0 times the base compensation from the date of employment as a member.
b. Each member may purchase additional coverage at special rates in multiples up to five (5) times base compensation through payroll deduction.
c. Optional dependent coverage of up to $25,000 for spouse and $10,000 for each dependent child is also available at special group rates.

32. COMPONENTS MANUFACTURING

Many decisions are yet to be made regarding the integration of the Saturn complex which were reviewed and discussed during the Agreement process. As these issues arise in the future, the parties agree to review the specifics of the component part(s) being considered to determine if Saturn can be competitive in quality and cost.

33. PROCEDURE TO MODIFY THE AGREEMENT

Once an Agreement is ratified and becomes effective, it will remain in full force and effect unless modified by the parties. However, in the event the parties wish to conduct formal negotiations on an entire Agreement once a full complement of members has been hired, such negotiations will be concluded no later than six months after the commencement of steady state as described herein. The parties are specifically empowered to make mutually satisfactory modifications, additions or deletions to the Agreement which are in line with the philosophy and mission of Saturn on an ongoing basis. In the event either party is unable to secure agreement on a modification(s) it desires, such party may institute this Procedure to Modify the Agreement.

A. Notice of Request to Modify the Agreement

The party seeking the modification(s) will furnish the other party a written Notice of Request to Modify Agreement in the form of a letter from the UAW SAC Advisor to the Vice President People Systems in the case of the Union, or vice-versa in the case of Management, listing the provision(s) the party wishes to modify or cancel and/or briefly describing any new provisions it may wish to negotiate. Thereafter, the parties will meet on this request and attempt to resolve the issues using the principles of conflict resolution.

B. Notice of Intent to Lockout or Strike

If after thirty (30) calendar days from the date the Request is received, the parties are unable to reach consensus, the initiating party for Saturn Corporation or the UAW SAC Advisor for the Union may serve a written Notice of Intent to Lockout or Strike in the same manner as described in "A" above. Thereafter, if a satisfactory agreement is not reached after negotiations for five (5) working days from receipt of this Notice, the moving party may initiate its action.

34. RATIFICATION

Provisions for ratification and notice thereof will be provided.

COMMITMENT OF PARTIES

Saturn and the Union acknowledge that the matters set out in this memorandum are neither all inclusive nor complete. The parties acknowledge that in arriving at this Agreement, additional matters have been extensively discussed. These matters serve as broad guiding principles of the parties to follow in fulfilling the mission of Saturn, and in their relationships with each other. It is the intention of the parties to rely upon those principles to provide guidance for future agreements.

INTERNATIONAL UNION, UAW
    Stephen P. Yokich
    Robert K. Farley
    Richard W. Danjin
    Michael E. Brown

UAW LOCAL 1853
    Michael E. Bennett

UAW LOCAL 1810
    Morris F. Hayes

SATURN CORPORATION
    Gerald A. Knechtel
    R. Timothy Epps
    Dennis G. Finn
    Richard A. Hoalcraft
    Daniel T. Koenn

Attachment #1. Reward System

Hire Rate and Progression Operating Technicians

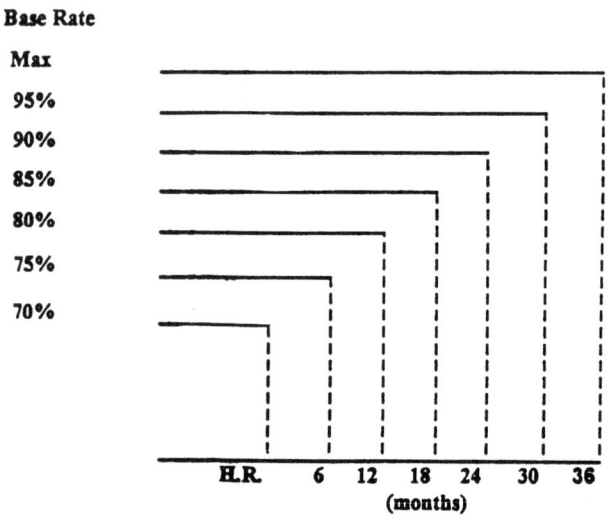

December 13, 1994

Mr. Richard G. LeFauve
President, Saturn Corporation
434 West 12 Mile, MDO1
Madison Heights, MI 48071

Dear Mr. LeFauve:

This letter is to reconfirm the support that the International Union, UAW, has for the Saturn Corporation. The parties recognize that the Corporation is marketing vehicles in a highly competitive market. As such, the job security of Saturn members is defined by the success that Saturn achieves within this market.

The Union continues to be fully committed to key fundamental principles which enhance the Corporation's success capabilities. These commitments include a full and active support of the partnership, maximization of programs that enhance the safety and well being of Saturn members, all efforts to make cost per car reductions to world class levels, and the requirement that continuous improvement be institutionalized and made effective in the day to day manufacturing operations.

The International Union looks forward to the continued success of the Saturn Corporation, its UAW members and above all, enthusiastic customers that become Saturn family members through their ownership of Saturn cars that are world leaders in quality, cost, and customer satisfaction.

Sincerely,

Stephen Yokich
Vice President and Director
UAW General Motors Department

December 13, 1994

International Union, United Automobile Aerospace and Agricultural Implement Workers of America, UAW

Attention: Mr. Stephen P. Yokich
            Vice President and Director
            General Motors Department

Gentlemen:

In the spirit of the recent negotiations, the General Motors Corporation, Saturn Corporation and the Union have recognized and agree to and re-commit the Saturn Mission and Philosophy laid down in the Memorandum of Agreement as it pertains to the future marketing, development, and design of product and processes, and the sourcing of any Saturn components. Further, it is understood all mutual practices, procedures, understandings, staffing and Agreements remain in full effect. Problems or issues arising out of the course of these events will be resolved as outlined in the Memorandum of Agreement with the overriding principle of the Mission and Philosophy applying.

Sincerely,

Richard G. LeFauve
President Saturn Corporation

December 13, 1994

International Union, United Automobile Aerospace and Agricultural Implement Workers of America, UAW

Attention: Mr. Stephen P. Yokich
            Vice President and Director
            General Motors Department

Gentlemen:

During the course of negotiations with the Saturn Corporation, it was agreed that certain General Motors employees who become Saturn members during the term of the 1985, and any subsequent Saturn Agreement and who have 10 or more years of credited service under The General Motors Hourly-Rate Employees Pension Plan will be provided with post-retirement health care and life insurance coverages under the GM-UAW Agreement in effect at the time the employee retires from Saturn Corporation.

Such post-retirement coverages would be provided if any of the following conditions are met at retirement from Saturn:

(1) The Saturn member has attained age 60.
(2) The Saturn member has attained age 55 but not age 60, and the total of the member's age and the member's combined years of GM and Saturn service (to the nearest 1/12 in each case) is 85 or more.
(3) The Saturn member has 30 or more years of combined GM and Saturn service.

Very truly yours,

GENERAL MOTORS CORPORATION
G. A. Knechtel, Vice President

DATE: December 13, 1994
TO: Bob Farley
SUBJECT: Retirement and Post-Retirement Health Care Provisions for Saturn Represented Team members with General Motors Credited Service of less than 10 years When They Came to Saturn

During the course of our recently concluded negotiations we discussed, for the subject Saturn team members (i) providing a one-time election with respect to retirement income and (ii) an adjustment in funding of the Saturn-UAW Retiree Health Care Fund.

With respect to the election concerning retirement income, over the period of the next six months, we will provide a package of information to each eligible subject team member. The purpose of this information is to allow each of these team members a one-time election to receive their retirement income from the GM-UAW Pension Plan. If this one-time election is not made, the team member will continue in the Saturn-UAW Pension Plan. We acknowledge that this election process is contingent upon the national parties to the GM-UAW Pension Plan making appropriate provisions to that plan to make this election process possible.

With respect to funding of the Saturn-UAW Retiree Health Care Fund for the subject Saturn team members, we have agreed to increase the funding level from 1% to 1.8% effective the first of the month following ratification of this agreement.

R. Timothy Epps
Vice President People Systems

December 13, 1994

Mr. Stephen P. Yokich
Vice President and Director
UAW General Motors Department
8000 East Jefferson Avenue
Detroit, MI 48214

Dear Mr. Yokich:

Saturn and the Union have agreed to the formation of a Saturn-UAW team that would meet periodically to jointly manage the functioning of the Saturn-UAW 1% Retiree Health Care Fund and the Saturn-UAW Pension Plan for UAW members.

The 1% Retiree Health Care Fund will be applied to post-retirement health care cost for Saturn retirees with less than ten years of credited service under the GM/UAW Pension Plan.

Jointly managing the pension plan means to engage in periodic reviews of the investment performance which may result in the placement of administration and investment responsibilities with companies other than General Motors Corporation.

It is proposed that such a team consist of up to three UAW representatives agreed upon by the Union and up to three persons designated by Saturn management. Please notify me of the people you designate to serve on the committee.

Sincerely,

R. Timothy Epps
Vice President
People Systems

December 13, 1994

Mr. Stephen P. Yokich
Vice President and Director
UAW General Motors Department
8000 East Jefferson Avenue
Detroit, MI 48214

Dear Mr. Yokich:

Saturn and the Union recognize the need to have certain UAW positions within Saturn appointed by the Union. As such, appropriate positions will be identified by the SAC and appointments jointly selected will be approved by the International Union SAC officer. Individuals selected and approved for these positions will be held accountable within their capacities to fulfill the stakes and equities of the UAW and Saturn partnership.

Any problems relating to the implementation of this letter may be raised by either Saturn or the Union, and it is understood that any necessary modification may be made by consensus agreement between Saturn and the Union.

Sincerely,

R. Timothy Epps
Vice President
People Systems

December 13, 1994

Bob Farley
UAW Coordinator

Dear Mr. Farley:

During these negotiations, the parties agreed to make revisions to the rotation supplement and to implement a special lump sum payment for Saturn/UAW members. These provisions provide for:

- The payment of a 2% special lump sum payment as described in the Guiding Principles (for both 4/10 and 5/8 scheduled members)
- Rotation supplement to be paid at 4% or 6% based on schedule

Memorandum of Agreement: Saturn Corporation

To facilitate the above provisions, the following vacation schedules will apply to Saturn/UAW members hired prior to 12/31/94:

5-Day Schedule

GM & Saturn Combined Length of Service	Vacation Entitlement
0 < 3	80 Hours
3 < 5	100 Hours
5 < 10	120 Hours
10 < 15	140 Hours
15 < 20	160 Hours
20 +	200 Hours

4-Day Schedule

GM & Saturn Combined Length of Service	Vacation Entitlement
0 < 10	120 Hours
10 < 20	160 Hours
20 +	200 Hours

R. Timothy Epps
Vice President People Systems

December 13, 1994

Mr. Bob Farley
UAW Coordinator
General Motors Department
International Union, UAW
8000 East Jefferson Avenue
Detroit, MI 48214

Dear Mr. Farley:

Per our discussions, the provisions of Paragraph (96a) (3) of the GM/UAW National Agreement have and do apply to Saturn UAW members who have joined Saturn and who may be employed into Saturn from GM/UAW in the future.

R. Timothy Epps
Vice President People Systems

July 23, 1995

Mr. Alfred S. Warren, Jr.
Vice President
General Motors Corporation
General Motors Building
Detroit, Michigan 48202

Dear Mr. Warren:

This will confirm that the discussions regarding the proposed Memorandum of Agreement between Saturn Corporation and the International Union, UAW, I advised you of the following:

> The UAW views Saturn as a special project designed to maintain small car production with a high degree of domestic content in the United States that will provide jobs having compensation and benefits which will maintain the standard of living now enjoyed by our members.

> The UAW considers the proposed Memorandum of Agreement as a "special case" because it is specifically designed as an integral part of the Saturn approach.

> Therefore, the UAW does not consider this Memorandum of Agreement as a precedent regarding the Union's policy at any other facility, including those at General Motors.

Sincerely,
Owen Bieber
President